Corporate Reorganization Law and Forces of Change

Corporate Reorganization Law and Forces of Change

SARAH PATERSON

OXFORD
UNIVERSITY PRESS

OXFORD
UNIVERSITY PRESS

Great Clarendon Street, Oxford, OX2 6DP,
United Kingdom

Oxford University Press is a department of the University of Oxford.
It furthers the University's objective of excellence in research, scholarship,
and education by publishing worldwide. Oxford is a registered trade mark of
Oxford University Press in the UK and in certain other countries

First Edition published in 2020

Impression: 1

Published in the United States of America by Oxford University Press
198 Madison Avenue, New York, NY 10016, United States of America

British Library Cataloguing in Publication Data

Data available

Library of Congress Control Number: 2020934583

ISBN 978–0–19–886036–5

Printed and bound by
CPI Group (UK) Ltd, Croydon, CR0 4YY

For Elizabeth

Preface

This book investigates the ways in which forces of change in the finance and non-financial corporate fields can produce different patterns of fact in large corporate reorganization cases, with the result that the participants in the cases mobilize and adapt corporate reorganization law in a variety of ways, according to the nature of the problem at hand. Little could I have known that, between submission of the manuscript and receipt of the uncorrected proofs, the paradigmatic example of a wholly unexpected force of change would be unleashed in both the US and the UK, in the shape of the COVID-19 crisis. As the US and the UK Governments have imposed business shutdowns and social distancing measures in an attempt to slow down the spread of the virus, firms on both sides of the Atlantic have experienced an unprecedented hard stop to cashflow, while liabilities have continued to accrue.

Professional and trade associations in both jurisdictions have responded with pleas to their Governments for action to deal with the impending economic crisis. A host of papers and webinars have followed, debating how corporate reorganization law might be used as part of the solution. As this book examines, the English administration procedure has historically been associated with an insolvency sale, rather than a corporate reorganization. In the early days of the COVID-19 crisis, drawing directly on the research underpinning this book, I wrote a paper for the UK Insolvency Lawyers' Association (ILA) demonstrating how the English administration procedure can be mobilized and adapted both to create liquidity and to create a breathing space from supplier action. Valuable comments were received and incorporated, and the paper was published by the ILA and supported by the City of London Law Society Insolvency Law Committee.[1] The initiative was boosted when Mark Phillips QC, William Willson, and Stephen Robins at South Square chambers, who had already been thinking along similar lines, effectively operationalized it with a consent protocol, which mapped out how management and monitoring could be arranged in the case.[2] In short, the argument in this book that corporate reorganization law is a tool which can be adapted in different,

[1] ILA, 'Changing the Narrative around Administration' (ILA, 26 March 2020) <https://www.ilauk.com/docs/ILA._03_.02.20.Rescue_Administration_paper%282002356353_.1%29_copy__1.pdf> accessed 6 June 2020; The City of London Law Society, 'Consultations and Responses' <http://www.citysolicitors.org.uk/clls/consultations-responses-2/> accessed 6 June 2020.

[2] Mark Phillips QC, William Willson, and Stephen Robins, 'Consent Protocol' (20 April 2020) <https://www.ilauk.com/news-events/news-view/saving-livelihoods-updated-consent-protocol> accessed 6 June 2020.

context-sensitive ways found immediate, practical expression in the ILA project to change the narrative around administration.

In the US, too, new policy papers have appeared suggesting how US corporate reorganization law could be adapted to respond to the COVID-19 crisis. David Skeel has produced a paper for the Brookings Institute, among other things advocating greater use of the pre-packaged bankruptcy technique and suggesting that section 363 could be mobilized for the purposes of corporate reorganization using what he describes as a 'sale to self'.[3] Jonathan Henes has called on Congress to codify what he calls 'one-day bankruptcy' cases:[4] cases in which the Chapter 11 plan is confirmed within 24 hours of commencing the case. This book argues that a rapid confirmation of a pre-packaged plan, or the mobilization of section 363 technology to achieve a corporate reorganization by a sale to the reorganizing financial creditors, may be an appropriate response when the purpose of the corporate reorganization is to deleverage a complex, leveraged capital structure. Importantly, it makes its case from multiple theoretical perspectives, arguing that both economically and progressively minded scholars ought to be able to agree to the use of these tools for this purpose. Yet it suggests that more complicated questions arise when landlords, unsecured trade creditors, or employees are implicated in the transaction. Thus, it suggests a way for all corporate reorganization law scholars to focus their lenses on the adaptations which Skeel and Henes have suggested.

Finally, days before the corrected proofs were due to be returned to the publisher, the UK Government introduced a new Corporate Insolvency and Governance Bill (the Bill) into the House of Commons, which it plans to fast-track through Parliament.[5] The Bill implements important reforms to English corporate reorganization law. The UK Government consulted on these reforms in 2018, and the proposals were discussed in the submitted manuscript of this book, so that it has been relatively straightforward to add early references to the Bill as the book is going to press. Yet, this book identifies the need to focus not only on the legislative drafting but also on the ways in which participants in the corporate reorganization process mobilize and adapt the tools which the legislation provides. It is clearly far too early to know how the new tools will be used. Nonetheless, this book suggests a way for scholars, practitioners, judges, and the legislature to think about any adaptations which emerge. The central argument of the text is that, whatever theoretical

[3] David A Skeel, 'Bankruptcy and the Coronavirus' (Brookings Institute, 21 April 2020) <https://www.brookings.edu/research/bankruptcy-and-the-coronavirus/> accessed 6 June 2020.

[4] Jonathan S Henes, 'Viewpoint: Congress Should Codify the One-Day Bankruptcy' (11 May 2020) <https://www.kirkland.com/publications/article/2020/05/codify-the-one-day-bankruptcy> accessed 6 June 2020.

[5] Corporate Insolvency and Governance Bill [HC] 2019–21.

or policy approach we adopt, we cannot use a single, universal or fixed conceptual framework to analyse the many different ways in which corporate reorganization law is mobilized and adapted in the twenty-first century. This argument assumes even greater significance as we grapple with the variety of corporate reorganization cases likely to emerge in the wake of the COVID-19 crisis.

Sarah Paterson
London School of Economics
6 June 2020

Acknowledgements

Although work started in earnest on this book in 2017, I have been working towards it for much longer than that would imply. Indeed, an early version of the insight that changes in fields proximate to corporate reorganization law may have narrowed the distance between economically and progressively minded scholars appeared in my article in the Oxford Journal of Legal Studies in 2014, 'Rethinking Corporate Bankruptcy Law in the Twenty-First Century'. I presented drafts of that article at a roundtable organized by Louise Gullifer and Kristin Van Zwieten at the Harris Manchester College Centre for Commercial Law, where the embryonic ideas benefitted from comments made by John Armour, Jennifer Marshall, and Jennifer Payne. It was this early work which led me, first, to unpack the forces of change which have given rise to the new landscape and, ultimately, to write this book.

I have benefitted from the insights of many participants at the Insolvency Lawyers' Association academic forums and conferences over the years and from discussions with fellow members of the ILA Technical Committee, with particular thanks to Jennifer Marshall, Gabrielle Ruiz, Joanne Rumley, Sonya Van de Graaff, and Inga West. A note of thanks is also in order for Hamish Anderson, Joe Bannister, Ashley Smith, and Jo Windsor for lively and insightful discussion of the UK Government reform proposals, and their implications for my developing thesis, and for fellow members of R3's General Technical Committee, where I am an academic member alongside Pete Walton. Many participants at INSOL academic forums (seamlessly coordinated by Ros Mason) offered valuable comments on particular ideas in development, including Gerard McCormack, Virginia Torrie, and Reinout Vriesendorp. And my work for the Secured Transactions Law Reform Project, for which I chair the Insolvency Working Group, proved invaluable in developing the sections on secured credit, with particular thanks to Hugh Beale, Louise Gullifer, Georgia Quenby, Magda Raczynska, and Duncan Sheehan. Felix Steffek and the team behind the 3CL events at Cambridge offered opportunities to develop the inter-disciplinary elements of some of the ideas. Tom Vickers read and commented on early drafts of a couple of the chapters; Ian Johnson was always willing to make time to challenge ideas; and Megan Sparber provided invaluable technical insights. Finally, many thanks to Adrian Walters and Christoph Henkel for their typical energy and commitment in developing the comparative insolvency and bankruptcy conferences, and to Andrew Dawson in picking up the baton. Many participants at the conferences offered valuable comments, but particular thanks are due to Adrian, Christoph, Ted Janger, Stephen Lubben, Stephan

Madaus, Bruce Markell, Nicolaes Tollenaar, and Jay Westbrook, all of whom provided particularly influential insights.

At the LSE, Eva Micheler organized a fabulous law and finance conference at which I was able to test out early ideas about the implications of the developing high-yield bond market for corporate reorganization law. David Kershaw read an early draft of the introduction with a critical eye, which paid dividends for the final book as a whole. Many other colleagues generously discussed particular aspects of my ideas, including (but certainly not limited to) Jo Braithwaite, Hugh Collins, Philipp Paech, Edmund Schuster, Joe Spooner, and Simon Witney. And Niki Lacey and Niamh Moloney provided all the necessary encouragement to see the project to the finishing line. I have been fortunate to discuss elements of the underlying research with Mark Roe during his time visiting Campus, and with Yannis Manuelides and other participants at LSE Financial Markets Group conferences. I am grateful to all the team at Oxford University Press for their skill in steering the book through production, particularly in the difficult weeks after submission, which saw the explosion of the COVID-19 crisis and, just as final corrections to the copy edit were being completed, a new Corporate Insolvency and Governance Bill. Finally, I am indebted to my parents-in-law, Kevin and Patricia Noon, for their tireless proofreading work. This is a more readable book as a result of their efforts. Of course, all views expressed, and all errors, are mine.

Contents

Table of Cases

NATIONAL COURTS

United Kingdom

United States

Table of Legislation

OTHER LEGISLATION

United States

EUROPEAN REGULATION

1
Introduction

1.1 Overview

Scholars viewing United States (US) corporate reorganization law through a predominantly economic lens, and scholars viewing it through a progressive lens, have fundamentally disagreed about almost every aspect of policy, content, and reform of corporate reorganization law.[1] The modern, theoretical debate started shortly after enactment of the US Bankruptcy Code in 1978 and took shape throughout the 1980s. Crucially, the debate responded to, and was shaped by, the ways in which the newly enacted corporate reorganization law provisions of the US Bankruptcy Code interacted with the wider organizational and institutional environment of the time in the fields of finance and non-financial corporates.[2] Indeed, all corporate reorganization law theory starts by observing the real world in which

[1] Corporate reorganization law refers to the part of corporate bankruptcy law which can be used to achieve a reorganization of the firm's liabilities, as opposed to a sale of its assets to a third party. The term 'bankruptcy' is used, in England, to refer to individuals, while the term 'insolvency' is used in relation to corporates. No such distinction is drawn in the United States. For ease of reference, the term 'corporate bankruptcy' is used for both England and the US in this book.

[2] The concept of a 'field' in the book is based on Neil Fligstein and Doug McAdams' definition of a strategic action field as '... a constructed mesolevel social order in which actors (who can be individual or collective) are attuned to and interact with one another on the basis of shared (which is not to say consensual) understandings about the purposes of the field, relationships to others in the field (including who has power and why), and the rules governing legitimate action in the field': Neil Fligstein and Doug McAdam, *A Theory of Fields* (OUP 2015) 9.

Corporate Reorganization Law and Forces of Change. Sarah Paterson, Oxford University Press (2020). © Sarah Paterson.
DOI: 10.1093/oso/9780198860365.001.0001.

corporate reorganization occurs. As one leading scholar recently commented, his own work was:

> . . . a product not only of the emerging scholastic work at that time, but also of the actual world—of firms, capital structures and players—that existed at that time.[3]

In England, large corporate reorganization was an almost entirely out-of-court affair right up until the 2000s.[4] It was investigated by a handful of legal scholars but, for the most part, did not occupy the legal academy. Yet, once again, corporate reorganization occurred out of court in England as a direct result of the firms, capital structures, and players that existed at the time.

Since the 2000s, almost every aspect of the landscape of firms and finance has changed in both the US and England. This book focuses on the new world of corporate reorganization which has emerged for large firms as a result.[5] Specifically, it focuses on the implications of the new world of corporate reorganization for the way in which corporate reorganization law is mobilized and adapted by the participants in the process. Its central concern is with the implications of these adaptations for scholars, practitioners, judges, and the legislature when they analyse the content of corporate reorganization law and the case for reform.

1.2 The US sections

1.2.1 The US corporate reorganization law debate

At its core, the debate among scholars adopting an economic approach to US corporate reorganization law and scholars adopting a progressive approach is a debate about the ways in which a capitalist economy promotes public interest and social welfare. Scholars adopting an economic approach argue that firms must fail in order to promote economic growth: the process which Joseph Schumpeter

[3] Thomas H Jackson, 'A Retrospective Look at Bankruptcy's New Frontiers' (2018) 166(7) U Pa L Rev 1867, 1868.

[4] References to England and English law throughout the book are to England and Wales, and the law of England and Wales, respectively. Although most of the English law analysis applies throughout the United Kingdom, there are some important differences in Scottish law (particularly Scottish secured transactions law) which are not discussed. At the same time, the number of Scottish and Northern Irish corporate reorganization cases is small compared to the number in England. Thus, for the most part, references are to England.

[5] This book is only concerned with large corporates. Small and medium-sized enterprises and owner-managed firms raise different issues from those considered here. A large company is taken to have liabilities of at least $100 million: Edward I Altman, 'The Role of Distressed Debt Markets, Hedge Funds, and Recent Trends in Bankruptcy on the Outcomes of Chapter 11 Reorganizations' (2014) 22 Am Bankr Inst L Rev 75, 88 fn 55.

famously labelled 'creative destruction'.[6] For these scholars, assets must be released from failing firms and reallocated to firms which are able to make better use of them. These economically minded scholars argue that this recycling of assets to highest and best use will promote innovation, the creation of new and better jobs, and ultimately economic growth. As Douglas Baird and Thomas Jackson put it, 'A principal characteristic of a market economy is, after all, that some firms fail, and postponing the inevitable or keeping marginal firms alive may do more harm than good.'[7] Economically minded corporate reorganization law scholars are aware of the dark side of creative destruction: that it may cause significant dislocations for employees, suppliers, and customers of the failed firm, and for the wider community in which the failed firm operates. Yet ultimately they are sceptical of the ability of the legislature and the law to intervene in this process in a way which does not hold back economic growth. And they argue that holding back economic growth is of greater detriment to society than the temporary dislocations which arise when a firm fails. In other words, in the end, economically minded corporate reorganization law scholars are of the view that both the public interest and social welfare are better served through the market mechanism than by legislative intervention. Thus, for scholars adopting an economic approach, corporate reorganization law exists solely to solve market failures which prevent assets from being allocated to highest and best use.

Progressive scholars, on the other hand, take the effect of dislocations for employees, suppliers, customers, and communities very seriously indeed. As Donald Korobkin puts it, they see bankruptcy law as '... a response to the many aspects of financial distress—moral, political, personal, social, and economic—and, in particular, to the grievances of those who are affected by financial distress'.[8] They are sceptical of the market mechanism to deliver results which are in the public interest, or which avoid social cost. They query whether the process of creative destruction will lead to the replacement of lost jobs and the opening up of new channels of supply for small suppliers. Even if it does, they are concerned about how long the process will take. They worry that any new jobs or opportunities for supply which are created will be inaccessible to the employees and suppliers of the failed firm. This may arise because the new firm is located somewhere which the employees cannot reasonably relocate to, or suppliers cannot reasonably supply to; or because the jobs require new skills which the old workforce does not currently have; or because suppliers of the failed firm must compete with existing suppliers

[6] Joseph Schumpeter, *Capitalism, Socialism, and Democracy* (George Allen & Unwin Ltd 1943) 81–86.

[7] Douglas G Baird and Thomas H Jackson, 'Corporate Reorganizations and the Treatment of Diverse Ownership Interests: A Comment on Adequate Protection of Secured Creditors in Bankruptcy' (1984) 51(1) U Chi L Rev 97, 102.

[8] Donald R Korobkin, 'Rehabilitating Values: A Jurisprudence of Bankruptcy' (1991) 91 Colum L Rev 717, 721.

of the new producer. Moreover, progressive scholars are concerned with the question of whether any new jobs or supply opportunities are of the same quality as the old ones.[9] And they focus on the risk of the potential hollowing out of entire communities if new producers are located in new areas, or even in new countries.[10] Overall, they do not subscribe to the view that the process of failure must take its course. Indeed, they have faith in the capacity of the legislature, and the law, to intervene actively to avoid or soften costly dislocations in the public interest. Thus, for scholars adopting a progressive approach, corporate reorganization law exists to avoid or reduce the social costs which result from corporate failure for weakly adjusting creditors, employees, and the community in which the distressed firm operates.

The most famous economic theory of corporate bankruptcy law is Thomas Jackson's creditors' bargain model.[11] For Thomas Jackson, corporate bankruptcy law existed solely to provide a strong automatic stay which prevented creditors from rushing to grab assets from the failing firm. Without the automatic stay, the grab race might have the result that the only viable option which remained for the failed firm would be a break-up sale of the remaining assets. In other words, because assets had been removed from the firm, creditors would be prevented from cooperative bargaining over whether a corporate reorganization or a liquidation would promote allocation of the assets to highest and best use.[12] A classic collective action problem emerged. Creditors had an individual incentive to rush to grab assets in order to recover their debts, yet this would potentially frustrate the allocation of assets to highest and best use. The vision was essentially procedural.[13] Corporate bankruptcy law existed solely to solve the market failure which prevented cooperative bargaining, by providing an automatic stay to prevent the grab race. The bargaining process could then be trusted to fulfil its role. Crucially, for the purposes of this book, Jackson did not envisage any specific corporate reorganization orientation in corporate bankruptcy law.

Jackson provided normative justification for the idea of a strong automatic stay of creditors' enforcement rights, based on the principle of consent. Using part of John Rawls' political theory methodology,[14] he argued that if creditors were placed

[9] Elizabeth Warren and Jay Lawrence Westbrook, 'Contracting Out of Bankruptcy: An Empirical Intervention' (2005) 118(4) Harvard L Rev 1197, 1232.

[10] Karen Gross, *Failure and Forgiveness: Rebalancing the Bankruptcy System* (Yale University Press 1997).

[11] Thomas H Jackson, 'Bankruptcy, Non-Bankruptcy Entitlements, and the Creditors' Bargain' (1982) 91 Yale LJ 857; Thomas H Jackson, 'Translating Assets and Liabilities to the Bankruptcy Forum' (1985) 14(1) J Legal Stud 73; Thomas H Jackson, *The Logic and Limits of Bankruptcy Law* (Harvard University Press 1986).

[12] In England, the term 'liquidation' typically applies only to a break-up sale of the assets of the firm, and not to a sale of the business and assets as a going concern. In the US, on the other hand, it typically refers to any sale transaction, as opposed to a corporate reorganization. In this book, it is used in the sense in which it is generally understood in the US.

[13] Douglas G Baird, 'Bankruptcy's Uncontested Axioms' (1998) 108(3) Yale LJ 573, 576–77.

[14] John Rawls, *Justice as Fairness: A Restatement* (second printing The Belknap Press 2001).

behind a veil of ignorance, and did not know whether they would be strong and fast creditors likely to succeed in the grab race for assets, or weak and slow creditors who would lose out, they would agree to the strong automatic stay. He thus used the idea of what he called the 'creditors' bargain' to provide normative justification for his limited vision of the content of corporate bankruptcy law.[15] This was an important part of Jackson's defence of his theory because economically minded scholars are sceptical of interference by corporate bankruptcy law in bargained for property and contract rights. In particular, they are concerned about the effect such interference will have on two sets of incentives. First, they are concerned about the effect which it will have on the incentives of other parties contracting with healthy firms in the economy, and thus the availability and cost of capital for these healthy firms. Secondly, they are concerned that it will create incentives for particular constituencies to favour a bankruptcy case as a result of the particular distributional consequences which follow from it, rather than because it will secure the allocation of assets to highest and best use.[16] Thus, Jackson needed to justify the role of the stay in preventing secured creditors from immediately taking enforcement action against the firm. Yet, notwithstanding the theoretical flourish of the veil of ignorance, his approach is fundamentally underpinned by the idea of a limited role for corporate bankruptcy law to solve the market failure which prevents assets from being allocated to highest and best use.

During her time as a Harvard law professor, Elizabeth Warren was probably the most high-profile critic of Thomas Jackson, Douglas Baird, and other scholars who adopted an economic approach.[17] Much of her work focuses on distributional questions in corporate bankruptcy. Elizabeth Warren saw a strongly redistributive role for corporate bankruptcy law, paying close attention to where losses fall and, in particular, seeking to ensure that losses do not fall on parties who had weak loss-adjusting capacity before the case, and who have weak bargaining capacity after the fall. Moreover, Elizabeth Warren, and her ally and co-author Jay Westbrook, also advocated strongly and consistently in favour of pro-reorganization content for corporate bankruptcy law, maximizing the chances that the firm could be saved.[18] In other words, their progressive vision was focused on how to preserve both value and the failing firm for the benefit of employees, weakly adjusting suppliers who may struggle to find alternative customers for supply, customers who may rely on the failing firm, and the community in which the failing firm was embedded.[19]

[15] Jackson, 'Creditors' Bargain' (n 11) 860.

[16] Jackson, 'Creditors' Bargain' (n 11) 868–71, 904.

[17] Elizabeth Warren, 'Bankruptcy Policy' (1987) 54 U Chi L Rev 775.

[18] Warren and Westbrook (n 9).

[19] Warren, 'Bankruptcy Policy' (n 17); Elizabeth Warren, 'A Theory of Absolute Priority' (1991) Ann Surv Am L 9; Elizabeth Warren, 'The Untenable Case for Repeal of Chapter 11' (1992) 102 Yale LJ 437; Elizabeth Warren and Jay L Westbrook, 'Searching for Reorganization Realities' (1994) 72(3) Wash ULQ 1257; Elizabeth Warren, 'Making Policy with Imperfect Information: The Article 9 Full Priority Debate' (1996–1997) 82(6) Cornell L Rev 1373.

Douglas Baird and other economically minded scholars railed against redistribution, the corporate reorganization policy goal, and the corporate reorganization law content. They pressed for market mechanisms to value the firm; raised serious concerns about the erosion of secured creditor power; argued against debtor control; and criticized the bargaining environment.[20] Thus, the economic versus progressive debate took shape.

1.2.2 Concepts in the US corporate reorganization law debate

Over time, the contours of the debate were drawn through a number of concepts which became the specific site of disagreement. First, progressive scholars argued that corporate reorganization law ought to promote the interests of the unsecured or junior creditor,[21] while scholars adopting an economic approach were sceptical of any attempt to influence the course of the case in the interests of this particular constituency.[22] Secondly, progressive scholars accepted the role of corporate bankruptcy law in solving collective action problems but also saw a specific role for law in promoting a reorganization,[23] while economically minded scholars saw a very limited role for corporate bankruptcy law beyond the boundaries of solving the collective action problem.[24] Thirdly, progressive scholars actively sought to tip power away from secured creditors who, they feared, might prefer a liquidation over a corporate reorganization,[25] while economically minded scholars were highly sceptical of any attempt to influence the allocation of assets.[26] Fourthly, progressive scholars supported strong debtor control rights in corporate reorganization law, in order to promote early action and the corporate reorganization transaction,[27] while economically minded scholars were highly sceptical of the incentives which this created, and were concerned that those responsible for the failure would preside over attempts to solve it.[28] Finally, progressive scholars supported an

[20] Douglas G Baird, 'The Uneasy Case for Corporate Reorganizations' (1986) 15 J Legal Stud 127; Douglas G Baird, 'Loss Distribution, Forum Shopping and Bankruptcy: A Reply to Warren' (1987) 54(3) U Chi L Rev 815; Michael Bradley and Michael Rosenzweig, 'The Untenable Case for Chapter 11' (1992) 101(5) Yale LJ 1043.

[21] Warren and Westbrook (n 9).

[22] Baird, 'Bankruptcy's Uncontested Axioms' (n 13) 590–91.

[23] Richard D Thomas, 'Tipping the Scales in Chapter 11: How Distressed Debt Investors Decrease Debtor Leverage and the Efficacy of Business Reorganization' (2010) 27(1) Emory Bankr Dev J 213.

[24] Jackson, 'Creditors' Bargain' (n 11); Jackson, 'Bankruptcy Forum' (n 11); Jackson, *Logic and Limits* (n 11); Baird and Jackson (n 7) 100–01.

[25] Warren, 'Making Policy' (n 19) 1390.

[26] Jackson, 'A Retrospective Look' (n 3) 1873: '... if secured creditors won outside of bankruptcy, there was no identifiable bankruptcy principle (beyond, to me, the flabby, unprincipled, "equality is equity" mantra) to change that outcome in bankruptcy'.

[27] Raymond T Nimmer and Richard B Feinberg, 'Chapter 11 Business Governance: Fiduciary Duties, Business Judgment, Trustees and Exclusivity' (1989) 6(1) Bankruptcy Dev J 1, 24; Thomas (n 23) 223.

[28] David A Skeel Jr, 'Creditors' Ball: The "New" New Corporate Governance in Chapter 11' (2003) 152 U Pa L Rev 917, 920–21.

uncertain litigation environment in Chapter 11, in order to strengthen the hand of junior creditors in bargaining for reorganization consideration,[29] while economically minded scholars worried about the transaction costs associated with a system which was 'widely thought to be cumbersome, costly, and complex'.[30] Thus, debate between progressive scholars adopting a pro-legal intervention approach and economic scholars adopting a market contractarian approach became encoded in a bundle of concepts which became the crucible of corporate reorganization law debate: the unsecured or junior creditor; collective action; secured creditor control rights; debtor control rights; and bargaining and litigation.[31]

These concepts clearly performed a descriptive function. The unsecured creditor described the creditor who did not have security, and thus ranked behind secured creditors, and the junior creditor described, more generally, the creditor who ranked behind senior creditors in the distributional order of priority. Collective action described the problem which arose when creditors could not cooperate together to achieve a reorganization transaction. Secured creditor control described the rights which creditors, by virtue of their security, had to enforce against the assets of the financially distressed creditor, and their ability, as a consequence, to influence the course of the case. Debtor control rights described the bundle of rights provided to the debtor in Chapter 11, which enabled management to exercise control over the course of the case. Finally, bargaining and litigation described the way in which the uncertain valuation environment in Chapter 11 encouraged the parties to bargain. Yet these concepts were more than merely descriptive terms. They also carried within them associated ideas, which theorists who were engaging them could mobilize to promote their own points of view. These associated ideas responded, in turn, to the real world of corporate reorganization at the time that the concepts were developed.

Chapter 11 was enacted in an era in which most large corporate reorganization plans implicated financial creditors and general, unsecured creditors and employees. Thus, the unsecured or junior creditors in a typical case included weakly adjusting trade creditors or employees. As a result, the unsecured or junior creditor represents, for the progressive scholar, the weakly adjusting trade creditor or employee worthy of special protection while, for the economic scholar, the unsecured or junior creditor represents the problem of interfering in the market mechanism beyond solving specific market failures. Furthermore, Chapter 11 was enacted at

29 Diane Lourdes Dick, 'Valuation in Chapter 11 Bankruptcy: The Dangers of an Implicit Market Test' (2017) U Ill L Rev 1487, 1501.

30 Mark J Roe, 'Bankruptcy and Debt: A New Model for Corporate Reorganization' (1983) 83 Colum L Rev 527, 528.

31 'Market contractarian', here, refers to the view that the parties will be able to bargain for the highest and best allocation of the assets, provided any relevant market failure can be addressed—see Jules Coleman, *Markets, Morals, and the Law* (OUP 1998) 243–46; Georg Vanberg and Viktor Vanberg, 'Contractarian Perspectives in Law and Economics' in Francesco Parisi (ed), *The Oxford Handbook of Law and Economics Volume 1: Methodology and Concepts* (OUP 2017) 247.

a time at which, if creditors did not wish to support a reorganization, their only real alternative was to push for a liquidation and a distribution of the proceeds. Thus, the collective action problem is a central concern for scholars from both camps, while progressive scholars worry particularly that secured creditors will prefer a liquidation over a corporate reorganization transaction. At the same time, in 1978, US firms had not typically encumbered all of their assets. Thus, firms had the ability to raise new finance secured over unencumbered assets to finance the corporate reorganization case. For the progressive scholar, this reduced the leverage which the secured creditor had over the course of the case and thus, implicitly, reduced the risks associated with the secured creditor's bias for a liquidation. A scholar adopting an economic approach, on the other hand, worried about the consequences of interfering with the secured creditor's bargained for rights.

Moreover, Chapter 11 was enacted at a time at which most managers still expected to spend much of their career with the same firm. As a result, managers of a financially distressed firm could be expected to focus on saving their jobs. Thus, progressive scholars saw real value in providing management with significant control rights, which they could be expected to use as a means of saving the firm. Economically minded scholars, on the other hand, worried a good deal about the incentives which debtor control rights created for entrenched managers. And Chapter 11 was enacted at a time at which the finance industry was only just beginning to move away from a relatively simple model of investment, in which reputation for what might be called 'good' standards of behaviour still mattered with clients and with peers. Thus, financial creditors could be expected to seek to avoid costly litigation, and to be willing to bargain, influencing the ways in which both progressively minded and economically minded scholars approached the bargaining and litigation concept. As a result, each of the concepts which have been identified—the unsecured or junior creditor; collective action; secured creditor control rights; debtor control rights; and bargaining and litigation—carry with them associated ideas relating to the particular organizational and institutional environment in which Chapter 11 was embedded at the time the concepts were developed.

1.2.3 The problem of engaging these concepts in the modern debate

For most of the 1980s and the 1990s, corporate reorganization law appeared to belong to the progressives. Chapter 11 practice promoted judicial valuations of the firm over market-based valuations. The hope was that this would produce higher valuations, and thus the allocation of greater reorganization consideration to unsecured or junior creditors. Chapter 11 did seek to solve the collective action problem through a strong automatic stay, which was important to both economically minded and progressively minded scholars, but it went further. It actively sought to tip the balance of power in the case away from secured creditors and towards the debtor, in the expectation that debtor management would prefer a corporate reorganization which would preserve their jobs. In this way, the firm would be saved for the employees, the general, unsecured supply chain, the customers, and the community in which the firm was located. Chapter 11 included a suite of significant powers for debtor management to control the corporate reorganization case, in the hope that this would incentivize management to file early, further increasing the prospects of a successful corporate reorganization transaction in the interests of employees, suppliers, customers, and the community. It created a complex and uncertain litigation environment in an effort to encourage creditors to coalesce around a consensually agreed corporate reorganization plan, and powerful rights for judges to impose the plan if recalcitrant creditors still could not be persuaded to agree. It set up a detailed committee machinery to enhance this bargaining environment. Overall, Chapter 11 provided the most fully developed legal mechanism to promote the corporate reorganization objective in the world.

However, since the 2000s, the balance of power in corporate reorganization appears to have shifted away from the debtor and its management. The victors appear to be economically minded scholars, who now observe a body of corporate reorganization law orientated to a greater extent around their pro-market vision. This has led to some despair among more progressively minded scholars and practitioners, the high-water mark being, perhaps, the final report of the American Bankruptcy Institute Commission to Study Reform of Chapter 11 (the ABI report). For the most part, the ABI report seeks to reassert a traditional, progressive vision, and to propose reforms designed to pull Chapter 11 back towards its progressive roots.[32] For example, the ABI report advocates for reforms designed to protect returns to unsecured or junior creditors, and proposes to tip the balance of power away from secured creditors and back towards the debtor. At the same time, the Loan Syndications and Trading Association (LSTA) has responded to the ABI report (the LSTA response) adopting strident, traditionally economic concepts.[33] Specifically, it argues that it ought not to be the role of Chapter 11 to intervene and affect the balance of power between secured creditors and the debtor in order to promote a corporate reorganization objective, and challenges the assertion that Chapter 11 has lost its way. The battle lines in the ABI report and the LSTA response have largely been drawn around modern corporate reorganization law using the concepts which have framed the economic versus progressive debate ever since Thomas Jackson launched his opening salvo in 1982.

[32] American Bankruptcy Institute Commission to Study the Reform of Chapter 11 2012–2014, *Final Report and Recommendations* (American Bankruptcy Institute 2014).

[33] LSTA, 'The Trouble with Unneeded Bankruptcy Reform: The LSTA's Response to the ABI Chapter 11 Commission Report' (LSTA October 2015).

Yet changes in what this book will call, borrowing from Patricia Thornton, William Ocasio, and Michael Lounsbury, 'logics', 'practices', and 'identities' in the finance and non-financial corporate fields, have profoundly changed the wider organizational and institutional environment with which corporate reorganization law interacts.[34] In a number of corporate reorganization cases, the purpose of the case is solely to reorganize the debtor's loan, bond, and equity finance arrangements. In these cases, the unsecured or junior creditors will be sophisticated, informed, and strongly adjusting financial creditors and not general, unsecured trade creditors and employees. A deep and liquid market for distressed debt has evolved, so that a creditor who does not wish to support a corporate reorganization transaction now has the chance to sell their claim in the secondary market to a party who does wish to support the reorganization effort. It is considerably more likely that a firm will have encumbered all of its assets, with consequences for secured creditor control, but this will interact with the new incentives which secured creditors may have as a result of the other changes in the finance field. It is considerably less likely that managers will expect to spend all of their career with the same firm, with consequences for their incentives in financial distress. And the world of work in the finance industry has changed dramatically, so that attitudes to the risk of litigation may be very different from attitudes in the 1980s.

These developments significantly undermine the utility of existing concepts as guides for analysing the content, and the case for reform, of corporate reorganization law. For example, it is difficult to believe that any progressive scholar would regard a US hedge fund invested in high-yielding, but risky, subordinated unsecured bond debt as needing particular protection in the interests of social welfare. And yet this will often be the identity of the unsecured or junior creditor in a reorganization of the debtor's loan, bond, and equity finance arrangements. Moreover, if a reorganization of the financial capital structure cannot be agreed, it becomes more likely that distress will spread to the general, unsecured trade creditors, employees, and customers (the groups which progressive scholars do wish to protect). Thus, the progressive scholar who continues to analyse the content of corporate reorganization law with the aim of protecting the unsecured or junior creditor in this context may take a seriously wrong turn.

While scholars have engaged with the new world of corporate reorganization, the literature is fragmented and partial. There is a general recognition that the facts of the typical Chapter 11 case have changed. As Thomas Jackson puts it, '... today's large bankruptcies have capital structures—and a set of players—very different from my 1980s paradigm of a large secured creditor or two and numerous, and diffuse, unsecured creditors'.[35] However, there is no systematic working out in the

[34] Patricia H Thornton, William Ocasio, and Michael Lounsbury, *The Institutional Logics Perspective: A New Approach to Culture, Structure, and Process* (OUP 2012) 128–47.

[35] Jackson, 'A Retrospective Look' (n 3) 1878.

literature of how corporate reorganization law is now mobilized and adapted, and the consequences for the fact patterns of the cases. Crucially, no distinction is regularly drawn between cases which reorganize the financial structure of the debtor and other types of cases. Indeed, there is a stubborn commitment to the idea of the typical case, even if there is an acknowledgment that the facts have changed.

Many scholars have identified that collective action problems are not as significant as they have been in the past.[36] However, the literature does not clearly connect the observation that collective action problems may have reduced in significance with the conditions in the finance field which have given rise to it. As a result, inadequate attention is paid to the fact that the conclusion that collective action problems are not as significant as they were thought to be in the 1980s is contingent on particular patterns of fact in the case. There is a significant body of literature on the rise of the distressed debt trader,[37] and Douglas Baird and Robert Rasmussen have briefly connected the new identities of the participants in the process with some of the concepts engaged in corporate reorganization law debate:

> The increasing role of hedge funds in owning the secured debt of distressed companies calls into question the long-standing assumption that senior investors are biased towards liquidation.[38]

However, Baird and Rasmussen move on to discuss a particular aspect of corporate reorganization practice which has developed as a result, and do not develop their insight generally. Similarly, both progressively orientated and economically orientated scholars have engaged with the changing incentives of management, but typically from their particular theoretical perspective and without connecting the development with the wider context of the corporate reorganization case.[39] And, other than limited work by the author, there has been very little literature

[36] See eg Douglas G Baird and Robert K Rasmussen, 'Anitbankruptcy' (2010) 119(4) Yale L J 648, 652–53; David A Skeel Jr and George Triantis, 'Bankruptcy's Uneasy Shift to a Contract Paradigm' (2018) 166 U Pa L Rev 1777, 1779; Anthony J Casey, 'The New Bargaining Theory of Corporate Bankruptcy and Chapter 11's Renegotiation Framework' (*SSRN*, 16 March 2019) <https://ssrn.com/abstract=335871> accessed 6 March 2020; Vincent S J Buccola, 'Bankruptcy's Cathedral: Property Rules, Liability Rules, and Distress' (*SSRN*, 3 December 2019) <https://ssrn.com/abstract=3353848> accessed 6 March 2020.

[37] See eg Chaim J Fortgang and Thomas Moers Mayer, 'Trading Claims and Taking Control of Corporations in Chapter 11' (1990) 12 Cardozo L Rev 1; Chaim J Fortgang and Thomas Moers Mayer, 'Developments in Trading Claims: Participations and Disputed Claims' (1993) 15 Cardozo L Rev 733; Paul M Goldschmid, 'More Phoenix than Vulture: The Case for Distressed Investor Presence in the Bankruptcy Reorganization Process' (2005) Colum Bus L Rev 191; Michelle M Harner, 'The Corporate Governance and Public Policy Implications of Activist Distressed Debt Investing' (2008) 77(2) Fordham L Rev 703; Michelle M Harner, 'Trends in Distressed Debt Investing: An Empirical Study of Investors' Objectives' (2008) 16(1) Am Bankr Inst L Rev 69.

[38] Baird and Rasmussen (n 36) 671.

[39] See eg Harvey R Miller and Shai Y Waisman, 'Is Chapter 11 Bankrupt?' (2005) 47 BC L Rev 129, 155; Baird and Rasmussen (n 36) 671.

connecting the changing sociology of the finance field with the bargaining environment in corporate reorganization.[40]

There are two principal reasons which account for this fragmented and partial approach in the scholarship to the dramatic changes in the wider organizational and institutional environment with which corporate reorganization law interacts. First, the article remains the preferred unit of analysis for corporate reorganization law scholars, which reduces the space and time which the scholar has to consider the underlying forces which account for the change, the detail of how those forces of change interact with corporate reorganization law, and the changes to the overall landscape which emerge as a result. Secondly, scholars tend to approach the changes in corporate reorganization law and practice from the particular theoretical perspective with which they identify. This means that their purpose is not generally to consider the implications of the change from other perspectives, with the result that any conclusions the scholar draws sometimes appear contingent on the political and ideological approach they have adopted rather than the changes in the finance and non-financial corporate field with which corporate reorganization law interacts. Overall, the result is that an incomplete picture of the landscape is painted by the scholarship. Thus, a gap emerges in the literature, demanding a more systematic working out of how the concepts which are engaged in corporate reorganization law debate connect with the real world of corporate reorganization. Fundamentally, there is a need for economic and progressive legal scholars to reassess the contours of their disagreement in the new world of corporate reorganization.

1.2.4 Building a new conceptual framework in the book

This is the gap which the book aims to fill. It seeks to do this in two, broad ways. First, as a book length project, it has the time and space for a systematic investigation of the dramatically different organizational and institutional environment which has unfolded. Secondly, as it is not the purpose of the book to weigh in on the wider question of how corporate reorganization law should promote public interest and social welfare, the book analyses the changes with which it is concerned from both the perspective of the economically orientated scholar and the perspective of the progressively orientated scholar. Crucially, it is this approach which reveals a field of action where the book will argue that both economically orientated and progressively orientated scholars ought to be able to agree on the content of corporate reorganization law, notwithstanding the different lenses which they train on it.

[40] Sarah Paterson, 'Market Organisations and Institutions in America and England: Valuation in Corporate Bankruptcy' (2018) 93 Chi-Kent L Rev 801.

Yet, it is emphatically not the purpose of the book to claim that a new type of typical large Chapter 11 case has entirely and permanently replaced all other types of Chapter 11 case. Nor is it the purpose of the book to claim that economically minded and progressively minded scholars ought to be able to agree on the content of all corporate reorganization law, regardless of how it is mobilized and adapted. As Chapter 11 has come of age, and as the finance field continues to undergo a period of unprecedented innovation and change, very different fact patterns emerge which corporate reorganization law is mobilized and adapted to meet in new and diverse ways. The views of scholars on both the content of corporate reorganization law and on the case for reform in some of these types of corporate reorganization case may crucially depend on whether they have selected an economic or a progressive approach. In other words, it is not the purpose of this book to claim the end of the debate between economic scholars and progressive scholars. Instead, it is a call for theorists to focus their particular lens on the very different ways in which corporate reorganization law is mobilized and adapted, taking care with the concepts which are engaged to describe the problems to which corporate reorganization law responds. Moreover, it is vital to keep in sight that sometimes scholars may be able to agree on the content of corporate reorganization law, even if they approach it from very different political and ideological perspectives. In other cases, however, they may disagree fundamentally on both content and the case for reform, depending on the lens through which they choose to view corporate reorganization law. This brings us to the comparative aspect of the book.

1.3 The English sections

This book is not limited to an examination of the need to better connect the US corporate reorganization law debate with the ways in which corporate reorganization law is now mobilized and adapted by the participants in the system. It also compares the US account with the development of corporate reorganization law and practice in England. It explores how and why reorganization of large corporates was achieved out of court and consensually in England right up until the 2000s. This has explanatory power for the finding that the same conceptual framework for analysing corporate reorganization law did not emerge in England as in the US. The book then explores (i) the ways in which the same shifts in logics, practices, and identities in the proximate fields of finance and non-financial corporates, which were explored in the US context, occurred in England through the 1980s and 1990s; and (ii) why, in the 2000s, this caused English practitioners to turn back to corporate reorganization legal tools developed in the nineteenth century, but little used since the Second World War. When this turn occurred in England, scholars, practitioners, and judges were not bounded by concepts developed in a different organizational and institutional environment. The book shows why this led to the emergence of different concepts in England for assessing corporate reorganization law cases from those which are typically engaged in the US. Finally, the book argues that these English concepts are well adapted to the modern mobilization and adaptation of corporate reorganization law to deleverage complex, financial capital structures.

This comparative analysis performs three roles in the book. First, it gives content to the claim, in the US sections of the analysis, that different approaches to corporate reorganization law can be developed if scholars, practitioners, judges, and the legislature begin by considering how the dominant problem with which they are concerned manifests itself in the relevant fact pattern. In other words, this is a more promising approach than attempting to fit old concepts to new facts in analysing the content of corporate reorganization law. Secondly, it provides a useful source of ideas for US scholars, practitioners, judges, and the legislature for different ways in which modern corporate reorganization law cases to deleverage complex, financial capital structures can be approached. In other words, there is a tendency to consider that the flow of ideas in corporate reorganization is always from the US to other jurisdictions. Yet the analysis in the English sections of the book suggests that modern US corporate reorganization practice does not always demand all of the tools which US corporate reorganization law offers, and that US scholars, practitioners, judges, and the legislature may also have something to learn from England. Finally, it offers a word of warning to English scholars, practitioners, judges, and the legislature.

The word of warning arises precisely because English corporate reorganization law is well adapted to deleveraging complex, financial capital structures. The book argues that modern English corporate reorganization law is well adapted for this purpose because scholars, practitioners, judges, and the legislature were not bounded by a priori commitments to concepts developed in a different organizational and institutional environment when modern corporate reorganization practice began to emerge. Yet, as already touched on and as is developed as the book progresses, corporate reorganization does not only take the form of deleveraging loan, bond, and equity financial capital structures. When the book was being written, there were a number of visible shifts and expansions in logics, practices, and identities in the finance and non-financial corporate fields which seemed likely to change the nature of the problem to be solved by corporate reorganization law. The book explores how these may, in turn, affect the ways in which corporate reorganization law is mobilized and adapted by the participants in the process. It argues that there is a very real risk that English scholars, practitioners, judges, and the legislature may struggle to adapt a conceptual framework which is well adapted for the deleveraging of complex, financial capital structures for these other mobilizations and adaptations of corporate reorganization law. In other words, a problem may arise in England in the future. Thus, the argument at the heart of the book is the need to adapt the conceptual framework used, in any jurisdiction, to analyse the content of corporate reorganization law when shifts in the fields proximate to it cause it to be mobilized and adapted in different ways. This argument assumes increased significance as the book goes to press, as the UK Government's response to the COVID-19 crisis profoundly alters the finance and non-financial corporate landscape, posing new challenges for English corporate reorganization law.

1.4 The future

This brings the challenge of prediction into focus. It is striking how often, in the account in this book, sophisticated predictions for the future of corporate reorganization law prove to have been wide of the mark. In 1989, Michael Jensen predicted the privatization of the reorganization of large, leveraged firms, on the basis that this would make sense for the financial creditors because there would be a good deal of firm value to preserve, if a rapid deleveraging of the capital structure could be achieved.[41] The account in the book reveals that in many ways Jensen was right: the book traces the rise of the exchange offer in the US, which is a market-based mechanism for achieving a reorganization of the firm's liabilities to financial institutions, and reveals an increasing focus on debt contracts as a method of allocating control rights to achieve a reorganization of financial liabilities in England. Yet, at the same time, the analysis reveals that Jensen was also wide of the mark. There is regular and contentious resort to legal process in the US. And significant resort to legal process to achieve a reorganization really only emerged for the first time as complex, leveraged capital structures developed in England.

The reason why Jensen's prediction has not wholly come to pass is that, while the rise of the leveraged capital structure was apparent at the time he was writing, many of the other complex changes in the finance field traced in this book were not apparent. Moreover, and significantly, the ways in which those changes would interact with each other was very difficult to foresee. Similarly, when it appeared for a time that corporate reorganization was being usurped by going-concern sales of distressed businesses to third party purchasers, Douglas Baird and Robert Rasmussen declared the 'End of Bankruptcy'.[42] In reality, since 2012, the corporate reorganization case has been very firmly back on the US agenda. Indeed, some of the factors which drove Baird and Rasmussen to make their prediction (notably the move away from the horizontally and vertically integrated firm, and the rising importance of intangibles) are the reasons why England needs to add new tools to its corporate reorganization law toolbox. As Georg von Wangenheim puts it:

[41] Michael Jensen, 'Active Investors, LBOs, and the Privatization of Bankruptcy' (1989) J App Corp Fin 34, repr (2010) 2(1) J App Corp Fin 77.

[42] Douglas G Baird and Robert K Rasmussen, 'The End of Bankruptcy' (2002) 55(3) Stanford L Rev 751.

> Law then evolves in an extremely wide and complex environment. Not only do rules from one legal area interact, and co-evolve, with rules from other areas, but also and perhaps in an even more important way, with non-legal phenomena—individual preferences and interests, technology, and social norms. In addition, legal evolution in one jurisdiction interacts with other jurisdictions. Given this complexity of legal evolution with co-evolving environments, all models in ELE are partial and study only a small segment of the co-evolution of law and its environment.[43]

This book was written at a time when a number of hugely significant, potential changes in the wider environment in which corporate reorganization is embedded were visible on the horizon. There were signs that concerns for climate change were gaining real popular support, with potentially dramatic consequences for firms in capitalist economies. In both the US and the UK, fundamental questions were being asked again about the purpose of the corporation: Milton Friedman's exhortation that, 'the social responsibility of business is to increase its profits' was under perhaps the most sustained attack it has suffered in the US and the UK for decades.[44] There was growing unease at the rise of leverage in the economy, in the structure and practices of the private equity industry, and in the future of the hedge fund industry. Indeed, Elizabeth Warren (who, at the time the book was being written, was running for the democratic nomination for the White House) proposed new, and wide-ranging, types of regulation of the finance industry. And new types of artificial intelligence (AI) were developing, with the potential for a dramatic change in the relationship between man and machine, which is beyond anything touched on in this book: AI has the potential to change not only the way in which finance and business is organized, but also the way in which the whole of society is organized. As the book goes to press, the paradigmatic example of an unforeseen force of change has emerged, in the shape of the COVID-19 crisis. It is impossible, against a tsunami of complex and unpredictable potential changes in the environment in which corporate reorganization law is embedded, to identify how corporate reorganization law might be mobilized and adapted going forwards.

This impossibility of identifying future uses of corporate reorganization law has several, important implications for the argument at the heart of this book. First, it highlights the crucial importance of focusing whichever lens is used to view corporate reorganization law on the different fact patterns which are observed over time. There is an understandable commitment to the search for fixed, universally applicable conceptual frameworks in the corporate reorganization law

[43] Georg von Wangenheim, 'Evolutionary Law and Economics' in Francesco Parisi (ed) *The Oxford Handbook of Law and Economics Volume 1: Methodology and Concepts* (OUP 2017) 162. 'ELE' is defined, at page 161, as 'evolutionary law and economics'.

[44] Milton Friedman, 'The Social Responsibility of Business is to Increase its Profits' *New York Times* (New York, 13 September 1970), s 6 (Magazine) 32.

academy. Yet the reality is that, as participants in the process mobilize and adapt corporate reorganization law in new ways to meet the problems of the day so, too, corporate reorganization law scholars must adapt the conceptual framework with which they analyse both corporate reorganization law content and the case for reform. Secondly, it underlines the crucial importance of the step of understanding the detail of the shifts in logics, practices, and identities in the fields proximate to corporate reorganization law as they unfold, and of analysing how these impact the ways in which corporate reorganization law is mobilized and adapted, before building a conceptual framework with which to analyse the new adaptation. This is apparent, for example, when the book considers the implications of the rise in so-called covenant-lite finance documents for corporate reorganization law, or the changing nature of collective action problems in full financial and operational reorganizations of large firms which are heavily dependent on intangible assets, and is likely to be crucial as the implications of the COVID-19 crisis for corporate reorganization law become apparent. Finally, it highlights the advantage which both the US and England have, as common law systems with expert judges who are able to revise the conceptual framework which they use in scrutinizing the outcome of the case in the context prevailing at the time. While economic scholars have often been sceptical of judicial discretion, and the detail of the US Bankruptcy Code may lead to a concern that judicial discretion has been constrained by the legislature, judicial flexibility can provide a powerful weapon in a rapidly changing world.

1.5 Organization of the book

Chapter 2 is a scene-setting exercise, offering a brief and highly selective review of one hundred years of corporate reorganization in the US and England. This provides some explanation for the very different ways in which corporate reorganization developed in each jurisdiction. Overall, Chapter 2 helps to sketch out the conditions which prevailed when the account in the book really begins in the 1970s.

Chapters 3–7 are each divided into a section exploring the US, followed by a comparison with the position in England. Each US section starts by exploring the associated ideas embedded in a particular concept which is regularly engaged in corporate reorganization law debate. It then analyses the extent to which a significant shift in logic and practice, or logic and identity, in the fields of finance or non-financial corporates have changed the fact pattern in the corporate reorganization law case. The implications of this change for the way in which corporate reorganization law is mobilized and adapted are then explored, before revisiting the implications for the ongoing utility of the original concept in theoretical debate. In each case, the analysis in the English section explores why the relevant concept identified in the US section had less or no salience in the English context. The way in which the shift in logic, practice, or identity in the finance or non-financial corporate fields with which the chapter is concerned unfolded in England is then identified and explored. The implications of this shift for English corporate reorganization law are examined, paying regard to the fact that scholars, practitioners, judges, and the legislature were not bounded by concepts developed for a different organizational and institutional environment as the new mobilization and adaptation of corporate reorganization law developed. Finally, the concepts for analysing corporate reorganization law cases which emerged in England as a result are identified and analysed.

Chapter 8 continues the exploration of recent shifts in logic, practice, and identity in the US and England. Specifically, it is still concerned with shifts in logic, practice, and identity in the finance and non-financial corporate fields which have impacted on concepts regularly engaged in corporate reorganization law debate. However, it is a little different from the structure of Chapters 3–7. This is because Chapter 8 is concerned with a shift in logic, practice, and identity which has impacted concepts engaged in corporate reorganization law analysis in the US and England in very similar ways. As a result, very similar issues arise in Chapter 8 for both the US and England.

Overall, the analysis in Chapters 3–8 reveals the field of action where the book argues that both economically minded and progressively minded scholars ought to be able to agree on the content of corporate reorganization law and the implications for reform. Chapter 9 then explains why the common ground which has been revealed in Chapters 3–8 is not the whole, or the end, of the story. First, it seeks to identify other ways in which corporate reorganization law has been mobilized and adapted to address different fact patterns in the decade since the 2008 financial crisis. It shows why analysis of the content, and case for reform, of corporate reorganization law is dependent on the lens through which these cases are viewed. Secondly, Chapter 9 investigates how expanding and changing shifts in logic and practice, and logic and identity, may cause the landscape to shift again, resulting in new debates among economically orientated and progressively orientated scholars. And thirdly, it suggests that some of the much more dramatic changes touched on in section 1.4 'The Future', which have the potential to reshape radically the finance and non-financial corporate fields, may have equally dramatic consequences for the ways in which corporate reorganization law is mobilized and adapted going forwards.

In common with the rest of the book, the significance of the different types of corporate reorganization case identified in Chapter 9 is explored, first, for the US, and secondly, for England. The analysis in Chapter 9 explores why English scholars, practitioners, judges, and the legislature need to be alive to the fact that a conceptual framework developed for assessing reorganization of complex, leveraged capital structures may require adaptation if corporate reorganization law is mobilized and adapted in new ways. In other words, Chapter 9 will identify the types of cases which give rise to this concern, and explore how and why it arises.

Finally, Chapter 10 applies the approach in the book to the corporate reorganization law reform debate in the US and in England. It will come as no surprise that the book is critical of the use of existing progressive conceptual frames to analyse the case for reform of Chapter 11, and of the use of existing economic conceptual frames to respond to progressive demands. It shows why the approach in the book, of thinking specifically about how the dominant concern of the theorist manifests itself in each of the diverse ways in which corporate reorganization law is now mobilized and adapted, may lead to different conclusions about the case for reform. Furthermore, it relates the reform agenda to the claim that the extent to which US scholars disagree about the content of corporate reorganization law may depend not only on which lens they use to view corporate reorganization law, but also on the specific way in which corporate reorganization law is mobilized and adapted to meet the specific fact pattern in the case. When it comes to the English corporate reorganization law reform agenda, Chapter 10 adopts a critical stance on the motivations which originally promoted the reform proposals, and on the somewhat unthinking tendency merely to turn to the tools of Chapter 11, without identifying why they might be needed in the English corporate reorganization law toolbox and how they might need to be designed as a result. Once again, it suggests that the first step is to relate the ways in which corporate reorganization law is actually mobilized and adapted by the participants in the process to the dominant concerns which have been identified, and to understand what reforms of corporate reorganization law may be needed once that relationship has been understood. The book ends with a call to abandon universal or fixed conceptual frameworks for analysing corporate reorganization law, and to turn instead to thinking specifically about the different ways in which corporate reorganization law is mobilized and adapted to respond to its wider environment.

2

Initial Conditions and Emergence of Corporate Reorganization in the United States and England

2.1 Introduction

The central insight in this chapter is that the different conditions prevailing in the United States (the US) and England in the early stages of industrialization offer significant explanatory power for the way in which corporate reorganization law and practice emerges in each jurisdiction. The purpose of this chapter is to explore that relationship in the US and English context. Specifically, the chapter investigates the relatively stable corporate reorganization law and practice which prevailed in each jurisdiction for much of the twentieth century, and the institutional logics, practices, and identities which gave rise to it.[1] This investigation provides the foundation for the rest of the book. Later chapters analyse how the wider organizational and institutional environment has changed, the new ways in which corporate restructuring law is mobilized and adapted by the participants in the corporate restructuring process as a result, and the implications for the corporate reorganization law debate.

This chapter argues that what the theorists and reformers of the 1970s and 1980s saw as the foundational normative concerns of US corporate reorganization law

[1] As identified in Chapter 1, the terms logics, practices, and identities are all borrowed from Patricia H Thornton, William Ocasio, and Michael Lounsbury, *The Institutional Logics Perspective: A New Approach to Culture, Structure, and Process* (OUP 2012) 128–47.

Corporate Reorganization Law and Forces of Change. Sarah Paterson, Oxford University Press (2020). © Sarah Paterson.
DOI: 10.1093/oso/9780198860365.001.0001.

and practice are all clearly visible in US corporate reorganization law and practice at the end of the nineteenth century and into the early twentieth century: the need to provide the debtor with a breathing space to reorganize its affairs; debtor control; priority funding for the case; the role of the court in encouraging bargaining and settlement; and valuation based on post-reorganization forecasts. As far as the US is concerned, the longevity of these concerns has considerable explanatory power for the struggle to reassess their relevance in a completely different organizational and institutional order.

Turning to England, this chapter reveals that the court debt restructuring procedure, which was laid down in the nineteenth century, gives way, in the middle of the twentieth century, to debt restructuring as a privately negotiated process rooted in contract. Indeed, resort to legal procedure is largely reserved for cases where a restructuring was not regarded as viable by the providers of finance. Once again, this structure, once it emerges, proves remarkably stable. As the book progresses, it reveals how the two-stage history of corporate reorganization law and practice in England has enabled participants to pull old tools out of the corporate reorganization law toolbox and adapt them to meet new goals and objectives. At the same time, it also explains why the English corporate reorganization legal tools do not do everything which the US tools can do, notwithstanding reform efforts which might have been expected to redesign them.

Once again, the account in this chapter reveals that the concepts which emerge to frame corporate reorganization throughout the twentieth century are clearly visible in modern corporate reorganization law and practice in England: where possible, restricting reorganization to financial creditors in order to preserve the cooperation of unsecured trade creditors; concern for minority hold-out power; weak moratorium protection; and strong deference to the will of the majority (unless there is some reason to doubt the majority motive in the context of the class of which they form part). Chapters 3–7 of the book argue that this conceptual framework has proved well adapted to modern corporate reorganization cases in the decade since the financial crisis. However, throughout the book, and particularly in Chapters 9 and 10, a question is raised as to whether England will be able to adapt its conceptual framework if expanding and changing institutional logics, practices, and identities cause the ways in which corporate reorganization law is mobilized and adapted to shift again. In the case of the US, the book is centrally concerned with connecting the conceptual framework used to analyse the content and reform of corporate reorganization law to current developments. In the case of England, the concern is the capacity to adapt existing conceptual frameworks to future developments of corporate reorganization law.

2.2 United States

2.2.1 Initial conditions and emergence of corporate reorganization

In the nineteenth century, the US embarked on a substantial programme of costly railroad construction. At the time, the US was at an early stage of industrialization. As a younger, more agricultural economy it had accumulated less capital for investment than Britain, which already had a mature industrial and commercial economy. Thus, much of the necessary capital to construct US railroads was raised from British investors, who favoured bonds over equity.[2] Although a corporate bankruptcy statute was on the books from early in the 1890s, it did not offer tools for the reorganization of corporate debt securities. Instead, these tools were reciprocally fashioned and supplied by the investment bankers of the day (notably J P Morgan), the courts, and the debtor's management, in a process known as 'equity receivership'.

At the time, it was usual for bondholders and other secured creditors to have security over particular pieces of equipment or infrastructure.[3] As a result, the collective action problem, with which modern corporate reorganization law scholars are familiar, was a particular concern. This is the concern that individual creditors have an incentive to rush to foreclose against the assets which provide security for their financing. While this may be in the best interests of the swiftest creditors, whose debts are well covered by the value of their security, it may also result in a break-up of the business. If this occurs, any prospect of saving the business as a going concern is lost, notwithstanding that this may be the best allocation of the relevant assets. Thus, a significant feature of the equity receivership was that, by the appointment of a receiver, the court of equity took all of the company's property into its possession. Where (as would usually be the case) the company had assets outside the state in which the receivership proceeding was opened, ancillary receiverships would be opened in all other relevant states. In this way, creditors were prevented from executing against particular assets, so that the railroad could be kept together and reorganized.[4]

In an equity receivership, a receiver (often a member of the incumbent management team, but sometimes a lawyer) was appointed over the debtor company. Committees were established to represent the railroad's bondholders and

[2] Rowena Olegario, *The Engine of Enterprise: Credit in America* (Harvard University Press 2016) 96.

[3] Peter Tufano, 'Business Failure, Judicial Intervention, and Financial Innovation: Restructuring US Railroads in the Nineteenth Century' (1997) 71(1) Bus Hist Rev 1, 11; Harvey R Miller and Shai Y Waisman, 'Does Chapter 11 Reorganization Remain a Viable Option for Distressed Business for the Twenty-first Century?' (2004) 78(2) Am Bankr Inst LJ 153, 165.

[4] David A Skeel Jr, 'An Evolutionary Theory of Corporate Law and Corporate Bankruptcy' (1998) 51 Vand L Rev 1325, n 110 1357.

shareholders, and the bondholders and shareholders were encouraged to hand their securities over to the relevant committee. Often, a committee was established for each class of debt and equity security. As Tufano puts it, 'Negotiations then proceeded until a single reorganization committee was formed, representing, in theory, all claimants.'[5] As far as the court was concerned, the object of the receivership was to protect the company's assets so that a plan of reorganization could be developed. The reorganization committee would attempt to formulate a reorganization plan pursuant to which the business and assets of the debtor would be sold to a new company. The former shareholders were required to contribute new money pro rata to their existing holding, in order to raise new finance, as a condition of receiving stock in the new company. This process was known as 'assessment'.[6] The existing bondholders, on the other hand, would agree to exchange their bonds for new bonds in the new company on new terms, including a lower interest rate, and would also often receive stock in the new company as further compensation. New bonds were also frequently issued to provide new money. Overall, the reorganization plan would reduce the debtor's fixed costs, provide new money (often essential if either the railroad had physically deteriorated or construction costs had proved considerably larger than originally anticipated), and enable the railroad to trade on with an appropriate capital structure. Pending agreement of the reorganization plan, receivers were permitted to issue interest-bearing 'receiver's certificates' which ranked in the order of distribution ahead of other debts, and which provided the necessary source of funds to operate the railroad whilst the reorganization plan was agreed.[7] When the plan was announced, the investment bank coordinating the reorganization committee normally decided what level of consent to the plan would be needed from bondholders and shareholders in order for the plan to become effective.

The level of acceptances was particularly important because the courts considered that they had no power to require dissenting creditors to take securities in the reorganization without a legislative mandate. Thus, they demanded that a cash price was paid for a dissenter's claim if he held out against the deal. The court thus played an important role in setting the 'upset price' or the minimum cash price which had to be paid to a dissenting security holder in order for the corporate restructuring to proceed. The upset price appears to have been loosely based on the anticipated post-reorganization earning potential of the railroad, and a discussion in an early twentieth-century Harvard Law Review piece suggests that the upset price was designed to ensure that the minority dissenters received value for their property, at a time at which the equity receivership process might chill rival bids

[5] Tufano (n 3) 12.
[6] ibid 14–15.
[7] Albro Martin, 'Railroads and Equity Receivership: An Essay on Institutional Change' (1974) 34(3) J Econ Hist 685, 699; Tufano (n 3) 8–9.

for the railroad.[8] Nonetheless, the upset price was also capable of being used to encourage the minority to accept the restructuring proposal. This is because the court could set a very low upset price so that dissenters would receive a low cash amount for their claim. The idea was that this would incentivize them to accept the exchange of their shares or bonds for the new instruments offered in the receivership.[9]

Thus, four significant points emerge. First, the equity receivership process was designed explicitly to address the collective action problem, preventing creditors from enforcing against individual assets, and giving the company a breathing space within which to work out a reorganization plan. Secondly, the modern practice of placing questions of value in the hands of the US bankruptcy courts is clearly visible in the earliest development of corporate reorganization practice in the US. Thirdly, the focus in determining value is on the post-reorganization earning potential of the enterprise, which seems to be rooted in concern for setting a fair value for the contractual and property entitlements of the minority. Finally, concern for minority protection was balanced by the ability of the courts to use the flexible weapon of the upset price to set a low value. In this way, they could seek to encourage bargaining and facilitate agreement of the debt reorganization plan, so that the debtor could emerge from the receivership with a capital structure fit for purpose. All of these elements are revisited as the book explores the development of modern US corporate reorganization law.

The investment banks, most notably the bank of J P Morgan, played a significant role in adapting the equity receivership process to meet the demands of nineteenth-century railroad reorganization, in a collaborative process with the courts, which understood the public interest nature of the mission at hand. The London investment banks were primarily focused, at the time, on government securities, and J P Morgan appears to have been critical in bringing the British investor and the US railroad together. As Ron Chernow identifies, competition to invest in the railroad securities was fierce, but British investors often had only the vaguest of ideas of even where the new railroad was to be located.[10] As the investors were remote from their investment, they depended upon J P Morgan to act as their intermediary, protecting their investment. At the same time, J P Morgan saw it as a key part of his role to protect that investment in order to secure his ability to return to the capital markets to raise funds for new projects. These capital raisings took place at a time before the establishment of government agencies to regulate the content of prospectuses or to enforce securities rules against issuers, and were promoted by men famously later named the 'robber barons'.[11] Thus, J P Morgan's capital-raising

[8] Samuel Spring, 'Upset Prices in Corporate Reorganization' (1919) 32(5) Harvard L Rev 489, 494.

[9] Tufano (n 3) 12.

[10] Ron Chernow, *The House of Morgan: An American Banking Dynasty and the Rise of Modern Finance* (Grove Press 1990) 29–30.

[11] Matthew Josephson, *The Robber Barons: The Great American Capitalists* (Harcourt, Brace & Co 1935).

ability depended uniquely on his reputation with the British investing community.[12] Moreover, the collective action problem discussed above was particularly acute in the railroad context because, if the railroad could not be kept together, there would be 'nothing but a streak of iron-rust on the prairie'.[13] At the same time, the collective action problem was heightened by the mixture of local and foreign creditors, because local creditors stood a better chance of victory in the race to enforce than distant creditors. Thus, in the US, the investment banker emerges as the key intermediary in financial restructuring. J P Morgan and his ilk perform the central role in establishing the reorganization committee, controlling the voting and strategic direction of the case, incentivizing bargaining, hiring new management, and taking board seats in the newly restructured railroad.

In the early stages of industrialization, as Alfred Chandler has compellingly shown in his ground-breaking work, the central unit of production was the small, family firm.[14] However, partly as a result of the development of nationwide transport links, large-scale enterprise, other than railroads, did begin to emerge towards the end of the nineteenth century. The geography of the US meant that the scale of these enterprises was very large indeed. Nonetheless, in many cases, the equipment which was required was inexpensive, while the innovations in production provided impressive cashflows. This meant that many of the early, large-scale enterprises were able to fund themselves out of retained earnings, perhaps with some limited working capital support from a commercial bank.

However, while this was typical of enterprises which developed by the forward and backward integration of methods of production and distribution, in other cases expansion was pursued through merger. This occurred, for example, in industries where large numbers of small manufacturing firms found themselves in the grip of competition, sometimes as a result of improved transport links. In this case, merger became necessary as these small companies drove prices down between themselves while supply steadily increased. At the same time, society nervously experienced the emergence of urban centres and of a national economy in the US. Concern initially focused on the railroads as the dominant institutions of their day, but soon shifted to concerns for cartel-like arrangements between enterprises located in the same industry: so-called industrial trusts. In an industrial trust, stockholders in individual companies passed their shares to a board of trustees, who made the operating and investment decisions for the companies going forward, in return for the issue of trust certificates.[15] As the trusts faced increasing attacks at federal and state levels, New Jersey passed legislation which offered the ability to

[12] Chernow (n 10) 23.

[13] See Miller and Waisman (n 3) 161 citing *Cent Trust Co of NY v Wabash* 29 F 618, 626 (ED Mo 1886).

[14] The account in this section of the development of American business is largely drawn from Alfred D Chandler, Jr, *The Visible Hand: The Managerial Revolution in American Business* (new edn, Harvard University Press 1977).

[15] ibid 319.

form a holding company, as Chandler puts it, 'simply by filing a few outline forms and paying a standard fee'.[16] Rural farmers contended with deflationary prices for agricultural produce, while the trusts enabled the industrial producers to maintain prices, so that the price of the fixed goods which farmers sought to purchase did not fall as rapidly as the price of the agricultural produce and products which they were selling.[17] Thus, political pressure mounted. This political pressure resulted in attempts to restrict informal cooperative arrangements between enterprises, culminating in the Sherman Antitrust Act of 1890, which prohibited the trust arrangements.[18] Yet, the Act had the effect of promoting, rather than discouraging, legal merger through the holding company route.[19] This mattered in the context of corporate reorganization because legal merger was a more costly exercise and resulted in large enterprises, other than railroads, requiring external sources of finance.

During this shift from a primarily agrarian economy, farmers and those in rural states remained highly sceptical of the emergence of a national economy and urban centres. They were particularly concerned about their continued access to reasonably priced credit, and the ability to survive bad harvests. Rural interest groups lobbied to keep banking local so that the unit bank emerged, located in a single state and without branches across state lines.[20] Sometimes state governments invested in the state banks which they chartered, buying stock, and sometimes they extracted payments from the banks in return for granting the charter.[21] In either case, they had little incentive to allow out-of-state banks to compete with their state banks.[22] In 1863, during the American Civil War, a National Banking Act had been passed which enabled the federal government to establish national banks. However, this only meant that the banks were chartered by the federal government and not by a state, and national banks were still caught by state restrictions on branching.[23] Both the typical state bank and the national banks were too small and too confined to act as the provider of capital to large enterprise, and it was often cheaper for large corporations to raise finance by issuing securities rather than paying for short-term bank credit.[24] As a result, the capital markets played a significant role in supplying the necessary financing for US enterprises. Fortunately, the railroad boom meant that the US had well-developed capital markets which these large enterprises could access. As discussed earlier in this section, British and other foreign

[16] ibid 319.
[17] Chernow (n 10) 72.
[18] Chandler, *The Visible Hand* (n 14) 319.
[19] ibid 330.
[20] Charles W Calomiris and Stephen H Haber, *Fragile by Design: The Political Origins of Banking Crises & Scarce Credit* (Princeton University Press 2014) 168.
[21] Olegario (n 2) 48.
[22] Calomiris and Haber (n 20) 163.
[23] ibid 179.
[24] Chernow (n 10) 303; Olegario (n 2) 95; Calomiris and Haber (n 20) 185.

investors had tended to prefer railroad bonds to railroad equities, regarding them as offering greater security. Thus, not only did the US have a well-developed equity capital market consolidated in New York, it also had a well-developed bond market. This meant that the new, large enterprises formed through merger had access to debt capital markets in order to raise funds.

Large enterprises began to tap these capital markets in the US just as the attractiveness of railroad securities declined, while abundant capital sought new investment opportunities. And as the capital markets deepened, enterprises which were generating significant cashflows emerged as investors in their own right.[25] This picture is important for corporate reorganization because it meant that large-scale enterprises (other than railroads) with complex capital structures comprising bond debt and equity emerged in the US very early in the twentieth century. At the same time, as noted earlier in this section, many of these enterprises were very large indeed, so that the reorganizations of the 1920s often involved hundreds, or even thousands, of different creditors comprising landlords, tort creditors, supply creditors, and other contracting creditors, as well as bondholders and stockholders. Although somewhat reluctantly, the courts did facilitate the adaptation of the equity receivership to meet the needs of these new enterprises. Thus, corporate reorganization in the US proceeded in much the same way in the early part of the twentieth century as it had at the end of the nineteenth century. This was particularly important because many of the mergers during the boom at the end of the nineteenth century did face financial difficulty. At this stage of industrialization, enterprise was developing dynamically on a formidable, but sometimes unstable, scale.[26] For example, the Distillers' and Cattle Feeders' trust incorporated using a holding company structure and concentrated production in a limited number of production facilities. Nonetheless, it sought to maintain a relatively high price for the whiskey which it produced so that a number of smaller concerns continued to compete with it. The company responded by buying out competitors and cutting prices, but this strategy was expensive so that eventually the company faced financial difficulties.[27] The equity receivership thus performed a central role in permitting US industry to learn from its mistakes, and to emerge with a capital and organizational structure fit for purpose at the beginning of the twentieth century.

Westward migration was a powerful force in promoting the development of the railroads which, as already explored, played a significant role in the development of large enterprises in the US. Better communication led to the development of new urban centres for these emerging large enterprises to serve. At the same time, as the nineteenth century progressed and Britain experienced the continuing

[25] Chandler, *The Visible Hand* (n 14) 317.

[26] Chernow (n 10) 24.

[27] Alfred D Chandler, Jr, 'The Beginnings of "Big Business" in American Industry' (1959) 33(1) Bus Hist Rev 1, 10–11.

development of the industrial revolution, the US enjoyed rapid growth as the provider of vital raw materials for the British, and as a major market for British products. Thus, large enterprise enjoyed buoyant domestic and international markets.

All of this required a stable work force. Yet, a defining feature of this period of US industrialization was a mobile population and scarce labour. As a result, there was considerable focus on identifying and retaining manpower. Indeed, as large enterprises began to emerge, a career manager could safely assume a job for life with the corporation. This, in turn, caused incumbent management to value stability of the enterprise over profit, and meant that if the company did face distress management had much to gain and little to lose from supporting the investment bankers and the courts in pushing through a financial restructuring. Senior management might be forced to share decision-making with the investment bankers for a period of time, but they would not lose their jobs, and would enjoy greater security after the successful conclusion of the corporate reorganization. It is important to note, in this context, that management rarely owned stock in the company, so that reorganization simply reinforced the ability of the company to pay their wages. At the same time, J P Morgan's skill lay in financial and not operational reorganization. He relied on able corporate managers who were familiar with the operational details of the industry.[28] Thus, the tripartite relationship between the investment banker, the debtor management, and the courts emerges in US corporate reorganization practice. This development of the career manager, focused on the stability of large national or international enterprises, went hand in hand with a focus on administration of the enterprise and the emergence of highly bureaucratized functions. This, in turn, increasingly resulted in promotion based on years of seniority rather than talent. This worked to reinforce the central role of the manager in US big business generally, and during a corporate reorganization specifically.

Thus, organizational and institutional conditions in the finance and non-financial corporate fields at the time at which reorganization of large enterprises first emerges in the US played a crucial role in determining the ways in which the participants in the system sought to shape the corporate reorganization process. The preoccupation with the courts in determining the right levels of protection for property and contract rights led to the development of the concept of the upset price to be paid to the dissenting minority in a corporate reorganization based on post-reorganization earning potential. Yet the courts also understood the need to address hold-out positions to facilitate a successful restructuring, and responded by using their power to set the upset price to facilitate bargaining and to encourage the minority to accept the reorganization plan. Thus, the participants in the system and the courts cooperated to adapt the legal tools of the time to the needs of business to reorganize.

[28] Chandler, *The Visible Hand* (n 14) 183.

The geography of the US, together with a mobile work force and the experience of western migration, made transport and communication a primary concern, which led to construction of railroads which, in turn, required significant capital. The initial sources of this capital were foreign, notably British, investors, and the raising of this foreign capital was mediated by investment bankers, notably J P Morgan. As a repeat player, J P Morgan saw his role as extending to the entire life cycle of the investment and, thus, investment bankers, together with lawyers, played a crucial role in the early corporate reorganizations in adapting legal tools. As British investors preferred bonds to equities, by the end of the century the US had developed debt capital markets in addition to equity capital markets. As large manufacturing enterprises began to emerge, facilitated in part by the development of the railroads, they were able to access these capital markets where necessary. And when the process of legal merger to produce industry giants encountered problems, they were able to adapt the equity receivership process developed in the railroad context to facilitate the reorganization of industrial concerns. At the same time, the career manager emerged, who rarely owned stock and who was focused on lifetime employment and thus the long-term stability of the enterprise, rather than profit. In most cases, the career manager was likely to play a key role in the corporate reorganization, and would be unlikely to lose anything other than the need to share decision-making with the investment banker for a period of time. As a result, a co-production story between advisers, managers, and the courts emerged.

2.2.2 Stability

Until the 1930s, the way in which market participants conceived of large corporate reorganization remained fairly stable. This is because the broad contours of the organizational and institutional structure of the finance and non-financial corporate fields remained the same, while no exogenous shock—in the form of legal reform requiring market adaptation of available legal tools—occurred until the 1930s. In the first place, the large investment banking houses consolidated their power over US corporates, operating according to what Ron Chernow has termed 'the Gentleman Banker's Code'.[29] As Chernow has identified, banks did not attempt to pitch to clients, which was regarded as an unseemly way for the gentleman banker to exercise power. Instead, a prospective client would need to arrive with proper letters of introduction. Furthermore, investment banks were (without overstating the case) broadly respectful of each other's sphere of influence, so that a client who wished to 'switch' investment bankers would frequently require the blessing of the

[29] Chernow (n 10) 24.

incumbent bank before securing the transition. Finally, again without overstating the strength of the claim, price competition was rare: competition was focused instead on quality of service.[30] J P Morgan and others continued to consolidate their power over companies for whom they arranged finance by taking seats on the board of directors in order to secure the flows of information which they required in order to look after their investor clients' interests.

Thus, a symbiotic relationship between banker and client emerged, so that it was only natural that the investment banker would continue to play a central role in any reorganization, and in the mobilization and adaptation of the available tools to achieve the desired ends. The era of the powerful banker and relationship banking meant that this was inevitable. A small problem emerged with the decision in *Northern Pacific Railway v Boyd*.[31] In *Boyd*, the court concluded that the practice of allowing only stockholders to participate in the newly reorganized entity through payment of new money or an assessment could no longer be supported, so that unsecured creditors should also be able to participate, possibly with an assessment, in any new stock offering.[32] However, although this was an inconvenience, the market was able to assimilate it in corporate restructuring plans, and equity receiverships continued to be used much as before.

At the same time, until the 1930s, to the extent that large US enterprises could not fund expansion or other projects from retained earnings, they frequently accessed bond markets, rather than commercial banks, for the necessary funding. A further, highly significant factor (explored in more detail in Chapter 5) was that certain aspects of US secured transactions law made it very difficult for a creditor in the US to take security over all, or substantially all, of the debtor's assets. As a result, it remained the case that secured creditors often did not have security over some of the debtor's most significant assets, and that debt was often unsecured. The federal equity receivership remained the legal procedure of choice until legislative amendments, in the 1930s and in the 1970s, began to change the landscape. First, in a series of 1930s cases the Supreme Court cast doubt on the ability to use the equity receivership to restructure a corporation other than a railroad or public utility.[33] Secondly, a number of practical problems with the equity receivership as a device for reorganizing industrial corporations were becoming evident. In an equity receivership, the equity receivers had only possession of, and not title to, the assets, so that it was necessary to commence an ancillary proceeding in every state and jurisdiction in which the corporation had property. Specific provisions ameliorated the effect of this for railroads, but it posed real challenges for the reorganization of

[30] ibid 23–24.

[31] *Northern Pacific Railway v Boyd* 228 US 482 1913.

[32] For a good description, see Alan D Morrison and William J Wilhelm, Jr, *Investment Banking: Institutions, Politics, and Law* (OUP 2008) 181.

[33] *Harkin v Brundage* 276 US 36, 48 S Ct 512 (1931); *Shapiro v Wilgus* 21 287 US 348 (1932).

industrial corporations. Moreover, the experience of the Great Depression had two particularly significant consequences for corporate reorganization law.

First, the experience of the Great Depression meant that many industrial companies needed to restructure their bonds, in order to reduce fixed costs. However, many of these corporations did not have sufficient cashflow to pay the upset price in a federal equity receivership. Thus, when many elements of equity receivership were codified in section 77 of the Bankruptcy Act in 1933, the first 'cram-down' mechanism was introduced pursuant to which creditors were divided into classes and it was possible for a reorganization to be approved with the vote of a two-thirds majority in each class.[34] Secondly, the experience of the Great Depression, and the backlash which followed against the investment bankers of the day, resulted in Chapter X of the Chandler Act of 1938. Chapter X not only prevented the company's bankers from advising the firm or as acting as trustee in the case, but it also handed the power to formulate the restructuring plan to the trustee.[35] The result was that market participants simply ignored the tool of Chapter X altogether, and turned instead to Chapter XI of the Chandler Act. Chapter XI had been conceived of as a process for small and medium-sized enterprises, but bankruptcy lawyers soon saw how it could be adapted to better meet their objectives in large corporate reorganization.[36] In other words, they left the tool explicitly designed for large corporate reorganization in the tool box, and took out another designed for a different purpose but which was readily adaptable. This is one of the starkest examples of corporate reorganization law as a tool or resource mobilized and adapted by the market which is encountered in the book. At the same time, other aspects of investment banker power were weakened, including by the passing of section 316(b) of the Trust Indenture Act of 1939, which prevented majority bondholders from imposing changes in principal, interest, or maturity date on the minority without court supervision.[37] This effectively prevented the private mediation of out-of-court settlements by investment bank intermediaries, and decisively drove the reorganization process into court.

The 1970s saw an overhaul of bankruptcy law in the US, largely motivated by concerns for rising consumer debt and the limitations of personal bankruptcy. However, professionals engaged in these reform efforts were able to demonstrate the shortcomings of the New Deal corporate reorganization laws, so that corporate reorganization law reform was also tackled.[38] It will be necessary to return to the investment bank as intermediary later in the account in the book, because

[34] Skeel (n 4) 1363.

[35] ibid 1368–1372.

[36] ibid 1374.

[37] Mark J Roe, 'The Voting Prohibition in Bond Workouts' (1987) 97 Yale L J 232, 250–52.

[38] Terence C Halliday, Susan Block-Lieb, and Bruce G Carruthers, 'Missing Debtors: National Lawmaking and Global Norm-Making of Corporate Bankruptcy Regimes' in Ralph Brubaker, Robert M Lawless, and Charles J Tabb (eds) *A Debtor World: Interdisciplinary Perspectives on Debt* (OUP 2012) 273–74.

the fate of that mechanism is a crucial part of the story of organizational and institutional change with which the rest of the book is concerned. Otherwise, the key ideas which informed the development of the federal equity receivership are clearly visible: strong debtor power to hold creditors at bay while a reorganization is agreed; a role for the US bankruptcy courts in encouraging bargaining and settlement; mechanisms for priority financing for the case; and valuation based on post-reorganization value. If anything, Chapter 11 in the new Bankruptcy Code took these central ideas and bolstered them with additional legal tools to increase the prospect of a successful reorganization.

Yet, it is an organizing principle of this book that, while Chapter 11 was being implemented, organizational and institutional changes in the finance and non-financial corporate markets were beginning to have a significant impact on how market participants conceived of, and approached, corporate reorganization law. This meant that, although in many ways Chapter 11 maintained ideas of what good corporate reorganization law should achieve which had been developed over the preceding seventy-five years, the ways in which participants would mobilize and adapt the law was about to undergo a profound change. The new organizational and institutional environment in the proximate fields of finance and non-financial corporates was to have a profound effect on the objectives of the participants, so that they mobilized and adapted corporate reorganization law in new ways. It is the purpose of this book to understand this story of adaptation, and its implications for corporate reorganization law theory.

2.3 England

2.3.1 Initial conditions and emergence of financial restructuring

Railways were also among the first non-financial corporations which influenced the development of large corporate reorganization law and practice in England. Personal connections were important in the raising of share capital and early financing relied heavily on investors local to the route of the line. Nonetheless, it also appears that, as knowledge of railways spread, so too did (as Reed puts it) 'deliberate investment of experienced railways capitalists',[39] facilitated by the development of stock exchanges to channel equity investment to the railways which needed it. Investors in railway shares pursued a range of occupations, from trade (including shopkeepers and small tradespeople, as well as merchants); manufacturers; gentlemen; and women. Loan capital was also an important source of financing (together with temporary loans such as bank advances and borrowing

[39] M C Reed, *Investment in Railways in Britain, 1820–1840: A Study in the Development of the Capital Market* (OUP 1975) 200—the account of railway finance in this section is largely drawn from Reed.

against promissory notes and balances due to other creditors, which appear to have provided sources of finance when the railway company had exceeded its legal borrowing powers). While there was some limited listing of railway debentures on the stock exchanges, railway companies generally obtained loans by advertisement, and personal connections remained important in the raising of loan capital. Scholars have struggled to identify the sources of loan capital, given scant surviving evidence, but it appears that railway debentures might have been attractive investments for institutional and trustee investors. Thus, just as in the US, many English railways had comparatively complex capital structures and a dispersed investor base, with similar implications for the development of corporate reorganization law and practice. However, the way in which reorganization law was mobilized and adapted by the participants in the system at this time was different from development in the US in some significant respects.

First, whereas railroad financing and construction happened at a time of weak federal law-making in the US (and at a time when significant policy development often occurred through the courts), the legislature was considerably more active in mid- and late Victorian Britain. Given Britain's early entry into industrialization through the industrial revolution, the Victorian parliaments took matters of commerce seriously. Victor Markham Lester has suggested that issues of financial distress were seen largely as a practical commercial problem, while the railways were seen in Britain, as in the US, as having a public as well as a private character.[40] In other words, the legislature was centrally concerned with providing the necessary tools to facilitate railway reorganization. As a result, legislation in England dealt with the collective action problem, which was at the heart of the development of the equity receivership as a tool of US railroad reorganization.

It was possible, in England, to take a mortgage over a railway 'undertaking' and the rates, tolls, and duties arising from that undertaking. In other words, whereas it was usual to have security over particular assets in a US railroad financing, a creditor in England could take a mortgage of the company's undertaking. However, crucially, in England no specific charge was created on the rolling stock—the mortgage was only on the profits arising from the use of the undertaking as a going concern. The creditors could appoint a receiver over a railway in order to collect in these sums, but they were not able to foreclose or sell against the assets of the railway. In this way, the collective action problem addressed through the US equity receivership was already largely addressed in railway legislation in England.[41] At the same time, and unlike the US position, the Railway Companies Act 1867 contained provisions which enabled the court to compel a minority of the railway's

[40] V Markham Lester, *Victorian Insolvency: Bankruptcy, Imprisonment for Debt, and Company Winding-Up in Nineteenth Century England* (OUP 1995) 9.

[41] This analysis draws upon William Williamson Kerr, *The Law and Practice as to Receivers Appointed by the High Court of Justice or Out of Court* (London: Sweet & Maxwell 1921).

creditors to accept a plan which had been approved by the majority.[42] This was later extended to companies other than railways in section 2 of the Joint Stock Companies Arrangements Act of 1870, although at that time a so-called 'scheme of arrangement' could only be proposed by a company in liquidation. In 1900, jurisdiction to sanction a scheme was extended to arrangements between the company in liquidation and its members, as well as its creditors, by section 24 of the Companies Act 1900. And, in 1908, the requirement for the debtor company to be in liquidation was lifted by section 120 of the Companies (Consolidation) Act 1908.

Thus, whereas in the US it was not possible for the court to require minority creditors to accept new securities in exchange for their claims in an equity receivership, in England the court could impose such a requirement via the legislative tool of the scheme of arrangement. Indeed, in *Alabama New Orleans Texas & Pacific Junction Railway*, the courts in England confirmed that it was possible for a scheme of arrangement, properly approved by the requisite majorities and sanctioned by the court, to deprive a dissenting creditor of his security.[43] A further distinction between the equity receivership and the English scheme of arrangement was the extent to which the court concerned itself with the details of the plan of reorganization. As explored in section 2.2.1 'Initial conditions and emergence of corporate reorganization', as the US courts had no ability to impose the plan on the dissenting creditors, initially resort was had to the court for the purposes of staying actions by creditors against the assets in order to preserve the possibility of a reorganization. The court also appears to have played a role in its discretion to fix the upset price (the cash price mandated to be paid to dissenters), which could both protect the minority (through the requirement to pay cash to those who did not support the plan) and encourage the minority to accept the plan (by fixing a low cash payment). Thus, the court did have some indirect influence on the success of the plan of reorganization via the mechanism of the upset price. However, beyond the fixing of the cash price, the US courts did not review the terms of the plan itself. In England, in contrast, before the court could approve or sanction the scheme, it was required to satisfy itself as to the reasonableness of the plan. Yet, from the earliest cases, the English courts showed a typically Victorian deference to commercial interests so that, unless there was some particular reason to be sceptical about the motivations of the majority, in general the courts would sanction a scheme which had received the requisite majority votes.[44] In other words, the idea of public enforcement of the private deal is clearly visible in the English jurisprudence from the 1870s.

[42] Railway Companies Act 1867 30 & 31 Vict c 127.

[43] *In Re Alabama New Orleans Texas & Pacific Junction Railway Co* [1891] 1 Ch 213; [1890] 12 WLUK 62.

[44] Lindley LJ put it this way in *In Re English, Scottish, and Australian Chartered Bank* [1893] 3 Ch 385; [1893] 7 WLUK 52: 'If the creditors are acting on sufficient information and with time to consider what they are about, and are acting honestly, they are, I apprehend, much better judges of what is to their commercial advantage than the Court can be.'

However, notwithstanding this early level of sophistication in corporate reorganization law, matters were to develop quite differently in England from the early part of the twentieth century until the twenty-first century. It is an organizing principle at the heart of this book that changes in the proximate fields of finance and non-financial corporates can change the ways in which the participants in corporate restructuring mobilize and adapt corporate reorganization law's tools. Nowhere is this more visible than in the relative decline of the importance of the sophisticated private and public character of the scheme of arrangement, and the rise of a largely privately ordered debt restructuring practice in England for most of the twentieth century. In order to understand this, it is necessary to understand something of both the early twentieth-century experience of industrialization in England and changes in the finance market.

First, while the US experienced the staggering rise of the large corporate in the early part of the twentieth century, companies simply did not develop on the same scale in England. The question of why, after such an early start in the process of industrialization, England's non-financial corporates did not develop on the scale of their US counterparts is hotly contested in the literature, with a variety of competing explanations and suggestions: England's small geographical size; the failure of business to invest in new technology in the second industrial revolution; English investment overseas; the failure of British banks to support domestic industry; focus on the family business; a failure to adopt modern corporate structures; a conservative choice of industries to develop; an out-of-date management structure; government policy; and allegations of a 'pervasively anti-industrial and anti-business culture'.[45] The important point to note is that retained earnings and cashflow from operations were even more significant sources of capital for English firms than for US firms. Moreover, to the extent that non-financial corporates did raise external finance, the sources of finance changed dramatically after 1913. Both the US and Britain experienced devastating bank failures at the end of the nineteenth century but, while US rural interests pressed for unit banking to preserve reliable sources of finance, in Britain benefits were seen in consolidation, so that the scale of operations could provide security against bank runs and ensure a steady supply of funds. A significant merger movement in banking followed which, for reasons explored later in the book, was not stopped by political intervention. As a result, five major banks emerged, dominating the banking industry in Britain.[46]

In the interwar years, the Big Five (Barclays, Lloyds, Midland, National Provincial, and Westminster, known later as the 'clearing banks' and now the Big Four (Barclays, Lloyds, HSBC, and Royal Bank of Scotland)) typically lent

[45] This list, and the description of Britain's alleged cultural attitude to business, is drawn from W D Rubinstein, *Capitalism, Culture, & Decline in Britain 1750–1990* (Routledge 1994) 1–9.

[46] For one account of the merger movement, see Michael Collins and Mae Baker, *Commercial Banks and Industrial Finance in England and Wales, 1860–1913* (OUP 2003, repr 2010) 107–11.

corporate overdrafts which were technically callable on demand and intended to finance periodic working capital needs. In practice, however, many of these were, as the bankers put it, 'hard core overdrafts' in which the borrower's account was allowed to remain perpetually in debit up to the agreed overdraft limit, and which could be used to purchase fixed assets. Many other companies were financed by loans which, although technically repayable on demand, were in practice rolled over from year to year.[47] If the borrower ran into difficulties, the bank would frequently continue to roll over the outstanding loan in the hope that the borrower might trade out of its difficulties. The banks did not see it as part of their role to provide risk capital to the firm, and consistently referred to their obligations to their depositors in determining the extent of acceptable risk which they were willing to take in a distressed situation. Nonetheless, this was an era of solid client relationships, when reputation for client care was important in the field, so that the bank was motivated both to try to retain its client and to preserve its own public reputation.[48] And this was an era of comparatively low leverage, so the fact that a debt exchange or similar reduction of financial liabilities was not on the table might not prove fatal. As developed in Chapter 5, it was usual for the bank to take security over all, or substantially all, of the customer's assets to secure further advances to a large, financially distressed borrower, so that in reality there was no need for a moratorium against enforcement by other creditors if the restructuring effort failed and a corporate bankruptcy process followed.[49] And, as the loan capital structure typically involved only parties who were well known to each other, private ordering was sufficient to implement any agreement which was required.

Where the bank concluded that a recovery was not in prospect it would appoint an accountant (normally the accountant who had headed the investigation into the company's affairs) as its 'receiver' or, if it had security over all, or substantially all, of the company's assets, as its 'receiver and manager'. A receiver and manager would take over the management of the company and would seek to realize the assets of the company for its appointor. The appointment of the receiver and manager shielded the bank from responsibility (and liability) for the sale. Reorganizations from within a receivership did occur, particularly if the bank was concerned about the company's management. Thus, in 1921 Sir Arthur Whinney, one of the leading accountants of his day, was appointed as receiver and manager of the Austin Motor Company primarily in order to force a change in the composition of the board after the Midland Bank lost confidence in the founder, Sir Herbert Austin. After

47 Committee of London Clearing Bankers, *The London Clearing Banks: Evidence by the Committee of London Clearing Bankers to the Committee to Review the Functioning of Financial Institutions* November 1977 (Longman Inc 1978) 99.

48 Daniel Prentice, 'Bargaining in the Shadow of the Enterprise Act 2002' (2004) 5 Eur Bus Org L Rev 153, 157 citing D Saphos, *Bank Liability on the Withdrawal of Credit and the Exercise of Default Remedies* (Oxford, D Phil 2002).

49 Randal C Picker, 'Security Interests, Misbehavior, and Common Pools' (1992) 59 U Chi L Rev 645; John Armour and Sandra Frisby, 'Rethinking Receivership' (2001) 21(1) Oxf J Legal Stud 73.

the board had been changed, other operational changes made, and creditors had voted unanimously to support the issue of three different debentures to refinance existing debt, the receiver subsequently left the company.[50] Yet this was rare. In general, receivership followed where confidence in management had been lost, and the bank was no longer willing to support the recovery effort.

Scholars have struggled to identify the extent to which industrial and manufacturing companies in England relied on the debt capital markets in the interwar years.[51] Yet, it is certainly the case that debenture stock was issued to the public by some of England's largest industrial and manufacturing concerns. Where mortgage debenture stock contained majority voting provisions requiring equivalent levels of support to the scheme of arrangement, a reorganization could be arranged by contract.[52] Yet, schemes of arrangement were still proposed in the years before the Second World War, in which debenture holders swapped their claims for new securities and/or cash, or the business and assets of the company were transferred to a new company which issued new securities and/or cash to the creditors in satisfaction of their claims.[53] As it transpired, however, the scheme of arrangement was largely to disappear from the landscape during the next major financial downturn in Britain.

In the early 1970s, the British finance industry suffered its first great shock after the stability of the first half of the twentieth century. So-called secondary banks (what would today be known as shadow banks) had been speculating heavily in the commercial property sector in Britain. Eventually, as interest rates rose to steady the market, the secondary banks found that they could no longer meet the interest payments on the loans which they had borrowed to finance their operations. However, the secondary banks had borrowed heavily from the commercial banks, which were now holding a significant number of non-performing loans. The Bank of England called all of the big banks together to form a lifeboat operation. One particularly troublesome case was the Stern Group, which had a massive portfolio of non-performing commercial loans. Kenneth Cork, probably the leading insolvency practitioner of his day, took charge of the Stern Group restructuring. In his memoirs he recounts his efforts to launch a scheme of arrangement for the company but, in the event, he struggled to gain sufficient support in order to be able to propose the scheme and call meetings of creditors to vote on it. Ultimately, Cork resorted to an informal structure, and used the muscle of the Bank of England to encourage the major banks to support the restructuring.[54]

[50] Roy Church, *Herbert Austin: The British Motor Car Industry to 1941* (Europa Publications Ltd 1979) 57–66.

[51] W A Thomas, *The Finance of British Industry 1918–1976* (Methuen & Co Ltd 1978) 15.

[52] *Goodfellow v Nelson Line (Liverpool) Ltd* [1912] 2 Ch 324; *British American Nickel Corp v O' Brien* [1927] AC 369—see De Forest Billyou, 'Corporate Mortgage Bonds and Majority Clauses' (1948) 57 Yale LJ 595.

[53] See *Dey v Rubber and Mercantile Corp Ltd* [1923] 2 Ch 528; *In re Garner's Motors Limited* [1937] Ch 594; *In re White Star Line, Limited* [1938] Ch 458.

[54] This account is largely taken from Kenneth Cork, *Cork on Cork* (Macmillan 1988) 195.

Perhaps, if the scheme of arrangement had proved successful in driving through the Stern Group restructuring, it would have been renewed as the tool of choice for participants in the corporate reorganization process in the 1980s and 1990s. Instead, the Stern experience simply reinforced the view of schemes as cumbersome and expensive. Furthermore, schemes suffered from a major procedural defect because the court would not give any ruling on whether creditors had been properly divided into classes for voting purposes until the very end of the process, at which point all the cost and expense of proposing and voting on the scheme had already been incurred. Overall, the better tool appeared to be an informal approach backed by Central Bank power. The Bank of England took this experience and set out, in a speech by Pen Kent (one of its directors), the principles which banks ought to adhere to when one of their customers was in trouble. These principles required banks to refrain from enforcing against the customer's assets while the restructuring efforts were in train; to lend new money on priority terms; to agree the date at which their losses would be calculated; and generally to behave fairly in securing a deal. In time, this became known as the 'London Approach'.[55] Significantly, it appeared at a time when another change was occurring in the proximate field of finance.

Until the 1970s, English corporates had typically borrowed on a bilateral basis from their bankers, but in the 1970s various initiatives gave rise to the syndicated loan. In a syndicated loan a lead bank arranges a group of banks to participate in making the loan, and an agent bank coordinates advances and repayments between the bank group and the borrower. As explored in Chapter 3, the syndicated loan was made possible by developments in the way in which interest was calculated and paid, and became the dominant form of large corporate financing for both working capital and longer-term needs in England after the 1970s. Bank finance also assumed particular significance during this decade because the British bond market suffered a significant decline, in part as a result of Britain's experience of exceptionally high inflation.[56] Thus, the London Approach performed an important function in codifying the principles by which the banks would act in a private restructuring at exactly the moment when complex loan debt became more common and coordination became more difficult. It also appeared at a time at which the Bank of England exerted considerable 'soft' power over the major British banks.

[55] Pen Kent, 'The London Approach' (1993) Q1 Bank of England Q Bull 110; John Flood, Robert Abbey, Eleni Skordaki, and Paul Aber, 'The Professional Restructuring of Corporate Rescue: Company Voluntary Arrangements and the London Approach' (1995) ACCA Research Report 45; Alice Belcher, *Corporate Rescue: A Conceptual Approach to Insolvency Law* (Sweet & Maxwell 1997) 116–22; John Armour and Simon Deakin, 'Norms in Private Insolvency: The "London Approach" to the Resolution of Financial Distress' (2001) 1 J Corp Law Stud 21.

[56] Margaret Ackrill and Leslie Hannah, *Barclays: The Business of Banking 1690–1996* (CUP 2001) 237–38; Christopher Coyle and John Turner, 'Law, Politics, and Financial Development: The Great Reversal of the UK Corporate Debt Market' (2013) 73(3) J Econ Hist 810; Brian R Cheffins, *Corporate Ownership and Control: British Business Transformed* (OUP 2010) 354.

This was an era in which the banks were expected to comply with the wishes of the Bank of England: stories (possibly apocryphal) abounded of stiff reprimands when they did not observe the rules of the game, so that it was said that all that was needed was the metaphorical 'raising of the Governor's eyebrows' to indicate displeasure.[57]

In time, the Bank of England withdrew from its role as enforcer of the London Approach, in part because it no longer felt that that role reflected its modern functions and purpose, and later because it lost its regulatory mandate. Yet the London Approach continued to be the dominant mechanism for encouraging debt restructuring in England because the syndicated loan market was a small market of repeat players. Thus, a bank which did not play by the rules of the game in a financial restructuring could be excluded from the next deal in the syndicated loan markets.[58] This is also something returned to in greater detail as the book progresses.

2.3.2 Stability

This system of private negotiation, and resort to legal process only for the purposes of changing management or achieving a sale of all or part of the business, was to prove remarkably stable in England until well into the 2000s, notwithstanding two significant reform efforts. The first major reform effort was launched towards the end of the 1970s. As Britain joined the European Community, her continental partners struggled to understand the receivership process, which appeared to be almost entirely a matter of contract. At the same time, cross-border trade was opening up after the collapse of many of the mechanisms which had restrained it. As a result, there was a pressing need for receivers to achieve recognition overseas, and the English approach of appointing the receiver without a court order could make this challenging.[59] Successive concerns had also been raised that receivers acted in the interests of the secured party but to the detriment of other creditors. In the event, the committee to investigate reform was headed by Kenneth Cork. Unsurprisingly, given Cork's experience in the Secondary Banking Crisis, the Cork Committee's report set out stringent criticisms of the scheme of arrangement process.[60] Ultimately the Committee concluded, 'that there is no means of substantially improving the present scheme of arrangement process for insolvent companies',[61] making two alternative suggestions. First, the Committee proposed a new procedure for small company debtors. Secondly, the Committee proposed a new corporate bankruptcy

[57] Flood and others (n 55) 30–31; Armour and Deakin (n 55) 40.
[58] Armour and Deakin (n 55) 46.
[59] Cork (n 54) 185, 187.
[60] *Insolvency Law and Practice: Report of the Review Committee* (Cmnd 8558 1982), paras 404–418.
[61] ibid para 422.

procedure, named administration, which they thought might, indirectly, facilitate the use of the scheme of arrangement procedure by large corporates.

It seems unlikely that Kenneth Cork saw anything significantly wrong with the system in which he was not only embedded, but dominant. Cork saw the process of receivership as generally low cost and efficient, and did not consider that banks acted solely in their own interests when one of their customers was distressed. The London Approach appeared highly effective in addressing the problems of unanimous voting in banking syndicates. Nonetheless, at the time, if there was no bank with a floating charge entitled to appoint a receiver, the only other available legal procedure in England was a liquidation. Liquidation was poorly adapted to achieve a sale of the business as a going concern, and it appears that this was the principal gap which Cork intended to fill when he suggested the introduction of administration.

An insolvency practitioner would be appointed as the administrator in the new administration procedure, which would also include a moratorium against secured creditor action and against the launch or continuation of legal proceedings against the company, in each case without either consent of the administrator or the consent of the court. As already noted, this prompted the Cork Committee to suggest that administration might be used indirectly to promote a scheme of arrangement. There is also some evidence that the big British banks thought that administration would be helpful to guard against the risk that one of their number did not fall into line, and took premature enforcement action.[62] And there is further evidence that Kenneth Cork saw a potential role for the administration moratorium in providing a breathing space in which the company could attempt to trade out of its difficulties. In his memoirs, Cork notes that the Committee did not imagine that appointment of an administrator would constitute an 'act of insolvency', and that 'an administrator should be brought in *before* a company was declared insolvent'.[63] Nonetheless, Cork imagined such an appointment in fairly limited circumstances, 'where for instance the directors were obviously incompetent or dishonest and the ordinary processes could not remove them; or where in the national interest the Government should take a hand, as happened in the case of Rolls-Royce, without going through the trauma of bankruptcy'.[64] And he envisaged that the 'more likely decision' than attempting to trade out of the company's difficulties would be 'to continue trading and then sell the business as a going concern, distributing the proceeds to the creditors and shareholders'.[65] In the event, administration was very

[62] Committee of London Clearing Bankers (n 47) 112.
[63] Cork (n 54) 195.
[64] ibid 195.
[65] ibid 196: '[The Administrator] might decide that the only thing to do was to put the company into liquidation; it might be to continue trading under a moratorium and "trade out" of the difficulty. For that the procedure would need to have been started early enough. The more likely decision would be to continue trading and then sell the business as a going concern, distributing the proceeds to the creditors and shareholders.'

firmly conceived of as an insolvency process in the Insolvency Act 1986; take up of administration was extraordinarily low; and the system continued generally as before. If a reorganization was agreed, it was generally agreed by contract using London Approach principles, and limited to financial debt, perhaps with contractually agreed plans to dispose of non-core assets to reduce indebtedness. If the restructuring efforts failed, the banks continued to appoint receivers and managers (now renamed administrative receivers) to realize the assets and distribute the proceeds.

A second reform effort was launched in the early 2000s, which was perhaps more directly influenced by experience of Chapter 11 in the US. Peter Mandelson, who was then Secretary of State for Trade and Industry in the UK, went on a trade visit to Silicon Valley.[66] On the trip, he was introduced to the tools available in Chapter 11: wrapping the company in the protective blanket of Chapter 11 while a plan of reorganization was negotiated; implementing the reorganization; and returning the company to the economy with a sustainable balance sheet. At the same time, concern was mounting with the process of administrative receivership and the paucity of returns to unsecured creditors. In the early stages of the case the banks would often appoint a firm with which they had a close relationship to act as 'investigating accountants' and to report on the wisdom of a restructuring. Concern arose that the accountant was incentivized to recommend a receivership. This was because it was usual for the investigating accountant to be awarded the receivership role in the event of appointment, and fees would ordinarily be more significant for appointment work than for investigation.[67] Concern also arose that the banks, as secured creditors, were incentivized to prefer an appointment and a quick sale over an uncertain restructuring, particularly where their security offered them good coverage of their debt. And where the banks were over-secured, concerns were raised that they lacked the incentives to monitor the receivers' costs. In this regard, concern was raised over the receiver's duties, which were almost exclusively to their appointor.[68] All of this gave rise, eventually, to the reform efforts of the Enterprise Act 2002.

Among other things, the Enterprise Act 2002 amended the Insolvency Act 1986 so that administrative receivership was all but abolished (administrative receivership did remain for certain categories of financing, such as project finance and capital markets transactions).[69] Administrators were required to consider their duties to all creditors and not just the secured creditor,[70] and a new

[66] 'Silicone Ballyhoo' *The Economist* (7 November 1998) 349(8093) 36; Gerard McCormack, 'Control and Corporate Rescue—An Anglo-American Evaluation' (2007) 56(3) Int'l Comp LQ 515, 524.

[67] John Flood and Eleni Skordaki, 'Insolvency Practitioners and Big Corporate Insolvencies' (1995) ACCA Research Report 43, 16.

[68] Riz Mokal, 'Administration and Administrative Receivership: An Analysis' (2004) 57 Cur Legal Probs 349.

[69] Insolvency Act 1986, s 72A–72H.

[70] ibid Sch B1 para 3(2).

hierarchy of purposes was introduced which required administrators to consider the possibility of a debt restructuring before a sale of the business or assets.[71] However, the banking community won an important concession in the process. Initially, the Government had intended that all administration appointments would be made by the court, but the banking community persuaded the reform committee that appointment should be possible out of court and, crucially, that the secured creditor should be able to control the identity of the appointee.[72] The significant fact was that the banking community, and the accountants who had built close personal relationships with them, saw little need for a radical overhaul of the way in which the system operated.[73] They tended to consider it an efficient system which secured good returns. In their view, where unsecured creditors lost out, it was simply because there was no value for them. At the same time, English scholars and practitioners were aware of mounting academic criticism of the US system as holding creditors at bay while value was depleted by irresponsible management, and in giving companies in Chapter 11 an unfair competitive edge against their more scrupulous industry rivals. There was no market appetite for a more Chapter 11-like system at the time. It also seems likely that this was the view of the judges who had presided over an insolvency system which, to them, seemed generally to work well. As a result, banks, and the accountants with which they maintained a relationship, mobilized the new administration tool in a way which was broadly similar to the way in which they had formerly mobilized the administrative receivership tool.

Yet significant organizational and institutional change was afoot in the finance field in England. Had the market participants been more aware of this at the time, they might have chosen to adapt the tools offered by the Enterprise Act reforms in a different way. This will form a significant part of the narrative in the remainder of the book, when it turns to explore the English experience of organizational and institutional change in the proximate fields of finance and non-financial corporates, and the impact of these changes on the ways in which corporate restructuring law is mobilized and adapted by the participants in the English law system.

[71] ibid Sch B1 para 3(1).

[72] A qualifying floating charge holder (QFCH: essentially a secured creditor who has a floating charge and security over all, or substantially all, of the company's assets) may appoint an administrator out of court, provided certain conditions are met (Insolvency Act 1986, Sch B1 para 14), or may make an application to court for an appointment (ibid Sch B1 para 12). On application to court by someone else, a QFCH may apply to court to have its own administrator appointed, and the court shall grant the application unless it thinks it ought to refuse 'because of the particular circumstances of the case' (ibid Sch B1 para 36). If an out-of-court appointment is made by someone else, notice must be given to the QFCH (ibid Sch B1 para 26), which enables the QFCH to appoint, or negotiate for the appointment of, its own nominee.

[73] See eg CMS, 'Company Rescue and Business Reconstruction—DTI/Treasury Review' (*CMS Law Now*, 1 March 2001) <https://www.cms-lawnow.com/ealerts/2001/03/company-rescue-and-business-reconstruction-dtitreasury-review?cc_lang=en> accessed 6 March 2020.

2.4 Conclusion

This chapter has explored how experience of railroad reorganization in the late nineteenth century laid the foundations of corporate reorganization law in both the US and England, but also how the very different organizational and institutional conditions in each jurisdiction at the time influenced very different developments of the law. In the US, the courts played a significant co-production role with investment bankers, and debtor management, in developing and implementing the equity receivership process. In England, statute provided the scheme of arrangement procedure, which was gradually adapted, through successive reform efforts, to provide the foundation for railway reorganization. At the same time, particular aspects of the statute explicitly relating to railway financing provided vital, additional tools.

Different organizational and institutional conditions in both jurisdictions in the middle of the nineteenth century produced profoundly different adaptations of corporate reorganization law and practice. In the US, the experience of the Great Depression resulted in significant distrust of investment bankers, so that investment banker power was neutered by the New Deal reforms and corporate reorganization law was put on a statutory footing. Certain problems with the equity receivership process were also resolved. Scholars saw significant problems with the New Deal corporate reorganization law, and when Congress came to reform bankruptcy law in the 1970s, these scholars pressed for the problems to be addressed. Yet, the foundational normative concerns of progressive scholars have all been clearly visible throughout the account in this chapter: the importance of debtor management; the need for strong moratorium protection; a role for the court in encouraging bargaining and settlement; minority protection and post-reorganization value; and the availability of priority financing for the case.

In England, the importance of concentrated bank debt, together with the limitations of the scheme of arrangement process, led to large corporate reorganization occurring out of court from the 1970s onwards. Initially, regulatory power and, later, the credible threat of market sanction, provided the necessary incentives to control hold-out positions. Yet, once again, the concerns of the modern era are also clearly visible: a strong focus on the views of the creditors themselves; restricting large corporate reorganization to financial debt; weak moratorium protection; and a limited role for the court in motivating the bargaining process.

This sets the scene for the rest of the book, in which a series of significant shifts in what, following Thornton, Ocasio, and Lounsbury,[74] are referred to as logics, practices, and identities in the proximate fields of finance and non-financial corporates, have led to new adaptations of corporate reorganization law by the participants in

[74] Thornton and others (n 1) 128–47.

the process in both the US and England. The argument is advanced that many of the concepts traditionally used to frame analysis of corporate reorganization law and practice in the US have less salience in this new organizational and institutional order, and need to be replaced, supplemented, or unravelled and reformulated. On the other hand, the argument is made that new concepts have emerged in England which are generally well adapted to the modern, wider, organizational and institutional environment. The concern for the adaptability of England's conceptual framework lies in the extent to which it has the potential to adapt as the wider organizational and institutional environment shifts again. This point is emphasized in many places in the book, and analysed in detail in Chapters 9 and 10, when the implications of further market adaptation for the future of corporate reorganization law are explored.

3
The Rise of Leverage

3.1 Introduction

It is an organizing principle of this book that the question of whether corporate reorganization law scholars can agree on the content of corporate reorganization law depends not only on the particular lens which they train upon it, but also on the particular fact pattern in the corporate reorganization case to which the law responds. Changes in logics, practices, and identities in the fields of finance and non-financial corporates have had significant implications for the facts in different types of corporate reorganization cases, and for the different ways in which participants in corporate reorganization cases mobilize and adapt corporate reorganization law in accordance with the relevant facts.[1] It thus becomes necessary to pay renewed attention to the fact pattern of the case in identifying the contours of the debate between economically minded and progressively minded scholars.

[1] As identified in Chapters 1 and 2, and used in the remainder of the book, the terms 'logics', 'practices', and 'identities' are all borrowed from Patricia H Thornton, William Ocasio, and Michael Lounsbury, *The Institutional Logics Perspective: A New Approach to Culture, Structure, and Process* (OUP 2012) 128–47.

Corporate Reorganization Law and Forces of Change. Sarah Paterson, Oxford University Press (2020). © Sarah Paterson.
DOI: 10.1093/oso/9780198860365.001.0001.

The past fifty years have been a time of particularly significant change in logics, practices, and identities in the finance and non-financial corporate fields. This chapter explores the first of the changes in logic and practice identified in the book. For most of the twentieth century, while the tax benefits of debt over equity were well understood, corporate borrowers remained relatively cautious about the amount of debt finance which they raised. However, since the 1970s, it has become considerably more likely that corporate borrowers will raise significant amounts of debt finance relative to their earnings. As will become apparent, the cautious approach to borrowing was generated by a logic of safety and stability, while the shift to greater levels of leverage has been generated by a logic of profit maximization.

Intuitively, a company which has a significant amount of debt relative to its earnings will not be as well placed to absorb any downturn in those earnings as an unleveraged competitor, because it has high debt service costs. Moreover, a company with high leverage may find that it is unable to refinance at the same leverage multiples when its loans and/or bonds mature if conditions in the credit markets have changed (eg as a result of changes in the general interest rate or economic environment).[2] Both of these situations give rise to financial distress: the firm has a business which is worth saving but does not have enough cash to pay its financial creditors.[3] Financial distress produces two types of cost. First, there are the direct costs of resolving the financial distress: advisory fees for lawyers, investment bankers, and other professionals, and the costs of any process or procedure used to resolve the situation. Secondly, there are indirect costs as customers and suppliers become nervous about dealing with the company because of its weakened financial condition; competitors see an opportunity to knock down a competitor and advertise aggressively to attract business away from the wounded firm; management of the struggling business takes short-term action to try to generate cash, perhaps cutting prices or taking risky action, which damages firm value in the longer term; or, conversely, so much money is diverted to meet debt service costs that management is unable to invest in the business. These are also the transmission mechanisms by which financial distress becomes economic distress.[4] It is therefore necessary to address financial distress as quickly and as cheaply as possible to limit

[2] Lawrence A Marsiello, 'From Hangover to Recovery? The Thoughts of a Turnaround Lender' in John Wm Butler Jr (Consulting Editor) *Navigating Today's Environment: The Directors' and Officers' Guide to Restructuring* (Globe White Page Ltd 2010) 30–31.

[3] Douglas G Baird, 'Bankruptcy's Uncontested Axioms' (1998) 108 Yale LJ 573, 581.

[4] For the distinction between financial and economic distress, see ibid 580:

> A firm may be troubled because it cannot succeed in the marketplace, since competitors produce a better product at a lower cost. On the other hand, a firm may be distressed because it cannot generate sufficient revenue to pay its debts. This first kind of adversity is called 'economic distress'. It exists regardless of a firm's capital structure … The second kind of trouble is 'financial distress'.

We might extend this description to cover firms whose competitors produce a better service at a lower cost.

direct and indirect costs, and to reduce the risk that financial distress becomes economic distress.

It will become apparent that where a complex, leveraged capital structure is the cause of the financial distress, the corporate reorganization case implicates particular participants. These participants then mobilize and adapt corporate reorganization law in specific ways to achieve the necessary deleveraging. Thus, a particular field of action emerges in which participants are motivated by new attitudes to debt to establish complex, leveraged capital structures, and in which participants mobilize and adapt corporate reorganization law in specific ways to facilitate a reorganization of these complex, leveraged capital structures in financial distress. The first step in analysing this field of action is to pay close attention to the way in which the case is described. The transaction is limited to debt and equity finance provided by sophisticated, informed, strongly adjusting institutional financial creditors and investors, rather than implicating the claims of trade creditors, employees, tort creditors, or customers of the firm. For reasons which will become apparent, it will be helpful to specify that it is sophisticated financial creditors and investors who are the participants in the process, rather than using generic terms such as 'unsecured creditors' or 'junior creditors'.

Although the terms unsecured creditor and corporate reorganization appear merely descriptive, in reality they have developed in the scholarly debate in the United States (US) in response to a typical Chapter 11 case in the 1980s. This would ordinarily take the form of a full financial and operational reorganization, and would implicate financial creditors, general, unsecured creditors, employees, and customers. As a result, the term unsecured creditor is often used as shorthand in the literature for a weakly adjusting, poorly informed creditor with little voice in the process and little capacity to absorb loss. Thus, the unsecured creditor becomes fundamental in the disagreement between economically minded scholars (who would not pursue redistributive policies in corporate reorganization) and progressive scholars (who would redistribute). This chapter suggests that none of these implicit, associated meanings is relevant when the unsecured creditor is a sophisticated financial lender or institutional bondholder in the reorganization of the debtor's debt and equity financing arrangements. In the first part of the chapter, the argument is made that continued use of the term unsecured creditor, rather than 'junior lender' or 'junior bondholder' or 'equity investor', when describing corporate reorganization cases, has obscured from view significant parts of the field where the distance between economically minded scholars and progressive scholars ought to have narrowed.

The second part of this chapter examines experience in England. The account reveals that, as a result of organizational and institutional changes in the finance field, participants have begun to mobilize and adapt England's corporate reorganization law tools, particularly in the decade since the financial crisis. This mobilization has occurred specifically for the purposes of reorganizing complex, leveraged capital structures. The participants in the process, and the courts, have not arrived at these cases bounded by a particular conceptual framework developed in the context of full financial and operational reorganizations, carrying the weight of particular a priori commitments to protecting the welfare of weaker trade creditors and employees in a corporate reorganization case. The legislative scheme is relatively light, and leaves significant discretion to the judges. In their turn, English judges have approached reorganizations of debt and equity raised from sophisticated financial institutions within a conceptual framework which is orientated to the realities of the marketplace. They have recognized that junior lenders and bondholders entered into the finance arrangements bargaining for the increased risk of a junior participation in a complex, leveraged capital structure. This has been reinforced in the finance contracts which are entered into when leveraged debt is raised. As a result, the approach which has emerged is highly pragmatic and well adapted for the use of corporate reorganization law as a tool to reorganize leveraged debt and equity finance.

The concern, in the case of England, is that the concepts which have emerged in the corporate reorganization law field in the decade since the financial crisis are intimately connected to reorganization of debt and equity finance provided by sophisticated financial institutions. Thus, the risk, in the English context, is that if expanding or changing logics, practices, and identities in fields proximate to the corporate reorganization field give rise to new types of corporate reorganization case, these will be obscured from view by the use of concepts which relate to a different fact pattern. This point is covered in detail in Chapters 9 and 10, when the book looks forward to the next decade, and considers the implications of the analysis in the book for the reform agenda. And it assumes heightened significance as the book goes to press in the midst of the COVID-19 crisis. For the moment, the analysis concentrates on the emergence of particular concepts in corporate reorganization law in England in an era of rising leverage multiples.

3.2 United States

3.2.1 The concept of the unsecured creditor

For scholars pursuing an economic analysis of corporate reorganization law, Chapter 11 exists to overcome market failures which prevent the resources of the financially distressed firm from being allocated to highest and best use. Chapter 11 contains a power for the judge to force a dissenting class of creditors to accept a reorganization plan, known as the 'cram-down' power.[5] The cram-down power

[5] 11 USC §1129(b).

exists either to incentivize bargaining, or to impose a bargain, in each case where bargaining for the most efficient allocation of resources would otherwise fail.[6] As will become apparent as the book progresses, bargaining in corporate reorganization may be difficult or even impossible because the parties may have radically different views as to what they will accept for themselves and what they are willing to give each other. If the senior secured creditors are not willing to permit the junior unsecured creditors to recover more than $250 million, but the junior unsecured creditors will not accept anything less than $500 million, then what Bradley Johnston calls 'the bargaining set' does not exist. Moreover, even where the parties have settled on a bargaining set, they may not be able to agree on what Johnston calls a 'common point' in the bargaining set.[7] Thus, bargaining may be impossible or, at the very least, costly, and market failure may take the form of a failure in bargaining. Viewed through an economic lens, the power of the judge to force a plan of reorganization onto a dissenting class in Chapter 11 seeks to solve the failure of bargaining.[8] For many scholars adopting an economic analysis of corporate reorganization law, where it becomes necessary to impose a plan of reorganization it should, to adopt Jules Coleman's term, 'mimic' the result the market would have produced if bargaining had been possible.[9] Thus, these scholars have suggested various market-based approaches to allocation of corporate reorganization value in a cram-down situation.[10]

Progressive scholars, on the other hand, have preferred the approach which US bankruptcy courts usually adopt in a Chapter 11 case. The concern is that market-based approaches may produce a valuation for the firm which has moved away from what might be called its intrinsic, or fundamental, value. The argument is that this may occur because other potential bidders in the same industry are excluded because they are also facing financial distress; or because credit markets are tight so that there is a lack of available financing for bidders; or because bidders heavily discount the price as a result of the immediate experience of distress. As a result, the market-based approach may produce no return for junior creditors in circumstances where a valuation based on post-reorganization cashflows would have produced a return. Crucially, in the 1980s and 1990s, the junior creditors were typically

[6] Jules Coleman, *Markets, Morals, and the Law* (OUP 1998) 29.

[7] J Bradley Johnston, 'The Bankruptcy Bargain' (1991) 65 Am Bankr LJ 213, 242–43, 245.

[8] Guido Calabresi and A Douglas Melamed, 'Property Rules, Liability Rules, and Inalienability: One View of the Cathedral' (1972) 85 Harvard L Rev 1089, 1105–1115.

[9] Coleman (n 6) 84.

[10] See eg Mark J Roe, 'Bankruptcy and Debt: A New Model for Corporate Reorganization' (1983) 83 Colum L Rev 527; Douglas G Baird, 'The Uneasy Case for Corporate Reorganizations' (1986) 15 J Legal Stud 127; Lucian Arye Bebchuk, 'A New Approach to Corporate Reorganizations' (1988) 101 Harvard L Rev 775; Philippe Aghion, Oliver Hart, and John Moore, 'The Economics of Bankruptcy Reform' (1992) 8 J L Econ & Org 523; Barry E Adler, 'Financial and Political Theories of American Corporate Bankruptcy' (1993) 45 Stanford L Rev 311.

general, unsecured creditors, such as trade creditors and employees,[11] many of whom were poorly placed to protect themselves *ex ante* and had limited bargaining power *ex post*. As a result, progressive scholars have typically preferred—and US bankruptcy courts have traditionally adopted—judicially supervised valuation exercises, in which expert valuers attempt to place a value on the business which reflects the intrinsic, or fundamental, value of the firm, rather than the price which the highest bidder would actually be willing to pay in the market at the time of the corporate reorganization transaction.[12]

Since this approach to valuation was crafted, US corporates have steadily shifted from a reliance on retained earnings to a reliance on borrowed money to finance their operations, and leverage ratios (the ratio of borrowed money to the firm's earnings) have steadily increased. As this chapter reveals, this has led to significant adaptations in the ways in which Chapter 11 is mobilized and adapted. This, in turn, fundamentally affects the ways in which corporate reorganization impacts general, unsecured trade creditors, employees, and customers, and requires the debate, among scholars who prefer a market-based approach to valuation and scholars who prefer judicially supervised expert valuation opinions, to be revisited. First, it is necessary to understand how and why the shift to borrowed money has occurred, and how corporate reorganization law interacts with the new environment.

3.2.2 The rise of leveraged capital structures

A number of different forces combined together to bring about the change in attitudes to borrowed money and leverage. First, there was a dramatic shift in the economic environment in which US corporates operated from the 1960s onwards. Towards the end of the 1960s, US inflation started to rise, partly as a result of the demands of the Vietnam War. This was compounded by the oil shock of the 1970s. High inflation led to concerns for future economic activity which depressed equity values,[13] leading investors to seek opportunities outside the stock market, while the inflationary environment incentivised anyone with a taxable income to increase their levels of debt.[14] At the same time, US corporates faced serious foreign

[11] Douglas G Baird and Thomas H Jackson, 'Corporate Reorganizations and the Treatment of Diverse Ownership Interests: A Comment on Adequate Protection of Secured Creditors in Bankruptcy' (1984) 51(1) U Chi L Rev 97, 107.

[12] See eg Kerry O'Rourke, 'Valuation Uncertainty in Chapter 11 Reorganizations' (2005) Colum Bus L Rev 403, 425: 'The Supreme Court has historically discouraged lower courts from making bankruptcy valuation decisions based on what third parties are willing to pay for a bankrupt enterprise.'

[13] Patric H Hendershott and Roger D Huang, 'Debt and Equity Yields, 1926–1980' in Benjamin M Friedman (ed) *Corporate Capital Structures in the United States* (The University of Chicago Press 1985) 147.

[14] John H Ciccolo and Christopher F Baum, 'Changes in the Balance Sheet of the US Manufacturing Sector, 1926–1977' in Friedman (ed), *Corporate Capital Structures* (n 13) 83.

competitive pressure, particularly from Japan.[15] As a result, there was a sharp and prolonged fall in the value of equity in US non-financial corporates after 1968, at the same time that the strategy of relying on retained earnings for growth came under pressure.

During this period, short-term money market instruments were seen to provide better protection against inflation than fixed rate, long-term bonds. This was because the interest rate on a typical thirty-day money market instrument only lagged inflation by around a month, while the fixed interest rate was locked in on a long-term bond, so that the only way in which an investor could adapt to rising rates was to sell the bond at a loss. As a result, long-term bonds had a negative after-inflation rate.[16] Initially, this drove many corporates to exploit the commercial paper markets as a source of finance, continually rolling over short-term borrowings to create functional long-term debt. The risks inherent in this strategy were revealed by a number of high-profile corporate bankruptcies in the 1970s when commercial paper borrowings could not be rolled over, notably the failure of the Penn Central railway and the failure of the retailer W T Grant. The Penn Central was able to take advantage of specific provisions for railroad reorganization in the US Bankruptcy Code in order to reorganize. W T Grant was unable to secure consent for a reorganization, and ultimately failed.[17] Other high-profile cases of distress followed.

At the same time, in the late 1970s, a young Michael Milken at Drexel Burnham Lambert was developing the idea of the junk bond. A junk bond is a bond which is subordinated to senior debt in right of payment on insolvency; which typically contains very few covenants; and which offers investors a high interest rate. Junk bonds had existed for some time (although not referred to in those terms). Indeed, Milken was heavily influenced by W Braddock Hickman's study of corporate bond performance from 1900 to 1943, in which Hickman had shown the benefits to the investor of a diversified portfolio of high-yield bonds,[18] and T R Atkinson's update for the period 1944–65.[19] Before Milken exploded onto the US finance market, junk bonds were largely so-called fallen angels: bonds which had originally been assigned an investment grade credit rating by the rating agencies, but which had subsequently been downgraded as a result of concerns with their issuer's credit worthiness. As Connie Bruck shows in her lively book, it was Milken

[15] Neil Fligstein, *The Architecture of Markets: An Economic Sociology of Twenty-First Century Capitalist Societies* (new edn, Princeton University Press 2002) 150.

[16] Benjamin M Friedman, 'Introduction: An Overview of the NBER's Research Project on the Changing Role of Debt and Equity in Financing US Capital Formation' in Friedman (ed), *The Changing Roles of Debt and Equity in Financing US Capital Formation* (University of Chicago Press 1982) 37.

[17] The accounts of Penn Central and W T Grant in this section are largely drawn from L J Davis, *Bad Money* (St Martin's Press 1982) 1–76.

[18] W Braddock Hickman, *Corporate Bond Quality and Investor Experience* (Princeton University Press 1958).

[19] Connie Bruck, *The Predator's Ball: The Inside Story of Drexel Burnham and the Rise of the Junk Bond Raiders* (Penguin Books 1989) 27–28.

who conceived of, and developed, the idea of bonds originally issued as high yield by issuers who would not have access to the investment grade market.[20]

Bruck also shows how Milken was able to develop his ideas. As a result of the economic experiences of the 1970s, the equity of many large US corporates appeared undervalued, fuelling the corporate raiders of the 1980s who sought to take over unwieldy conglomerates, often with a view to breaking them up and using the sum of the parts to finance the acquisition debt. Milken's high-yield bonds provided a crucial source of financing for these takeovers. As Chapter 4 develops in more detail, in the debt capital markets the providers of bond capital had shifted, from the 1950s onwards, from pre-Second World War retail investors to institutional investors. Pension funds, mutual funds, and insurance companies had become the dominant providers of bond capital in the US. Milken found ready investors for his high-yield bonds amongst pension funds, mutual funds, insurance companies, offshore banks, college endowments, and high-yield funds.[21] When the savings and loans crisis resulted in the passage of the Garn-St Germain Depository Institutions Act in 1982, savings and loans were able to join as investors in Milken's financings.[22] Overall, the explosion of the junk bond market in the 1980s is an important part of the story of the growth in leverage, and of the increased frequency of large corporate reorganization when the leveraged capital structures of the 1980s resulted in financial stress in the 1990s.

Finance scholarship also played a significant role in endorsing the shift to borrowed money. Hickman's study in the 1950s has already been touched upon. In 1958, Modigliani and Miller published their famous theorem that, given certain assumptions, the mixture of debt and equity in a firm's capital structure did not affect its value.[23] Modigliani and Miller's theorem suggested that corporates had a choice of capital structure, and the assumptions to the theorem gave a clue as to how and why corporates might select between debt and equity. In 1968, Edward Altman published work on how to assess the likelihood that a highly leveraged company would face bankruptcy.[24] In 1976, Jensen and Meckling suggested that it was possible to reduce the so-called 'agency costs of debt' (the risk that in distress directors would support risky behaviour in an effort to save their jobs, which might also be in the interests of shareholders but which might increase losses for lenders) through the terms of the debt contract.[25] And in the mid-1980s, Jensen

[20] ibid 10–11, explaining that these issuers could not access the investment grade markets 'Because of their small size, or their lack of credit history, or their leveraged capital structure'.

[21] ibid 11.

[22] Although there is some suggestion in the literature that they may not have been as significant as investors in junk bonds as is sometimes suggested—see Benjamin M Friedman, 'The Risks of Financial Crises' in Martin Feldstein (ed) *The Risk of Economic Crisis* (The University of Chicago Press 1991) 40.

[23] Franco Modigliani and Merton H Miller, 'The Cost of Capital, Corporation Finance and the Theory of Investment' (1958) 48 Am Econ Rev 261.

[24] Edward I Altman, 'Financial Ratios, Discriminant Analysis and the Prediction of Corporate Bankruptcy' (1968) 23(4) J Finance 589.

[25] Michael C Jensen and William H Meckling, 'Theory of the Firm: Managerial Behavior, Agency Costs and Ownership Structure' (1976) 3(4) J Finan Econ 305.

published highly influential work on the corporate governance benefits of debt,[26] arguing that debt disciplined management, and prevented them from making irresponsible investments, because they would lack free cashflow, which had to be applied to service the debt burden. In other words, the benefits to the firm of debt finance outweighed its costs.

The way in which directors thought about the financing of the firm was further revolutionized by the shareholder value revolution. Before the 1930s, large industrial corporates had tended either to be owned by their founders or had had representatives of the investment banks which had floated their securities on their boards of directors. In other words, there was a party on the board of directors representing the interests of the shareholders. Through a combination of organizational change and the post-depression New Deal reforms, investment banks ceased to participate on boards, and shareholdings had been diversified away from founders. In the 1930s, Berle and Means' highly influential work showed the risk for investors where share ownership was dispersed and there was no one on the board to monitor management's commitment to shareholders.[27] In other words, there was a growing concern that the management of the large US corporate wasn't responsible to anyone. This was reinforced by seminal work in sociology, which encouraged debate on the highly bureaucratized nature of the large US corporate enterprise.[28]

Milken had provided many examples of disastrous investments by large public companies, and the rallying cry of the leveraged buyouts of the 1980s was that they would take US corporates out of the hands of complacent, bureaucratic managers and into more entrepreneurial hands.[29] As the merger wave of the 1980s gathered pace, companies with straightforward balance sheets and good cashflows looked increasingly vulnerable, so that there was an incentive to leverage the capital structure in order to avoid becoming a takeover target.[30] With a growing focus on the virtues of concentrating on shareholder value, pressure mounted to distribute earnings to shareholders rather than to retain them.[31] The 1980s were thus a highly significant time for institutional change in the fields of finance and non-financial corporate borrowers. This is perhaps best demonstrated by the gentrification of the junk bond. Milken's own career was to end ignominiously with a prison term for securities fraud. Yet his legacy survived and was accepted into the mainstream of

[26] Michael Jensen, 'Agency Costs of Free Cashflow, Corporate Finance, and Takeovers' (1986) 76(2) Am Econ Rev 323.

[27] Adolf A Berle and Gardiner C Means, *The Modern Corporation and Private Property* (Macmillan 1935).

[28] David Riesman with Nathan Glazer and Reuel Denney, *The Lonely Crowd: A Study of the Changing American Character* (Yale University Press 1961); William H Whyte, *The Organization Man* (Simon and Schuster 1956).

[29] Bruck (n 19) 186–90; 272.

[30] Ron Chernow, *The House of Morgan: An American Banking Dynasty and the Rise of Modern Finance* (Grove Press 1990) 692–93.

[31] M Friedman, 'The Social Responsibility of Business is to Increase its Profits' *New York Times* (New York, 13 September 1970) s 6 (Magazine) 32.

finance. In time, the vocabulary of the field changed, so that the junk bond market became known, once again, by the less pejorative term, the high-yield bond market.

The business of banking was also changing dramatically. As Chapter 2 explored, US restrictions on bank branching and consolidation meant that banks were small in size right up until the 1990s, so that commercial banks simply did not have the capacity to make the size of loan required by a mega-sized US corporate expanding nationally and internationally. At the same time, the reforms in the Glass-Steagall Act of 1933 famously forced banks to choose between commercial and investment banking. Domestic regulation, designed to solve the problem of US balance of payments, increasingly drove US multinationals overseas to raise funds.[32] The suggestion that Glass-Steagall did not prohibit securities underwriting outside the US caused a so-called 'Eurodollar market' to explode.[33] The Eurodollar market enabled US banks, which were prohibited from domestic underwriting, to underwrite dollar issuances in Europe (notably in London) for their multinational clients. Technological innovation in communication and information, and legal wizardry in banks' legal structures, also helped to overcome the geographical barriers imposed by the New Deal reforms.[34] And states themselves began to avoid the restrictions on national banking, not least in order to find merger partners and purchasers to rescue failing banks.[35]

The pressure for deregulation was overwhelming and, when it came, it came quickly. Caps imposed on the interest which banks could charge on deposit accounts (discussed in Chapter 4) were finally dismantled with the passage of the Garn-St Germain Depositary Institutions Act of 1982.[36] States steadily dismantled restrictions on interstate banking, and the final remaining barriers were dismantled at a federal level with the passage of the Riegle-Neal Interstate Banking and Branching Efficiency Act of 1994.[37] Finally, the Gramm–Leach–Bliley Act of 1999 effectively dismantled the Glass-Steagall Act of 1933.[38] A number of large commercial banks were to emerge, with a rich range of investment strategies, acting as significant providers of capital to large US enterprises. These expanding banks now needed to find profitable opportunities for expanding sources of funds.

Fortunately, there was a relentlessly growing demand for debt finance in the US. First, the commercial banks were able to participate in financing the leveraged

[32] Chernow (n 30) 541.

[33] ibid 544–45. As Gary Burn puts it, 'The prefix "Euro" is a misnomer, in that it defines what is an *offshore currency*, held and used *outside* the country where it acts as legal tender, and traded in a market which exists outside the system of state-prescribed banking jurisdiction': Gary Burn, 'The State, the City and the Euromarkets' (1999) 6(2) Rev Int'l Pol Econ 225, 226.

[34] Edward J Kane, 'De Jure Interstate Banking: Why Only Now?' (1996) 28(2) J Mon, Credit & Banking 141, 143–44.

[35] ibid 146.

[36] Robert DeYoung, William C Hunter, and Gregory F Udell, 'The Past, Present, and Probable Future for Community Banks' (2004) 25(2/3) J Finan Serv Res 85, 93.

[37] ibid 96.

[38] ibid.

takeovers of the 1980s.[39] Secondly, the leveraged takeovers of the 1980s laid the foundations for the modern buyout, or private equity, industry. In a private equity investment, the professional investors (ordinarily limited partners in the private equity fund) are locked in for the time-limited life cycle of the private equity fund. They trade return for liquidity. The General Partner of the fund establishes holding companies to acquire a target group of companies and to borrow significant amounts of debt to fund the acquisition. The plan is to trade the group after acquisition and (ideally) to find ways to grow value followed by a trade sale, stock market listing, or sale to another private equity firm after three to seven years, producing outsized returns for the private equity investors. The acquisition debt is guaranteed by the operating group companies, and secured against their assets.[40]

Leverage performs a central function in the private equity industry. First (and controversially) it magnifies investor returns, enabling the industry to promote its spectacular return history. Secondly, it is part of a governance package intended to closely align managers with shareholders, so that the high fixed costs of the acquisition debt cause managers to focus only on value-maximizing projects. And finally (possibly) it may enable private equity firms to exploit pricing differences in equity and debt markets.[41] Private equity investment has exploded on both sides of the Atlantic, with the result that some extremely large corporations are privately owned companies with complex, leveraged capital structures. The innovation has also driven other large, publicly traded companies to leverage up, not only to avoid becoming a 'take private' target, but also in an attempt to replicate the investor benefits of the private equity industry. This has had significant implications for the fact pattern in a corporate reorganization case to deleverage the capital structure.

3.2.3 Leveraged capital structures and the corporate reorganization case

As already identified, a finance company with a leveraged capital structure may face greater difficulties in coping with a temporary reduction in earnings during a downturn in its operating group. This is because it must constantly find cash to meet its debt service obligations, or may face greater challenges when it comes to refinance if conditions in the credit markets have changed. Moreover, the company is suffering financial, as opposed to operational, stress as a result of its leveraged

[39] Chernow (n 30) 666; Bruck (n 19) 13 notes that, when Coastal Corporation acquired American Natural Resources company for $2.46 billion, $1.6 billion of the financing was provided by bank loans and $600 m was provided by high-yield bond issuance.

[40] For a more complete account, see Louise Gullifer and Jennifer Payne, *Corporate Finance Law: Principles and Policy* (2nd edn, Hart Publishing 2015) 765–67.

[41] Cem Demiroglu and Christopher M James, 'The Role of Private Equity Group Reputation in LBO Financing' (2010) 96 J Finan Econ 306, 308.

capital structure.[42] In other words, if it is able to reduce the fixed costs of its debt service by, for example, swapping debt for equity, the rest of the group may very well be healthy and there may be no need for a more far-reaching operational or managerial restructuring in the operating group companies. Leveraged capital structures posed challenges for many of the corporate reorganizations of the 1990s, but the corporate reorganizations which followed typically implicated both financial and trade credit.[43] In other words, the cases were what might be called thoroughgoing financial and operational reorganizations. And, as Chapter 6 explores, US management also turned to Chapter 11 for strategic purposes: to reject collective bargaining arrangements with labour, or to deal with mass tort claims. The important point is that, in the majority of cases, the Chapter 11 plan of reorganization expressly implicated non-adjusting or weakly adjusting general, unsecured creditors, employees, customers, or (sometimes) tort claimants, all bundled into the term 'unsecured creditors'.[44]

In the decade since the financial crisis there has been a growing appreciation that, if the corporate reorganization can be confined to the debt and equity finance provided by sophisticated financial institutions, then it may be possible to prevent distress spreading to the operating group. Far more attention has been paid to the value-destructive consequences of trading in Chapter 11 while a corporate reorganization plan is negotiated: high advisory costs for the lawyers, investment bankers, and other finance professionals necessary to guide the company through the corporate reorganization process; management distraction; lost customers as a result of uncertainty around the company's future and on its service levels during a bankruptcy process; lost opportunities for new business during the bankruptcy case; creditor action in refusing supply, or reducing debtor days, or demanding cash on delivery; and the significant implications of having resorted to bankruptcy for confidence in the company after it has reorganized. At the same time, many modern businesses in both the service and manufacturing sector are contract businesses, which may be harder to keep together for any period of time than a business with a significant number of physical assets, as suppliers cancel contracts and customers move away from the firm. Thus, speed is of the essence. As Michael Jensen highlighted in a piece in 1989, where high debt service costs motivate the

[42] For the distinction between operational and financial stress, see Ian Ratner, Grant Stein, and John C Weitnauer, *Business Valuation and Bankruptcy* (John Wiley & Sons, Inc 2009) 3.

[43] For an example, see the analysis of the National Convenience Stores Incorporated reorganization in Stuart C Gilson, *Creating Value through Corporate Restructuring: Case Studies in Bankruptcies, Buyouts, and Breakups* (John Wiley & Sons Inc 2001) 66.

[44] For a description of what is meant by non-adjusting or weakly adjusting creditors, see Warren and Westbrook's description ' … creditors who have little meaningful opportunity to negotiate with their debtors or adjust their prices to reflect risks': Elizabeth Warren and Jay Lawrence Westbrook, 'Contracting Out of Bankruptcy: An Empirical Intervention' (2005) 118 Harvard L Rev 1197, 1203.

reorganization transaction there may be a great deal of firm value left to preserve, but only if action can be taken quickly.[45]

What is needed, then, is a rapid reorganization of the debt and equity finance provided by the financial institutions. If the renegotiation of the capital structure of the firm involves only the institutional shareholders and financial creditors, it is most likely to affect other constituencies only if it results in excessive transaction costs or cannot be achieved at all. In their ground-breaking work in 1998 Bruce Carruthers and Terence Halliday noted that:

> ... at the moment of bankruptcy, every credit relationship, which is to say every financial relationship with other companies, banks, the state, consumers, suppliers, workers, and even communities, is *simultaneously* thrown into doubt. In principle, every player in the organizational network is at the bankruptcy table.[46]

Yet, where the balance sheet is to be restructured via a reorganization of debt and equity finance provided by financial institutions in a modern case, often only the institutional shareholders and financial creditors are implicated and present at the bankruptcy table.[47]

As Chapter 4 explores in more detail, these shareholders and financial creditors in a complex, leveraged capital structure are sophisticated parties, who had the full range of investment opportunities available to them.[48] The fact that the capital structure may need to be flexed to deal with changes in the economic environment was foreseeable, and the participants were informed, strongly adjusting, diversified, and hedged—in other words, they had the knowledge and bargaining power to adjust their investment terms and secure credit protection in advance. As Merton Miller put it in the Nobel Memorial Prize Lecture in 1990:

> The high promised yields that might be earned during the good years were understood as compensation for the possible bad years in time and bad bonds in the total junk bond portfolio. The high nominal yields, in short, were essentially risk premiums.[49]

[45] Michael Jensen, 'Active Investors, LBOs, and the Privatization of Bankruptcy' (1989) J App Corp Fin 34, repr (2010) 2(1) J App Corp Fin 77.

[46] Bruce G Carruthers and Terence C Halliday, *Rescuing Business: The Making of Corporate Bankruptcy Law in England and the United States* (Clarendon Press 1998) 6.

[47] For an example, see the analysis of the Flagstar Companies, Inc reorganization in Gilson (n 43) 110.

[48] It is possible that individual retail investors may hold equity directly in large, publicly traded firms—see Diane Lourdes Dick, 'Valuation in Chapter 11 Bankruptcy: The Dangers of an Implicit Market Test' (2017) U Ill L Rev 1487. However, as Chapter 4 explores, institutional shareholders are likely to dominate. In any event, retail investors are likely to be relatively sophisticated and to have diversified investment portfolios, given that most retail investment will be made via professional fund managers. In short, this is no longer an era of so-called widows and orphans stock.

[49] Merton H Miller, 'Leverage: Nobel Memorial Prize Lecture 1990' in Jagdeep S Bhandari and Lawrence A Weiss (eds) *Corporate Bankruptcy: Economic and Legal Perspectives* (CUP 1996) 3.

Financial distress is when the risk happens.This has crucial implications for the concept of the unsecured creditor in the traditional debate between scholars viewing US corporate reorganization law through an economic lens and scholars viewing it through a progressive lens.

3.2.4 Implications for the concept of the unsecured creditor

The scholarly lens must now be trained on a field of action in which corporate reorganization law is used solely to adjust debt and equity finance in a complex, leveraged capital structure. Moreover, the unsecured creditors in these reorganizations are sophisticated, informed, strongly adjusting financial creditors. The problem is a capital structure which (and this is crucial) all the financial creditors knew may need adapting if the economic environment changed. In other words, institutional junior unsecured lenders or bondholders have taken advantage of the pricing associated with a complex, leveraged capital structure. They have taken the risk (which they deal with by diversification and hedging) that they will bear losses if the capital structure subsequently requires reorganization. For scholars adopting an economic analysis, the problem to be addressed by corporate reorganization law is the problem of cooperation in bargaining for a new capital structure. For progressive scholars, social cost arises if the cost of the reorganization of the liabilities owed to the institutional financial creditors is excessive, or the law lacks the tools to facilitate the reorganization of these liabilities, so that at best distress shifts to the general, unsecured creditors or, at worst, the business fails. Thus, scholars adopting an economic analysis and scholars pursuing a progressive agenda ought to be able to coalesce around providing the participants with legal tools which reduce the transaction costs associated with bargaining for a reorganization in these types of cases.

Yet, the persistence of concepts for analysing corporate reorganization law which are closely related to the full financial and operational reorganizations of the 1980s and 1990s has obscured this common ground. It is helpful to unpack this argument a little more by examining three of the ways in which a modern capital structure may be deleveraged: the exchange offer; a section 363 sale; or a Chapter 11 reorganization case.

3.2.4.1 The exchange offer

The finance market has, since the 2008 financial crisis, worked to facilitate the rapid reorganization of leveraged capital structures, and the exchange offer has become increasingly popular as a method of achieving the deleveraging transaction. The exchange offer is a market system for reorganizing debt and equity finance provided by financial institutions, while containing the threat power of hold-out creditors. In an exchange offer, new bonds are offered in exchange for outstanding bonds, typically with a lower coupon or principal amount and shorter maturity, but with improved seniority. The exchange offer obviously implicates value because the offer must be sufficiently attractive to persuade the relevant majorities in each class to accept it. At the same time, it avoids what will shortly be revealed can be a costly and unpredictable valuation fight in a Chapter 11 case, while providing a method of dealing with a recalcitrant minority. It is, in effect, a way for the financial institutions to bargain for the new capital structure among themselves, while limiting the threat position of potential hold-out creditors. Thus, in some ways, the increasing popularity of the exchange offer reflects Michael Jensen's 1989 prediction that the leverage model would lead to the privatization of the bankruptcy process.[50] Michael Milken and the team at Drexel Burnham Lambert originally pioneered the unregistered exchange offer using section 3(a) 9 of the Securities Act 1933 as a way of loosening interest payment obligations in the high-yield bond issues which they had placed, without going through the costly process of registering a security with the US Securities and Exchange Commission before it could be offered to bondholders. As Bruck explains, Milken understood the increased risk of bankruptcy, as a result of high debt service obligations or changed credit market conditions at refinancing, in a leveraged capital structure, and focused on the concept of the 'flexible balance sheet'.[51]

The exchange offer appears to undermine Chapter 11's foundational normative concern with minority unsecured creditor protection, which can be traced all the way back to the era of the equity receivership. A key motivation for the codification of the equity receivership in the 1930s was the concern that the equity receivership plan might have been designed to further the interests of the investors which the investment bank (often J P Morgan) represented. The corollary to this was the concern that local creditors, and others who were not within the investment bank's sphere of influence, might have been prejudiced by the deal. And, crucially, the equity receivership dominated at a time at which most investors were retail investors. Thus, the New Deal reforms to corporate reorganization law sought to shift bargaining power away from the powerful investment bank intermediaries and, implicitly, the creditors who they represented, and section 316(b) of the Trust Indenture Act 1939 prevented majority creditors from imposing changes in principal, interest, or maturity date on the minority without court supervision. In other words, a corporate reorganization plan compromising principal or interest, or extending maturities, would require a Chapter 11 plan.

Yet the modern mobilization and adaptation of corporate reorganization law tools specifically to reorganize the liabilities of a leveraged group owed to sophisticated financial institutions raises quite different issues from the mobilization of

[50] Jensen, 'Privatisation of Bankruptcy' (n 45). However, it will become apparent that, in other ways, Jensen's prediction was wide of the mark. As the book unfolds it will reveal that this is because he underestimated other shifts in logic, practice, and identity which would increase the transaction costs associated with corporate reorganization bargaining.

[51] Bruck (n 19) 75–76.

the equity receivership to compromise liabilities owed to retail investors. The participants in modern leveraged capital structures are sophisticated institutional investors who understand and bargain for the risk of leverage, and have the full range of investment opportunities packaged in complex, modern investment portfolios. Crucially, the exchange offer is limited to reorganizing debt and equity finance provided by sophisticated financial institutions, and does not implicate general, unsecured debt, employee claims, or the like. Thus, while protection of minority unsecured creditors retains some salience, it is of reduced salience when compared with a full financial and operational reorganization implicating weakly adjusting, poorly informed, general unsecured creditors and stakeholders, even for scholars sympathetic to a more progressive orientation. Once this is understood, it is apparent that, provided only the debtor's liabilities to sophisticated financial institutions are reorganized, the central concern should be to reduce the transaction costs in achieving the deleveraging, whichever lens is focused on the case.

Out-of-court reorganization typically reduces transaction costs, both by saving on legal and other advisory and administrative costs, and by reducing some of the other indirect costs associated with a Chapter 11 filing. The exchange offer attempts to exploit this cost saving, while providing a more streamlined mechanism for achieving the reorganization of debt and equity finance provided by financial institutions. Thus, it may be appropriate to relax the section 316(b) restriction. William Bratton and Adam Levitin have suggested that section 316(b) would be better replaced by an approach focused on whether there are reasons to be sceptical that the majority has voted for the deal, or whether they were motivated by separate, individual preferences.[52] Bratton and Levitin's approach retains some concern for minority protection, in providing the opportunity to challenge financial creditors who are acting for ancillary purposes unrelated to the interests of the class of which they are a part. This is an idea which is developed in later chapters. For the moment, the short point is that the analysis here supports their argument.

3.2.4.2 The section 363 sale

The second way in which debt and equity finance can be reorganized is via the section 363 sale. Where section 363 is used in this way, financial creditors which are 'in the money' establish a new company to place a bid for the group's business and assets, in which they own equity and other securities. The bidding company is able to facilitate release of these creditors' claims against the seller in consideration for the purchase (a process known as credit bidding). The first bidder is sometimes known as the stalking horse bidder. If other bidders emerge to compete

[52] William W Bratton and Adam J Levitin, 'The New Bond Workouts' (2018) 166 U Pa L Rev 1597. See also Mark J Roe, 'The Voting Prohibition in Bond Workouts' (1987) 97 Yale L J 232; and Robert Gertner and David S Scharfstein, 'A Theory of Workouts and the Effects of Reorganization Law' (1991) 46 J Finance 1189.

with the stalking horse bid, an auction is held (ordinarily at the office of the distressed corporate's lawyers), which other bidders may attend (and the stalking horse bidder is sometimes paid a break fee if a rival bid is successful). In simple terms, where firm value is sufficient to support a payment of all or some of a financial creditor's claim, the creditor is 'in the money'. Where firm value is insufficient to support any payment to the financial creditor, the creditor is 'out of the money'. In a leveraged capital structure, where no one is likely to outbid financial creditors who are in the money, this can provide an effective method of reorganizing the firm's debt and equity finance arrangements. Crucially, the transaction mobilizes a market-based, auction price as the benchmark for valuing the firm. This is because the reorganizing creditors' bid can only be beaten if someone offers more for the business and assets of the firm in an auction process. This contrasts with the approach to valuation which is adopted in a Chapter 11 plan, and may be part of the explanation for an increasing number of section 363 sales as a means of reorganizing debt and equity finance since the 2008 financial crisis.

If the court is asked to cram a Chapter 11 plan of reorganization down on a dissenting class of financial creditor or equity investor, it typically measures the plan against the post-reorganization value of the firm based on predicted future earnings of the firm after the reorganization, adjusted by an appropriate discount rate to give a present value (discounted cashflow (DCF) methodology).[53] As identified at the beginning of the chapter, this is because corporate reorganization often occurs at a time at which the economy has slowed and many other companies are also reorganizing by selling assets, so that there may be a great deal of supply and tighter distribution of debt capacity in the economy, depressing prices below the price which a DCF analysis would imply. The concern, in other words, is that the transaction is occurring at a low point in the cycle, so that value may have moved away from what might be called the intrinsic, or fundamental, value of the firm. The concept of post-reorganization value thus seeks to ensure that all creditors in the case receive consideration which reflects the prospects of the company after the reorganization, rather than allocating consideration in the transaction only to those creditors where the current market price of the firm is sufficient to cover some or all of their claim.

However, there has been increasing unease at the speculative nature of DCF valuations in modern finance markets. Each class of creditor appoints its own valuation expert. The concern arises that the valuation expert for the senior creditors will do all they can to argue for a low post-reorganization value (in order to deleverage the firm as much as possible, and provide the senior creditors with the lion's share of the equity in the new capital structure). On the other hand, the concern arises that the valuation expert for the junior creditors

[53] For a crisp description of DCF methodology, see O'Rourke (n 12) 421.

will do all they can to argue for a high post-reorganization value for the firm (in order to secure an allocation in the new capital structure for the junior creditors). While the resulting valuation dispute is presented with some cynicism in the literature, recent work by Oliver Hart and John Moore suggests that the very complexity of the settlement mechanism may drive the result. Hart and Moore's work focuses on complex mechanisms for settling future disputes in contracts.[54] They suggest that where a mechanism is complex, and permits a range of outcomes to be defended, *ex post* inefficiencies may result because the range of outcomes will enable each party to feel aggrieved that things are not going their way. In other words, it may be that the complexity of the mechanism itself, together with what Christian Zehnder calls the parties' 'self-serving biases', mean that the parties genuinely have a greater sense of entitlement.[55] Whether the parties genuinely believe in radically different value allocations, or cynically exploit the uncertainty of the valuation process, these valuation fights are notoriously expensive, and as will be seen in Chapter 9, there are reasons to suspect they may become more common.

It is suggested here that where the transaction reorganizes a complex, leveraged capital structure, and implicates only strongly adjusting financial creditors and investors, a current market price or current market value approach to valuation is to be preferred to a post-reorganization value approach, whether viewed through an economic or a progressive lens. Provided the valuation approach is clear to the parties *ex ante* they can price for it, adjust their portfolios, and hedge accordingly. Admittedly, this may cause some increase in the price of subordinated unsecured debt, but that is not necessarily a bad thing. As already discussed, a complex, leveraged capital structure may result in a costly reorganization transaction, so there may be merit in creating better incentives for debtors to concentrate on how much debt they take on. In any event, as explored in the second part of this chapter, English courts have largely adopted a current market price or current market value approach in assessing reorganizations of debt and equity finance provided by financial institutions. Nonetheless, a mezzanine loan and high-yield bond market has developed in England. Thus, the use of section 363 sale technology to achieve a deleveraging of a complex, leveraged capital structure among sophisticated financial creditors ought not to be objectionable, whether viewed through an economic or progressive lens. This leads, finally, to the implications of the developing argument for Chapter 11 reorganization.

[54] Oliver Hart and John Moore, 'Contracts as Reference Points' (2008) 123(1) Q J Econ 1.

[55] Christian Zehnder, 'New Directions of Incomplete Contracts: Reference Points, Communication, and Renegotiation' in Philippe Aghion, Mathias Dewatripont, Patrick Legros, and Luigi Zingales (eds) *The Impact of Incomplete Contracts on Economics* (OUP 2016) 383.

3.2.4.3 Chapter 11 plan of reorganization

In this case, it is suggested that not only should the use of exchange offers and section 363 technology be supported as methods of reorganizing debt and equity finance provided by financial institutions, but also that a current market price or current market value approach should be adopted in assessing a Chapter 11 plan of reorganization for these types of reorganization transactions. This both reduces the opportunities for the parties cynically to exploit uncertainty to drive a better bargain and addresses the problem that an overly complex mechanism may cause each party legitimately to feel entitled to the outcome which best serves its own interests. In many cases, it will be possible to use an auction process to establish current market price.[56] But even where this is not possible,[57] market price methodologies reduce many areas of challenge in the valuation process: it may be more straightforward to use 'comparable companies' analysis as a reference point, in which the valuer looks at recent transactions by companies in the same or similar sectors in establishing value, and more emphasis can be placed on current operating results, avoiding the weight put on highly speculative post-reorganization cashflow forecasts in current Chapter 11 valuation debates.[58] Once again, it is suggested that both scholars adopting an economic analysis (many of whom, as already identified in section 3.2.1 'The concept of the unsecured creditor', broadly support a market-orientated approach to valuation) and progressive scholars (who are more concerned with what might, following Coleman, be called questions of 'desert and entitlement')[59] ought to be able to agree with this approach where only sophisticated, informed, strongly adjusting financial creditors and investors are implicated.

3.2.5 Summary of the argument in section 3.2

Overall, it is suggested here that when financial liabilities which are owed to sophisticated financial institutions and investors in complex, leveraged capital structures are sufficient to absorb the losses, there are good reasons for prioritizing reduction of renegotiation costs over shifting bargaining power to unsecured creditors. This supports a more permissive approach to both exchange offers and section 363

[56] Douglas G Baird and Robert K Rasmussen, 'The End of Bankruptcy' (2002) 55 Stanford L Rev 751, 786–88; Gennady Zilberman, 'Bankruptcy Section 363(b) Sales: Market Test Procedures and Heightened Scrutiny of Expedited Sales May Prevent Abuses and Safeguard Creditors without Limiting the Power of the Courts' (2010) 5 Brook J Corp Fin & Com L 241.

[57] For example, where there is a concern that the benefits of a marketing process in establishing value are outweighed by the risks of the marketing process (such as causing further harm to the company's reputation as its financial difficulties become more widely appreciated), potentially having a depressing effect on value, or even making a sale transaction impossible to achieve.

[58] See also Kenneth Ayotte and Edward R Morrison, 'Valuation Disputes in Corporate Bankruptcy' (2018) 166 U Pa L Rev 1819.

[59] Coleman (n 6) 93.

sale transactions as methods of implementing a reorganization of debt and equity finance provided by sophisticated financial institutions. And it further supports a new approach to the principles of valuation in Chapter 11, which moves away from assessing entitlement to consideration in the reorganization based on post-reorganization value assessed using DCF methodology towards a current market price or current market value approach. Crucially, the argument holds whether an economic or a progressive approach is adopted in the analysis. Of course, if corporate reorganization law supplies the tools to facilitate a reorganization of financial debt and equity in complex, leveraged capital structures, concerns may be raised about the borrower-level and social costs high leverage implies. There is both underinvestment risk[60] and the increased risks implicated in attempting periodically to flex the capital structure if it proves unsustainable in prevailing economic conditions. Thus, the decision may be taken to restrict the incentives to create complex, leveraged capital structures *ex ante*, and the mechanisms which are provided to facilitate their reorganization *ex post*. These wider concerns are revisited later in the book. For the moment, assuming that benefits are seen in the expansion of credit and no decision has been taken actively to seek to reduce leverage in the market for credit, then it makes sense to provide the market with tools which can be mobilized and adapted to facilitate a reorganization of a complex, leveraged capital structure.

3.3 England

3.3.1 Why concern for the unsecured creditor assumed less significance in England

As noted briefly in Chapter 2, England's experience of volatile and damaging inflation in the 1970s (considerably more volatile and higher than US inflation) set the corporate bond market into a serious decline from which it was not to recover until recent times.[61] As a result, banks were the most important source of external debt finance for many large corporates in England, which had working capital or fixed investment needs which could not be met from retained earnings or equity raising. At the beginning of the 1970s, large corporates typically borrowed on a bilateral

[60] Underinvestment occurs in a highly leveraged firm where firm insiders have private information about profitable opportunities which outside investors are not willing to fund, and lack the internal cashflow to fund the opportunity as a result of the leveraged capital structure—see Edward M Iacobucci and George G Triantis, 'Economic and Legal Boundaries of Firms' (2007) 93 Virg L Rev 515, 548.

[61] Margaret Ackrill and Leslie Hannah, *Barclays: The Business of Banking 1690–1996* (CUP 2001) 237–38; Christopher Coyle and John D Turner, 'Law, Politics, and Financial Development: The Great Reversal of the UK Corporate Debt Market' (2013) 73(3) J Econ Hist 810; Brian R Cheffins, *Corporate Ownership and Control: British Business Transformed* (OUP 2010) 354.

basis from their relationship bank. If the borrower ran into difficulties, the bank was frequently prepared to provide the company with some breathing space, in order to see whether it could trade out of its difficulties.

Nonetheless, in the extremely difficult economic conditions of the 1970s, a breathing space was not sufficient for many large corporates to achieve turnarounds in their fortunes. During this era, as Stuart Slatter identifies, both Labour and Conservative Governments stepped in to help with the rescue of large, uncompetitive firms which were significant employers; major defence contractors; or high-technology industries.[62] Slatter describes how the state became involved in the rescue of British Leyland; Chrysler (UK); Alfred Herbert; Massey-Ferguson; Rolls-Royce; Ferranti; Sinclair Radionics; Kearney Trecker Marwin; Cambridge Instruments; and International Computers. Government intervention in these situations prevented or lessened the dislocations for employees, suppliers, and customers which would otherwise have occurred. By the end of the 1970s, change was on the horizon, both in the structure of the finance industry and in the authorities' preferred method of incentivizing the rescue of a large, failing firm. Yet, at the end of this period of change, social norms in the finance industry continued to play a more significant role in large company rescue than corporate reorganization law.

Minos Zombanakis was a banker with Manufacturers Hanover Trust Company of New York, posted in Rome, and representing the bank in the Middle East.[63] He appears to have negotiated £5 million in start-up funding to open a London office, where he is said to have played a significant role in the development of the syndicated term loan (although just how significant his role was is a matter of some controversy). In a syndicated term loan, the interest rate paid by the borrower is re-fixed periodically (typically every three to six months), depending on the cost of funds of the group of banks, or syndicate, which makes advances to the borrower. A group of 'reference banks' within the syndicate reported their cost of funds to the agent bank (the bank which coordinates advances to, and repayments from, the borrower), shortly before the interest rate fixing date.[64] The market developed so that a syndicated loan could be a term loan or a revolving loan. A term loan could be either a bullet term loan, in which the principal amount was repaid at maturity, or an amortizing term loan, in which case the principal amount was repaid periodically. In a revolving loan, the principal amount was notionally paid back and redrawn at the end of each interest period. Syndicated loan finance was to be the

[62] Stuart Slatter, *Corporate Recovery: Successful Turnaround Strategies and their Implementation* (Penguin 1984) 248–51.

[63] The story of Zombanakis in this part is largely drawn from Chris O' Malley, *Bonds without Borders: A History of the Eurobond Market* (Wiley 2015) 47–48.

[64] In modern syndicated loans a screen rate may be used instead of a reference bank quotation system. This system is undergoing significant change as the book goes to press, as a result of the withdrawal of the LIBOR rate following evidence of 'rate rigging'.

most significant source of both working capital and longer-term finance for large English corporates for the foreseeable future.[65]

As single bank (or bilateral) loans were replaced by loans advanced by a syndicate of banks, sums borrowed began to increase and the process of negotiation in distress changed. It was now more likely that a reorganization of the capital structure would be needed in distress, in which banks swapped their claims for other debt or equity interests. Thus, coordination problems became a very real concern. Chapter 2 outlined how the Bank of England promulgated new principles (known as the London Approach) to govern these multi-bank workouts, which were translated by the British Bankers' Association into written principles published in 1990.[66] The principles of the London Approach were used to motivate corporate reorganization where a large firm had borrowed significant amounts of money, typically from a large syndicate of banks (in a speech in 1993 Pen Kent, then Director for Finance and Industry at the Bank of England, referred to syndicates of upwards of twenty banks).[67] The aim was normally to contain the discussion within the bank group, and actively to prevent the involvement of trade creditors so as not to destabilize the business.[68] Typically, around 15 per cent of the equity was left with the original shareholders.[69] There was an appreciation that putting a company into any corporate bankruptcy proceeding might cause considerable commercial damage to the company. Indeed, in a leading article on administrative receivership (the principal corporate bankruptcy process in England in the 1990s), John Armour and Sandra Frisby noted that administrative receivership appointments were largely confined to small and medium-sized enterprises (SMEs), with annual turnover of less than £5 million.[70] Overall, a London Approach reorganization of a large corporate was likely to be confined to the debtor's bankers, and it was unusual for it to implicate the debtor's general, unsecured creditors. Thus, the general, unsecured creditor was not on the stage on which London Approach reorganizations played out. To the extent that general, unsecured creditors were asked to forbear during the reorganization process (eg by stretching debtor days to create much needed liquidity), this would be achieved consensually as part of a cash management strategy, often worked out during the 1990s with specialist help from turnaround experts.

65 Ackrill and Hannah (n 61) 237–38.

66 John Flood, Robert Abbey, Eleni Skordaki, and Paul Aber, 'The Professional Restructuring of Corporate Rescue: Company Voluntary Arrangements and the London Approach' (1995) ACCA Research Report 45, 27.

67 Pen Kent, 'The London Approach' (1993) Q1 Bank of England Q Bull 110, 112.

68 Flood and others (n 66) 7.

69 John Armour and Simon Deakin, 'Norms in Private Insolvency: The "London Approach" to the Resolution of Financial Distress' (2001) 1 J Corp Law Stud 21, 36.

70 John Armour and Sandra Frisby, 'Rethinking Receivership' (2001) 21(1) Oxf J Legal Stud 73, 92.

3.3.2 The rise of leveraged capital structures in the UK

British banks were, however, facing many of the same pressures in making money as US financiers. In the cosy, non-inflationary world of times gone by, English banking operated as a virtual oligopoly. Each bank had its list of customers which it serviced, interest rates were essentially fixed across the market, and there was very little competition on price. The authorities appear to have tacitly supported this arrangement in return for informal control rights over the banking sector. Several factors brought this world to a juddering halt. First, the UK moved away from a system of direct credit controls (in which the central bank would impose liquidity and special deposit requirements on UK banks, and would specifically ask them to observe particular lending ceilings from time to time) towards a modern system of monetary policy (where money supply was controlled either through asset purchases or changes in the rate of interest charged by the central bank).[71] This undid the informal bargain between the banks and the authorities and, starting with the Competition and Control measures implemented in 1971, radical steps were taken to improve the competitive environment in UK banking.[72] Secondly, the development of the Eurodollar market in London meant that British banks faced competition from foreign banks (particularly US banks), while they faced competition for deposits at home from other domestic financial institutions such as building societies (the functional equivalent of US savings and loans) and trustee savings banks.[73] Thirdly, the inflation of the 1970s, rapid changes in technology, and major recessions all posed new challenges.[74] And finally, Big Bang on 27 October 1986 radically reformed stock trading in Britain, leading to the development of organizations resembling universal banks.[75]

The upshot of all of these changes was that, by the end of the 1980s, British banks and other financial institutions competed with each other fiercely in attracting deposits and in the pricing of loans. At the same time, after the Second World War, several factors had incentivized many of the founding families, which still dominated some of England's biggest industrial and manufacturing concerns, to divest their shares: tax; concern about profitability; and an increasingly regulated market. At the same time, tax also incentivized individual investment in pension funds and insurance funds, so that institutional investors emerged to buy the shares. Thus, a small group of large institutions emerged as investors in the equity of British

[71] Charles W Calomiris and Stephen H Haber, *Fragile by Design: The Political Origins of Banking Crises and Scarce Credit* (Princeton University Press 2014) 142–43.

[72] For a description of the 'cartel' arrangements in place before the Competition and Control measures, and of the scale of the dismantling, see Committee of London Clearing Bankers, *The London Clearing Banks: Evidence by the Committee of London Clearing Banks to the Committee to Review the Functioning of Financial Institutions* (Longman, Inc 1978) 175.

[73] Ackrill and Hannah (n 61) 160.

[74] ibid 204–05.

[75] ibid 212–13.

business, including banks.[76] The newly emerging institutional investors demanded that directors focused on shareholder value in business operations, and gradually shifted from merely relying on a steady dividend stream to concentrating on earnings. British banks now found themselves focusing not so much simply on size (which had hitherto been a virtue in itself) but also on profitability.[77]

This focus on profitability also led to questions about the efficiency of UK diversified conglomerate groups when compared with large corporates focused on core competencies.[78] As a result, during the 1980s, management buyouts (MBOs; where an existing management team partnered with a private equity firm to spin off a non-core activity financed by loan debt) and management buy-ins (MBIs; where an external management team was brought in) began to grow in deal size as well as volume.[79] While the US leveraged buyout industry was booming, thanks to Milken's high-yield bond innovation, a high-yield bond market did not develop immediately in Britain. Yet, a management team pursuing a buyout was likely to need to rely heavily on debt finance in order to fund the acquisition. In England, this need for debt finance was solved by importing the idea of mezzanine financing: loan debt which ranked junior to the senior loan but above equity in a corporate bankruptcy.[80] Sometimes, the mezzanine debt was simply contractually subordinated to the senior debt, in an agreement between all of the lenders setting out how their claims would be treated in times of stress. This agreement is known as the intercreditor agreement. Sometimes, the debt was also structurally subordinated. In other words, it was advanced to holding company borrowers further away from the operating companies in the organizational structure than the borrower of the senior debt, without the benefit of operating company guarantees or security interests. And, sometimes, the senior loan was itself tranched into senior debt and 'second lien' debt. In short, the loan market in England developed in ways which enabled the buyout industry to get started, and the leveraged capital structure emerged.

This process gathered pace when a market for high-yield bonds began to develop in England. Initially the investors in high-yield bonds issued by English borrowers were almost entirely US investors already familiar with the asset class at home.[81] The English banks demanded that high-yield bonds were structurally, as well as contractually, subordinated to their senior bank debt, but experience of this

[76] Cheffins (n 61) 19.

[77] Committee of London Clearing Bankers (n 72) 165.

[78] Much of the account of the early development of the private equity industry in Britain in this section is drawn from Sebastien Canderle, *Private Equity's Public Distress: The Rise and Fall of Candover and the Buyout Industry Crash* (2011).

[79] John Coyne, 'Divestment by Management Buy-Out: Variant and Variety' in John Coyne and Mike Wright (eds) *Divestment and Strategic Change* (Philip Allan/Barnes & Noble Books 1986) 140.

[80] Canderle (n 78) 49.

[81] For a more detailed account of the development of the high-yield bond market in England, see Sarah Paterson, 'The Adaptive Capacity of Markets and Convergence in Law: UK High Yield Issuers, US Investors and Insolvency Law' (2015) 78(3) Mod L Rev 431.

structure in the telecoms industry downturn in the 1990s prompted a boycott of the European high-yield market by high-yield investors, so that it became more common for both high-yield bonds and mezzanine loans to be only contractually subordinated. In fact, the precise structuring of the high-yield bond, and its relationship to the rest of the capital structure, has ebbed and flowed as the amount of money searching for investment in the asset class has increased and decreased. Indeed, this is a highly sensitive segment of the finance market, which is sometimes open for business and sometimes not. Nonetheless, it has become a more important part of leveraged capital structures in England, particularly since the 2008 financial crisis. The growth in mezzanine finance, coupled with the early development of the high-yield bond market, meant that by the beginning of the 2000s British leveraged buyout associations had matured from funding MBOs to entire 'take private' deals, in which a highly leveraged company was established by the leveraged buyout association specifically for the purpose of taking private publicly listed companies. Thus, the large corporate leveraged buyout began to be a feature of the English landscape. A European private equity industry emerged, including names such as 3i, Bridgepoint, Candover, BC Partners, Cinven, Apax, and Permira, and the European operations of large, US-based houses such as Blackstone and Texas Pacific Group.[82]

The private equity house takes increased bankruptcy risk because it is operating over a relatively short time horizon: private equity fund investment is illiquid but time limited so that the private equity house is incentivized to achieve an 'exit', perhaps by relisting the company or by selling it in a trade sale. Yet, lenders to a private equity portfolio group are also likely to concentrate on the ability to flex the capital structure, if changing conditions make it unsustainable before an exit is achieved. The borrower is then free to return to the debt markets to releverage if conditions improve once more. Thus, the idea of the flexible capital structure becomes central to the English leveraged buyout investment. Publicly traded companies in England, like their peers in the US, began to borrow techniques from the private equity industry, including leveraging the firm's capital structure. Until this point, the London Approach had proved highly effective in incentivizing banks to bargain for a large corporate reorganization.[83] Yet, as leverage multiples grew, leaving a hefty chunk of equity with the existing shareholders became unfeasible. And, as explored in Chapter 4, new types of investor entered the leveraged finance field, who did not have a relationship with the Bank of England and who were not active

[82] This list is drawn from Canderle (n 78) 126–27.

[83] See eg the report of a Royal Bank of Scotland presentation at the IBC Sixth Insolvency Conference London, 1997, in Muir Hunter, 'The Nature and Functions of a Rescue Culture' (1999) 104(4) Comm L J 426, 447: 'The Royal Bank of Scotland, which made its own separate presentation, emphasized the Bank's special interest in equity participation as its chief reward for the rescue, and stated that it had a special department (Specialized Lending Services, or "SLS") for rescues'.

in the primary loan markets. New ways of deleveraging a complex, leveraged capital structure needed to be found.

3.3.3 Leveraged capital structures and English corporate reorganization law

Although investors in Europe do now invest in the high-yield bond asset class, US investors continue to provide important liquidity to the market. As a result, high-yield bond issues by English corporate borrowers are ordinarily governed by New York law, and are issued on Rule 144A terms which enable sophisticated US investors to invest in them without implicating all of the machinery of US securities laws.[84] This means that English Rule 144A offerings are not bound by section 316(b) of the Trust Indenture Act 1939, so that they can include majority voting provisions on core terms such as payment terms. At the same time, it means that some of the motivation for an exchange offer in the US, in terms of avoiding the complex and costly registration requirements of the Securities Acts, does not apply. Furthermore, in order for bondholders to be persuaded to exchange their bonds, it is generally necessary to offer paper at a more senior level in the capital structure. In England, it has (until recently) been rare for banks in the senior debt to allow the necessary permitted baskets for additional senior indebtedness to make this possible.[85] Instead, where it is too difficult to achieve contractual renegotiation of a complex, leveraged capital structure, market participants have turned to the scheme of arrangement to deal with a recalcitrant minority.

The scheme of arrangement has been on the statute books since the end of the nineteenth century but, as explored in Chapter 2, had rarely been used in large corporate reorganization after the Second World War.[86] In the main, this was because the London Approach developed instead as a highly successful mechanism for promoting all-bank workouts. The scheme also suffered from a major problem. In a scheme of arrangement, creditors are divided into classes for the purposes of voting on the scheme, and two court hearings are held: an initial hearing to call the meetings of creditors to vote on the scheme (each class of creditors must have a separate meeting), and a second court hearing, after the meetings have been held, at which the court is asked to sanction the scheme. There had been very little twentieth-century jurisprudence on how class meetings should be constituted, leading to market uncertainty about how to approach the issue. At the same time, the court did not decide on class composition at the initial hearing in the scheme

[84] Rule 144A is promulgated under the Securities Act of 1933.

[85] Danelle le Cren and Jeff Norton, 'Problems at the Border' (2015) 34(4) Int'l Fin L Rev 52, 54.

[86] Andrew Wilkinson, Adrian Cohen, and Rosemary Sutherland, 'Creditors' Schemes of Arrangement and Company Voluntary Arrangements' in Harry Rajak (ed) *Insolvency Law: Theory & Practice* (Sweet & Maxwell 1993) 322; Hunter (n 83) 441.

process. Instead, it considered class composition after the scheme had been voted on at the final hearing, at which the court is asked to sanction the scheme. This meant, as Alice Belcher puts it, '... a whole scheme [could] have been negotiated, voted on and come to a final hearing before the court express[ed] its dissatisfaction with the classification of creditors'.[87] At the same time, the problems with relying on the London Approach to reorganize a highly leveraged, modern capital structure, now that market conditions had changed, were becoming all too clear. Thus, in a decisive move relatively unbounded by existing jurisprudence, the courts shifted to deciding issues of class composition at the initial hearing to launch the scheme, rather than waiting until the final hearing after meetings had been called and voting had taken place. In 2002, a Practice Statement was issued in which it was stated that the court would consider issues relating to composition of class meetings at the initial hearing and, where possible, seek to ensure that the judge hearing the first application, 'should retain carriage of the scheme throughout'.[88] This was a crucial development, removing one of the principal obstacles to use of the scheme as a reorganization tool, given other features which make it particularly well adapted for the task.

The scheme is a Companies Act procedure, so that some of the negative connotations of a corporate bankruptcy procedure for general, unsecured creditors and employees of the operating subsidiaries can be avoided.[89] The use of a Companies Act procedure can signal to these constituencies that no corporate bankruptcy is envisaged, and that they are not implicated in the reorganization transaction. The scheme procedure is relatively rapid (about six weeks in total). Court involvement is relatively limited and the court is unlikely to interfere if the majority of financial creditors support the scheme, so that execution risk is minimized.[90] Finally, and significantly, guarantee obligations of the operating subsidiaries for the finance company's financial liabilities can be released in the finance holding company scheme of arrangement.[91] This means that it is not necessary to place the operating subsidiaries into any kind of process at all. The scheme of arrangement does not offer a moratorium on creditor action (although it can be used to implement a moratorium), but in England this problem is solved by moratorium provisions contained in the intercreditor agreement between the financial creditors. The scheme's fitness for purpose is perhaps most nicely illustrated by a borrower who is neither US nor English, but who sought to use US or English tools as alternatives to flex its capital structure. DTEK is a Ukrainian power company which

[87] Alice Belcher, *Corporate Rescue: A Conceptual Approach to Insolvency Law* (Sweet & Maxwell 1997) 109.

[88] Practice Statement (Companies: Schemes of Arrangement) [2002] 1 WLR 1345.

[89] Companies Act 2006, ss 895–899.

[90] *Re English, Scottish and Australian Chartered Bank* [1893] 3 Ch 385; [1893] 7 WLUK 52.

[91] *In re Lehman Brothers International (Europe) (in administration) (No* 2) [2009] EWCA Civ 1161; [2010] Bus L R 489.

had issued New York law-governed, high-yield bonds. It simultaneously launched an offer to exchange its bonds for new bonds in New York, and a scheme of arrangement to achieve the same economic transaction in England. When it failed to gain sufficient support for the exchange offer, it abandoned it and resorted to implementation via a scheme.[92] This nicely illustrates both the equivalence of the exchange offer and the scheme, as tools to flex the capital structure to reduce fixed costs while maintaining liquidity in the debt, and the efficiency of the scheme to enforce the majority deal. However, it is possible that trading conditions will be such that a more radical flexing of a leveraged capital structure may be needed. The scheme of arrangement is less well adapted to address this issue, and participants in the process and their counsel have sought to mobilize and adapt English corporate reorganization law in new ways, specifically to meet the demands of this situation. For the reasons developed below, this has led to the emergence of a new conceptual framework for testing the fairness of the corporate reorganization plan in English corporate reorganization law.

3.3.4 The concept of the counterfactual, or next best alternative, emerges in England

In the nineteenth century, the scheme of arrangement was designed as a method of enforcing a transaction, which had been approved by a majority of creditors in an investment, on the minority in the same class. This was central to the courts' conclusion that a scheme of arrangement could deprive minority creditors of security: the risk of being crammed down by a majority in a class was seen as a corollary of having invested in debt as one of a number of creditors. In other words, the principle which underpins the architecture of the scheme process is one of majority rule. Valuation is not really congruent with the decision to impose the plan on the minority. Instead, the nature of the court's inquiry focuses on whether there are reasons to doubt the will of the majority, perhaps because the majority investors have particular characteristics which affect their preferences so that the decision to support the transaction is motivated by exogenous considerations and not the attractiveness of the reorganization transaction itself. Thus, the court does not substitute its own view on whether the scheme is reasonable. Rather, the question is whether the scheme is one which the particular class of creditor could reasonably have approved, or whether there is reason to doubt that the majority vote was taken in the interests of the class.[93] Crucially, the development of the scheme

[92] Linklaters, 'DTEK Exchange Offer and Scheme of Arrangement: Facilitating High-Yield Debt Restructurings' (*Linklaters*, 1 May 2015) <https://www.linklaters.com/en/insights/publications/2015/january/dtek-exchange-offer-and-scheme-of-arrangement-facilitating-high-yield-debt-restructurings> accessed 6 March 2020.

[93] *In re Anglo-Continental Supply Co Ltd* [1922] 2 Ch 723; [1922] 7 WLUK 9.

of arrangement in the nineteenth century did not contemplate that investors in one class of debt security could ask the court to impose the reorganization on investors in a different class of debt security. When US legislators implemented the ability for a court to force dissenters to take securities in a plan of reorganization in the 1930s, they overtook England by permitting not only the imposition of a plan of reorganization on a minority *within* a class, but also the imposition of a plan of reorganization on a *dissenting* class (provided at least one other impaired class had consented to it).

Just as Wall Street has had to work around the fact that Chapter 11 is not naturally adapted to flexing a leveraged capital structure which is unsustainable in prevailing economic conditions, so, too, the highly innovative participants in the City of London needed to work around the limitations of the scheme. Thus, they sought to mobilize and adapt the English pre-packaged administration tool to achieve a reorganization of liabilities to financial institutions where there is insufficient value to offer enough to each class to achieve a largely consensual deal through a scheme of arrangement. A pre-packaged administration sale is a transaction in which the assets are marketed before the debtor is placed into the English administration process and insolvency practitioners, known as the administrators, are appointed. Before appointment, the administrators-in-waiting shadow the marketing effort so that, if they are appointed as administrators, they can be content that they can move immediately to a sale to the winning bidder in the auction. Where a pre-packaged administration is used as a reorganization tool, an auction of the finance company's shares in the operating parent is typically run for around six weeks before the finance company is placed into the administration process. This auction process establishes the current market price for the operating parent company shares. Creditors who are in the money (that is, where the value of the parent company shares established via the auction is sufficient to cover all or part of their debt) incorporate a new company in which they hold the equity and debt. This new company bids in the auction. When the administrators are appointed, the new company is able to procure that the in the money creditors release their claims against the finance company in consideration for the purchase of the operating parent company shares. Thus, the operating group is reorganized under the new holding company in which the in the money creditors hold the shares, and the creditors who are out of the money are left stranded in an empty shell: functionally a debt-for-equity swap transaction.

If the senior creditors who are receiving equity and debt in the new holding company are able to reach agreement on the plan consensually, then no court hearing is necessary. This is because it is possible to appoint an administrator out of court as a matter of English law.[94] Thus, the bidding company can be established, the finance

[94] Insolvency Act 1986, Sch B1 paras 14 and 22.

holding company placed into administration, and the shares in the operating parent transferred without any court hearing. In this case, it will be for the junior bondholders, lenders, or equity proactively to mount a challenge. However, sometimes a scheme of arrangement is needed to achieve the reorganization among the senior lenders. There is no problem, in principle, with proposing a scheme of arrangement to only some of the company's creditors, but it is possible for junior creditors to appear at the final hearing to object to the scheme on the basis that they should have been allocated scheme consideration. At this point, the question is not limited to the integrity of the majority class votes, but also extends to whether it is fair to exclude the junior creditors from the scheme.

The first, modern case in which this issue arose was the reorganization of MyTravel, a package holiday company.[95] In *MyTravel*, the company proposed a scheme of arrangement which offered junior bondholders a relatively slim allocation of consideration, against the threat of an even slimmer allocation of consideration in a sale of the operating parent company shares to a senior creditor bidding vehicle if they did not agree to the proposal.[96] At this time, the US approach to valuation in a US Chapter 11 reorganization was poorly understood in England, and arguments about valuation were not well articulated in the case. Mr Justice Mann approached the question of whether the bondholders were entitled to an allocation of consideration in the scheme by comparing the scheme with what would happen if the scheme did not proceed (which will be referred to as the counterfactual).[97] At this point, it is important to rehearse some of the history of the scheme of arrangement noted in Chapter 2. Schemes of arrangement have their roots in the Joint Stock Companies Arrangement Act of 1870. This was passed after doubts were expressed as to whether the court could approve a liquidator's compromise with creditors so as to bind dissenting creditors, and only applied to compromises within liquidation. In 1906, the Loreburn Law Amendment Committee saw no reason why the power of the court to approve a creditor compromise should be limited to circumstances in which the company was in liquidation. As a result, the Companies Act 1907 extended the power to approve a creditor scheme to circumstances in which the company was not in liquidation.[98] Thus, the scheme developed as an alternative to a liquidation proceeding, and English courts approach

[95] *In re MyTravel Group Plc* [2004] EWHC 2741 (Ch); [2005] 1 WLR 2365.

[96] It is worth noting that, in the MyTravel case, the directors proposed to implement the sale transaction themselves, rather than placing the company into administration and relying on an administrator to execute the sale. Most subsequent cases have proceeded on the assumption that, if a sale transaction is required, as it will be an insolvent sale (because it will not generate enough proceeds to pay all the financial creditors) it will be conducted by an insolvency practitioner acting as administrator.

[97] *In re MyTravel Group Plc* (n 95) [55].

[98] See Andrew J O Wilkinson and Adrian L Cohen, 'Creditors' Schemes of Arrangement and Company Voluntary Arrangements' in Alison Clark (ed) *Current Issues in Insolvency Law* (Stevens & Sons 1991) 122.

questions of fairness with a strong regard to the counterfactual if the scheme of arrangement is not approved.

In *MyTravel*, Mr Justice Mann expressed the view that the relevant counterfactual was liquidation, which in England generally means a break-up sale of the assets rather than a sale of the business and assets as a going concern.[99] He determined that the bondholders would receive no distribution in this counterfactual. Although the Court of Appeal subsequently set aside his comments on valuation made at the initial hearing for the scheme,[100] the bondholders nonetheless saw the writing on the wall for their prospects of successful challenge, and accepted the company's plan of reorganization. Subsequently, Counsel for the bondholders, Michael Crystal QC, together with Riz Mokal, wrote two important articles discussing the US approach to valuation in a cram-down situation.[101] A lively debate ensued in the English market about the approach which England ought to adopt. The debate moved from discussing the straightforward application of a liquidation counterfactual, to questions about whether the US approach to valuation ought to be adopted in determining fairness of the allocation of consideration in a cram-down scheme twinned with a pre-packaged administration sale.

This came to a head in the *Re Bluebrook* case, in which a pre-packaged administration sale (to strand the junior creditors) was coupled with a scheme of arrangement (to impose the deal on a dissenting minority of senior creditors) and the junior creditors appeared at the sanction hearing for the scheme to object to the transaction on valuation grounds.[102] Once again, Mr Justice Mann presided. The company and the senior lenders did not rely solely on the results of a marketing process to establish current market price. In addition, they submitted valuation evidence prepared by PricewaterhouseCoopers LLP (PwC) which indicated that the value of the business and assets as a going concern fell short of the value of the senior debt. This evidence was prepared using a range of valuation methodologies, including a valuation prepared using DCF methodology. However, in providing this valuation evidence, the company and the senior lenders did not concede that the court should consider post-reorganization value in assessing the fairness of the scheme. Instead, the valuation evidence sought to ascertain value on a current market value basis. As a result, PwC applied a discount factor to their DCF valuation, which was intended to reflect the fact that uncertainty in the market, and the post-2008 financial crisis

99 It is worth noting that MyTravel was regulated by the Civil Aviation Authority in the UK, which had announced its intention to withdraw MyTravel's operating licence if the scheme was not concluded; this may have justified the use of liquidation as the relevant comparator rather than a going concern sale of the business and assets.

100 *Re MyTravel Group Plc* [2004] EWCA Civ 1734; [2004] 12 WLUK 456.

101 Michael Crystal QC and Riz Mokal, 'The Valuation of Distressed Companies: A Conceptual Framework' (2006) 3 Int'l Corp Rescue Issues 2 and 3.

102 *Re Bluebrook Ltd* [2009] EWHC 2114 (Ch); [2010] BCC 209. For a fuller analysis of the Bluebrook case, see Sarah Paterson, 'Bargaining in Financial Restructuring: Market Norms, Legal Rights and Regulatory Standards' (2014) 14(2) J Corp Law Stud 333, 351–52.

credit crunch, would have a depressing effect on the price which anyone would pay for the business at the time of the scheme. The valuation evidence therefore primarily sought to support the results of the market testing process in indicating what a purchaser would be prepared to pay for the business in prevailing market conditions, rather than to interrogate the question of whether that current market price undervalued the business.

The junior lenders criticized the market price and valuation evidence. They instructed their own valuation expert, LEK, which introduced evidence based on a Monte Carlo simulation—a relatively complex valuation technique involving repeated calculations to produce a range of outcomes which are then mapped as probabilities of a particular result. Mr Justice Mann was critical of the use of the Monte Carlo simulation; in particular, he did not consider that the range of possibilities arrived at through a Monte Carlo simulation provided the valuation guidance which the court needed for the purposes of assessing the fairness of the scheme. Furthermore, in his view the junior lenders had not articulated their criticisms of the market price and current market value approach as clearly as they could have done. He neatly summarised his view at paragraph 49 of the judgment:

> All in all, therefore, I do not give the LEK valuation as much weight as I give the other exercises. As an exercise of assessing what a third- party purchaser would pay it is very unconvincing. One cannot assume that he would pay something in the high probability range. Purchasers do not work like that. Subjective assessments are much more weighty factors, and the scheme companies' exercises tend to reflect that better. The most that it does in the present case is to give pause for thought on this point: are the purchasers in fact getting too good a deal (too much unfair value) because in the present market sales are unlikely to take place, and when economic conditions change the same group will be perceived to be more valuable, and the purchasers will ultimately reap the benefit of that? This is not quite the way the case is put, but I can see that in some circumstances it might be.

This paragraph gets to the heart of the matter. The argument is that establishing value, and assessing the fairness of a scheme to reorganize the debtor's liabilities to financial institutions, by reference to market price when markets are depressed will cause the senior lenders to recover more upside than they deserve when the markets recover. Having articulated the concern in this way, Mr Justice Mann turned to consider it. However, he had already expressed his reservations about the LEK evidence. Furthermore, he noted that, even if the discount factor which PwC had applied were to be stripped out of their DCF valuation (so that the valuation was not linked to current market conditions), the valuation still fell short of the amount which would be needed to indicate a return for the mezzanine lenders. In these circumstances, Mr Justice Mann was not persuaded that the valuation evidence before him indicated that the junior lenders were getting a raw deal. Counsel for the mezzanine lenders had drawn his attention to the fact that all of the valuation evidence had been presented by counsel, and that no cross-examination of the valuation experts had taken place. Nonetheless, he considered that the LEK evidence was insufficient to overturn the evidence submitted by the scheme companies and the senior lenders. Overall, it was clear that the English court remained minded to assess the fairness of a deleveraging scheme by reference to the amount a purchaser would be prepared to pay for the business in prevailing market conditions.

As a result, the market moved to indicate, in the original finance documents, the valuation principles which should be implicated when an enforcement sale is required to implement a reorganization of the debt and equity finance provided by the financial institutions. In England, the Loan Market Association (LMA) provides a suite of documents which are ordinarily used as the starting point for negotiation in a leveraged loan transaction. The Loan Market Association is a trade association for participants in the loan market, founded by banks operating in the loan market in 1996.[103] As already discussed, the intercreditor agreement contractually subordinates the junior debt, and establishes the payment waterfall in distress. However, it also sets up the mechanism by which guarantees and security provided by the operating subsidiaries can be released in an enforcement sale transaction.[104]

These release mechanisms now enable the finance parties to select between market price and market value in a sale transaction, which can, in turn, be used to implement a non-consensual reorganization of the debt and equity finance provided by the financial institutions. However, crucially, even where the market value option is chosen, it is market value in 'prevailing market conditions'.[105] In other words, the concept which has developed in English law-governed intercreditor agreements is release of junior lender or junior bondholder claims where the current market price or current market value of the firm breaks above them. This is, in turn, based on the theory that if no reorganization of the debtor's liabilities to financial institutions can be agreed, the counterfactual is that the finance company will be placed into administration or liquidation and either the shares in the operating parent sold, or the business broken up and the assets sold. English law thus adopts a considerably more straightforward approach to issues of valuation than that which is generally adopted in a Chapter 11 case in the US.

In 2018, the UK Government published proposals to reform English corporate bankruptcy law, which included a new procedure closely modelled on the scheme

[103] The Treasurer's Wiki, Association of Corporate Treasurers, <https://wiki.treasurers.org/wiki/Loan_Market_Association> accessed 6 March 2020.

[104] Chris Howard and Bob Hedger, *Restructuring Law and Practice* (2nd edn, LexisNexis 2014) 354–57 paras 6.237–6.239.

[105] ibid 232 para 5.2(c).

of arrangement, but facilitating cross-class cram-down.[106] While the book was being written, no update had been issued about the 2018 proposals. However, as the book is going to press in the midst of the COVID-19 crisis, the UK Government has introduced a new bill, which it plans to fast-track through parliament and which, among other things, takes forward certain of the 2018 reform proposals.[107] This includes the addition of a new Part 26A to the Companies Act 2006, largely replicating the scheme of arrangement procedure, but incorporating a power for the court to cram a compromise or arrangement down on a dissenting class.[108] It is too early to know how participants will mobilize and adapt this new tool, and when participants may prefer to use a scheme twinned with pre-packaged administration as a method of imposing a plan on a dissenting class. What is important, for the purposes of this chapter, is that the new Part 26A procedure provides that the court may sanction the compromise or arrangement against the wishes of a dissenting class, provided that that class is not worse off than they would be in the event of the 'relevant alternative'.[109] In most cases, the relevant alternative will be either an insolvent going concern sale or an insolvent piecemeal sale, in either case implicating current market price or current market value. Thus, where Part 26A is used, it will continue to implicate a relatively straightforward approach to valuation when the court considers whether to sanction a reorganization of the debtor's loan, bond, and equity finance, certainly when compared with the usual approach of the US bankruptcy court.

It is suggested here that the entirely common-sense development of the approach to valuation in reorganization of debt and equity finance provided by financial institutions in England has resulted in a system defined by concepts which are well adapted to deleveraging a complex capital structure, implicating only sophisticated financial creditors and investors. From an economic perspective, both the finance documents and the English courts place a great deal of emphasis on current market prices and values, thus mimicking the price which the market would have put on the transaction if bargaining had been possible. From a progressive perspective, the reorganization can be achieved rapidly and at relatively low cost, reducing the chances that distress will spread to the operations, imposing losses on non-adjusting and weakly adjusting creditors. In other words, the English courts have cooperated with senior creditors and debtors to set down concepts which are well adapted to the reorganizations of the past decade.

[106] Department for Business, Energy & Industrial Strategy, *Insolvency and Corporate Governance: Government Response* (Department for Business, Energy & Industrial Strategy 26 August 2018) paras 5.114–5.276..

[107] Corporate Insolvency and Governance Bill [HC] 2019–21.

[108] ibid Sch 9, inserting new Part 26A into Companies Act 2006.

[109] New Part 26A of the Companies Act 2006, s 901G, which provides that the relevant alternative is 'whatever the court considers would be most likely to occur in relation to the company if the compromise or arrangement is not sanctioned'.

3.3.5 Summary of the argument in section 3.3

Overall, banks in the senior debt in English law-governed, complex, leveraged capital structures worked to establish a market approach to allocation of consideration in transactions reorganizing the debtor's loan, bond, and equity finance. This approach was based on current market price (usually established via a short auction process for the shares which the finance company holds in the parent of the operating group) or current market value (established using market-based valuation techniques). The courts, recognizing the development of the scheme of arrangement and pre-packaged administration as tools to achieve the rapid and low-cost deleveraging of a complex, leveraged capital structure implicating only sophisticated financial creditors, and relatively unbounded by existing concepts which had emerged in a different era, have worked with senior creditors and their advisers to establish principles which facilitate the deleveraging transaction. Thus, the concepts of the counterfactual (what would happen if no reorganization could be agreed) and current market price and value (reflecting the expectation that what would happen would be an insolvent sale of the shares which the finance company holds in the operating parent) have emerged as the framework within which the reorganization is tested. The argument has been developed that both economically minded and progressively minded scholars ought to be content with this conceptual framework. To the extent that there is a concern in England, it is whether these concepts will be used uncritically in the future if expanding and shifting logics, practices, and identities in the finance and non-financial corporate fields cause corporate reorganization law to be mobilized and adapted in new ways in England in the future. This is a concern which will be raised many times over in the chapters which follow, and which is revisited in detail later in the book.

3.4 Conclusion

For the moment, then, the case is made that where the reorganization is to flex a complex, leveraged capital structure between sophisticated financial creditors, plenty of latitude can be provided to the parties to establish how the reorganization is to be implemented. Indeed, the court can act as something of a supporting player, helping to implement the deal if recalcitrant creditors hold out against it. This avoids the social costs involved if renegotiation costs spiral, or (worse still) the deleveraging transaction cannot be consummated at all.

In the US, Chapter 11 has proved less well adapted to a straightforward flexing of the capital structure among financial institutions, and market participants have developed the exchange offer and section 363 sale to achieve a rapid and lower-cost implementation of the transaction. This chapter has argued in favour of the adaptation of these market-orientated transactions, for the purposes of reorganizations implicating only strongly adjusting, informed, financial creditors and investors. Yet it has gone further. It has also suggested that, whatever the ongoing debate around current market price and value in Chapter 11 in general, in a reorganization implicating only sophisticated financial creditors and investors, both scholars adopting an economic analysis and progressive scholars ought to be able to agree that current market price and current market value are the right concepts against which to assess the reorganization plan.

The English scheme of arrangement has proved itself best in class for a rapid, low-cost enforcement of a majority deal to flex the liabilities of an over-leveraged company to financial institutions. However, it does not address the situation in which financial liabilities are sufficient to absorb the loss, but firm value is such that majority support for the reorganization cannot be achieved on acceptable terms in each class of financial creditor and investor. City lawyers have mobilized and adapted the pre-packaged administration for this situation. This has been supported by the development, in the English courts, of a conceptual framework for assessing the treatment of junior bondholders, lenders, and the equity by reference to the counterfactual (what would happen if a reorganization could not be agreed) and market price/current market value for the shares in the operating group (based on the assumption that an insolvent sale of the shares would be the most likely counterfactual). This conceptual framework has been reinforced by amendments to the LMA intercreditor agreement, which is typically used as the starting point in negotiations for a leveraged finance package.

The new Part 26A of the Companies Act will also adopt a counterfactual approach to the valuation question, functionally similar to the approach taken in a scheme of arrangement twinned with a pre-packaged administration sale.[110] Once again, a straightforward approach is supported where only strongly adjusting, informed financial creditors and investors are implicated. To the extent that there is a concern with the English law approach, it is whether current developments in logics, practices, and identities in the fields of finance and non-financial corporates may cause corporate reorganization law to be mobilized and adapted in the future in ways which implicate a wider range of creditors and liabilities. This leads to the concern that new valuation concepts may be needed if this were to occur. And it leads to the general concern that the conceptual frameworks adopted by English scholars, practitioners, judges, and the legislature may not prove sufficiently flexible to facilitate the emergence of new valuation concepts if they are required. This aspect of the debate arises many times as the rest of the book unfolds, and is considered in detail in Chapters 9 and 10.

[110] ibid.

4
The Rise of Trading

4.1 Introduction

Chapter 3 explored how the rise of leverage in non-financial corporate capital structures has resulted in the emergence of a number of corporate reorganization cases which are limited to rearranging the loan, bond, and equity finance of the firm. The argument was advanced that better analytical purchase is gained when the participants in these cases are described as sophisticated financial creditors and investors (rather than secured and unsecured creditors). Specifically, the argument was made that, because the term unsecured creditor developed against the background of full financial and operational corporate reorganization cases, the concept brings with it certain inherited ideas. It was then argued that these inherited ideas do not apply to capital reorganizations limited to debt and equity finance provided by sophisticated financial institutions. It was suggested that continued use of the term 'unsecured creditor' in corporate reorganization law debate is part of the reason why scholars adopting an economic approach and scholars adopting a progressive approach have struggled to observe the shorter distance between them in this type of reorganization case. Thus, it was suggested that the first step in identifying common ground is to change the term used to describe the participants in the case.

Corporate Reorganization Law and Forces of Change. Sarah Paterson, Oxford University Press (2020). © Sarah Paterson.
DOI: 10.1093/oso/9780198860365.001.0001.

This chapter addresses the relationship between corporate reorganization law and a second, profound shift in logic and practice in the field of finance. This is the shift in the way in which lenders and bondholders regard the lending decision. Initially, the focus is on the lending decision as the advance of money compensated by an interest rate and repayment at maturity. However, the logic of this conservative view of lending depends on stable, relatively uncompetitive finance markets. This chapter charts the rise of more challenging and competitive markets, in which the logic of the lending decision becomes maximizing returns. At this point, it becomes important to be able to trade positions before maturity, in order to balance portfolios and maximize profits. This change in logic and practice has occurred on both sides of the Atlantic. As this chapter reveals, it has motivated participants in the finance field to mobilize and adapt corporate reorganization law in new ways in cases of financial distress.

In this chapter, the argument is made that concepts in corporate reorganization law in the United States (US), organized around collective action problems, need significant adaptation for a reorganization among sophisticated, strongly adjusting financial creditors and investors, where the debt trades in secondary markets. The dominant challenge for corporate reorganization law in this context is the problem of holding out by strongly adjusting, informed financial creditors and not the risk that creditors will take enforcement action against the firm, rendering a reorganization impossible. Once again, the first stage in analysing the new terrain is to take care in how the corporate reorganization case is described. Unlike some other, recent contributions, the purpose is not to suggest a new, universal conceptual framework in which collective action problems are permanently replaced by hold-out problems. Rather, the suggestion is that, in reorganization cases implicating only sophisticated, informed financial creditors and equity holders where the debt trades in secondary markets, hold-out problems may be a greater concern than collective action problems for both scholars adopting an economic approach and scholars adopting a progressive approach to corporate reorganization law. As is explored in Chapter 9, other types of corporate reorganization case persist, in which collective action problems may be as important, or more important, than the hold-out issue. Indeed, as this book goes to press, it appears that collective action problems may be a very real concern in COVID-19-related corporate reorganization cases. Furthermore, by focusing on the importance of debt trading, it will be more straightforward to adapt the approach in the future if shifts occur in logics, practices, or identities in the distressed debt market. Once again, better analytical heft is gained by focusing both on the concepts used to describe the field and on the associated ideas embedded within those concepts as a result of the particular fact pattern to which they respond. The first step in Chapter 3 was to replace the term unsecured creditor with a term which better describes the terrain (sophisticated financial creditor and investor). In this chapter, the focus is on the importance of a new concept: traded debt.

At the same time, it will become apparent that the more recent development of modern corporate reorganization law in England and Wales has enabled terms and concepts to emerge which are better adapted to traded debt markets. This chapter identifies, once again, that to the extent there is a concern about the development of English corporate reorganization law, it is whether it will be able to adapt if expanding logics and practices in the field of finance cause corporate reorganization law to be mobilized and adapted in the future in a way which implicates a wider range of participants and liabilities. Specifically, as this book goes to press, English corporate reorganization law faces the challenge of adapting to the particular problems posed by the Government response to COVID-19. As before, English scholars, practitioners, judges, and the legislature need to be alive to the fact that English corporate reorganization law, and the concepts which are engaged in it, have developed in the past decade from the point of view of achieving a reorganization of the debtor's liabilities to financial institutions. Moreover, and crucially, this has occurred in an environment of deep and liquid secondary markets for distressed debt.

4.2 United States

4.2.1 The concept of the collective action problem

As identified in Chapter 2, in the nineteenth century it was usual for secured lenders to US railroads to have security over particular pieces of equipment or infrastructure.[1] As a result, nineteenth-century participants in railroad reorganization were familiar with concerns for collective action: that individual secured creditors might have an incentive to enforce against their secured assets, which would be in their individual best interests, but would not be in the best interests of creditors as a whole because it would make a collectively value-maximizing reorganization difficult or impossible to achieve. Thus, a significant feature of the equity receivership was that, by appointment of a receiver, the court of equity took all of the assets into its possession. Ancillary receiverships would be opened in all states in which the railroad had assets. In this way, creditors were prevented from executing against particular assets, so that the railroad could be kept together while attempts were made to agree a reorganization.[2]

It is, therefore, unsurprising that this feature was preserved when many aspects of the equity receivership process were codified in the 1930s. Thus, the strong

[1] Harvey R Miller and Shai Y Waisman, 'Does Chapter 11 Reorganization Remain A Viable Option for Distressed Business for the Twenty-First Century?' (2004) 78(2) Am Bankr LJ 153, 165.

[2] David A Skeel Jr, 'An Evolutionary Theory of Corporate Law and Corporate Bankruptcy' (1998) 51 Vand L Rev 1325, n 110 1357.

automatic stay is a central feature of the modern US Bankruptcy Code. Thomas Jackson most famously focused on the role of the stay in preventing the 'grab' race for assets, so that a corporate reorganization can be achieved.[3] This aspect of Jackson's theory is uncontroversial. Until recently, most corporate reorganization scholars have agreed on the existence of the collective action problem, and on US corporate reorganization law's role in solving it. In other words, a debtor can resort to Chapter 11 in order to benefit from the strong automatic stay, which will keep its business and assets together while it negotiates with its creditors.

However, since the 1970s, participants in both loan and debt capital markets have shifted from a hold-to-maturity to a trading strategy. This chapter reveals why this requires a reappraisal of the orientation of the traditional corporate reorganization law debate around the collective action problem. Once again, the argument is made that a new orientation of the debate is needed for reorganization of liabilities owed to financial institutions in traded markets, whether one views corporate reorganization law through an economic or a progressive lens. First, it is necessary to understand how and why the shift to trading strategies has occurred, and the ways in which corporate reorganization law interacts with the new environment.

4.2.2 The rise of traded debt

For much of the first half of the twentieth century, households would deposit all of their wages and savings with US banks. Moreover, a peculiar feature of US banking before the 1950s was that corporate customers were required to hold so-called compensating balances with their bankers. These were essentially fixed deposits held with the bank as the price of accessing its services.[4] Thus, banks had reliable sources of deposit capital which could be used for the process of making loans. This meant that banks pursued a relatively homogeneous strategy: taking deposits from customers and lending them to other customers in the form of loans. Banks' profits came from the difference between the interest which they paid on customer deposits, and the interest rate which they received on the loans which they advanced. Banks worked hard to keep their relationships with both the deposit and loan customers on whom their business depended.

The first shift in this steady hold-to-maturity system occurred when households began to keep assets away from the banking system during the Great Depression, as a result of fear of bank runs.[5] This problem was particularly acute for smaller banks, leading to the introduction of Regulation Q within the Glass-Steagall Act

[3] For the classic account, see Thomas H Jackson, 'Bankruptcy, Non-Bankruptcy Entitlements, and the Creditors' Bargain' (1982) 91 Yale LJ 857.

[4] Martin Mayer, *The Bankers* (Weybright and Talley 1974) 163.

[5] Ben S Bernanke, 'Nonmonetary Effects of the Financial Crisis in the Propagation of the Great Depression' (1983) 73(June) Am Econ Rev 257, 264.

of 1933. Regulation Q prohibited interest on what Americans call checking accounts (and the English call current accounts), and capped the interest US banks could offer on deposits. It was intended to prevent bank runs by preventing larger banks from attracting deposits from unstable smaller banks by increasing interest rates, and it was supported by many small banks, which saw it as a way to prevent competition.[6] Yet, in the late 1960s and early 1970s, money market rates regularly exceeded the Regulation Q cap, so that US retail customers were strongly incentivised to invest money with emerging money market funds rather than deposit it with a bank.[7]

The growing reluctance of corporate treasurers to hold compensating balances with their banks also increased pressure on sources of funds.[8] Moreover, corporates began to diversify away from banks to other sources of investment. In the 1960s, deep and active commercial paper markets emerged in which large corporates could raise short-term money from finance companies.[9] While commercial paper is structured as a short-term investment, some large corporates effectively sought to use it as a form of long-term financing, continuously rolling over their commercial paper issues. Indeed, as noted in Chapter 3, it was this practice which was to contribute to the massive corporate bankruptcies of Penn Central and W T Grant in the 1970s. After the New Deal reforms of US securities markets following the Great Depression, there was a growth in direct private placements of securities (mainly high-grade corporate bonds and notes) to the large insurance companies, which were growing in importance as significant investors. Private placements avoided many of the registration requirements of the 1930s securities laws legislation, and the transactions could also be completed more rapidly and with more certainty than a public offering.[10] Large corporates were increasingly able to access this private placement market as a source of external finance.

Inevitably, faced with both competition for deposits as the principal source of capital, and with competition as a supplier of capital, US banks looked for alternatives. The first serious innovation was the development of the Certificate of Deposit (the CD) by First National City Bank.[11] The CD enabled the banks to circumvent the stringent cap on interest rates on short-term deposits set by Regulation Q. A CD could be issued with a maturity date of, for example, six months, at a

[6] Charles W Calomiris and Carlos D Ramirez, 'Financing the American Corporation: The Changing Menu of Financial Relationships' (February 1996) NBER Historical Working Paper 79, 30.

[7] Robert DeYoung, William C Hunter, and Gregory F Udell, 'The Past, Present, and Probable Future for Community Banks' (2004) 25(2/3) J Finan Serv Res 85, 92.

[8] Ron Chernow, *The House of Morgan: An American Banking Dynasty and the Rise of Modern Finance* (Grove Press 1990) 538.

[9] Calomiris, Himmelberg, and Wachtel define commercial paper as 'unsecured, short-term negotiable promissory notes sold on the open market': see Charles W Calomiris, Charles P Himmelberg, and Paul Wachtel, 'Commercial Paper, Corporate Finance, and the Business Cycle: A Microeconomic Perspective' (September 1994) NBER Working Paper 4848, 6.

[10] Vincent P Carosso, *Investment Banking in America: A History* (Harvard University Press 1970) 367.

[11] The account of the CD is drawn from Mayer (n 4) 192–95.

higher interest rate reflecting its longer maturity. It could then be bought and sold in the secondary market some time after it was issued, making it effectively a short-term deposit with an interest rate considerably higher than the maximum amount that Regulation Q allowed. The CD market expanded rapidly, and a deep and liquid market emerged. At the same time, a Wall Street banker named George Garvin developed as a broker to match banks with excess reserves on deposit with the Federal Reserve, with banks which needed reserves.[12] Slowly the so-called 'inter-bank' market developed, and banks switched from focusing on retail and commercial deposits as their principal source of loan capital to wholesale borrowing in the money markets.

In the debt capital markets, the providers of bond capital shifted, from the 1950s onwards, from pre-Second World War retail investors to institutional investors. A number of factors accounted for this: the wage controls of the Second World War, which favoured the payment of non-wage compensation to employees; changes in tax laws; changes in collective bargaining; and changes in pension fund legislation.[13] By the 1950s, pension funds, mutual funds, and insurance companies had become the dominant providers of bond capital. Yet, until the 1970s, most of these investors in the public markets were still hold-to-maturity investors.[14] In other words, they bought a bond and held it until its maturity date, receiving periodic interest or 'coupon' payments. This worked well enough in a market of small portfolio management firms and insurance companies who had bought a private placement; the early US mutual fund industry was founded on the dominant logic of a trustee function, in which wealth was guarded for future generations and the buy-and-hold investment strategy made sense.[15]

However, trading activity was fuelled, in the late 1960s, by rising inflation. As noted in Chapter 3, inflation emerged as a serious concern in the US in the late 1960s as a result of the impact of the Vietnam War, and gathered pace during the oil shock of the 1970s. Investors were forced to manage portfolios actively to cope with the inflationary environment. This gave an immediate fillip to the emerging trading houses such as Salomon Brothers, who were able to deal with block trades of securities on the scale which these investors required.[16] Meanwhile, Milken structured his operations in the high-yield bond market to promise his investors liquidity.[17] He maintained an extensive network of investors upon whom he could rely, and who relied on him. This co-dependent structure enabled him to develop a ready market for trading the high-yield bonds which he sponsored, buying back

12 The account of the historical development of traded Fed Funds draws on Mayer (n 4) 206–09.

13 Calomiris and Ramirez (n 6) 36.

14 ibid 38.

15 Michael Lounsbury, 'A Tale of Two Cities: Competing Logics and Practice Variation in the Professionalizing of Mutual Funds' (2007) 50(2) Academy of Management J 289, 290.

16 Chernow (n 8) 585.

17 Connie Bruck, *The Predator's Ball: The Inside Story of Drexel Burnham and the Rise of the Junk Bond Raiders* (Penguin Books 1989) 46.

bonds where necessary to maintain market liquidity. The era of buying a security and holding it to maturity was coming to an end. Institutional investors held large positions but prized the flexibility, at any time, either to trade securities to adjust a diversified portfolio, or to trade out of underperforming assets. At the same time, these trading activities increasingly provided investment banking houses with the market information which they required for their other activities.[18]

A new focus on risk at the core of the investment decision was also to contribute to the shift to trading strategies. In March 1952, a short article appeared in the Journal of Finance by a twenty-five-year-old graduate student from the University of Chicago named Harry Markowitz.[19] Markowitz focused on how to select a portfolio of stocks and bonds, rather than on how to select individual securities. His key insight was to focus on the role of risk in the process of investing. Specifically, Markowitz focused on the relationship between diversification and risk: that the riskiness of the portfolio could be established by the covariance of the holdings within it. In other words, a portfolio of very risky holdings could have an overall lower risk, provided that the individual assets within the portfolio did not move in lock step with one another. Markowitz's insights, and the developments in portfolio theory which followed his work, brought a new level of mathematical precision to the process of compiling and maintaining a portfolio. For a significant number of investors, it gave rise to a more scientific process of trading securities within a portfolio.

The development of sophisticated portfolio investment techniques has been enormously significant to the way in which market participants approach both monitoring and default risk. Once an investor is thinking in portfolio terms, it may not matter if an individual security defaults, provided the investor has sufficient diversification across his portfolio. In other words, portfolio theory has been crucial to the rise of more speculative, results-orientated, traded investment practice. Furthermore, as investors moved towards a portfolio approach to investment, they saw it as their job, and not the job of the chief executive officer of the company, to diversify risk, adding fuel to the deconsolidation trend already encountered in Chapter 3. This was further fuelled by the increasing importance of securities analysts in the new world of the institutional investor. Securities analysts disliked the conglomerate, which they found difficult to value, so that divestitures had a favourable impact on stock analyst valuation.[20] Finally, sophisticated institutional creditors expected to hedge their positions as part of their trading strategy. Thus,

[18] Alan D Morrison and William J Wilhelm Jr, *Investment Banking: Institutions, Politics, and Law* (OUP 2012) 21.

[19] Harry Markowitz, 'Portfolio Selection' (1952) 7(1) J Finance 77. The account of Markowitz in this section is drawn from Peter L Bernstein, *Capital Ideas: The Improbable Origins of Modern Wall Street* (John Wiley & Sons, Inc 2005) 41–60.

[20] Dirk Zorn, Frank Dobbin, Julian Dierkes, and Man-shan Kwok, 'Managing Investors: How Financial Markets Reshaped the American Firm' in Karin Knorr Cetina and Alex Preda (eds) *The Sociology of Financial Markets* (OUP 2005) 271.

the development of the derivative market, particularly the establishment of the International Swaps and Derivatives Association (ISDA) in 1985 and the promulgation of market standard derivative contracts, played a vital role in facilitating an active secondary market in debt.

A further innovation arose as banks looked for other sources of income in order to meet the return requirements of their shareholders in the changing environment. One way in which banks sought to do this was by adding fees for structuring transactions to interest income.[21] This coincided with the development of modern securitization techniques, so that banks could package up loans and sell them to a securitization vehicle.[22] This model of banking was to become known as the 'originate-to-distribute' model, and it was to fuel an active secondary market in corporate loans. The 1990s also saw the highly significant development of international regulatory capital rules for banks, with the introduction of the Basel Accord (Basel I) in 1988, which took effect in 1992. Investment banks, notably J P Morgan, worked on developing the value at risk (VaR) measure, which sought to identify the maximum amount a financial portfolio could lose at a given level of confidence. J P Morgan used the VaR measure in two internal risk management tools: RiskMetrics for market risk (1994) and CreditMetrics for credit risk (1997). When Basel II introduced a considerably more sophisticated system of regulatory capital, certain banks were permitted to use these internal risk measurement tools in calculating their capital requirements. These internal measurements were sensitive to different types of debt and, importantly, enabled banks to reduce their capital requirements through securitization and other types of structured finance products. Thus, both technological innovations in the monitoring of market and credit risk and the regulatory capital consequences of risk led to innovation in securitization and structured finance products.[23]

As many authors have shown, US mortgage securitization developed over the very long run.[24] However, both the extraordinary depth of the modern market, and the ability to securitize a wider range of assets depended on modern innovations. These innovations were aimed at managing default risk. Specifically, they sought to find better ways to structure the securities to match investors with lower appetite for risk with the default-free component of the asset pool, and those with a higher appetite for risk with the risky cashflow generated by the asset pool.[25] Of course, many of these innovations in mortgage securitization led to the sub-prime

[21] Neil Fligstein and Doug McAdam, *A Theory of Fields* (OUP 2015) 152–53.

[22] Rowena Olegario, *The Engine of Enterprise: Credit in America* (Harvard University Press 2016) 180–81.

[23] This development of the history of regulatory capital is drawn from Georges Dionne, 'Risk Management: History, Definition, and Critique' (2013) 16(2) Risk Man Ins Rev 147.

[24] See eg Kenneth A Snowden, 'Mortgage Securitization in the United States: Twentieth Century Developments in Historical Perspective' in Michael D Bordo and Richard Sylla (eds) *Anglo-American Financial Systems* (Irwin Professional Publishing 1995) 261.

[25] Fligstein and McAdam (n 21) 147; Olegario (n 22) 194–95.

mortgage collapse which was at the heart of the 2008 financial crisis. Yet, they also enabled securitization of a wider class of assets to develop, including collateralized loan obligations and collateralized debt obligations which can be used to securitize commercial bank loans.

In short, the model of relationship banking, in which banks relied on a symbiotic relationship with clients in order to secure the deposits which they needed to fund their loan activities, began to come to an end. At this point, banks would be ready to trade in and out of particular exposures where it made sense, on a portfolio basis, to do so. Through the 2000s, this broke down the barriers which had made corporate lending something which only banks undertook, and new sorts of funds emerged as major players in the loan markets. The conventional account of what makes banks different is their specialization both in monitoring the firms they lend to and in enforcing the detailed debt contracts which they have entered into.[26] This made sense in a hold-to-maturity market, which emphasized both the negotiation of the terms of a loan agreement which the originating lenders would be enforcing and the monitoring function of the bank. However, once much of the business of banking shifted from relationship to transaction business, in which bank lenders transferred loans to securitization vehicles on a portfolio basis, both of these factors distinguishing banks from other lenders became less significant. This rapidly opened up the business of making commercial loans to other types of firm.

4.2.3 The rise of traded debt and the corporate reorganization case

The shift from debt as a held-to-maturity to a tradeable asset, coupled with the arrival of a range of providers of loan and debt capital with a rich range of investment strategies, explicitly gives rise to the concern that the loans of financially distressed borrowers will either trade at a deeply discounted price or will not trade at all. As a result, the ability to reduce the transaction costs associated with financial distress becomes a priority concern for traded loan and bond markets. In times of stress, it is important to have the ability to reorganize capital structures which are causing financial distress, so that debt securities remain liquid. In periods of buoyancy a debtor, who has perhaps even recently undertaken a comprehensive reorganization of its capital structure to reduce fixed costs, may re-enter the debt markets and raise debt again.

This willingness of banks and other financial creditors to trade has led to the massive explosion of firms specializing in buying distressed debt.[27] Players in this

[26] Eugene F Fama, 'What's Different about Banks?' (1985) 15(1) J Mon Econ 29.

[27] Particularly after the 1991 amendment to the US Bankruptcy Rules—see Harvey R Miller, 'Chapter 11 in Transition—From Boom to Bust and into the Future' (2007) 81(4) Am Bankr LJ 375, 389.

market may be pursuing a range of strategies. Some are hoping to swap the debt which they acquire for equity in the reorganization transaction, making a significant profit when the business is sold a few years after the reorganization has completed (known as a 'loan-to-own' strategy). Others are simply hoping to trade the debt when the reorganization takes place, or seems more likely.[28] Nonetheless, most of these event-driven trades rely on the reorganization becoming more likely (so that the price of the debt in the distressed market goes up) or completing (so that the distressed debt trader is allocated equity). This is highly significant, because it enables those who do not want to support the reorganization to trade out, and those who do support it to trade in. Thus, it enables lenders who wish to reshape their portfolio to monetize their position, while reorienting the creditor body around those who support a reorganization transaction.

At the same time, the need for tools to reduce the transaction costs associated with renegotiation is significantly heightened in the world of traded debt. First, it is significantly less likely in modern reorganizations of the debtor's liabilities to financial institutions that the parties to the transaction will be those who originally advanced the funds. This leads to problems of identifying the creditors before the negotiation can begin. Furthermore, traded debt exacerbates three problems in modern reorganization negotiations identified by Bratton and Levitin: conflicted voting, hold-out strategies, and misjudgement in the face of complexity.[29] In past eras, banks and public bondholders largely pursued homogeneous investment strategies, and thus shared the same concerns in default. Today, financial creditors may have very different objectives for the reorganization, depending on which parts of the capital structure they are invested in, and their overall strategy for the trade. This leads to the problem of conflicted voting, in which financial creditors are not voting on the basis of the investment decision for the particular debt security or loan. Rather, the financial creditors are motivated by another position which they have in the debtor's capital structure; or another investment opportunity which they can see; or a position which they are developing in a competitor's capital structure. The hold-out problem arises because creditors see the potential to trade in (or refuse to trade out), and to hold up a deal which the majority has largely coalesced around, until they receive some sort of side payment or *quid pro quo* to go away. And finally, there is the very real possibility that, while the majority of creditors are agreed on the investment decision, a minority of creditors may simply misjudge the appropriate response to the complex situation and refuse

[28] Paul M Goldschmid, 'More Phoenix than Vulture: The Case for Distressed Investor Presence in the Bankruptcy Reorganization Process' (2005) Colum Bus L Rev 191, 212, 269–71; Michelle M Harner, 'The Corporate Governance and Public Policy Implications of Activist Distressed Debt Investing' (2008) 77 Fordham L Rev 703, 715–18.

[29] William W Bratton and Adam J Levitin, 'The New Bond Workouts' (2018) 166 U Pa L Rev 1597, 1607.

to vote in favour. This risk is heightened when new players enter the situation, and must understand the assessments which other creditors have already made.

4.2.4 Implications for the concept of the collective action problem

Insofar as corporate reorganization law is concerned, this means that the collective action problem becomes less significant because creditors have another exit route besides enforcement which is quicker, offers a certain price, and removes the risk of the reorganization transaction. It also increases the prospect that any firm which the market perceives to have going concern value will be susceptible to reorganization. Thus, both the tool of the automatic stay and the tools which management can mobilize to steer creditors towards a reorganization and away from a liquidation have less force in a reorganization of the bond, loan, and equity capital structure when distressed debt trades. Instead, lenders and bondholders want to know that corporate reorganization law provides the tools to enable liabilities to financial institutions to be flexed in periods of stress, in order to keep positions liquid and tradeable.

This shift towards actively thinking about the ability to adapt the complex, leveraged capital structure while the debt is trading therefore has profound implications for the job which financial creditors want corporate reorganization law to do. In a hold-to-maturity market dominated by retail investors it was likely that downturns in the company's fortune would implicate a wide range of creditors, some of whom may prefer a sale over a reorganization, giving rise to the familiar tools of Chapter 11 to facilitate a corporate reorganization transaction. This, in turn, motivated the central debate between scholars adopting an economic approach, who argue that corporate reorganization law should be concerned with the efficient reallocation of assets to highest and best use, and progressive scholars, who are concerned to save the firm for weakly adjusting, general, unsecured creditors, customers, and employees. Yet these concerns are on the margins where the reorganization is negotiated between sophisticated, strongly adjusting financial creditors and investors to flex the loan, bond, and equity capital structure of the firm in order to meet prevailing economic conditions, when the debt is trading. Here social cost arises if (i) the transaction costs associated with the reorganization are so large that financial creditors and investors resist early adaptation of the capital structure, increasing the likelihood that a problem of high leverage will become an operational problem; or (ii) no mechanism emerges to reorganize the loan, bond, and equity finance at all. Thus, what is needed is an effective mechanism to reduce the transaction costs associated with renegotiation by addressing the coordination problems, conflicted voting, hold outs, and misjudgements associated with traded debt in complex, leveraged capital structures. The dominant logic of the reorganization is to reorganize the complex, leveraged capital structure of the group as speedily and cheaply as possible.

This has had a significant impact on the way in which financial creditors and investors perceive the corporate reorganization system. In the US, Chapter 11 is poorly adapted to the low-cost flexing of the group's liabilities to financial institutions. First, it assumes a renegotiation within a bankruptcy process. Yet where only institutional financial creditors and investors are to be implicated in the renegotiation this potentially imposes both the (significant) direct costs associated with a Chapter 11 filing and the indirect costs of bankruptcy in terms of damage to relationships with customers, suppliers, and other contracting parties. Secondly, it prioritizes the role of the automatic stay which, as already identified, may not be needed in a flex of the capital structure between financial creditors and investors in a traded market. Thirdly, it introduces a comprehensive range of tools for an operational restructuring, which may be wholly unnecessary for the type of reorganization in question. And finally, by requiring that any amendment to principal payment is ruled on by a court, it severely limits the ability of the financial creditors and investors to allocate the risks of flexing the capital structure among themselves. These issues arise because Chapter 11 was designed to address collective action problems: that individual creditors may have incentives to rush to grab assets, rendering a corporate reorganization impossible. It assumed the presence of the original secured lender and unsecured bond and trade creditors in the bankruptcy process, and focused on providing the tools necessary for this type of corporate reorganization. Yet, it is poorly adapted for the reorganization of liabilities owed to financial institutions in the presence of rapidly traded debt. Once again, this only becomes clear when real attention is paid to the way in which the particular fact pattern in the reorganization case is described.

4.2.4.1 The exchange offer

As Chapter 3 identified, the market has turned to the exchange offer, which builds on a technique pioneered by Michael Milken. In an exchange offer, bondholders are asked to agree to a contractual exchange of their bonds for new bonds with new terms. The exchange offer must also deal with the risk that a minority will hold out against the deal, in the hope of forcing better terms. The hold-out risk is generally addressed by making it a term of the exchange offer that the majority will change the terms and conditions attaching to the old bonds by, for example, removing covenant protection or changing the interest rate. This has the effect that those bondholders who do not accept the exchange will find themselves with bonds attracting significantly worse economic terms. As Chapter 3 also explored, an exchange offer must navigate section 316(b) of the Trust Indenture Act 1939, which prohibits majority amendment of bond payment terms. It has already been argued that this has little salience in modern debt markets. Indeed, Chapter 3 concluded in agreeing with Bratton and Levitin's assessment that section 316(b) ought to be repealed and replaced with a more general capacity to enquire into the legitimacy of the majority vote itself. In particular, the focus would be on whether the majority had individual preferences motivating their support for the deal, unrelated to the terms of the deal itself.[30] The shift to a traded market adds further support for a reform along these lines, because the reform would restrict the ability for funds to trade into the situation on a litigation strategy, explicitly intending to hold up the reorganization and demand enhanced reorganization consideration as the price of support. The crucial point for these purposes is that the principle which underpins section 316(b) must be adapted in the new world of traded debt which has emerged in corporate reorganization.

4.2.4.2 The pre-packaged plan and the section 363 sale

Sometimes the exchange offer combined with an exit consent does not prove sufficient to implement the reorganization of the debtor's liabilities to financial institutions, and it becomes necessary to resort to corporate reorganization law's tools.[31] However, in this case, the ways in which Chapter 11 is mobilized and adapted by financial creditors have changed to meet the specific needs of a reorganization of liabilities owed to financial institutions, when the financial institutions are also trading the liabilities. First, there has been a significant rise in so-called pre-packaged plans, in which creditors file for Chapter 11 once they are assured of the requisite majorities in each class to support the plan, and ask the court to move rapidly to confirm the plan of reorganization.[32] This reflects the fact that the tool which the creditors need to implement the transaction is the court's power to deal with hold outs, by cramming the new capital structure down on dissenting minorities. The objective of filing for Chapter 11 in these cases is not to benefit from the protective blanket of the automatic stay during renegotiation; the detailed tools for corporate reorganization; or the bankruptcy judge as mediator. Pre-packaged plans have been supported by the development of so-called restructuring support

[30] ibid 1665–73.

[31] Contrary to Michael Jensen's prediction in 1989, corporate reorganization has not been wholly privatized, notwithstanding the incentives implied by the leverage model. This is partly because of the need to deal with the increased hold-out threat which has emerged, in rapidly traded markets. Michael C Jensen, 'Active Investors, LBOs, and the Privatization of Bankruptcy' (1989) J App Corp Fin 34, repr (2010) 2(1) J App Corp Fin 77.

[32] See Stuart Gilson, 'Managing Defaults: Some Evidence on How Firms Choose between Workouts and Bankruptcy' in Jagdeep S Bhandari and Lawrence A Weiss (eds) *Corporate Bankruptcy: Economic and Legal Perspectives* (CUP 1996) 308, 321: 'Prepackaged bankruptcy is a hybrid of private restructuring and chapter 11—one that potentially incorporates the best features of both methods'; and John McConnell and Henri Servaes, 'The Economics of Pre-Packaged Bankruptcy' in Bhandari and Weiss (eds) 322, 323:

> A prepackaged bankruptcy should be viewed as an administrative extension of an informal reorganization. It is not likely to be useful in resolving complex, litigious disputes among hundreds of creditor groups with sharply divergent interests—the kind we often see in a traditional, highly contentious chapter 11 reorganization. (For example, cases involving extensive claims held by trade creditors are not likely to lend themselves to this new method).

agreements, which can be used to bind parties who trade into the situation in the future to the terms of the reorganization bargain.[33]

Secondly, as Chapter 3 explored, section 363 of Chapter 11 has been exploited to achieve a reorganization of the debtor's liabilities to financial institutions. In a section 363 sale which is functionally a reorganization of debt and equity raised from financial institutions, the financial creditors who are consenting to the plan form a new company which purchases the business and assets of the debtor group. The consideration for the purchase is the release of existing debt claims (so that the process is known as credit bidding). In a situation of pure financial distress caused by an inappropriate capital structure, majority creditors have determined for themselves the appropriate adjustment to debt and equity, and are looking to the bankruptcy judge to secure it against those who may otherwise hold up a largely consensual deal. In this case, financial creditors do not wish to risk the chance that hold-out creditors may use the bankruptcy forum to slow down the process, launch a valuation case, and increase transaction costs. Section 363 avoids this risk, both because it requires relatively short notice to creditors, and because it implicates a sale transaction. Thus, value is established through the market, rather than through professional valuation opinions. As a result, the section 363 process deals effectively with the increased risk of hold-out creditors in rapidly traded markets, where the more complete machinery of a Chapter 11 corporate reorganization case is not required.

4.2.4.3 The intercreditor agreement

There has also been considerable focus on addressing the risk of hold-out positions through the terms of the intercreditor agreement, which is negotiated between financial creditors when the loans and debt securities are originally advanced and issued. There is no market standard documentation used in the US loan market as the starting point for negotiation,[34] but intercreditor agreements adopt common features in allocating control rights in distress. First, they often provide a contractual stay on enforcement rights by junior creditors. Secondly, they may contain mechanisms to release junior creditors' security interests in an enforcement sale. And finally (and perhaps most controversially), they may restrict junior creditors' voting rights in a corporate reorganization case.[35] All of these mechanisms reduce the risk that debt is purchased for very low values by parties who then seek to exploit a hold-out position to recover an outsized return.

US bankruptcy judges, brought up in a tradition of strongly interventionist mandatory corporate reorganization law, have been somewhat suspicious of these

[33] Douglas G Baird, 'Bankruptcy's Quiet Revolution' (2017) 91 Am Bankr LJ 593.

[34] Tom Young, Lukas Becker, and Danielle Myles, 'Brother, Can you Spare Me a Loan?' (2012) 31(2) Int'l Fin L Rev 20.

[35] Edward R Morrison, 'Rules of Thumb for Intercreditor Agreements' (2015) U Ill L Rev 721.

contracts. Moreover, the idea of contracting around corporate reorganization law has been strongly associated with an economic perspective.[36] Yet, if a context-sensitive approach is adopted to the facts of the reorganization case, it is apparent that there is ample reason to uphold a bargain reached by sophisticated financial creditors and investors who traded in and out of a wide variety of investments on a portfolio basis, and who can trade out of the position if they do not favour the reorganization transaction. This analysis holds whatever theoretical or policy approach is taken to the question. Put differently, it may not be legitimate or even practical to allocate control rights in distress when corporate reorganization implicates general, unsecured creditors, but it may be considered legitimate when the participants in the process are sophisticated financial creditors and investors in traded markets, and the pressing concern for corporate reorganization law is to reduce the hold-out problem.

For scholars adopting an economic approach, there are powerful reasons, based on party autonomy and consent, to respect the bargain which the financial creditors have entered into. For scholars viewing the case through a progressive lens, the intercreditor agreement reduces social cost by addressing the heightened hold-out financial creditor problem, thus reducing the transaction costs associated with a reorganization of the liabilities to financial institutions, and reducing the risk that financial distress morphs into operational distress. To the extent that the intercreditor agreement increases senior financial creditor power, provided this is to the detriment of sophisticated, subordinated financial creditors who are strongly adjusting and informed, and not to the detriment of weakly or non-adjusting retail or trade creditors, progressive scholars should not be too concerned.

4.2.5 Summary of the argument in section 4.2

Thus, profound institutional change in the field of finance from a hold-to-maturity to a traded debt market has had a profound effect on the facts of the reorganization case, and on the ways in which financial creditors select, mobilize, and adapt corporate reorganization law's tools to address them. Chapter 11 is poorly adapted to the flexing of the capital structure, increasing the risk of coordination problems, conflicted voting, hold outs, and misjudgements. This has resulted in the rise of exchange offers, pre-packaged plans, and section 363 sales. New concerns arise in this landscape. First, there is the question of whether US corporate reorganization law could be adapted to provide a more streamlined option for reorganizing loan, bond, and equity finance, which would avoid some of the pathologies which arise as a result of working around Chapter 11 through the adaptations explored here.

[36] See eg Alan Schwartz, 'Contracting for Bankruptcy Systems' in F H Buckley (ed) *The Fall and Rise of Freedom of Contract* (Duke University Press 1999) 281–301 .

More significantly, it raises the question of whether Chapter 11 should be more permissive in the extent to which it allows financial creditors to set up contractual mechanisms which can be used to adapt the financial capital structure.

Once again, concerns do still arise for corporate reorganization law. Yet, they do not engage the traditional normative debates between bankruptcy scholars as to whether corporate reorganization law should be limited to providing the environment for a reorganization to be agreed, or whether it should go further in making distributional choices. Instead, the central normative concern centres on whether easily accessible tools for flexing the capital structure in times of stress supports high leverage in good times. Specifically, the question is whether leverage should be permitted to rise to levels which all of the creditors know may not be sustainable in the future on the basis that, if that comes to pass, the capital structure will be flexed to meet the prevailing conditions of the time to maintain liquidity.

There is risk in the economy-wide spread of highly leveraged structures. There is the risk that leverage causes persistent underinvestment. This may have the result that distress does not take the form of financial distress caused by an inappropriate capital structure, but becomes distress in which the inappropriate capital structure has damaged the business (as arguably occurred in the case of the toy retailer, Toys R Us).[37] Indeed, as this book goes to press, it appears likely that the particular problems for firms with highly leveraged capital structures in responding to the COVID-19 crisis will come under scrutiny. Furthermore, there is the possibility that, even with the assistance of legal tools, the problems of coordination, conflicted voting, hold outs, and misjudgements prevent implementation of the reorganization of the loan, bond, and equity finance, so that a corporate bankruptcy which should have been avoided follows. These concerns may be heightened further if the distressed debt market becomes constrained.

It has already been identified that the ability for financial creditors who no longer support the reorganization to trade with financial creditors who do support it, is fundamental to the analysis in this chapter. Yet, the depth and liquidity of secondary markets in the past decade may be the result of post-2008 financial crisis monetary policy, so that there is no guarantee that the distressed debt market will always be open, or will always operate in the same way. And if there is one lesson which should be learnt from the 2008 financial crisis, it is that even the deepest and most liquid capital markets can suffer a shock. At the same time, one of the most significant changes to the Basel regulatory capital regime after the financial crisis has been to require banks to reassess each asset annually for the purposes of calculating their capital requirements. This means that if the credit quality of a borrower declines, banks will be required to hold greater amounts of capital, which

[37] Bryce Covert, 'The Demise of Toys R Us is a Warning' (*The Atlantic*, July/August 2018) <https://www.theatlantic.com/magazine/archive/2018/07/toys-r-us-bankruptcy-private-equity/561758> accessed 6 March 2020.

may fuel trading in the distressed debt market. These two, diametrically opposed, potential forces for change provide just one example of the crystal ball challenge of predicting how the finance market may develop over the next ten years. This problem of prediction is further heightened by the uncertainty surrounding the consequences of the COVID-19 crisis. Some of these issues will be revisited at the end of the book. For the moment, the important point is that, although analysis of corporate reorganization law may be currently formulated in a way which takes account of the concept of traded debt, it may equally be necessary to reformulate it in the future, if conditions in the distressed debt market change.

4.3 England

4.3.1 Why concern for collective action problems assumed less significance in England

As noted in Chapters 2 and 3, at the time at which corporate bankruptcy scholarship began to emerge in England, large corporate reorganization was almost entirely an out-of-court affair, motivated by the principles of the London Approach. Several aspects of London Approach reorganizations reduced the salience of collective action problems in England. First, a London Approach reorganization typically implicated a single syndicate of banks. While the syndicate might have been quite large, the banks in the syndicate generally had the same strategy for the corporate reorganization case (to recover, after the reorganization, as much of their investment as possible). Secondly, the London Approach set down principles of co-operation expressly designed to reduce collective action problems. The main tenets of the London Approach were that banks should: (i) remain supportive on hearing that a company to which they had an exposure was in financial difficulty (keeping their facilities in place and not rushing to put the company into a corporate bankruptcy process); and (ii) work together to reach a *collective* view on whether and how the company should be reorganized.[38] Thirdly, these principles of collective action were supported by enforcement mechanisms: initially the regulatory power of the Bank of England; subsequently, the informal power of the Bank of England; and, finally, fear that failure to observe the principles of collective action might lead to the exclusion of a bank from the primary syndicated loan markets.[39] In short, corporate reorganization law had little role to play in addressing collective action problems during efforts to reorganize large corporates in England.

[38] Pen Kent, 'The London Approach' (1993) Q1 Bank of England Q Bull 110, 111.

[39] John Armour and Simon Deakin, 'Norms in Private Insolvency: The "London Approach" to the Resolution of Financial Distress' (2001) 1 J Corp Law Stud 21, 33–34, 46.

4.3.2 The rise of traded debt in England

Nonetheless, the syndicated term loan had changed the investment proposition for English bankers. They had traditionally advanced short-term loans, often in the nature of an overdraft, even to large corporate borrowers. Yet, they were now locked into their loan with the borrower. As a result, detailed mechanisms were developed to enable banks to trade out of their participations in English law syndicated loan agreements. There are three mechanisms by which a lender's portion, known as its participation, in a syndicated loan can be traded. First, the participation in the loan can be assigned. In this case, as a matter of English law, the new lender assumes any rights which the existing lender has, but the existing lender retains any obligations. Furthermore, an assignment may be either an absolute (or legal) assignment,[40] or an equitable assignment. If the assignment satisfies the requirements of an absolute assignment, and is notified to the borrower, then the borrower must pay any outstanding obligations directly to the transferee in order to get a good discharge. Secondly, the participation can be novated to the new lender, in which case the new lender assumes both the existing lender's rights and its ongoing obligations under the loan agreement. Finally, the lenders may enter into a sub-participation agreement, in which the original lender remains the lender of record, but accounts to the sub-participant for any receipts. The most common form of sub-participation is a funded sub-participation arrangement, in which the sub-participant pays the existing lender an amount equal to any outstanding amounts of the loan facility. It is notable that these mechanisms include mechanisms which enable the fact of the transfer to remain hidden from the borrower. Thus, the syndicated loan amalgamates some of the logic of relationship banking and some of the logic of tradability inherent in public debt markets.

As Chapter 3 explored, from the 1970s onwards, the banking environment became gradually more competitive in England, and British banks faced pressure from institutional shareholders to improve bank profitability. Just as in the US, this caused British banks to focus on profitability in their operations, and an active mortgage securitization market developed in England from the mid-1980s. Securitization issuance rapidly increased from the mid-1990s, as a result of increased demand from investors and of technological innovation which assisted the securitization process.[41] At the same time, English banks faced the same international regulatory capital demands as their US peers. The increasingly sophisticated risk management techniques of the investor community drove the development of tranching and other techniques already encountered in the US context. And the broadening of the asset class from mortgages, consumer loans,

[40] Law of Property Act 1925, s 136.

[41] Miguel Segoviano, Bradley Jones, Peter Linder, and Johannes Blankenheim, 'Sensitization: Lessons Learned and the Road Ahead' (2013) IMF Working Paper WP/13/255 54–55.

and credit cards to collateralized debt and loan obligations began to happen in England too.[42] As a result, loans gradually became a tradeable asset class in England, just as they had become in the US. British banks no longer assured their liquidity by short-term lending, but by the ability to trade loan assets, either as part of a rebalancing of their portfolio or when a borrower faced distress.

As this market began to converge with the US market, US distressed debt traders began to look to the English market for investment opportunities as part of their diversification strategy. The distressed debt traders burst onto the scene in England in the administration of Barings in 1997. The City Disputes Panel had negotiated a scheme of arrangement with Barings bank and its bondholders. This deal had been struck in a very English way: behind closed doors and with an eye on the acceptability of the economic package to all concerned. The US funds considered that the deal paid far too much regard to giving a little to everyone and, as a result, seriously mispriced the deal for some classes of credit. Once the debt traded into their hands, to the horror of the English market, they voted the deal down and held out for another two years for a new plan which they regarded correctly priced the various tranches of debt.[43]

This was a rude awakening for a market that was still a somewhat gentlemanly world of 'my word is my bond'. At this time, the distressed debt traders were known, in the English market, by the somewhat pejorative term 'vulture funds'. After Barings, large corporate borrowers saw the risk that debt would trade into the hands of these vulture funds at times of financial stress, upsetting the possibility of reaching an accommodation with a group of broadly supportive banks, and risking a far more dramatic reorganization. As a result, they attempted to restrict the ability of certain funds to trade in (using so-called 'black lists') or sought to mandate who a loan could be traded to (using so-called 'white lists'). The British banking industry strongly resisted these attempts and the courts supported a permissive reading of transfer rights in syndicated loan agreements.[44] Whereas liquidity had once been assured by the short-term nature of British bank lending, it was now assured by the tradability of the loan, and by the development of a secondary market for loan assets, particularly when the borrower was distressed. As a result, the British banks infrequently accepted limitations on tradability, particularly when the borrower was in breach of its loan agreement, both to ensure the particular bank's ability to trade and to support the general development of the secondary market for loans. The vulture funds opened offices in London, and were gentrified in the usual way by a change in the vocabulary of the field, so that they were renamed distressed debt investors. In time, these changes also had the same

[42] Chris O'Malley, *Bonds without Borders: A History of the Eurobond Market* (Wiley 2015) 145–49.

[43] For a more detailed account, see Sarah Paterson, 'Bargaining in Financial Restructuring: Market Norms, Legal Rights and Regulatory Standards' (2014) 14(2) J Corp Law Stud 333.

[44] *Essar Steel Limited v The Argo Fund Limited* [2006] EWCA Civ 241; [2006] 2 All ER (Comm) 104.

effect which they had had in the US, in making loan debt attractive for institutions which would have traditionally confined themselves to the bond market.

4.3.3 The rise of traded debt and English corporate reorganization law

These changes finally destroyed the crumbling foundations on which the London Approach was built. Market practice in London dictated that changes to core terms such as price and maturity in the loan market required unanimous bank consent. Yet, the same issues which made a financial restructuring more challenging to agree in the US now entered the London market: coordination problems; the risk of hold outs; and the risk of misjudgement in complexity. Overall, the close relationship between a borrower and its lead bank broke down, so that the process of agreeing a restructuring was also harder in human terms. British banks no longer thought of loans as relationships with customers, but rather as a portfolio of transactions. As a result, they embraced the distressed debt market, which enabled those who did not want to support the reorganization to monetize the transaction. The extent to which the market favoured this approach to distress was demonstrated, once again, by a change in vocabulary in the field. Yet, this time, a new, pejorative term was adopted for what would have been an entirely acceptable financial restructuring in times gone by: amend and extend became amend and pretend. Sometimes adaptation of the financial capital structure could be achieved through privately negotiated contract. There is nothing in English law to prevent this. Moreover, the fact that the principal English corporate bankruptcy law process, administration, was regarded as poorly adapted to reorganize the operations of the business, and more often than not resulted in a sale of the business or assets, provided a useful stick to incentivize a restructuring agreement. Nonetheless, just as experience in the US had shown, sometimes a legal tool is needed to drive through the bargain.

At this point, as explored in Chapter 3, English borrowers and their advisers turned back to the nineteenth-century scheme of arrangement tool. As already noted, this had lain dormant as a corporate reorganization mechanism for most of the twentieth century, when corporate reorganization had been a largely out-of-court, contractual transaction. In a scheme, an initial court hearing is held at which creditors are divided into classes for the purposes of voting on the plan. Each class then votes on the scheme. A majority in number, and three-quarters majority by value, of those present and voting, is needed in each class for the scheme to be sanctioned by the court.[45] The rapid trading of debt claims in distress raises the particular issue of keeping negotiations on track if a lender or bondholder trades

[45] Companies Act 2006, s 899.

out before the scheme is launched. In order to deal with this, it is common to draft a so-called 'lock-up' agreement, once the parties are coalescing around a deal, in which each signatory agrees that it will not sell its debt claim unless the buyer signs up to the terms of the lock-up agreement. This obviously raises the concern that the parties to the lock-up agreement may be treated as a separate class in the scheme of arrangement. As explored in Chapter 3, there is no ability to impose a scheme of arrangement on an entire dissenting class in a scheme. Thus, if lock-ups did have an impact on class composition, the utility of the scheme as a reorganization mechanism would be severely compromised.

4.3.4 The concepts of rights and of interests develop in English corporate reorganization law

As Chapter 3 explored, unlike the US courts, the English courts have come to the scheme of arrangement mechanism relatively unbounded by concepts developed in a different corporate reorganization era. Indeed, the courts have played a vital role in developing concepts which support the comparatively low-cost flexing of a complex, leveraged capital structure through the scheme of arrangement. Thus, the English courts have shown themselves alive to the fact that, if a single class votes against the plan, then the reorganization of the loan, bond, and equity finance will fail. As a result, they have worked to develop a conceptual framework which limits this risk. Specifically, the courts have focused on the concept of rights, rather than the concept of interests, as determinants of scheme class.

As introduced in Chapter 3, a Practice Statement from 2002 makes clear that the purpose of the initial scheme hearing is for questions of class composition to be drawn to the attention of the court.[46] The principle is, first, 'that those whose rights really are so dissimilar that they cannot consult together with a view to a common interest should be treated as parties to distinct arrangements—so that they should have their own separate meetings' but, secondly, 'that those whose rights are sufficiently similar to the rights of others that they can properly consult together should be required to do; lest by ordering separate meetings the court gives a veto to a minority group'.[47] Rights, in this sense, means the rights which creditors are releasing or giving up in the scheme, and any new rights which replace them. The courts have determined that ordinarily the fact that some creditors have locked up behind the scheme goes to their interests and not their rights, with the result that the lock-up is not sufficient to place them in a separate class.[48] In this way, the power

[46] Practice Statement (Companies: Schemes of Arrangement) [2002] 1 WLR 1345.

[47] *Re Hawk Insurance Co Ltd* [2001] EWCA Civ 241; [2001] 2 BCLC 480 [33].

[48] *Telewest Communications Plc (No 1)* [2004] EWHC 924 (Ch); [2004] BCC 342; *McCarthy & Stone Plc, McCarthy and Stone (Developments) Limited* [2009] EWHC 712 (Ch); [2009] 3 WLUK 383; *Metrovacesa SA, Re* [2011] EWHC 1014 (Ch); [2011] 3 WLUK 918.

of creditors who have refused to lock up to hold up the scheme is contained. The courts can consider whether the fact that creditors had entered into a lock-up has affected their individual preferences at the final hearing to sanction the scheme. In other words, the courts have the flexibility to determine whether the creditors ultimately voted for the scheme not because it was an arrangement that 'an intelligent and honest man, a member of the class concerned and acting in respect of his interest, might reasonably approve',[49] but rather because they would suffer a claim for breach of contract if they withdrew their support. Thus, the approach of the English courts reflects the approach recommended by Bratton and Levitin, and discussed in the first part of this chapter.[50] It does this by focusing on whether individual preferences may make the views of the majority suspect, rather than more dramatic methods of minority protection, such as section 316(b) of the Trust Indenture Act 1939 in the US context, or confining locked-up scheme creditors to a separate class in the English scheme of arrangement context. Crucially, by distinguishing between the concept of rights and the concept of interests, the English courts leave this question to the final stage of the reorganization, at which point they can take a nuanced and specific approach in considering whether there is any reason to override the majority vote.

Moreover, when the English courts come to consider the majority vote, they have identified a high hurdle for interference. Modern courts have referred, with approval, to dicta in the nineteenth-century case of *Re English, Scottish, and Australian Chartered Bank* that 'If the creditors are acting on sufficient information and with time to consider what they are about, and are acting honestly, they are, I apprehend, much better judges of what is to their commercial advantage than the Court can be'.[51] Thus, it is extremely unlikely that the courts will interfere in an arrangement as a result of the execution of a lock-up agreement negotiated between sophisticated financial creditors. This strong deference to the concept of majority rule makes the scheme of arrangement well adapted to achieving a reorganization of a complex, leveraged capital structure in the context of a rapidly trading market.

Of course, as Chapter 3 identified, a limitation on the scheme of arrangement is that it cannot be used to impose a reorganization plan on an entire dissenting class, unless it is twinned with a pre-packaged administration sale. As briefly discussed in Chapter 3, when a pre-packaged administration sale is used in this way, the finance holding company is placed into administration, and the creditors who are in the money bid their debt, in consideration for the purchase of the shares in the operating parent. This potentially enables the debtor group to deal with the hold-out threat of a creditor who trades into the situation and gains a blocking

[49] *Re National Bank Ltd* [1966] 1 WLR 819 (Ch) 829 citing J B Lindon, Brian Parker, Hugh Williams, and Lord Wrenbury, *Buckley on the Companies Acts* (13th edn, LexisNexis 1957).
[50] Bratton and Levitin (n 29) 1665–73.
[51] [1893] 3 Ch 385.

position. Pre-packaged administrations are not a creature of statute but have developed through the ingenuity of English lawyers. This development was supported by the courts, when they recognised the pre-packaged administration in a number of cases, and by the bodies which regulate insolvency practitioners, when they made pre-packaged administration subject to specific regulations. Pre-packaged administrations remain controversial in mid-market company restructuring, where they are commonly used to write off trade debt while the business continues in the hands of owner-managers. Yet, they have attracted much less attention in the large corporate reorganization field, precisely because the reorganization is usually confined to financial creditors. Indeed, in the latest regulatory investigation of pre-packaged administration,[52] pre-packs for reorganizations of loan, debt, and equity finance were expressly carved out of the reform proposals. Thus, English corporate reorganization law has been much less concerned with the consequences of imposing a new capital structure on sophisticated, strongly adjusting, financial creditors. This has equipped the market well to deal with the hold-out issue in traded markets.

As already highlighted, one area in which English corporate reorganization law has lagged behind the US is that it has lacked a single procedure explicitly designed to achieve cross-class cram-down of a new capital structure. It has already been noted in Chapter 3 that, just as the book is going to press, the UK Government has introduced a new bill, which it plans to fast-track through Parliament and which will, among other things, add a new Part 26A to the Companies Act 2006.[53] The new Part 26A is heavily modelled on the scheme of arrangement procedure, but includes a cross-class cram-down mechanism. This preserves the benefits of scheme-like technology in providing a rapid and low-cost implementation tool which reduces the risk of hold-out creditors in rapidly traded markets, while adopting a relatively simple approach to valuation (discussed in Chapter 3) which enhances the effectiveness of the tool.

4.3.5 Summary of the argument in section 4.3

Thus far, the argument has been advanced that the central concepts in US corporate reorganization law were fixed at a time at which corporate reorganization implicated not only financial creditors but also general, unsecured creditors, employees, and customers, with the result that the scholarship has struggled to adapt these concepts to cases which implicate only sophisticated, strongly adjusting financial

[52] The Graham Review into Pre-Pack Administration, <https://www.gov.uk/government/publications/graham-review-into-pre-pack-administration> accessed 6 March 2020.

[53] Corporate Insolvency and Governance Bill [HC] 2019–21, Sch 9, inserting new Part 26A into Companies Act 2006.

creditors and investors. It has been noted that ideas inherited from an earlier era can obscure the ways in which shifts in logics and practices in proximate fields interact with corporate reorganization law, and the implications for the corporate reorganization law debate. To the extent that there is a concern for the adaptability of corporate reorganization law concepts in England, it is that they have been developed at a time when only sophisticated, strongly adjusting, financial creditors are typically implicated in corporate reorganization, and at a time when debt trades widely in deep and liquid distressed debt markets. Thus, the concern has been raised that scholars, practitioners, judges, and the legislature may struggle to adapt these concepts for cases which implicate a wider range of participants, or when debt trades less successfully. This issue becomes clearer in Chapter 9, which considers how current developments in logic and practice in the fields of finance and non-financial corporates may implicate different participants in the corporate reorganization process, who may mobilize and adapt corporate reorganization law in new ways. As Chapter 9 develops, this may mean that the corporate reorganization concepts examined in Chapters 3–8 of this book may need to be adapted again.

4.4 Conclusion

This chapter has examined how the shift in investment logic, from a hold-to-maturity strategy to trading strategies, has impacted the ways in which corporate reorganization law is mobilized and adapted in the US and in England. It has been argued that concepts in US corporate reorganization law, which were developed to address the collective actions problems which arise when individual creditors are incentivized to rush to enforce against the assets of the borrower, have less significance than the problems of coordination, conflicted voting, hold outs, and misjudgements in rapidly traded debt markets. Consequently, the analysis in this chapter supports Bratton and Levitin's suggestions for reform of the approach to majority voting in section 316(b) of the Trust Indenture Act of 1939.[54] It has also suggested reasons to be circumspect about limiting both pre-packaged Chapter 11 plans and section 363 sales as methods of implementing a reorganization of debt and equity finance. A more flexible approach to the finance documents in financial capital structure reorganization has also been advocated, together with the possibility of a more streamlined version of Chapter 11. The point has been made, again, that this is not to ignore the fact that new normative concerns arise, but that these normative concerns have more to do with whether an environment of highly leveraged, rapidly traded debt should be supported than with protecting the hold-out power of minority unsecured creditors in distress. Once again, it must be

[54] Bratton and Levitin (n 29) 1665–73.

emphasized that it cannot be assumed that deep and liquid distressed debt markets, offering opportunities to trade, will always be available. The analysis in this chapter might be very different if distressed debt trading becomes more difficult in the future.

Turning to England, it was found, once again, that because modern corporate reorganization law only really started to develop during the 2000s, it is generally well adapted to facilitating the sort of low-cost flexing of complex, leveraged capital structures which have dominated corporate reorganization practice in recent times. Specifically, it is well adapted to cope with the coordination, conflicted voting, hold out, and misjudgement problems posed by rapidly traded debt markets. In particular, this chapter explored how the English courts have narrowed the concept of rights, and expanded the concept of interests, in order to address these challenges in the scheme process. It has been suggested, once again, that to the extent there is a concern for the adaptive capacity of English corporate reorganization law's concepts, that concern is located in how corporate reorganization practice may develop as a result of certain changes in logic and practice in the fields of finance and non-financial corporates which may lead to a wider range of participants and liabilities being implicated in corporate reorganization in the future. Once again, this is an idea which will be revisited later in the book.

5
The Rise of Secured Credit

5.1 Introduction

Thus far, the book has explored two shifts in the organizational and institutional structure of the finance field: the shift from a market in which leverage ratios were low to a market in which high leverage is significantly more common; and the shift from a hold-to-maturity market to a traded market. As Chapter 3 identified, a borrower with a highly leveraged capital structure is more likely to face financial distress than a borrower with lower levels of leverage. As Chapter 4 identified, in a traded market the party which originates the loan or invests in a bond does not assume that it will retain an exposure to the borrower at maturity or, if earlier, on renegotiation or default. As a result, the lender is more likely to trade monitoring protection for yield, so that the mechanisms by which lenders monitor borrowers are weakened. If the risks of financial distress are higher, but levels of monitoring are lower, then security assumes a greater role in protecting the particular lender who has the economic interest in the loan or bond at the relevant time. Thus, both of the shifts in logic and practice explored in Chapters 3 and 4 give rise to a greater need for non-financial corporate borrowers to offer a wider range of assets as security for borrowings, and for lenders to be confident in the enforceability of their security in default.

Corporate Reorganization Law and Forces of Change. Sarah Paterson, Oxford University Press (2020). © Sarah Paterson.
DOI: 10.1093/oso/9780198860365.001.0001.

Security does not merely provide stronger economic protection when the firm faces distress. Perhaps more importantly, it can provide the secured creditor, who holds the investment at the moment of default, with bargaining leverage in reorganization negotiations. Where a firm has a complex, leveraged capital structure, it is possible that the borrower will manage the debt burden until some other shock occurs, and will only then find that it has insufficient cash to meet its debt service burden. In this case, flexing the capital structure to reduce the fixed costs associated with the debt may enable the borrower to trade on. This is the situation with which this part of the book is primarily concerned and, as will become apparent, in this situation security may play a significant role in providing the lender with bargaining leverage in reorganization negotiations. It is not surprising, therefore, that the changes in the fields of finance and non-financial corporates discussed in Chapters 3 and 4 have led to changes in secured transactions law in the United States (US), with significant implications for the balance of bargaining power in attempts to reorganize the debtor's debt and equity finance in times of distress.

This chapter explores how changes in secured transactions law in the US have shifted control rights in corporate reorganization towards secured creditors. Scholars viewing corporate reorganization law through an economic lens are largely content with this development, but it is a matter of great concern for progressive scholars. Yet, once again, the argument will be made that where these control rights arise in the context of a reorganization of the debtor's debt and equity financing arrangements among financial institutions in traded markets, they should not be of significant concern for the progressive scholar. Crucially, the liquidation preference of secured creditors is unlikely to be a significant issue. Instead, it will become apparent that the real issue is junior financial creditor holdout power, whichever lens is used to view the problem to be addressed. Once again, the argument is that this new common ground has been concealed by a failure to concentrate systematically on the concepts which have laid the foundations of the corporate reorganization law debate. Whereas Chapter 3 identified the need to replace concepts with others which better describe the case, and Chapter 4 was concerned with inserting a new concept vital to analysis of the field, in this chapter the focus is on unravelling an existing concept (secured creditor control) and reformulating it to take better account of the wider organizational and institutional environment.

Turning to England, the chapter explores how the English courts have generally supported the allocation of control rights in distress to senior financial creditors. It reveals why this has contributed to making English corporate reorganization law well adapted for the problem of reorganizing a complex, leveraged capital structure. Once again, to the extent that there is a concern about English corporate reorganization law, it will be with the question of whether new conceptual boundaries may be needed for senior financial creditor control if shifts in logics, practices, and identities in the finance and non-financial corporate fields cause corporate reorganization law to be mobilized and adapted in new ways in the future. Once again, as this book goes to press, specific concerns arise as COVID-19 poses new challenges for corporate reorganization law. For the moment, however, the focus of this chapter is on the emergence of particular concepts in corporate reorganization law in England as complex, secured capital structures have developed in the era of leverage.

5.2 United States

5.2.1 The concept of secured creditor control

Questions of secured creditor control in Chapter 11 have traditionally sharply divided scholars adopting an economic analysis of corporate reorganization law and scholars adopting a progressive approach. Once again, for those in the economic camp, corporate reorganization law exists to solve market failures which prevent bargaining. It is thus essentially a procedural device which clears the way for the parties to negotiate towards the wealth-maximizing solution to the firm's financial difficulties (or, in certain circumstances, to impose a market bargain when negotiation is impossible or transaction costs are too high). It does not serve to determine the terms of the bargain itself. Indeed, as explored in Chapters 3 and 4, where Chapter 11 does step in to impose a transaction many scholars viewing corporate reorganization law through an economic lens argue that the imposed transaction should, as much as possible, mimic the transaction which would have been achieved if consensual bargaining had been possible.[1] In this framework, scholars adopting an economic approach pay high regard to the pre-bankruptcy distribution of entitlements of the creditors, and the strategic power which those entitlements provide in the corporate reorganization negotiations. Insofar as secured credit is concerned, as Thomas Jackson recently put it, '... if secured creditors won outside of bankruptcy, there was no identifiable bankruptcy principle (beyond, to me, the flabby, unprincipled, "equality is equity" mantra) to change that outcome in bankruptcy'.[2]

Progressive scholars, on the other hand, worry about the bargain itself, in addition to the procedural conditions required for bargaining. Insofar as secured credit is concerned, they worry that secured creditors will have an incentive to prefer a liquidation over a corporate reorganization transaction, which will result in the secured creditor recovering all, or most, of its secured debt, but will result in reduced returns, or no return, for unsecured creditors.[3] Thus, a crucial aspect of

1 Jules Coleman, *Markets, Morals, and the Law* (OUP 1998) 84.
2 Thomas H Jackson, 'A Retrospective Look at Bankruptcy's New Frontiers' (2018) 166(7) U Pa L Rev 1867, 1873.
3 Harvey R Miller and Shai Y Waisman, 'Is Chapter 11 Bankrupt?' (2005) 47 BC L Rev 129, 173.

Chapter 11 for progressive scholars has been the mechanisms which tip the balance of power away from secured creditors towards the debtor in order, they hope, to facilitate the corporate reorganization transaction. As this chapter explores, traditionally it has been difficult for a US lender to take security over all of the borrower's assets. Instead, ever since the era of railroad financing and the equity receivership, it has been common for secured lenders in the US to have a security interest in particular assets. This gives rise to the collective action concern which was identified in Chapters 2 and 4: that lenders with the benefit of security over particular assets will race to enforce against those assets, preventing a corporate reorganization transaction emerging which preserves value for creditors as a whole.

Value is not the only reason progressive scholars have a preference for corporate reorganization. The concern arises that, even if a sale of the business and assets can be achieved, jobs and facilities may move out of the immediate community to other parts of the country. This concern is heightened because many companies in the modern economy are service companies, and jobs and facilities can be moved with relative ease to another part of the country. The US is a geographically vast country, so that suppliers, employees, and even customers may struggle to follow the business to its new location. At the same time, the impact on the community which is left behind can be dramatic. Although many of the tools of corporate reorganization can also be used in a sale transaction (most notably the mechanism for assuming, rejecting, and assigning contracts), it is also thought that the debtor may assume a greater number of liabilities in a corporate reorganization transaction than in a sale transaction. Overall, the significant point is that Chapter 11 actively seeks to tip the balance of power towards the debtor, in the expectation that the debtor will prefer a corporate reorganization transaction, and away from the secured creditor, who might otherwise be expected to press for an individually economically rational liquidation sale which would not be in the interests of creditors as a whole.

Thus, Chapter 11 provides a series of debtor-friendly provisions: a strong automatic stay; a broad power to raise new finance for the corporate reorganization case; the recovery or return of property transferred out of the debtor's possession prior to commencement of the Chapter 11 case; expansion of the debtor's administrative powers; and, most importantly of all, the debtor's exclusive right to propose a plan of reorganization and to solicit acceptances of its plan for 120 days, subject to termination, contraction, or extension for cause.[4] This last power is significant, because it effectively holds creditors at bay unless they agree to the plan of reorganization, while professional and other costs of the case accrue. Thus, creditors have a practical incentive to engage in negotiation and to try to come on board with the debtor's reorganization plan.

[4] This list is largely drawn from Miller and Waisman (n 3) 143–44.

As this chapter explains, significant changes to secured transactions law in the US have led to significant changes in the balance of power between the secured creditor and the debtor in the Chapter 11 case. While this has been widely debated in US scholarship, there has been insufficient focus on the detail of the ways in which changes in secured transactions law have interacted with corporate reorganization law. This has obscured what ought to be common ground between economically minded and progressively minded scholars on the question of secured creditor control. In order to develop this argument, it is necessary to start with a sustained inquiry into the nature of the changes in secured transactions law and the consequences of these changes for the ways in which corporate reorganization law is mobilized and adapted by the participants in the process.

5.2.2 The rise of secured credit

In the early twentieth-century decision of *Benedict v Ratner*,[5] Justice Brandeis was faced with a case in which the debtor had assigned its account receivables (which an English lawyer would refer to as book debts). The terms of the assignment provided that, prior to default, the borrower was entitled to collect the debts and use the proceeds as it chose. No consent was required from the secured party, and the debtor's customers were not notified of the assignment. Justice Brandeis refused to recognize the priority of the assignee, stating:

> Under the law of New York, a transfer of property which reserves to the transferor the right to dispose of the same or to apply the proceeds thereof for his own use is, as to creditors, fraudulent in law and void.

As a result, it was difficult for a lender or bondholder to take security over receivables in the US, notwithstanding that, for a number of debtors, receivables are likely to be one of the most significant assets available to them as collateral. Lenders developed a number of workarounds for this and other issues, but what emerged was disparate and lacked overall coherence. This led, in 1951, to the development of Article 9 of the Uniform Commercial Code (UCC), under the auspices of two sponsoring organizations: the American Law Institute and the National Conference of Commissioners on Uniform State Laws. The UCC proposal recommended that it should be possible to take a valid security interest where the debtor was free to dispose of the collateral without consent (as with inventory), or collect collateral and use the proceeds (as with receivables). It also made other suggestions to improve the ease of taking, and perfecting, security interests.

5 268 US 353 (1925).

In order for these recommendations to take effect, it was necessary for the individual states to adopt them. In the event, Article 9 of the UCC was not widely adopted until 1962. Although the revisions in the 1960s did make it substantially easier for American lenders to acquire a perfected security interest in certain classes of assets falling within Article 9, it remained challenging for an American lender to obtain a security interest over substantially all of the assets of the company: a so-called 'blanket lien'. As the second part of this chapter will reveal, this contrasted with the position in England where it was possible for lenders (principally banks) to take a combination of fixed and floating security over all of the assets of a non-financial corporate borrower from late in the nineteenth century. A number of reasons contributed to the challenges for the US secured lender.

First, the perfection requirements in US secured transactions law were complex and frequently litigated. Section 544(a) of the US Bankruptcy Code (the so-called 'strong arm' clause) provides the bankruptcy trustee or debtor-in-possession the status of a hypothetical judicial lien creditor, entitling him to avoid security interests that are unperfected at the start of the bankruptcy case. Most security interests under Article 9 are perfected by filing a financing statement, but both the place of filing rules and the description requirements have traditionally been notoriously challenging. Thus, it was not unusual for a lender to find that a significant portion of its collateral package had not been properly perfected.[6] A further limitation on taking valid security over all of the non-financial corporate borrower's assets was that certain types of assets were excluded entirely from Article 9's scope.[7] Significantly, Article 9 of the UCC did not apply to most security interests in deposit accounts (although some states did make non-uniform amendments to state law to bring deposit accounts within Article 9). There were real, practical difficulties in relying on common law to take security over a deposit account, so that frequently a debtor's deposit account would be unencumbered.[8]

Moreover, US secured transactions law traditionally imposed significant limitations on the extent to which a lender's security interest could attach to assets coming into the estate after commencement of the bankruptcy case.[9] As explored in the second part of this chapter, in English law the floating charge continues to attach to property coming into the estate which is within the scope of the charge, even after insolvency proceedings have been commenced. In contrast, the usual rule in US bankruptcy was that a pre-petition security interest could not reach property coming into the estate after the bankruptcy petition,[10]

[6] On this point, and for a more detailed examination of the history of the developments, see Sarah Paterson, 'Finding Our Way: Secured Transactions and Corporate Bankruptcy Law and Policy in America and England' (2018) 18(2) J Corp Law Stud 247, 257.

[7] ibid 258.

[8] G Ray Warner, 'The Anti-Bankruptcy Act: Revised Article 9 and Bankruptcy' (2001) 9 Am Bankr Inst L Rev 3, 45; Bruce A Markell, 'From Property to Contract and Back: An Examination of Deposit Accounts and Revised Article 9' (1999) 74 Chi-Kent L Rev 963, 968–69.

[9] Paterson (n 6) 259–60.

[10] 11 USC § 552(a).

other than proceeds, products, offspring, profits, or rent of the pre-petition collateral.[11] At the time the US Bankruptcy Code was enacted, the definition of 'proceeds' in Article 9 of the UCC was relatively limited, so that once again a pot of assets was likely to exist which fell outside the scope of the security package. This was further compounded by complex rules on the ability to assert a security interest in monies coming into the estate before the bankruptcy case commenced, where they have been co-mingled with monies coming into the estate after commencement.

Overall, then, for much of the period with which this book is concerned, it has been very difficult for a lender to take a security interest in all, or substantially all, of a US debtor's assets. In a hold-to-maturity market with low leverage, in which large, non-financial corporate borrowers did not frequently rely on commercial banks for significant borrowings, and in which local bankers typically lent to local borrowers, the finance market was able to cope with these limitations. This organizational and institutional structure of the field of finance had significant implications for the way in which modern US corporate reorganization practice evolved in the 1980s and 1990s. First, it was entirely possible that the non-financial corporate borrower would have unencumbered cash available to finance the bankruptcy case. As a result, when debtors filed for Chapter 11, they were frequently able to use free cash to finance operations while they exploited their exclusive right to propose a plan of reorganization. Secondly, to the extent that cash in the business was not sufficient to support operations, the American non-financial corporate borrower typically had a pool of unencumbered assets to offer as security for a new, so-called 'debtor-in-possession' (DIP) loan.

Section 364 of Chapter 11 of the US Bankruptcy Code expressly permits the distressed company to obtain financing after it has petitioned for Chapter 11 on either an unsecured basis or, after notice and a hearing, in exchange for priority. It is possible for the security interest to 'prime', or rank ahead of, existing security. However, this requires the debtor to show that no other financing is available, and that the interests of pre-petition secured creditors which would be primed by the new security are 'adequately protected', which can be challenging to demonstrate. Crucially, section 364 also expressly permits a secured claim in unencumbered property, and so the limitations on the ability of existing lenders to take security over all of the assets were significant in providing a ready pool of unencumbered assets which could be used for this purpose. As a result, a deep market for third-party providers of so-called DIP finance developed in the US in the 1990s, enabling management to tap the necessary financing to operate the business while they developed a reorganization plan in the safety of Chapter 11. The third-party specialist providers had an interest in committing DIP finance for the Chapter 11 case. The very fact that the DIP finance facility was available for drawing would often give

[11] 11 USC § 552(a) and (b).

creditors, suppliers, and customers the necessary confidence to continue to deal with the business in Chapter 11. This meant that relatively good cashflow could be achieved, and the DIP financier might be able to continue to collect fees for what was effectively standby financing.[12] At the same time, the fees charged could be significant. Where third-party DIP finance was available, it reduced the power of the debtor's existing lenders to dictate the strategy for the case, because the debtor was not reliant on the existing lenders for funding in order to trade through the Chapter 11 case. Even if the existing lenders ultimately provided the attractive DIP financing, they were aware that the debtor had other options, so that their strategic power was reduced.

As a result, both the availability of free cash and the development of the DIP finance market led to a lively literature which alleged that managers of large, distressed, US corporates were mobilizing the tools of Chapter 11 in order to hold their creditors at bay and dissipate the company's few remaining assets. For the secured lender, the concern was that by the time they were able to take control of their collateral much of the remaining value in the business would have disappeared. Perhaps the most celebrated case was that of Eastern Airlines, in which Frank Lorenzo was alleged to have taken over the company in a 1980s-style highly leveraged buyout, and flown the company's planes around the world under Chapter 11 bankruptcy protection until the business had no value.[13] However, as the finance field moved from a hold-to-maturity market to a traded market, in which monitoring assumed lower significance and other types of protection assumed greater significance, and as leverage in large, US corporates grew, it is unsurprising that pressure mounted to make the legal tools for taking and perfecting security in the widest range of assets more straightforward. Ultimately, this pressure led to the 2001 revisions to Article 9 of the UCC. These changes in the field of secured transactions law, when coupled with the other organizational and institutional changes in the field of finance discussed in Chapters 3 and 4, were to have profound implications for the ways in which corporate reorganization law was mobilized and adapted to reorganize complex, leveraged capital structures.

The first, crucial change was the significant amendments to the perfection requirements in Article 9. The 2001 amendments relaxed many of the UCC's complex description requirements, so that a more limited list of information was required for a valid security interest, and so that it became possible simply to state that the security interest was in 'all assets'.[14] The place of filing rules were also significantly simplified, so that most financing statements were required to be filed in the state where the borrower was located.[15] Thus, overall, it became considerably less likely

[12] For an example, see the description of the funding of Interstate Stores in Philip B Nelson, *Corporations in Crisis: Behavioral Observations for Bankruptcy Policy* (Praeger 1981) 112 and n 45.
[13] See Robert K Rasmussen, 'The Efficiency of Chapter 11' (1991) 8 Bankr Dev J 319, 319–21.
[14] UCC § 9-504(2).
[15] UCC § 9-301(1).

that the debtor would be able to rely on secured creditor error to carve out a portion of unencumbered assets. Secondly, new classes of collateral were added to Article 9 in 2001, including health-care receivables, commercial tort claims, and deposit accounts.[16] The addition of deposit accounts was particularly significant. Notably, instead of filing a financing statement a lender is now able to obtain 'control' in one of three ways: (i) where it is the bank that maintains the deposit account, by automatic control and perfection;[17] (ii) by ensuring that the bank which maintains the deposit account and the borrower enter into a 'control agreement' which provides that the bank will comply with the secured party's instructions to pay out the funds in the deposit account without further consent by the debtor;[18] or (iii) by providing that the borrower becomes the bank's customer with respect to the account.[19] Crucially, there is no need to maintain day-to-day operating control of the account to obtain priority. The perfection of a security interest in a deposit account is thus now a relatively straightforward matter, making it considerably easier for lenders to take blanket liens.

Also of significance is a subtle but important change in the extent to which security may be said to attach to assets coming into the estate after commencement of the case. It will be remembered that this is limited to proceeds, products, offspring, profits, or rent of the pre-petition collateral, and that, at the time the US Bankruptcy Code was enacted, the definition of 'proceeds' in Article 9 of the UCC was relatively limited. The 2001 revisions now apply the concept of proceeds to future property that is generated by or related to the original collateral. This, once again, makes it more likely that a lender will be able successfully to assert a security interest in a greater proportion of the borrower's assets. This is compounded by some relatively technical changes, including changes to the co-mingling rules. Thus, it is now considerably more likely that a large US non-financial corporate borrower will have encumbered all, or substantially all, of its assets before the commencement of the corporate reorganization case.

5.2.3 The rise of secured credit and the corporate reorganization case

The emergence of blanket security has profound implications for the balance of bargaining power between the debtor and the secured creditor, the effectiveness of the moratorium, and the course of the corporate reorganization case. First, it is now significantly less likely that the borrower will have unencumbered cash

16 UCC § 9-102.
17 UCC § 9-104(a)(1).
18 UCC § 9-104(a)(2).
19 UCC § 9-104(a)(3). For a detailed discussion of the requirements, see Markell (n 8) 984–86.

which it can use in operating the business, while it prepares a reorganization plan. Chapter 11 provides that a debtor which seeks to use cash which is the subject of a security interest requires either the consent of the secured party,[20] or the consent of the court. The court will only grant consent if it is satisfied that the creditor has been provided with 'adequate protection' of its security interest.[21] Section 361 of the US Bankruptcy Code provides a non-exclusive list of methods of providing adequate protection: (i) cash payments; (ii) replacement security; or (iii) other protection that will result in the realization of the 'indubitable equivalent' of the secured creditors' interest in the property. As the 2001 revisions make it more likely that all of the debtor's assets will be subject to a valid security interest, it also makes it less likely that the borrower will be able to satisfy the court that it has provided adequate protection to the secured creditor. This provides the secured creditor with significant ability to exercise leverage over the non-financial corporate borrower in the course of the case and, when combined with the other changes in the organizational and institutional structure of the finance field, has profoundly shifted both the balance of bargaining power between the debtor and secured creditor in Chapter 11 and the extent to which the debtor is able to rely on moratorium protection while it prepares its plan of reorganization. Crucially, it has enabled secured financial creditors largely to dictate the form in which the corporate reorganization will be implemented, with milestones and other contractual provisions in the secured debt documents to control the course of the case.

Moreover, together with changes in regulatory capital rules following the 2008 financial crisis, these changes have had an impact on the availability of third-party DIP finance. The unattractive capital treatment of DIP loans following post-2008 financial crisis regulatory reform, together with the lack of unencumbered assets to support them, has led to a hollowing out of the market for third-party DIP lending. It is thus now considerably more likely that the only source of DIP financing will be the existing lenders.[22] As discussed in section 5.2.2 'The rise of secured credit' above, it was always the case that existing lenders had an incentive to provide the valuable DIP finance, which was reasonably assured of repayment, carried attractive pricing, and in many cases was not even drawn down. However, because the debtor had other options, the existing lender's strategic bargaining power over the terms of the DIP finance was constrained. Once existing lenders are the only potential providers of DIP finance, they have the ability to dictate their terms. The existing lenders are, therefore, able to insert significant control rights over the case in the DIP loan agreement itself. Interestingly, Bratton and Levitin suggest that the lack of available DIP finance has some explanatory power for the rising popularity

[20] 11 USC § 363.

[21] 11 USC § 361, 362(d), 363(e), and 364(d).

[22] See eg David A Skeel Jr, 'Creditors' Ball: The "New" New Corporate Governance in Chapter 11' (2003) 152(2) U Pa L Rev 917; Harvey R Miller, 'Chapter 11 in Transition—From Boom to Bust and into the Future' (2007) 81(4) Am Bankr LJ 375, 390.

of exchange offers as a method of flexing the capital structure and, as is explored in more detail in Chapter 6, it also appears to be part of the explanation for a rise in popularity of section 363 sales over corporate reorganization plans.[23] Yet, as credit conditions have loosened after the 2008 financial crisis, and creditors in the case have become more willing to provide new finance, the DIP finance contract has become significant in providing the secured creditor with another source of bargaining leverage, in detailed provisions dictating how the reorganization case is to proceed.

Furthermore, the controversial practice of 'rolling up' the new DIP loan into the pre-petition secured loan has emerged. In effect, the new, post-petition loan is used to repay the old, pre-petition loan. As the new loan is subject to US bankruptcy court approval, it is possible for the secured creditor, at a stroke, to remove any concerns with perfection and validity of its pre-petition security, and to insulate the loan from some aspects of reorganization. Roll-ups come in two varieties. In a so-called 'creeping roll-up' the new loan is used to repay pre-petition revolving credit advances as they mature. Alternatively, in a first-day roll-up the new loan is used to refinance the entire amount of the pre-petition loan.[24] In both cases, the motivation for the loan is to protect the secured creditor's priority position. Yet, if the secured creditors are denied the ability to roll up, the concern arises that they will decline to provide the DIP finance with significant implications for the debtor's options.

5.2.4 Implications for the concept of secured creditor control

Unsurprisingly, these changes in the ways in which corporate reorganization law's tools have been adapted have attracted a great deal of attention. A significant body of literature adopting an economic analysis broadly welcomes the changes as addressing the problems with debtor control, which were widely criticized in the Chapter 11 cases in the 1980s and 1990s.[25] Yet other authors, and the recent American Bankruptcy Institute Commission to Study Reform of Chapter 11, worry that it has shifted the delicate balance struck between debtor and secured creditor control and the utility of moratorium protection too far in favour of the secured credit lobby.[26] In part, this is because the concept of secured creditor control continues to be implicitly associated with concern for secured creditor liquidation

[23] William W Bratton and Adam J Levitin, 'The New Bond Workouts' (2018) 166 U Pa L Rev 1597, 1601.

[24] For a useful discussion, see Daniel J Bussel and Kenneth N Klee, 'Recalibrating Consent in Bankruptcy' (2009) 83 Am Bankr LJ n 209 and accompanying text.

[25] Douglas G Baird and Robert K Rasmussen, 'The Prime Directive' (2007) 75 U Cin L Rev 921, 939.

[26] Miller and Waisman (n 3) 170; American Bankruptcy Institute Commission to Study the Reform of Chapter 11 2012–2014, *Final Report and Recommendations* (American Bankruptcy Institute 2014).

bias: that secured creditors will exercise their strategic control rights to implement a sale transaction, rather than a corporate reorganization, to the detriment of unsecured creditors. This framing of the concept of secured creditor control in the corporate reorganization case gives rise to the traditional normative concern of Chapter 11 to reduce secured creditor control, in order to push against the secured creditor's liquidation bias. Thus, the concern arises to steer the parties towards a corporate reorganization transaction which will maximize value for a wider group of creditors, including weakly adjusting, general, unsecured creditors worthy of protection. In order to interrogate this, it is necessary, once again, to start by carefully describing the fact pattern in a typical reorganization limited to debt and equity finance provided by financial institutions.

First, this part of the book is concerned with a borrower who is suffering financial distress as a result of a complex, leveraged capital structure. Although Chapter 9 explores some recent innovations in the finance field which affect the analysis, for the moment it will be assumed that the secured creditor has negotiated restrictive covenants in the finance documents which enable it to bring the debtor to the bargaining table if there is reason to believe that the capital structure may be unsustainable in changing economic conditions. At this point, as already discussed, in many cases there will be value in the business and operations of the borrower, and the aim of the transaction will be to limit the reorganization to the loan, bond, and equity finance, implicating only strongly adjusting, sophisticated financial creditors and investors. If secured creditors do not wish to support the reorganization, it is highly likely that they will be able to trade in the secondary market with creditors who do support it. This offers the exiting secured creditors a more certain and rapid method of monetizing their position than attempting to push for a liquidation transaction. On the other hand, if the secured creditor continues to believe there is sufficient value in the business to repay their claim, they are probably best advised to support the reorganization of the debtor's debt and equity financing arrangements but only—and this is crucial—if the reorganization can be implemented relatively expeditiously and without damagingly high transaction costs. Thus, control rights which enable the secured creditor to be reasonably assured of rapid implementation of a reorganization constrain the secured creditor's liquidation bias, and reduce the risk that financial distress will spread to the operations of the group, implicating weakly adjusting general, unsecured creditors, employees, customers, and the like.

5.2.4.1 The section 363 sale

This does not mean that secured creditors will necessarily prefer a plan of reorganization as the means of reorganizing the debtor's loans, bonds, and equity. As discussed in Chapter 4, section 363 may offer certain advantages over a plan of reorganization. There are advantages, both in terms of speed of execution and because section 363 implicates the price which bidders are willing to pay in current market conditions over speculative efforts to establish the intrinsic, or fundamental, value of the firm using discounted cashflow methodology. Furthermore, by opting for the section 363 sale transaction, which requires the consent of the secured creditors, but not of unsecured bondholders or the equity holders, the unsecured bondholders and the equity holders have significantly less leverage than they would have had over a corporate reorganization plan. Thus, the secured creditors may set milestones as a condition for the use of cash collateral, or set milestones in the DIP finance documents, which enable them to dictate the form of the transaction, and may push for a section 363 sale transaction where that is the form of transaction which they prefer. This gives rise to the concern that unsecured creditors lose the advocacy of the debtor, and may not recover as much as they would have done in a plan of reorganization implicating a discounted cashflow (DCF) valuation.

However, even for progressive scholars, this does not raise the same concerns for secured creditor control where the unsecured creditor constituency is a class of subordinated, unsecured bondholders, mezzanine lenders, or equity holders in a complex, leveraged capital structure. In Chapters 3 and 4 it was suggested that, in this case, corporate reorganization law should be more concerned with reduction of transaction costs and hold-out power than with unsecured creditor protection, given that the compromised creditors are informed, strongly adjusting financial creditors. This argument holds where the consequence of secured creditor control is to prefer a form of transaction to deleverage the capital structure with lower transaction costs, even if it results in a potentially lower allocation of value to unsecured junior bondholders or mezzanine lenders than a Chapter 11 plan of reorganization. And the argument has already been made, in Chapters 3 and 4, in favour of simplifying the approach to valuation in Chapter 11 in a reorganization of loan, bond, and equity finance, in order to reduce the socially wasteful transaction costs associated with more complex valuation fights. Of course, progressive scholars may continue to be concerned if the selection of the sale transaction results in a lower allocation of value to general, unsecured creditors and employees than would be the case in a plan of reorganization. However, the argument is made that they ought not to be concerned if the selection of the sale transaction results in rapid, low-cost deleveraging of the capital structure; it only impacts junior unsecured lenders, bondholders, and equity who took the risk and reward of that complex, leveraged capital structure; and it reduces the risk that distress in the financial arrangements will spread to the business and operations of the firm. Once again, it is essential to take care to avoid extending existing theory uncritically to new fact patterns. And, once again, the first step is to replace general concepts which have become associated with specific theoretical concerns and commitments (in this chapter, secured creditor control) with a more specific description of the relevant facts (senior, secured creditor control of a deleveraging of a complex, leveraged capital structure).

5.2.4.2 Chapter 11 plan of reorganization

To this end, the suggestion that a Chapter 11 plan of reorganization and a section 363 sale can be functionally equivalent methods of implementing a reorganization requires a little more unpacking, in the context of secured creditor control. As the account in the book so far has shown, where the finance market considers that a debtor's problem is the wrong capital structure, the transaction may implicate a debt-for-equity exchange, and thus a change of control transaction. It is also likely that debt will trade in the distressed debt market in anticipation of this transaction. One possibility is that, after the debt has traded into the hands of those who support the transaction, a reorganization will be negotiated and confirmed in Chapter 11, pursuant to which the debt will be swapped for equity in the debtor by the parties who traded into the debt (a strategy known as 'loan-to-own'). Alternatively, it is possible that, rather than trade into the debt, the new investor will bid for the debtor group's business and assets in a section 363 sale, either alone or in combination with post-petition secured creditors, and will become the new equity owner of the business via the sale transaction. And it is also possible that the fulcrum security holders, some of whom may have traded in after the financial distress became apparent, will purchase the debtor company's assets as the equity owners of the new bidding vehicle in a section 363 sale, in consideration for a release of their debt claims against the seller in a process known as credit bidding. The crucial point is that, in each case, while the transaction results in a change of control via the debt-for-equity swap, if the transaction arises out of the need to deleverage the loan, bond, and equity capital structure, it is possible for general, unsecured trade creditors and employees to be kept whole, whichever form of transaction is selected.[27] Thus, the only parties affected by the form of the transaction are financial creditors and investors. Each of the transactions deleverages the capital structure, and the result of the deleveraging is, in each case, a change of control. It is possible that junior unsecured lenders and bondholders may receive a lower allocation of reorganization consideration in a section 363 sale based on market price than in a plan of reorganization based on market value calculated by an expert valuer using discounted cashflow methodology. Yet, the argument has already been made in favour of a market price approach in any reorganization of the debt and equity financing provided by sophisticated financial institutions, even where a plan of reorganization is used to implement the transaction. If this recommendation were to be adopted, one of the remaining differences between the forms of transaction would be eliminated, and they would frequently be genuine equivalents.

[27] See eg Brad B Erens and Timothy W Hoffmann, 'The Triumph of the Trade Creditor in Chapter 11 Reorganizations' (2013) 9(1) Pratt's J Bankr L 3, 17–30; David A Skeel Jr and George Triantis, 'Bankruptcy's Uneasy Shift to a Contract Paradigm' (2018) 166 U Pa L Rev 1777, 1779; Jackson (n 2) 1878.

Moreover, as noted briefly in Chapter 3, there is interesting emerging work in the finance literature which suggests that section 363 sale transactions may dominate when credit conditions are tight.[28] Stuart Gilson, Edith Hotchkiss, and Matthew Osborn tentatively suggest that this is because it will be cheaper for the acquirer to obtain acquisition finance in tight credit markets than for a reorganizing debtor to obtain exit financing. They do not find that the selection of the section 363 sale is associated with inefficient liquidation because they find a high incidence of going concern sales, and they do not find returns to junior creditors to be lower than in a plan of reorganization.[29] Their account also illustrates the potential risks for financial creditors attempting to mobilize the section 363 sale to achieve a reorganization of financial liabilities via credit bidding, as rival bidders may emerge during the auction process. Indeed, they suggest that a reorganization of debt and equity provided by financial institutions is still more likely to be concluded using a plan of reorganization than via a section 363 sale transaction. Thus, the section 363 sale transaction is selected at times when it may not be possible to deleverage in other ways, and is replaced by the less risky Chapter 11 plan of reorganization when credit markets improve.

Emerging empirical evidence appears to support Gilson, Hotchkiss, and Osborn's analysis of the factors driving selection of the 363 sale transaction. The high point of the ratio of section 363 sales to all Chapter 11 cases came immediately after the Great Recession in 2008, when credit conditions were exceptionally tight,[30] while, in their review of bankruptcy in 2018, Jones Day noted:

> Twenty-five public and private companies with assets valued at more than $1 billion obtained confirmation of chapter 11 plans or exited from bankruptcy in 2018. Continuing a trend begun in 2012, many more of these companies (19) reorganized than were liquidated or sold.[31]

In other words, the choice of a section 363 sale versus a plan of reorganization does appear to be counter-cyclical.[32] Despite some comment in the literature at the start of the twenty-first century that section 363 sales would render corporate reorganizations obsolete, that does not seem to have come to pass.[33]

[28] Stuart Gilson, Edith Hotchkiss, and Matthew Osborn, 'Cashing Out: The Rise of M&A in Bankruptcy' (*SSRN*, 9 May 2019) <https://ssrn.com/abstract=2547168> accessed 6 March 2020.

[29] For an alternative view, see Lynn M LoPucki and Joseph W Doherty, 'Bankruptcy Fire Sales' (2007) 106 Mich L Rev 1, 3–4, 10.

[30] Jared A Wilkerson, 'Defending the Current State of Section 363 Sales' (2012) 86 Am Bankr LJ 591, 600.

[31] Jones Day, 'The Year in Bankruptcy: 2018' (February 2019) <www.jonesday.com/en/insights/2019/02/the-year-in-bankruptcy-2018> accessed 24 July 2020.

[32] Wilkerson (n 30) n 45 and accompanying text.

[33] Douglas G Baird and Robert K Rasmussen, 'The End of Bankruptcy' (2002) 55 Stanford L Rev 751, 751–52.

5.2.5 Summary of the argument in section 5.2

It is suggested that it is relevant for the common ground between an economic analysis and a progressive analysis that the unsecured creditors who receive a potentially lower allocation of value in the market-based section 363 sale are sophisticated, risk-adjusting investment professionals. It has already been noted that a transaction to sell all of the debtor group's business and assets to senior secured creditors may not implicate any loss for general, unsecured creditors. There is evidence in the literature that in some cases the senior secured creditors may use the section 363 process to assume and pay the debts of some general, unsecured creditors while leaving others behind.[34] This may raise traditional, progressive concerns for maximizing returns for weakly adjusting creditors who lack voice in the process, and the selection of a sales transaction versus a corporate reorganization. In other words, the claim here is that both scholars adopting an economic approach and scholars adopting a progressive approach should be able to agree on moving towards a market price approach in valuation for the flexing of a complex, leveraged capital structure, and should not worry too much if the transaction is implemented using section 363 or a confirmed plan of reorganization. Yet, arguably, different normative concerns arise where weakly adjusting, general, unsecured creditors are implicated and, in this case, the traditional debate between law and economics scholars and progressive scholars about the consequences of a more market-orientated approach continues to apply. Once again, the purpose of this book is not to shut down the corporate reorganization law debate. Rather, the book argues that the distance between the two camps is narrower where the reorganization implicates only sophisticated, strongly adjusting financial creditors and investors; it emphasizes the need to be specific about the ways in which the corporate reorganization case is described; and it demands careful focus on the implications of the detail of the case for the concepts of corporate reorganization law.

5.3 England

5.3.1 Why concern for secured creditor control assumed less significance in England

Whereas the blanket lien has only appeared as a serious force in reorganization in the US in recent times, it has been a central feature of the English finance market since the end of the nineteenth century. In 1870, the English Court of Appeal determined that, where a company charged its 'undertaking and all sums of money

[34] Bussel and Klee (n 24) 731.

arising therefrom', the word 'undertaking' captured all present and future property of the company,[35] effectively recognizing the ability of the secured creditor to bring all of the property and assets of the company within the scope of the security package. A conceptual problem remained with a fixed charge over the company's undertaking because the chargee's consent was required for any disposals (so that a charge over the undertaking would effectively paralyse the business). Transactional lawyers dealt with this issue by including an express right, in the finance documents, for the company to deal with the charged assets in the ordinary course of business until default, winding up, or cessation of business where the charge was over all of the company's undertaking, present and future. In due course, the courts began to imply this term into such all-encompassing charges and they gradually became known as 'floating charges'.[36] In 1906, the Loreburn Committee considered, but ultimately did not recommend, abolition of the floating charge.[37] Thus, by the end of the nineteenth century, the ability of a lender to take security over all, or substantially all, of the assets of an English company with comparative ease was well established.

This environment of full security was a critical part of the development of English restructuring law and practice. As discussed in previous chapters, from the 1980s onwards, large, listed public corporates in England typically raised debt finance by borrowing from a syndicate of banks. Most of these large, listed public company borrowers were able to borrow on unsecured terms. Secured debt theory suggests that this is because public corporations already publish a significant amount of information about their business, so that the monitoring benefits of security are less important, and because the costs of negotiating security outweigh its benefits for a large corporate with good cashflows.[38] Nonetheless, where a large, publicly traded corporation faced financial distress it was often required to provide security as a condition of further advances. Thus, it was not unusual for a large corporate in restructuring negotiations to encumber all of its business and assets in favour of its bank creditors.[39]

As Chapter 2 briefly noted, in 1982, the report of the Cork Committee recommended various reforms to English corporate bankruptcy law. Following the Committee's recommendations, in 1985–86, a new procedure of administration was introduced. However, this was primarily to deal with the (rare) situation where there was no creditor with a floating charge willing to appoint a receiver. Indeed, in many ways it was modelled on the existing secured creditor receivership remedy.

[35] *Re Panama New Zealand and Australian Royal Mail Co* (1869–70) LR 5 Ch App 318.

[36] For a more complete account of the history see Paterson (n 6) 249–50. See also John Armour, 'The Chequered History of the Floating Charge' (2004) 13 Griffith L Rev 25.

[37] *Report of the Company Law Amendment* Committee (Cm 3052, 1906).

[38] Gerard McCormack, 'The Priority of Secured Credit: An Anglo-American Perspective' (2003) JBL 389, 403–04.

[39] J R Lingard, *Corporate Rescues and Insolvencies* (2nd edn, Butterworths 1989) 49.

The committee to investigate reform was headed by Kenneth Cork, probably the leading insolvency practitioner of his day, who enjoyed a close, professional relationship with many of Britain's large clearing banks. It is, therefore, perhaps unsurprising that the broad boundaries of secured creditor control which already existed were largely preserved in the new system. There was some concern that banks were providing limited new money in restructuring negotiations, taking full security over all of the assets of the debtor company, and subsequently placing the debtor company into insolvency proceedings with an improved position compared with other creditors. The 1985–86 reforms sought to address this issue, first, by providing the ability to disqualify directors who were found to be unfit, and, secondly, by making directors potentially personally liable for debts incurred in trading if they ought to have concluded that there was no reasonable prospect of avoiding insolvent liquidation.[40] As a result, the thought was that directors would need to be satisfied that any new, secured financing was sufficient to rescue the company and not simply 'a marginal increase in facilities' by which the bank's security 'is materially improved'.[41]

Notwithstanding this concern in the literature about the motives of the banks in granting rescue facilities, and periodic Government and public concern that banks were mobilizing England's corporate bankruptcy law tools to achieve a rapid enforcement of secured debt, there was little solid empirical evidence and little scholarly discontent with the overall approach, particularly in the large corporate arena.[42] Early pioneers of English corporate bankruptcy scholarship included Professor Roy Goode, Professor Ian Fletcher, and the leading Queens' Counsel, Gabriel Moss. One does not discern, from this scholarship, a widespread concern for secured creditor control of large corporate reorganization. Indeed, there was a great deal of scepticism of the US system, which was seen, as Moss put it, as akin to leaving the alcoholic in charge of the pub,[43] and as promoting wildly anti-competitive effects. Raymond Nimmer and Richard Feinberg have argued that the policy choices in Chapter 11 reflect a belief that the underlying causes of financial distress are '... circumstantial and reflect conditions not ineptly created by management'.[44] Yet, writing in 1988, Kenneth Cork noted, 'Sheer incompetence at board level was the basis of almost every failure.'[45] Moreover, writing about the innovation of the new administration process, he stated:

[40] The Company Directors Disqualification Act 1986 and the Insolvency Act 1986, s 214. For a discussion, see Lingard (n 39) 49.

[41] Lingard (n 39) 39.

[42] For the strongest defence, see John Armour and Sandra Frisby, 'Rethinking Receivership' (2001) 21(1) Oxf J Legal Stud 73.

[43] Gabriel Moss, 'Chapter 11: An English Lawyer's Critique' (1998) 11 Insolv Intell 17.

[44] Raymond T Nimmer and Richard B Feinberg, 'Chapter 11 Business Governance: Fiduciary Duties, Business Judgment, Trustees and Exclusivity' (1989) 6 Bankr Dev J 1, 24.

[45] Kenneth Cork, *Cork on Cork* (Macmillan 1988) 38.

> ... an administrator should be brought in *before* a company was declared insolvent, where for instance the directors were obviously incompetent or dishonest and the ordinary processes could not remove them; or where in the national interest the Government should take a hand, as happened in the case of Rolls-Royce, without going through the trauma of bankruptcy.[46]

In other words, Cork firmly conceived of resort to legal process as reserved for cases where trust had been lost in the directors, or government finance was needed. It is worth recalling that, at this stage, Chapter 11 was embroiled in many controversies in the US. Overall, the English academy appears to have been relatively content with the balance of power in the English system of large corporate reorganization.

Major rebalancing of secured creditor control rights could have emerged in the reform efforts of 2002. These were explicitly motivated by the visit of the then Secretary of State for Trade and Industry, Peter Mandelson, to Silicon Valley, and by the US system which Mandelson was exposed to on the visit.[47] Specifically, Mandelson appears to have been impressed by the tools of Chapter 11 which could protect the business while it was working out a plan of reorganization.[48] However, in the event, the reforms did very little to shift the balance of power away from secured creditors. Although the creditor-friendly administrative receivership procedure was largely abolished, English corporate bankruptcy law remained management-displacing, and the banks successfully lobbied for secured creditor control over the identity of the insolvency practitioner. English corporate bankruptcy law remained a tool for secured creditors to enforce against the business and assets when corporate reorganization efforts had failed.

There was significant academic analysis of why the reforms had failed to achieve a genuine shift of control rights away from secured creditors, with scholars divided over the result.[49] However, the battleground, in the English debate, was really whether secured creditors had sufficient incentives to achieve a going concern rescue of the business as opposed to a break-up sale of the assets, if the debtor was placed into corporate bankruptcy proceedings. The debate focused less on whether incentives were sufficiently tilted towards corporate reorganization. Banks remained the dominant financiers of large corporate Britain and although, with the benefit of hindsight, the days of out-of-court reorganization of large corporates

[46] ibid 195.

[47] 'Silicone Ballyhoo' *The Economist* (7 November 1998)349(8093) 36; Gerard McCormack, 'Control and Corporate Rescue—An Anglo-American Evaluation' (2007) 56(3) Int'l Comp LQ 515, 524.

[48] For the consultations leading to the reforms, see The Insolvency Service, *A Review of Company Rescue and Business Reconstruction Mechanisms* (HMSO 1999); The Insolvency Service, *A Review of Company Rescue and Business Reconstruction Mechanisms: Report by the Review Group* (HMSO 2000); The Insolvency Service, *Productivity and Enterprise Insolvency—A Second Chance*, Cm 5234 (HMSO 2000).

[49] See eg Sandra Frisby, 'In Search of a Rescue Regime: The Enterprise Act 2002' (2004) 67 Mod L Rev 247, 248; cf Riz Mokal, 'Administration and Administrative Receivership—An Analysis' (2004) 57 CLP 349.

were numbered, by and large it still worked relatively effectively at the time. Indeed, Peter Miller and Michael Power, writing in 1995, described the field as, 'the legally created market for insolvency administration and the extra-legal market for corporate rescue'.[50] To the extent that banks did resort to a corporate bankruptcy procedure, in most large corporate cases they sought to sell the business as a going concern, saving jobs and keeping much of the operations intact. Thus, no immediate problem of social cost emerged for scholars of a more progressive leaning. This resulted in some bemusement, until the 2000s, with the emphasis US scholars put on reorganizing the company, as opposed to saving the business. The reason for rehearsing this history here is because it is critical to understand that, when English lawyers and market participants needed to start to craft legal tools to facilitate these reorganizations, they were not constrained, when looked at in the round, by particular conceptions of secured creditor control. The English system had been based on a combination of highly pragmatic market incentives: for the debtor to restructure; for the creditor to retain its relationship with the debtor and to try to recover its money over the long run; and for both the debtor and the creditor to maintain their public reputations. The English corporate bankruptcy system is often described as secured creditor-friendly, but this is to look at only one part of what was a complex overall organizational and institutional environment.

5.3.2 The rise of secured capital structures in England

As previous chapters have already explored, complex, leveraged capital structures have emerged in large private and public companies as a result of a number of factors. These include the development of mechanisms to enable loan participations to trade effectively; access by English borrowers to high-yield markets; growing corporate bond markets; and increasing leverage. Unsurprisingly, in a culture of full security, it is significantly more likely in England that all of the loans and bonds in a complex, leveraged capital structure will benefit from a security package over all, or substantially all, of the borrower's business and assets. Most commonly, a security trustee holds the benefit of the security for all of the lenders and bondholders. The security will comprise a fixed and floating charge over the debtor's assets, together with a comprehensive guarantee and security package from the operating companies. In a complex, leveraged capital structure, detailed ranking of the loan and debt instruments will need to be worked out. The most senior loans or bonds will rank first on insolvency (and thus command the lowest interest rate as the most secure financing) and junior instruments will rank in successively

[50] Peter Miller and Michael Power, 'Calculating Corporate Failure' in Yves Dezalay and David Sugarman (eds) *Professional Competition and Professional Power: Lawyers, Accountants and the Social Construction of Markets* (Routledge 1995) 56.

more subordinated positions. Merely addressing ranking is not, however, sufficient where an incidence of security is powerful enforcement rights. It is also necessary to determine which lenders and bondholders will have the ability to exercise the enforcement rights associated with the security, and how those rights will be regulated between the parties. In England, this balance of power is worked out in the intercreditor agreement.

5.3.3 Secured capital structures and English corporate reorganization law

The intercreditor agreement has little role to play in a scheme of arrangement implementing a largely consensual deal voted on by the requisite majority of creditors in each class—the classic renegotiation of the loan, bond, and equity finance arrangements which is at the heart of this book. This is because, from the nineteenth century onwards, the English courts have been content that a scheme of arrangement could discharge a dissenting creditor's security interest. This conclusion is based both on legislative mandate and on the the fact that the creditor has invested with a number of other creditors in the company's debt and thus can be bound by the will of the majority.[51] As a result, in a classic consensual scheme of arrangement, no particularly difficult issues arise as a result of security interests. Similarly, where the restructuring agreement is agreed consensually, and implemented solely in contract, the parties can agree, as part of the contractual arrangements, the mechanisms for security release. However, as discussed in Chapters 3 and 4, to date it has not been possible in English law for a court to impose a scheme of arrangement on a dissenting class of creditor.[52] As a result, the workaround described in Chapters 3 and 4 has been developed, in which the finance company borrower is placed into administration and its assets (the shares in the parent of the operating group) are sold to a new company owned and capitalized by those creditors receiving an allocation in the new capital structure. The idea is to strand the dissenting class (either or both of the junior debt holders and the equity) in the old finance holding company which is now an empty shell. However, in order for this to be effective, it is obviously crucial that the participating creditors are able to initiate the transaction, and that the guarantee and security interests which the stranded creditors have against the operating companies can no longer be enforced.

[51] *Potteries, Shrewsbury, and North Wales Ry Co v Minor* (1870–71) L R 6 Ch App 621; *Re Dynevor Dyffryn and Neath Abbey Colleries* (1879) 11 Ch D 605; *Re Empire Mining* (1890) 44 Ch D 402; *Re Alabama, New Orleans, Texas and Pacific Junction Ry* [1891] 1 Ch 213.

[52] As discussed in Chapters 3 and 4, the Corporate Insolvency and Governance Bill, which has been introduced just as this book is going to press, inserts a new Part 26A into the Companies Act 2006, closely modelled on the scheme of arrangement but with a cross-class cram-down power: Corporate Insolvency and Governance Bill [HC] 2019–21, Sch 9, inserting new Part 26A into Companies Act 2006.

A pre-packaged administration sale of the shares which the finance holding company holds in the operating parent would not achieve this result. Given the argument in this book that the ability to flex the capital structure in times of stress has been crucial in supporting other developments in debt finance designed to magnify returns, the ability to tackle this issue has been of some importance.

5.3.4 The concept of contractual senior secured contingent control rights emerges in England

The account in the book has already revealed that the forces which drove corporate reorganization into court in America in the 1930s, and away from private bargaining, did not occur in England. Indeed, the private bargain has been of crucial importance throughout the history of financial restructuring in England. As the account in the book has established, for a significant part of the twentieth century financial restructuring has occurred entirely as a matter of private negotiation. When the scheme of arrangement was developed at the end of the nineteenth century, it was very much a mechanism for enforcement of the majority deal. It is perhaps, therefore, not surprising that participants in the City of London turned to the debt documents to address the issue of enforcement rights and release of security. When multi-tranche capital structures first emerged in the early wave of leveraged buyouts, senior, secured lenders wanted to know that they would not be prevented from pursuing an enforcement by junior, secured creditors who would not make a return on a sale, and who would therefore wish to hold on for another day, in the hope of improving value by refusing to release the guarantees and security granted to them by the operating companies. The concern is similar to the concern with the operation of Chapter 11 in the 1980s: that the senior creditors would be held at bay so that, by the time they were able to enforce, value would have dripped away and they would make a reduced return compared with the return they would have made on an expeditious enforcement. Yet, in the English context, the focus was explicitly on the incentives of the junior financial creditors to hold up the deal, rather than concern for secured creditor liquidation bias. As a result, the early intercreditor agreements contained provisions providing senior creditors with the ability to control initial decisions on enforcement after default, and to instruct the security trustee to release guarantees and security granted to junior creditors on an enforcement sale.

As is common with new technology in contracts, the early clauses facilitating senior secured creditor control of enforcement action contained what appeared to be a significant drafting error. In order to understand this, it is necessary to start with a brief reminder of the structure of a buyout transaction, which was described in Chapter 3. A buyout transaction is usually structured by one or two finance companies holding shares in a holding company for the operating group, with a chain of operating subsidiaries beneath it. Ordinarily, all of the material group operating companies guarantee the leveraged buyout financing, and grant security over their business and assets for the guarantee obligations. Security enforcement can take the form of appointment of an administrator in one of the finance holding companies, and the sale of the shares in the parent company for the operating group, so that all of the operating group companies arrive in the ownership of the bidding company. At this point, it is necessary to release the guarantees and security provided by all of the operating group companies in favour of the junior financial creditors. The earliest versions of the intercreditor agreement for leveraged loans did provide the senior secured creditors with an exclusive period in which they were able to instruct the security trustee to release guarantees and security on an enforcement sale. Yet, at the same time, the drafting also seemed to limit the release authority of the security trustee to the guarantees and security granted by the company whose shares were transferred, and not the guarantees and security granted by the rest of the operating companies below it.

This obviously provided a powerful impediment to a sale transaction as a method of dealing with a dissenting class of creditor in a reorganization of the debtor's loan, bond, and equity financing. The ability effectively to impose a plan on a dissenting class is important not just to enable implementation of the transaction, but also as a credible contingency plan to encourage bargaining. And the ability to impose such a transaction, given the terms of the intercreditor agreement, was challenged by a group of lenders in an early flexing of the capital structure of a leveraged buyout transaction after the 2008 financial crisis. At first instance, Mrs Justice Proudman considered that the clause was unambiguous and should be construed in accordance with its terms, so that it was only possible for the security trustee to release the guarantees and security granted by the immediate company in the sale chain.[53] This handed considerable hold-out power to junior financial creditors to negotiate for a return in the transaction, on the basis that a reorganization among the financial creditors could not be implemented without their consent. Unsurprisingly, given the crucial nature of the decision, not just for the case in question but for other cases where the debt documents used the same contractual drafting, the case was appealed.

The Court of Appeal adopted a pragmatic and commercial approach, and construed the clause as permitting the release of guarantees and security granted by all the operating group companies.[54] The English courts have traditionally paid high regard to bargains struck between well-advised, sophisticated, financial creditors. Indeed, they have referred, in numerous cases since the financial crisis, to their reluctance to interfere in such bargains.[55] At the same time, in

[53] *HHY Luxembourg Sarl v Barclays Bank Plc* [2010] EWHC 2406 (Ch); [2010] 9 WLUK 401.

[54] *HHY Luxembourg Sarl v Barclays Bank Plc* [2010] EWCA Civ 1248; [2010] 10 WLUK 543.

[55] For just one example, see *Belmont Park Investments Pty Ltd v BNY Corporate Trustee Services Ltd & Anor* [2011] UKSC 38; [2012] 1 AC 383 [79].

the case of schemes of arrangement twinned with pre-packaged administration sales, they are acting against the backdrop of relatively thin statutory provisions when compared with their US bankruptcy judge peers. Thus, there is less argument in England that the intercreditor agreement is interfering with mandatory provisions of the legislative regime. English judges have met the development of intercreditor technology in a decade of reorganizations implicating only sophisticated financial creditors, unbounded by a history of the court-implemented financial and operational restructurings common in the US in the 1980s and early 1990s. As a result, not only have they seen little reason to interfere with the terms of the intercreditor agreement which financial creditors have agreed, but they have also actively supported the development of intercreditor technology with a highly pragmatic, and what might be called following John Adams and Roger Brownsword, a realistic approach.[56]

It is a principle of contractual interpretation in English law that, where a clause has an unambiguous meaning, it should be given effect in accordance with its terms. Commercial sense is only brought into account where a clause is capable of more than one interpretation.[57] And Mrs Justice Proudman had considered the scope of the release clause to be unambiguous. Yet, the Court of Appeal showed itself alive to the real intent behind the contractual provision. They combined a realistic approach to interpreting the clause, with a strong instinct to uphold the fundamental bargain which they considered the financial creditors had made, in order to facilitate the deleveraging transaction. A similar conceptual framework is apparent in the first instance decision of Mr Justice Eder in the *Stabilus* case, in which he supported distribution of equity through the proceeds waterfall in the intercreditor agreement.[58] Thus, a conceptual framework of upholding what the courts see to be the realistic objective of the intercreditor agreement, heavily orientated toward constraining junior financial creditor hold-out power, played a vital role in the development of corporate reorganization law in England since 2008. As discussed in earlier chapters, in the era of the London Approach incomplete contracting had not posed any particular problems, because the London Approach itself facilitated the privately negotiated contractual bargain. The intercreditor agreement now provides a privately negotiated governance structure for facilitating the transaction, following the London Approach's demise. Since its establishment

[56] John N Adams and Roger Brownsword, 'The Ideologies of Contract' (1987) 7(2) J Legal Stud 205.

[57] *Rainy Sky SA v Kookmin Bank* [2011] UKSC 50; [2011] 1 WLR 2900.

[58] *Saltri III Ltd v MD Mezzanine SA SICAR (t/a Mezzanine Facility Agent)* [2012] EWHC 3025 (Comm); [2013] 1 All ER (Comm) 661. For an analysis of the 'fundamental importance' of this to the English restructuring market in 'effectively dispelling the notion that has been made historically by certain practitioners and Queen's Counsel that there is a presumption under English law that secured assets will be sold, on enforcement, for cash consideration unless the documents provide otherwise', see Chris Howard and Bob Hedger, *Restructuring Law and Practice* (2nd edn, LexisNexis 2014) 463 paras 7.65–7.66.

in 1996, the Loan Market Association (LMA) has developed a suite of finance documents to act as the starting point in leveraged loan negotiations. Unsurprisingly, the release mechanisms in the LMA intercreditor agreement clearly contemplate all operating subsidiaries in the group.

The allocation of control rights in the intercreditor agreement negotiated between the parties has not been without controversy in England, with concerns that the LMA has adopted a firmly pro-senior creditor stance which reduces the prospects for junior creditors to achieve a 'fairer' deal.[59] Indeed, the LMA is rooted in the original clearing bank structure of the English market. And the English market continues to have a more pro-senior creditor (historically clearing bank) cast as a result of its organizational and institutional history. Thus, the assignment of control rights based on current market value of the firm provides less bargaining power for the junior creditors than they typically have in a Chapter 11 valuation fight. This influences not only how reorganization consideration will be allocated between the parties, but also the scope for the junior creditors to renegotiate for any return at all. Moreover, where a marketing process is carried out to establish the market value of the firm, the contract may be relatively complete (because it will be difficult to dispute that the point specified in the contract on which control rights are to pass has been reached). As a result, the contractual mechanism reduces the scope for the parties to work from what Hart and Moore call different 'reference points' in order to defend different views on what each is entitled to.[60] In other words, it provides a conceptually different bargaining environment from that prevailing in Chapter 11 in the US. Yet, there is little concrete evidence that this has held back the leveraged loan and debt capital markets in England. Moreover, the approach is consistent with work on optimal financial contracting, given that the junior creditors allocate control rights to the senior creditors when the current market value of the company is low and where the junior creditors otherwise have an incentive to hold up renegotiation.[61] Thus far, the argument has been made that this reduces transaction costs and increases the prospects of a rapid deleveraging, improving the bargaining environment for scholars adopting an economic analysis and reducing the social cost associated with more complex reorganizations or enforcement transactions for those sympathetic to a more progressive orientation. Thus, it is suggested that scholars of all stripes should support the approach adopted by the LMA intercreditor agreement, and the approach of the English courts towards it.

59 Jennifer Tang, 'A Confused Industry' (2010) 29 Int'l Fin L Rev 20.

60 Oliver Hart and John Moore, 'Contracts as Reference Points' (2008) 123(1) Q J Econ 1. .

61 Philippe Aghion and Patrick Bolton, 'An Incomplete Contracts Approach to Financial Contracting' (1992) 59(3) Rev Econ Stud 473; Hans B Christensen, Valeri V Nikolaev, and Regina Wittenberg-Moerman, 'Accounting Information in Financial Contracting: The Incomplete Contract Theory Perspective' (2016) 54(2) J Account Res 397, 407.

5.3.5 Summary of the argument in section 5.3

Thus, the courts have played a vital role, specifically in a permissive and pragmatic reading of the enforcement and guarantee and security release mechanisms, and generally in upholding the terms of the intercreditor agreement, in constituting an environment in which relatively low-cost and speedy reorganizations of the capital structure of leveraged borrowers can occur. The English courts appear to have acknowledged the need to uphold the enforcement sale as a method of imposing the reorganization on an entire class of secured credit, where the scale of financial distress does not leave room for some consideration to be allocated to each class of financial creditor. The drafting of the LMA's intercreditor agreement has now been clarified to resolve any ambiguity in favour of implementation of a new capital structure through the enforcement sale. Once again, in the absence of legislative time spent on the question of reform in a different organizational and institutional environment, participants have worked to adapt existing tools to achieve new objectives and the court has, where necessary, supported market innovation and private bargaining by adopting and endorsing those adaptations. Crucially, because English corporate reorganization has historically been significantly more likely to implicate a fully secured capital structure, and because assets are not transferred free of guarantee and security interests in an enforcement sale, an intercreditor agreement is put in place with detailed allocation of control rights in distress between senior financial creditors and junior financial creditors. This deference to the financial documents has once again enabled an approach to develop which is well adapted to the specific challenges of reorganizing a complex, leveraged capital structure.

It is a central argument of this book that private bargaining *ex ante* to regulate the flexing of a leveraged capital structure if it becomes unsustainable between sophisticated financial creditors raises different normative concerns from a reorganization which implicates trade, contract, and other liabilities. This is because the financial creditors know that the risk of the high-reward strategy of increasing leverage is an increased risk of financial distress, and that in order to support the leveraged capital structure and to maintain liquidity in the debt to avoid financial distress leading to operational distress, it may become necessary to adapt the capital structure in the future. Thus, the issues associated with sophisticated secured financial creditors imposing loss on general, unsecured creditors do not arise. Given that the financial creditors are aware of the risk of the leveraged capital structure *ex ante*, they have incentives to impose a contractual mechanism for the renegotiation in order to reduce transaction costs. However, while the structural framework for renegotiation can be negotiated in advance, sophisticated financial creditors also recognize that the precise economic structure of the deal cannot be worked out until the transaction is implemented. At this stage, the numbers involved are of such significance (and to some extent subjective interpretation) that the detailed implementation of the deleveraging transaction, if it is ever required, is likely to be highly contestable and contested. This makes it impractical to ask the security trustee, which is not a particularly highly remunerated party, to take on the litigation risk involved in implementing a fully worked-out contractual framework without the help of the court. Thus, the court takes on an essential role as enforcer and enabler of the renegotiation mechanism which the parties have worked out in advance. In other words, the parties mobilize the courts to oversee the implementation of the contractual mechanism. This does not raise significant concerns for senior, secured creditor control where only sophisticated financial institutions are involved who either negotiated the transaction, or who bought into it and who priced the deal accordingly (although the court will want to guard against out-and-out collusive and abusive behaviour in order to maintain the integrity of the debt capital and loan markets).

On the other hand, the ability to control the timing and choice of enforcement options, and to release guarantees and security granted in favour of a class of creditor, and thus to impose a new capital structure against the wishes of a dissenting class, provides a vital tool in supporting the ability to adapt the capital structure. This book has consistently argued that such a mechanism is essential to support the growth of leveraged debt financing and the rest of the institutional environment which surrounds it. Once again, there has not been a modern tradition of using corporate reorganization law to facilitate a full financial and operational reorganization of a large corporate in England (although, as Chapter 9 will explore and as already foreshadowed, this may yet change over the next decade). Thus, when participants in the English process started to mobilize corporate reorganization law to facilitate a reorganization of complex loan, bond, and equity capital structures, they were not bounded by particular concerns for the balance of power between the debtor and secured creditors as a way of protecting general, unsecured creditors. Indeed, it was clear to them that the battleground was between senior financial creditors and junior financial creditors and equity. Equally, it became readily apparent that the real risk in implementing the transaction in a timely and cost-efficient manner was junior financial creditor hold-out power. And finally, the English corporate reorganization law statutes are comparatively thin, leaving participants ample ability to adapt them through privately bargained contracts, while the English courts have a long tradition of upholding bargains between well-advised, sophisticated financial creditors. As a result, the intercreditor agreement has been able to develop as a highly effective method of allocating contingent control rights on distress.

5.4 Conclusion

Chapter 11 has traditionally been concerned to hold secured creditor power in check, out of fear that a secured creditor will prefer a rapid enforcement sale which is in its own interests, but which does not maximize value for other, unsecured creditors, shareholders, and stakeholders. This chapter has identified that, for much of the twentieth century, it has been difficult for a creditor to take security over all, or substantially all, of a debtor's assets in the US. This meant that, if the debtor faced financial difficulties and filed for Chapter 11 protection, it usually had significant unencumbered assets, including cash, which it could use to fund the case. Moreover, it was likely to have other assets which it could pledge as collateral for so-called debtor-in-possession financing to finance the case. The logic in providing debtor-in-possession financing was usually the high rate of interest which could be charged for what was relatively safe, secured financing. In an ideal situation, the debtor-in-possession financier would hope that the very existence of a new, standby loan facility would provide confidence to trade suppliers and others dealing with the company, resulting in improvements in the trading terms which suppliers were prepared to offer, which in turn improved the debtor's cashflow. As a result, in many cases the standby debtor-in-possession facility was not actually drawn down.

Increasing tolerance for higher leverage ratios, and increasing focus on loan debt as a tradeable instrument, led to increasing pressure for reform to make it more straightforward to take and perfect security over the full range of a debtor's assets. Ultimately, this resulted in significant reform to US secured transactions law in 2001, so that it is now much more likely that a debtor entering Chapter 11 will have fully encumbered all of its assets. This has had a number of consequences for corporate reorganization law and practice. It is more likely that a secured creditor will have security over the debtor's receivables, and will be able to make demands about the course of the corporate reorganization case in return for the debtor's use of cash collateral in trading the business. It is also more likely that the only providers of debtor-in-possession financing will be the existing creditors. There are two main incentives for existing creditors to provide this funding, other than ensuring that the corporate reorganization transaction can be implemented. First, through roll-up and other techniques the creditors are able to protect the priority position of their pre-filing debt. Secondly, the DIP financing agreement provides a further mechanism for setting out control rights for the course of the case. Both of these incentives have led to concern for rising secured creditor control, and the risk that secured creditors will prefer value-destructive enforcement sales. It has been suggested in this chapter that, where a sale is used to implement a transaction which is functionally a reorganization, implicating only sophisticated financial creditors and shareholders, this issue is of less concern, even for progressive scholars. This is particularly the case if the choice of transaction saves costs. And the argument has been advanced that the pattern of reorganizations implemented via a section 363 sale transaction, versus a Chapter 11 plan of reorganization, suggests a search by secured creditors for the form of transaction with lowest costs. It is admitted that a sale transaction may implicate other general, unsecured creditors, and in that case the traditional debate about secured creditor power is more salient. As ever with a fact-sensitive approach, detail matters.

Turning to England, the account in this chapter revealed a much longer history of full security. Against this background, it is unsurprising that fully secured, complex, leveraged capital structures are common in England. However, the concern remains that junior secured creditors will attempt to hold up the capital structure renegotiation in return for a better deal. The chapter explored the ways in which participants in the system have used the intercreditor agreement to design contingent decision-making mechanisms for distress. The chapter identified that these typically allocate significant control rights to senior secured creditors. Yet, the intercreditor agreement also envisages that the court will act, if necessary, as the ultimate arbiter of any dispute over the detailed implementation of the renegotiation machinery. This chapter has revealed that the English courts have been proactive in enforcing senior, secured creditor control rights in the privately negotiated bargain. It has been suggested that this is because they have arrived at financial capital structure reorganization cases unbounded by a history of full financial and operational restructurings pitching secured creditors against general, unsecured creditors. Moreover, it has been emphasized that the English courts have a long tradition of upholding bargains made between sophisticated financial creditors. And, finally, the courts have benefitted from relatively generous legislative boundaries in developing a way forward. Thus, England has dealt effectively with the allocation of control rights between senior and junior financial creditors. As ever, the question will be whether this will fix certain concepts in reorganization in England which may be poorly adapted to new situations implicating both fully or strongly adjusting creditors and non-adjusting, or weakly adjusting, creditors. Once again, this is an issue to which later chapters will return.

6
The Fall of the Lifetime Manager

6.1 Introduction

Thus far, the account in the book has focused on shifts in logics and practices in the finance and non-financial corporate fields, the implications of these shifts in logics and practices for the facts of the corporate reorganization case, and the ways in which participants in the corporate reorganization process mobilize and adapt corporate reorganization law to address them. In this chapter and the chapters which follow it, the focus will be on the implications of shifts in what will loosely be called the logics and identities of the participants in the process for the analysis of certain motivating concepts in corporate reorganization law. This chapter particularly explores shifts in the identities of both the non-financial debtor firms, and of the individuals who manage them, and the significance of these shifts for the concept of debtor control in Chapter 11.

Chapter 5 of the book identified that scholars in the progressive tradition support the concept of debtor control in Chapter 11 cases on the basis that debtor control promotes corporate reorganization over a business or asset sale, which secured creditors might otherwise prefer. It further identified that scholars adopting an economic approach are sceptical of debtor control rights for this purpose, preferring to leave selection between potential transactions to the creditors. Recent significant shifts in logics and practices in the field of secured debt were examined. The argument was made that, once these shifts were unpacked and the ways

Corporate Reorganization Law and Forces of Change. Sarah Paterson, Oxford University Press (2020). © Sarah Paterson.
DOI: 10.1093/oso/9780198860365.001.0001.

in which they interacted with corporate reorganization law analysed, there was reason to suggest that both scholars adopting a broadly economic orientation and scholars adopting a more progressive approach ought to be able to accept increased secured creditor control in cases limited to the claims of sophisticated financial institutions. Consistent with the organizing principle of this book, the crucial step was unpacking the concept of secured creditor control as it applied in the specific example of a reorganization of loan, bond, and equity financing arrangements, rather than extending existing concepts of secured creditor control uncritically to all types of corporate reorganization case.

Progressive scholars also promote allocation of debtor control rights as a means of incentivizing early filing for the corporate reorganization case.[1] This chapter examines the relevance of the concept of debtor control rights to incentivize early filing in light of shifting identities in the field of non-financial corporate debtors. The argument is made that changes in the socially constructed identities of both debtor firms and the individuals who manage them suggest reasons to question the concept of allocating control rights to the debtor as a means of incentivizing early filing. And a query is raised as to whether this formulation of the debtor control rights concept holds in other contexts too.

The argument is made that the debtor control concept is relevant in a different way in a case limited to the loan, bond, and equity financing arrangements. Once negotiations to achieve the reorganization have started, leaving management in day-to-day control of the group avoids signalling distress to general, unsecured creditors, employees, and customers. These groups might otherwise take action, which would increase pressure on the firm and increase the likelihood that financial distress cannot be contained in the debt and equity finance provided by financial institutions. Once again, it is suggested that this analysis holds whether an economic or a progressive approach is adopted. Overall, the crucial step is to avoid using the concept of 'debtor control rights' in a way which necessarily implicates inherited ideas, and without considering how that concept may have changed as a result of changes in the underlying identities of the firms and of the individuals who manage them. Once again, therefore, the purpose of this chapter is to unravel the concept of debtor control rights, and to reformulate it in the specific context of a reorganization limited to debt and equity financing provided by financial institutions.

The account in the book has already revealed that English corporate bankruptcy law did not develop with a commitment to a particular conception of debtor control, or of tipping the balance of a case towards corporate reorganization. Instead, corporate reorganization was a largely out-of-court affair, with legal process

[1] See eg Richard D Thomas, 'Tipping the Scales in Chapter 11: How Distressed Debt Investors Decrease Debtor Leverage and the Efficacy of Business Reorganization' (2010) 27 Emory Bankr Dev J 213, 215.

reserved for cases where reorganization efforts had failed. When this chapter turns to examine England, it reveals that, as a result of shifts in the finance and non-financial corporate fields, participants in the process have mobilized and adapted corporate reorganization law to achieve a reorganization of debt and equity financing arrangements in ways which also take into account the relationship between management displacement and signalling. Yet, they have done this without bringing on board the baggage of other inherited ideas associated with the concept of debtor control rights in the United States (US) literature. Once again, to the extent that there is a concern for English corporate reorganization law, it is whether it promotes a sufficiently adaptable concept of debtor control for cases in which financial distress has spread to the operations of the group. Once again, Chapters 9 and 10 will return to this issue.

6.2 United States

6.2.1 The concept of debtor control rights

A major reason why progressive scholars support debtor control rights is their hope that, by offering debtor management the ability to control the course of the case, management will be incentivized to file for Chapter 11 proactively before distress has deepened and the liquidity issues facing the group are so significant that corporate reorganization becomes impossible.[2] Debtor management is then able to promote a corporate reorganization plan in the interests of all creditors, including weakly adjusting creditors who otherwise lack bargaining power in the process.[3] Thus, the concept of debtor control rights becomes closely associated with the twin ideas of proactive filing and promoting the corporate reorganization case.

This concept of debtor control responds, in turn, to a particular idea of a director or senior manager in a large corporate in the US in the 1970s and 1980s. In his ground-breaking work, Alfred Chandler maps the emergence of bureaucratized management practices in large US corporates in the early twentieth century.[4] He shows how a worker moving up through the ranks of US industry expected to have a job for life with the firm. As a result, managers might be expected to prefer conservative firms with low leverage to secure their jobs and lessen the probability of bankruptcy. This has important implications for the incentives which the architects of the US Bankruptcy Code might have expected, in 1978, to result from debtor

[2] ibid 215; Harvey R Miller, 'Chapter 11 in Transition—From Boom to Bust and into the Future' (2007) 81(4) Am Bankr LJ 375, 386–87.

[3] Thomas (n 1) 225; Raymond T Nimmer and Richard B Feinberg, 'Chapter 11 Business Governance: Fiduciary Duties, Business Judgment, Trustees and Exclusivity' (1989) 6 Bankr Dev J 1, 51.

[4] Alfred D Chandler Jr, *The Visible Hand: The Managerial Revolution in American Business* (new edn, Harvard University Press 1977).

control of the process. The provisions of the Code, which enabled management to keep their jobs through the corporate reorganization process and which handed them the almost exclusive right to design the corporate reorganization plan, interacted with a management team which would have expected to remain employed with the same firm for their entire working lives, remunerated by a good salary and a number of firm-specific perks in the form of a company car, golf, and social club membership. Although it was accepted that the debtor's management was not neutral in the process, it was expected to be the party best placed to promote a corporate reorganization transaction in the interests of all creditors, employees, and customers.

As noted in earlier chapters, this world of the lifetime manager was held up as part of the cause of declining US competitiveness in the changing world of the 1960s and 1970s. The influential work of Berle and Means suggested that the secure US leaders of industry were able to sit comfortably on cashflows with little regard for their ultimate investors.[5] A well-known sociological work of the 1950s blamed the declining fortunes of US industry on the image of the 'other directed' (as opposed to 'inner directed') middle manager, where 'much time in the office is ... spent in sociability: exchanging office gossip ("conferences"), making good-will tours ("inspection"), talking to salesmen and joshing secretaries ("morale")'.[6] In 1976, Jensen and Meckling concentrated on so-called agency costs: the risk that management would indulge in a number of rent-seeking actions.[7] This book has already explored how this ultimately contributed to something of a revolution in attitudes about what a company is for, from the regular employer providing secure work for its workforce to a focus on so-called shareholder value. This, in turn, was used by Milken and the original architects of the leveraged buyouts of the 1980s to defend the somewhat brutal takeover battles as removing companies from sluggish, bureaucratized managers and placing them into the hands of a new breed of owner-managers.

Nonetheless, debtor control remained relevant in corporate reorganization in the US, albeit perhaps not in the ways in which the original architects of the US Bankruptcy Code imagined. Until the 1970s, America's non-rural economy was dominated by large manufacturing and industrial concerns, many of whom had heavily unionized workforces. The account in the book so far has referred, many times, to the fact that, after the boom years of the 1950s and early 1960s, the US faced something of a crisis as inflation rose, hurting profits, and as foreign (notably

[5] Adolf A Berle Jr and Gardiner C Means, *The Modern Corporation and Private Property* (Macmillan 1933).

[6] David Riesman with Nathan Glazer and Reuel Denney, *The Lonely Crowd: A Study of the Changing American Character* (Yale University Press 1961) 126, 136.

[7] Michael C Jensen and William H Meckling, 'Theory of the Firm: Managerial Behavior, Agency Costs and Ownership Structure' (1976) 3(4) J Finan Econ 305.

Japanese) companies began to compete with US industrial giants.[8] Unions fought hard to maintain labour's power and rights in an economic environment fraught with challenges, to the disapproval of politicians in Washington but also, significantly, to the disapproval of much of the public. This emboldened employers in confronting the unions, which had the benefit of powerful collective bargaining rights enshrined in US federal law.[9] The newly minted Chapter 11 appeared to offer a solution to terminating labour agreements without observing the cumbersome collective bargaining agreements for unionized workforces enshrined in labour law. Chapter 11 permitted the debtor to terminate an executory contract whenever termination would further the debtor's reorganization.[10] There is no definition of an executory contract but the so-called Countryman definition is frequently adopted, in which the term 'generally includes contracts in which performance remains due to some extent on both sides'.[11] A collective bargaining agreement appeared to fall squarely within this definition, and US management sought to mobilize and adapt corporate reorganization law as a tool to address costly re-negotiation with labour. As Ronald Mann has compellingly shown,[12] the question arose as to how to balance two competing federal policies enshrined in statute: the federal policy of protecting labour through the specific bargaining procedures in collective bargaining agreements; and the federal policy of enabling a debtor to terminate unprofitable contracts in bankruptcy, in order to reorganize its operations and return to financial health.

As Mann shows, this battle between two competing policies was decisively solved in favour of the corporate reorganization objective in the case of *Bildisco*, where the Supreme Court determined that a collective bargaining agreement was an executory contract for the purposes of the US Bankruptcy Code.[13] As a result, the firm was able to terminate its labour agreements without undergoing the costly bargaining process otherwise required. Clearly, this decision profoundly shifted the bargaining power between the unions, on the one hand, and the directors and management, on the other, in a corporate reorganization. Yet, as Mann shows, it seems likely that the Supreme Court in *Bildisco* was heavily influenced not only by political, but also by public, perceptions of organized labour at the time. There was a sense that the US's prosperity and place in the world were both under threat, and that organized labour was standing in the way of renewed progress. In other words, management was able to mobilize and adapt corporate reorganization law explicitly to reduce the size of the workforce without debate and negotiation, as a

[8] Neil Fligstein, *The Architecture of Markets: An Economic Sociology of Twenty-First Century Capitalist Societies* (new edn, Princeton University Press 2002) 150.

[9] 29 USC § 158(d)(1984).

[10] 11 USC § 365(a)(1984).

[11] Alan N Resnick and Henry J Sommers (eds), *Collier on Bankruptcy*, Vol 3 (16th edn, LexisNexis 2002) para 365.02.

[12] Ronald J Mann, *Bankruptcy and the US Supreme Court* (CUP 2017) 99–123.

[13] *In re Bildisco* 682 F 2d 72.

result of two things. First, the provisions promoting debtor control facilitated the proactive use of Chapter 11 in this way. Secondly, the wider organizational and institutional environment enabled management to co-produce—with the US bankruptcy court—a way of mobilizing and adapting Chapter 11 to achieve the strategic objective.

A further challenge facing US business at the time was the rapid deregulation of significant sectors such as airlines, trucking, natural gas, petroleum, railroad freight transportation, and telecommunications. Deregulation was first promoted under President Jimmy Carter, and then under President Ronald Regan. For over forty years, airline regulators strictly controlled routes; entry to the industry; and the number of carriers which could compete in any given market.[14] Yet, by the 1960s, changes in demand, in fuel prices, and in the general economic environment were to usher in a sudden and dramatic period of deregulation. Inevitably, many US airlines found themselves with workforces and labour prices which were unsustainable, as they competed on price across all aspects of their business. The *Bildisco* judgment had caused public debate and legislative reform, so that specific provisions and requirements for the rejection of collective bargaining agreements were incorporated into the US Bankruptcy Code.[15] Yet, the US Bankruptcy Code continued to offer an expedited form of collective bargaining, engaged most recently in the *General Motors* and *Chrysler* bankruptcies.[16] Moreover, in seeking corporate bankruptcy protection in order to terminate labour agreements, the debtor is handed a major competitive advantage. And the moratorium protection, coupled with the generous period which management is given to propose a corporate reorganization plan, effectively enables the company to continue to operate without paying the interest on its debt, thereby reducing fixed costs.

As a result, the management of significant numbers of US airlines were proactively to turn to Chapter 11 to deal with the challenges of deregulation, specifically implicating employees and other creditors with weak bargaining power. Companies in the same industry, which had not yet filed for bankruptcy protection, found themselves at a competitive disadvantage and, in some cases, appear to have been forced to file for corporate bankruptcy protection too. And crucially, as Kevin Delaney convincingly demonstrates in his analysis of the *Continental Airlines* bankruptcy, financial creditors appear to have supported the use of Chapter 11 to reduce labour costs, notwithstanding the risks associated with the filing, and were ultimately repaid in full.[17] In Delaney's terms, Chapter 11 was used strategically to deal with one class of creditor (the workforce), but unlike the reorganizations

[14] Aisling J Reynolds-Feighan, *The Effects of Deregulation on US Air Networks* (Springer-Verlag 1992) 1–3.

[15] 11 USC § 1113.

[16] Mann (n 12) 121–23.

[17] Kevin J Delaney, *Strategic Bankruptcy: How Corporations and Creditors Use Chapter 11 to their Advantage* (University of California Press 1998) 82–125.

examined in this part of the book, the class which was singled out for compromise was a class of non-adjusting or weakly adjusting creditors.

This gives rise to a complex debate. One might have expected at least some progressive scholars to criticize the use of corporate reorganization generally, and the concept of debtor control specifically, where it is used to shift the costs of reorganization onto a non-adjusting or weakly adjusting creditor group, which has little power in the process. Indeed, in progressive theory terms it might be said to be a straightforward redistribution of income away from workers towards financial creditors and the owners. On the other hand, one might also have expected scholars broadly sympathetic to the law and economics movement to approve of providing tools which facilitate the rapid downsizing of an overblown workforce on efficiency grounds. As Oliver Williamson puts the argument (albeit referring to a different era), 'The incentive to challenge the union in the first place and the efforts to organize labor subsequently were principally geared to achieving efficiency, the rewards for which, once the new methods were imitated by rivals and rates of return were driven down to competitive levels, were diffused throughout society.'[18] Instead, in the literature of the time, progressives broadly supported debtor control, and scholars adopting an economic approach were broadly critical of it, and little focus emerged on the specific consequences of debtor control in the fact pattern of the corporate reorganization case.

It is, of course, always challenging to place scholars in theoretical boxes and, as Susan Rose-Ackerman has shown, progressivism is a broad church.[19] Many of these strategic corporate reorganizations, while undoubtedly brutal, do appear to have achieved their objectives, in that major airlines such as Continental were able to survive the highly competitive environment which emerged (albeit many airlines were forced to return to the US bankruptcy courts in the 1990s, when rising oil prices, and concern over travel after the US declared war on Kuwait, gave rise to another period of intense stress). And the shift of bargaining power in Chapter 11 in reality reflected a shift in commercial bargaining power away from labour as a result of deregulation. This shift in commercial bargaining power caused some employees to agree to other bargains outside Chapter 11 which were even more disastrous. Donald Barlett and James Steele identify a pattern of requesting employees to reduce their wages, in return for stock in the company, only for the company eventually to file for bankruptcy. They describe the case of Transcon Lines in which 88 per cent of the 4,000 employees agreed to reduce their wages by 12 per cent for five years, in return for 49 per cent of the company's stock, only for the company to file for bankruptcy one year later.[20] Arguably, the workers would

[18] Oliver E Williamson, *The Economic Institutions of Capitalism: Firms, Markets, Relational Contracting* (The Free Press 1985), 235.

[19] Susan Rose-Ackerman, *Rethinking the Progressive Agenda: The Reform of the American Regulatory State* (The Free Press 1992).

[20] Donald L Barlett and James B Steele, *America: What Went Wrong?* (Andrews and McMeel 1992) 116–17.

have been better off with the harsh realities of a judicially supervised, early strategic corporate reorganization case. Thus, it is perfectly possible that some progressive scholars would have supported the ways in which the *Bildisco* judgment was proactively mobilized by management in deregulating industries. And it may also be that law and economics scholars are sceptical of the reliance on the flexibility of corporate bankruptcy judges to achieve the result in these cases, and would hold that labour law should have been amended to expedite collective bargaining, rather than relying on strategic applications of corporate reorganization law.

Kevin Delaney gives a further example of what he calls 'strategic bankruptcy' in the 1990s (for the purposes of this book, strategic corporate reorganization). He examines the *Manville Corporation* bankruptcy, in which Chapter 11 was used to deal with mass tort liability. In the specific example of *Manville*, Delaney shows that it was Manville's financial creditors, and not its management, who pressed proactively to use Chapter 11 to address growing tort liabilities.[21] Once again, the financial creditors received full repayment, while the tort victims were left vulnerable to a long-term compensation plan which depended on the accuracy of future forecasting of asbestos claims for its ability to pay out claims, and which capped the amount which victims would recover. Management of other businesses exposed to mass tort or other litigation claims have also adopted the strategic use of Chapter 11 proactively to deal with the threat facing the business. As this book goes to press, Purdue Pharma is trading in Chapter 11 with a view to addressing mass tort liability arising out of its manufacture of the opioid painkiller, OxyContin,[22] and Pacific Gas and Electric, the utility company for the San Francisco Bay Area, continues to trade in Chapter 11 after litigation following deadly fires in the state in 2017.[23]

The interesting point, from the perspective of the approach in this book, is that there is very little micro-analytical debate between progressives and law and economics scholars in the literature paying attention to the specific facts of the strategic corporate reorganization cases of the 1980s and the 1990s (other than repeated references to Eastern Airlines), the use of Chapter 11 to compromise tort and mass litigation liabilities, and the implications of the specifics of the cases for a generalized concept of debtor control. Once again, debtor control becomes associated with promoting early and desirable corporate reorganization by progressive scholars, and with value-destructive efforts to hold creditors at bay by economic scholars, in each case without much attention being paid to the specific fact pattern in the strategic corporate reorganization case, and of the specific ways in which corporate reorganization law is mobilized and adapted by the participants in the

[21] Delaney (n 17) 60–81.

[22] Jan Hoffman and Mary Williams Walsh, 'Purdue Pharma, Maker of OxyContin, Files for Bankruptcy' *The New York Times* (New York, 15 September 2019).

[23] Myles McCormick and Ed Crooks, 'PG&E Files for Bankruptcy Protection after Wildfires' *Financial Times* (New York, 29 January 2019).

process to address it. One of the most furiously debated issues with the debtor control rights concept is the extent to which it leaves the party responsible for failure in control during the reorganization discussions. Chapter 11 is based on the view, as Raymond Nimmer and Richard Feinberg put it, that more often 'the underlying causes are circumstantial'.[24] Against this background, the benefit of retaining the existing directors is that those who know the business best, and the problems which it faces, are motivated to file early and are then able to navigate through the corporate reorganization case. Progressive scholars are broadly prepared to accept that the benefits of incentivizing filing, and keeping know-how within the debtor, outweighs the risks. On the other hand, scholars viewing corporate reorganization law through an economic lens are highly sceptical of the debtor-in-possession concept.[25] They hold up the somewhat egregious example of Eastern Airlines, in which Frank Lorenzo allegedly filed for Chapter 11 and held creditors at bay for many months until any value remaining in the business had virtually disappeared. In this chapter, the suggestion is made that a new approach is needed to this debate, as a result of shifts in the socially constructed identities of management of large US corporates. It is necessary to start by unpacking the changing attitude of management to their role, and the implications of this for the corporate reorganization case.

6.2.2 The fall of the lifetime manager in the US

As already identified, one of the most significant changes in the wider organizational and institutional environment in which corporate reorganization law is mobilized has been the rise of the private equity firm. A crucial aspect of the private equity industry is the close alignment of shareholder and director incentives. Directors of a private equity business can expect a reasonably sizeable stake in the equity of the business. The aim of the investment is to trade the company for a number of years (generally around three to seven years), and then to achieve an 'exit' for the investor. This is typically achieved by listing (or relisting) the company on the stock exchange, a trade sale, or a sale to another private equity firm. It is assumed that if directors hold an equity stake in the company they will also be focused on exit as a method of realizing their own returns. The directors may stay with the company for a period after exit, but their focus is unlikely to be on lifetime employment. Instead, these directors are focused on exit events as both an endorsement of their success as private equity managers in the job market and as a chance to become extremely rich, often in industries where they would not otherwise have expected substantial remuneration packages. As Chapter 3 explored,

[24] Nimmer and Feinberg (n 3) 24.

[25] Michael Bradley and Michael Rosenzweig, 'The Untenable Case for Chapter 11' (1992) 101 Yale LJ 1043.

leverage plays a vital role in the private equity model, improving investor returns by the substantial amount of debt which is used to finance the buyout. Once again, one of the risks of leverage is an increased likelihood of financial distress, either because the firm may struggle to generate sufficient cash to meet substantial debt service obligations in an economic downturn or because, even if it is able to continue to generate sufficient cash, it is not left with enough cash to invest in its business, so that it finds itself at a competitive disadvantage. It may also struggle to refinance its debt at maturity if credit conditions have changed. Thus, in modern times, the private equity portfolio group emerges as an entirely new type of large corporate in financial distress, focused on adapting the balance sheet to meet the demands of a more stressful time.

Turning to leveraged public companies, a similar analysis emerges. Public company directors are heavily orientated around the idea of shareholder value. Indeed, executive directors of large public companies are often what might be called professional directors: focused on progression through the ranks of listed companies via their ability to communicate with institutional shareholders, rather than on progression through a particular industry or sector.[26] Increasingly, in order to demonstrate this commitment to shareholder value, public companies have borrowed private equity techniques. Thus, it is highly likely that managerial remuneration will depend, in some way, on the performance of the company's share price. Directors of large, publicly traded companies are unlikely to see themselves as associated with a particular firm for the rest of their careers. As a result, they will be focused on the need to preserve shareholder value, in order to maintain their currency in the professional director job market.

6.2.3 The fall of the lifetime manager and the corporate reorganization case

While proactive Chapter 11 filings to deal with mass tort liability and other serious litigation claims do continue to be made, they raise specific issues and are hardly examples of debtor control as a way of incentivizing a transaction which is in the best interests of weakly adjusting creditors who would otherwise lack bargaining power in the process. The ability to adapt corporate reorganization law to shift bargaining power with unions was important in the General Motors and Chrysler bankruptcies after the 2008 financial crisis, and US firms do still turn to Chapter 11 to address labour costs.[27] Indeed, while it is too early to say what the

[26] Sarah Paterson, 'The Paradox of Alignment: Agency Problems and Debt Restructuring' (2016) 17(4) Eur Bus Org L Rev 497, 500.

[27] See Mann (n 12) 121–23 and Michelle M Harner, 'The Corporate Governance and Public Policy Implications of Activist Distressed Debt Investing' (2008) 77 Fordham L Rev 703, 719.

consequences of the COVID-19 crisis will be for jobs and the workforce, it must be possible that firms will mobilize Chapter 11 to reduce labour costs in response to the economic effects of shutdown and social distancing. Nonetheless, to date labour costs have not been a major preoccupation in the majority of recent corporate reorganization cases.

As widely covered in the relevant literature, union power was severely diminished by the experience of the 1980s, and a considerably smaller proportion of the US workforce now works in unionized employment. In contrast, many US companies today are little more than 'a good idea, a handful of people ... and a bunch of contracts',[28] and keeping the employees travelling up and down in the lift is often a more significant concern in a reorganization limited to debt and equity financing arrangements than reducing the workforce. This is a significant reason for the shift from seeking corporate bankruptcy protection while a plan of reorganization is negotiated to pre-negotiating the reorganization of the firm's debt and equity finance. Corporate reorganization procedures are then mobilized to deal with the remaining, recalcitrant financial creditors, or even avoided altogether if the transaction can be implemented via the exchange offer. This also helps to explain, in part, the market preference for implementing a reorganization of debt and equity finance via a rapid section 363 sale rather than through a Chapter 11 reorganization plan. All of these methods help to ensure that a strong message can be given to the workforce, so that it can be retained rather than dismissed. In other words, in a typical reorganization limited to debt and equity finance, far from compromising employee claims, the trick is to persuade employees that there is nothing in the case which ought to concern them.

Turning to consider how the socially constructed identities of the directors of these companies and corporate reorganization law interact in renegotiation of the capital structure, a very different picture emerges from that which might have been anticipated in large corporates which were expected to provide lifetime employment for their leaders. The directors of private equity portfolio companies are likely to have worked in anticipation of an exit, and realization of their equity. In other words, the role of the chief executive officer of one of these companies is perhaps better conceptualized as an investor role, rather than as one of an employee with a long-term commitment to build the firm, as Karen Ho puts it, 'as a permanent social institution'.[29] Where a complex, leveraged capital structure becomes unsustainable in current market conditions, the director's equity stake will be significantly diluted at best, or written off at worst, in a reorganization of the capital structure. Furthermore, the director risks his reputation in the job market as a result of the corporate reorganization case. This means that directors are unlikely proactively to

[28] John Micklethwait and Adrian Wooldridge, *The Company: A Short History of a Revolutionary Idea* (The Modern Library 2003) 183.

[29] Karen Ho, *Liquidated: An Ethnography of Wall Street* (Duke University Press 2009) 124.

seek a reorganization until they are effectively forced to do so. However, once the reorganization discussions become unavoidable, the directors may be incentivized to support a reorganization plan which significantly deleverages the balance sheet, so that any equity allocation which they receive ranks behind as little debt as possible. Where directors are not allocated equity in the transaction, they are likely to be incentivized through cash bonuses, often tied to milestones for renegotiating the capital structure.[30] In other words, rather than being motivated simply by retaining their jobs, the directors are likely to be motivated by the consequences of the reorganization transaction for their financial investment in the firm. As Harvey Miller and Shai Waisman put it:

> At the outset, management, fearing a loss of control in the current environment, is often reluctant to commence a Chapter 11 case ... Conversely, once a Chapter 11 case has commenced, management often has every incentive to cooperate with lenders. Perhaps senior management is simply reading the proverbial 'writing on the wall'. At the outset of many cases, it is often obvious that creditors will eventually own the reorganized debtor.[31]

The analysis might be different, of course, if the private equity firm itself has an incentive to seek proactive use of corporate reorganization law. Thus far, the incentives of the directors of the portfolio group in which the private equity firm is invested have been considered. Yet the equity in that group is held by the private equity firm on behalf of its investors, and mechanisms do exist for the private equity firm to intervene if it disagrees with the approach adopted by the directors of the portfolio company. In other work,[32] this author has explored an argument raised by some scholars, that private equity firms do indeed have incentives to adopt a proactive approach. The argument is that private equity firms invest in a number of portfolio groups, and must return frequently to the debt markets to raise acquisition financing. In these circumstances, the argument is that they are motivated to adopt a proactive approach, in order to reduce lender losses, so that they will be able to continue to borrow for future acquisitions.[33] If this analysis holds, debtor control would continue to facilitate early action, before distress has spread to the operations of the group, and

[30] Jared A Ellias, 'Regulating Bankruptcy Bonuses' (2019) 92(3) South Cal L Rev 653.

[31] Harvey R Miller and Shai Y Waisman, 'Is Chapter 11 Bankrupt?' (2005) 47 Boston Coll L Rev 129, 155; David A Skeel Jr, 'Creditors' Ball: The "New" New Corporate Governance in Chapter 11' (2003) 152(3) U Pa L Rev 917, 927.

[32] Sarah Paterson, 'The Rise of Covenant-Lite Lending and Implications for the UK's Corporate Insolvency Law Toolbox' (2019) 39(3) Oxf J Legal Stud 654.

[33] Matthew T Billett, Redouane Elkamhi, Latchezar Popov, and Raunaq S Pungaliya, 'Bank Skin in the Game and Loan Contract Design: Evidence from Covenant-Lite Loans' (2016) 51 J Finan Quant Anal 839, 843.

while the group has operating liquidity to see it through the corporate reorganization negotiations.

However, as the author's other work highlights, the difficulty with this analysis is that private equity firms must also return to the market to raise new funds from the investors who provide the equity capital for the leveraged buyout transactions. A private equity firm typically raises a private equity fund for around ten years. The private equity firm must then return to the market to raise new funds if it is to continue in operation.[34] This means that, as well as worrying about its ability to continue to access debt markets, the private equity firm must also worry about its ability to raise new funds. The decision to invest in a private equity firm is a highly personal one, focused on the talent of the private equity firm to generate the required levels of return and to justify the high fees associated with this sort of investment.[35] Crucially, investment in a private equity fund appears to be a significantly more personal decision than the decision by banks or other institutional lenders and bondholders to finance the portfolio company. Indeed, the debt-financing decision appears to be driven by the general state of the loan and debt capital markets, and the available investment opportunities, to a significant degree.[36] Thus, the reaction of investors provides a powerful disincentive for the private equity firm to come to the table any earlier than it need to, for fear that proactive use of the Chapter 11 process will result in a heavy dilution or total loss of the equity investment, ultimately hindering attempts by the private equity firm to raise a new fund.

As noted in Chapter 3, many public companies have adopted a leveraged capital structure and it is, therefore, possible that a public company may require a reorganization of its debt and equity finance. Yet, once again, even if corporate reorganization law provides debtor-friendly tools, it is unlikely that the directors will seek a proactive reorganization of the firm's loan, bond, and equity finance where that may result in dilution or write-down of the equity held by the existing institutional shareholders. It is also highly likely that director and shareholder interests will be aligned in a public company via compensation which is linked to the performance of the share price, and by director share option schemes. In other words, directors in leveraged public companies are now likely to have the same personal incentives to hold off a reorganization of the leveraged capital structure until it becomes inevitable, but to support a deleveraging, for which they are properly incentivized, once that stage is reached.

34 Steven Neil Kaplan and Per Strömberg, 'Leveraged Buyouts and Private Equity' (*SSRN*, June 2008) 5, <https://ssrn.com/abstract=1194962> accessed 6 March 2020.

35 Ludovic Phalippou, 'Investing in Private Equity Funds: A Survey' (*SSRN*, 18 April 2007) 6–7, <https://ssrn.com/abstract=980243> accessed 6 March 2020.

36 BIS Annual Economic Report, *Debt and the Financial Cycle: Domestic and Global* (BIS 29 June 2014).

6.2.4 Implications for the concept of debtor control rights

This creates an entirely different organizational and institutional environment from that which prevailed when senior management were largely salaried and anticipated a job for life with a single employer. In this old world, the concept of debtor control as a means of promoting the policy objective of early filing for corporate reorganization made some sense. By promising the directors the ability to control the course of the case, the directors were incentivized to file proactively. And by providing the directors with strong, debtor-friendly tools, the directors believed that they would be able to promote a corporate reorganization plan in which they retained their positions. Although the practical realities of this were heavily debated in the empirical literature, with at least one large study finding that directors were frequently replaced in large corporate reorganization cases, and often at the instigation of the creditors,[37] the generalized logic of the approach nonetheless made sense in the organizational and institutional environment of the time. On the other hand, in the new order, where creditors are likely to emerge as the owners of the financially distressed business after the reorganization case, and directors think of themselves as investors, there is little incentive for an early filing. Yet, once the writing is on the wall, the directors can be given financial incentives to cooperate in the rapid flexing of the capital structure.

Recent literature has been critical of the use of financial incentives to motivate directors to progress the capital structure reorganization case. Indeed, there has been some attempt to regulate bonus payments to senior managers in Chapter 11, so that they must achieve something more than merely keeping the managers in their post during the negotiations.[38] Yet, when the way in which corporate reorganization law interacts with its wider organizational and institutional environment is unpacked, the conclusion is that, for the most part, financial incentives are replacing non-financial incentives in motivating the reorganization transaction. And, once again, the argument in this book is that a rapid and low-cost reorganization of the capital structure should be the dominant normative concern, rather than protection of strongly adjusting, junior unsecured bondholders, mezzanine lenders, and shareholders.

It is a controlling principle of this book that in a financially distressed company with an overleveraged capital structure, the public interest lies in a rapid flexing of the balance sheet before distress spreads to the operating companies. In this way, losses will be limited to the sophisticated, strongly adjusting, financial creditors who bargained for the risk, and will not spread to non-adjusting or weakly adjusting trade, labour, or tort creditors, or customers. However, the concept of

[37] Lynn M LoPucki and William C Whitford, 'Corporate Governance in the Bankruptcy Reorganization of Large, Publicly Held Companies' (1993) 141 U Pa L Rev 669, 723.

[38] Ellias (n 30).

debtor control does not hold out much promise for the proactive commencement of the reorganization discussions. Fortunately, financial creditors have ample contractual mechanisms to provide for this, through covenants which, once breached, force the directors to negotiate. Thus, some scepticism is needed for the suggestion that a simple concept of debtor control should apply in these cases. Moreover, caution should be exercised before rebalancing the emerging power of creditors in Chapter 11 cases back towards the debtor. This analysis holds for scholars sympathetic to either a progressive or to a more economically orientated agenda. Chapter 9 returns to explore this point in more detail, when it examines recent developments in finance contracts.

This is not to say, however, that the concept of debtor control is of no relevance in a reorganization of loan, debt, and equity finance. In order to examine this, it is necessary to start with the question of the trade-off between director culpability and director knowledge. This takes on a different cast in many of the reorganizations with which this part of the book is concerned. In a private equity acquisition, the majority of the directors of the operating portfolio companies will have played no part in the strategic decision to leverage the capital structure. It is the case that these directors may have had to approve the grant of guarantees and security for the acquisition debt, but the strategic decision is one which is largely imposed on them and which, in many cases, may make them uneasy. It is difficult to argue, in many of these cases, that the fault for the complex, leveraged capital structure lies with the portfolio group operating management. This means that it is highly likely that little blame will be attached to these managers by the financial creditors if the capital structure proves unsustainable. Moreover, the fact that the complex, leveraged capital structure may become unsustainable, and may require reorganization, was known to the financial creditors and the equity at the time at which it was put in place.

This latter point applies equally to a public company. In a public company scenario, the directors of the main public company board may be more directly implicated in the decision to adopt a complex, leveraged capital structure. Yet they did so with the explicit cooperation of the lenders and bondholders, and with the implicit support of the institutional shareholders, who could have traded out if they had concerns. Once again, all parties at the bargaining table were aware that the downside of a complex, leveraged capital structure was that it may prove unsustainable if the wider environment shifted. Moreover, these parties had a wide range of alternative investment opportunities open to them. Thus, the directors may not be held responsible for overleverage by the financial creditors and equity investors at the bargaining table during the reorganization discussions, albeit they may suffer widespread public opprobrium for being closely associated with the decision to leverage the capital structure if a reorganization cannot be achieved among the financial institutions, and the business fails. In this case, the losses will not be confined to the shareholders and financial creditors who were complicit in the decision to leverage the capital structure, but will fall on general, unsecured creditors, and employees. These creditors may be weakly placed to absorb the losses which arise, and may have been dimly, or wholly, unaware of the capital structure of the firm and the implications of complexity and leverage.

This last point gives a clue to the crucial importance of leaving management in control in a reorganization of financial liabilities owed to financial institutions. A fundamental objective is to avoid action by general, unsecured creditors and customers, who become concerned about the financial condition of the debtor. General, unsecured creditors may reduce debtor days; demand cash on delivery; or cancel contracts. Employees may seek alternative employment. Customers may find alternative suppliers. And other important stakeholders, such as credit insurers, may take action against the firm. These types of general, unsecured creditor, employee, customer, and stakeholder action will have the result that financial distress will steadily move into the operations of the business. This may make a reorganization of the loan, bond, and equity finance more difficult to achieve, or lead to a requirement for a much more significant financial and operational reorganization. More dramatically, it may have the result that the business fails completely.

Thus, it is crucial to avoid signalling to general, unsecured creditors, employees, customers, and other important stakeholders that there is anything to concern them. Ian Molho describes signalling as 'situations where it is possible to credibly transmit private information from the informed to the uninformed party via the use of publicly observable "signals"'.[39] Parties form 'probabilistic beliefs' about the relationship between what Molho calls 'the observed signal' and the unobservable variable which the party is trying to assess.[40] Suppliers, customers, and employees associate Chapter 11 filing with financial loss and disruption. If a Chapter 11 filing is imminent, they may take action to protect themselves. By leaving the debtor in control, they are given the signal that a reorganization is being worked out among the institutional financial creditors and equity. This is a further explanation for the rise of exchange offers, pre-packaged Chapter 11 plans, and section 363 sales, as methods of implementing a reorganization. All of these transactions avoid signalling anything other than business as usual to general, unsecured creditors, employees, customers, and other crucial stakeholders, until the reorganization is worked out among the financial institutions. Once the debtor files the pre-packaged Chapter 11 plan, or launches the section 363 sale, all of these other parties can be reassured that the Chapter 11 filing is solely for the purposes of implementing a reorganization of liabilities among financial institutions, and that they will not suffer loss or other inconvenience. In this way,

[39] Ian Molho, *The Economics of Information: Lying and Cheating in Markets and Organizations* (Blackwell Publishers Ltd 1997) 61.

[40] ibid 64.

the financial creditors seek to contain the transaction within the loan, bond, and equity finance, and to minimize the impact of the reorganization on the business and operations of the debtor group.

6.2.5 Summary of the argument in section 6.2

Overall, the argument in this chapter is that the concept of debtor control is historically associated with early and proactive promotion of the corporate reorganization case. Yet the argument is that it does not hold out much promise for incentivizing proactive commencement of reorganization discussions, given shifts in the socially constructed identities of firms, and of the individuals who manage them, in the large, non-financial corporate field. This is not to say, however, that the debtor-in-possession concept fulfils no function in a reorganization of a complex, leveraged capital structure. Indeed, it is essential in a deleveraging transaction among financial institutions that, to the greatest extent possible, general, unsecured creditors, employees, customers, and other important stakeholders are given a business as usual message. Leaving the debtor in control of the day-to-day operations of the firm, and avoiding the launch of any legal process until the reorganization is ready to be implemented, signals that it is business as usual for all of these parties. Thus, the ambition is to contain the transaction within the loan, bond, and equity finance, and to seek to minimize the impact of the transaction on the business and operations of the debtor group.

Once again, it has been argued that both scholars adopting an economic approach and scholars viewing corporate reorganization through a progressive lens ought to agree with this role for the debtor-in-possession concept in a reorganization among financial institutions. For economically minded scholars, the debtor-in-possession concept reduces the indirect transaction costs of general, unsecured creditor, employee, customer, or other stakeholder action which may make bargaining over a more appropriate capital structure impossible. For progressively minded scholars, it facilitates a reorganization which is limited to strongly adjusting financial creditors. Thus, it prevents distress spreading to the operations of the group and implicating general, unsecured creditors, employees, and customers. And the question of whether the directors are responsible for the financial distress has much less salience where the cause of the distress is a complex, leveraged capital structure rather than mismanagement of the debtor's operations, at least for so long as the case proceeds as a renegotiation limited to financial creditors and the equity. Once again, the important step is to interrogate the concept of debtor control in a twenty-first-century reorganization of a complex, leveraged capital structure, rather than importing ideas which have historically been associated with it, but which are no longer relevant to the facts of the case at hand.

6.3 England

6.3.1 Why England did not approach the concept of debtor control in the same way

English corporate bankruptcy law has no general commitment to a particular conception of debtor control in corporate bankruptcy legal process. As earlier chapters have identified, until comparatively recently, most large English corporates were financed by bank loans provided by large British, and latterly European, banks. When borrowers ran into trouble, the banks would attempt to rollover loans, extend maturity dates, or waive covenants, in order to provide the company with the time to trade out of its difficulties. These efforts were ordinarily coupled with efforts by the debtor to sell non-core assets or divisions to pay down debt, and sometimes by organized programmes to slim the size of the workforce, using labour law. Thus, reorganization of large corporates in England was an out-of-court affair, enforced through social norms in the finance and non-financial corporate fields. Even when England moved towards reorganization via the exchange of loan debt for other types of claim, for a time the reorganization was still arranged out of court and implemented by privately negotiated contract. The principal corporate bankruptcy tools of the day were only used when the banks had lost faith in the borrower and its management. It is therefore scarcely surprising that these tools were management-displacing.

England, of course, also experienced brutal economic conditions in the 1970s. In the 1978–79 'Winter of Discontent' the country experienced hugely unpopular, widespread strikes for higher wages, involving mainly public sector employees. When the right-wing Conservative party came to power in 1979, as a result, in part, of public dissatisfaction with the economic and industrial relations conditions of the 1970s, the new Prime Minister, Margaret Thatcher, expressly set out to weaken union power. This took three broad forms. First, as in the US, the Thatcher government set out to deregulate many areas of the labour market. Secondly, it launched a comprehensive legislative regime designed to weaken union power. And finally, it won decisive victories against extended and sometimes brutal strikes in coal mining and printing.[41]

However, and crucially, corporate reorganization law was not implicated in this battle in England in the way in which it was implicated in the US. One reason for this lies not in the differences in corporate reorganization law, but more fundamentally in differences in labour relations between the two jurisdictions. Both US and UK labour relations have traditionally been decentralized,

[41] Charles G Hanson, *Taming the Trade Unions: A Guide to the Thatcher Government's Employment Reforms, 1980–90* (MacMillan 1991) 1–111.

in the sense that bargaining occurred directly between management and labour, and no government agency extended the collective bargains to non-union settings. Yet, the detail of decentralized labour relations has traditionally been profoundly different in the two jurisdictions. The first part of this chapter identified that union formation, union recognition, and collective bargaining processes were entrenched in federal legislation in the US. That is why, when management sought to take on union power in the 1980s in the rapidly changing economic environment of the time, it turned to another federal legislative scheme to provide the necessary implementing power. In contrast, trade unionism had a long, deep commitment to voluntarism in the UK.[42] At the time, employers were free to recognize trade unions or not, and collective bargaining was informal and largely non-binding. This meant that the nature of the fight to reduce union power was different. Furthermore, in the US the fight was largely led by management, who needed to find sources of power. In contrast, in the UK, it was largely driven by the Thatcher government, which was able to turn to legislative power to achieve many of its objectives.

Similarly, the experience of deregulation was very different in the UK from that prevailing in the US. Both the US and the UK had been concerned to ensure that market participants enjoying a natural monopoly would not exploit the consumer, primarily through tariffs and prices, and, following the Great Depression, that economic depression and industrial decline were addressed. In the US, the activities in question were typically left to private enterprise, but close regulation was imposed with the establishment of a complex network of regulatory agencies and authorities.[43] As Toninelli puts it, 'This was regulation strongly supported by the electorate but fiercely opposed by the business community.'[44] Indeed, opposition increased throughout the 1970s and 1980s as industries struggled with increasing regulatory and administrative costs in an increasingly competitive era. The dismantling of parts of the regulatory state which followed thus had significant impacts on the industries in question. In the UK, the response to the same issue, from the 1940s onwards, had been the establishment of large, nationalized industries.[45] It is thus impossible to separate the twin ideas of deregulation and of privatization in the Thatcher years.

[42] Richard B Freeman, 'The Future for Unions in Decentralized Collective Bargaining Systems: US and UK Unionism in an Era of Crisis' (1995) 33(4) British J Industrial Relations 519, 522.

[43] Pier Angelo Toninelli, 'The Rise and Fall of Public Enterprise: The Framework' in Pier Angelo Toninelli (ed) *The Rise and Fall of State-Owned Enterprise in the Western World* (CUP 2000) 7.

[44] ibid 13.

[45] Toninelli, *The Rise and Fall of Public Enterprise* (n 43) 18 lists the Bank of England, the coal industry (1946), the railway system, inland waterways, civil airlines, the electricity industry (1947), the gas industry (1948), the iron and steel sector (1949), the postal services (1969), and the automobile, ship-building, and aerospace industries (1974–77).

Thatcher was committed to moving away from government command and control of the economy, which she saw as the root of the UK's decline during the 1970s. The nationalized industries had vague objectives and limited abilities to set prices to clear markets, irrespective of increases in marginal costs or of how costs varied across areas of action. They were hit especially hard by rising prices of fuel, raw materials, and other types of purchased inventory throughout the 1970s. And ideological objections to the use of nationalized industries for redistributive purposes, and to removing industry from the competitive pressure of the market, gained ground throughout the 1970s.[46] Yet Thatcher was equally committed to protecting the privatized companies as they emerged from government control, in order to protect her privatization programme as a whole. This meant that many of the UK's deregulating industries experienced deregulation more slowly and gently than their US counterparts. A good example of this is the comparison between deregulation in the airline industry in Britain and in the US. The first part of this chapter explored how deregulation in the US arrived rapidly and brutally, demanding an immediate and decisive response from management, who turned to US corporate reorganization law. The pressure of US deregulation was felt in Britain, but other factors came into play. First, Britain's domestic airline market had never been as tightly regulated as the domestic airline market in the US. Secondly, further deregulation in Britain faced particular challenges because of the small domestic base. Finally, and perhaps most importantly of all, the Thatcher Government was committed to the privatization of British Airways (BA), the national flag carrier, and, as Alan Dobson puts it, 'felt that it had to nurture BA in the short-term to enable it to make the transition successfully from a protected nationalized industry to private enterprise'.[47]

Nor have English debtors turned to corporate reorganization law in substantial numbers to address mass tort or other significant litigation liabilities. Once again, in part this is because the English procedures do not offer some of the tools for the debtor which are available in Chapter 11. Nonetheless, perhaps just as significantly, England has had very different experience of mass tort and class action litigation from the US. While England was one of the first countries in the European Union to introduce specific 'group action' provisions seeking damages for product liability, the procedure has been rarely used and group action cases are much less common than in the US.[48] Many of the cases which have commenced have settled

[46] The account of issues in Britain's nationalized industries draws on Robert Millward, 'State Enterprise in Britain in the Twentieth Century' in Toninelli (ed) *The Rise and Fall of Public Enterprise* (n 43) 157, 169.

[47] Alan P Dobson, *Flying in the Face of Competition: The Policies and Diplomacy of Airline Regulatory Reform in Britain, the USA and the European Community 1968–94* (Avebury Aviation 1995) 181.

[48] David Wilkinson, 'Mass Tort Treatment of Pharmaceutical Product Liability Cases in England' (2006) 73 Def Counsel J 264.

before trial, or been withdrawn as a result of lack of state funding. Thus, English companies have not turned in large numbers towards corporate reorganization as a way of dealing with mass tort claims. Overall, in contrast with the position explored in the US, England did not experience a period of proactive resort to the bankruptcy process by debtor management in order to address the challenges of deregulation and mass tort liabilities.

6.3.2 The fall of the lifetime manager

England has, however, experienced the same rise of the private equity industry as the US. Furthermore, directors of publicly traded companies in England now operate against similar incentives to those of their US counterparts: a need to focus on shareholder value; shareholder value as the currency of the job market; and the likelihood that they will move between publicly traded companies across the course of a career. At the same time, the account in the book so far has shown how and why market incentives are no longer sufficient, in all cases, to achieve a privately negotiated reorganization of a complex, leveraged capital structure. This has had explanatory power for the reasons why participants in corporate reorganization have only now begun to resort to law in England. In short, the landscape of the portfolio career manager is very similar in England to the landscape already sketched out for the US.

6.3.3 The fall of the lifetime manager and English corporate reorganization law

The first part of this chapter revealed that, while debtor control does not perform the function of incentivizing proactive commencement of a modern, large corporate reorganization case, it is critical to avoid signals to general, unsecured trade creditors, employees, customers, and other crucial stakeholders that they ought to consider protecting their position. This has been widely understood in England, perhaps precisely because resort to legal process has traditionally functioned as a powerful signal that financial creditors have lost faith in the management or in the business, and a sale or break-up transaction is likely to follow. It has thus been essential to avoid signalling to all of these other creditor and customer groups that they are implicated in the firm's financial difficulties. In this dramatically different, wider organizational and institutional environment, participants in the English process, and the lawyers who advise them, have been able to mobilize and adapt the scheme of arrangement, and the scheme of arrangement and pre-packaged administration, as largely management-in-possession procedures.

6.3.4 The debtor-in-possession concept emerges in England

Insofar as the scheme of arrangement is concerned, the case is not launched until the reorganization among the financial institutions is ready to be implemented, with day-to-day operation of the business continuing as usual until then. When the scheme of arrangement is launched, no insolvency practitioner, or other officer, is appointed. Furthermore, the scheme is a Companies Act, and not an Insolvency Act, procedure so that headlines that the debtor has filed for bankruptcy can be avoided. Adopting Molho signalling terminology, the probabilistic beliefs of general, unsecured creditors, which associate filing for an administration process with their own financial loss, are avoided.[49] In this way, the hope is that general, unsecured creditors can be encouraged to trade with the business to the greatest extent possible in the usual way, avoiding problems with financial liabilities spreading to problems in the business and operations.

As earlier chapters have explored, while a scheme of arrangement can be used to impose a plan of reorganization on a majority within a class, it cannot be used to impose a plan of reorganization on a dissenting class.[50] Earlier chapters have also explored how participants in the English process, and the lawyers who advise them, have to date overcome this difficulty by 'twinning' the scheme of arrangement with a pre-packaged administration sale of the shares in the operating group to a new company owned by the reorganizing creditors and equity holders. In this case, an insolvency practitioner, known as an administrator, is appointed to the finance holding company which holds the shares in the parent of the operating group. However, functionally, this remains a largely debtor-in-possession procedure. The administrator is only appointed to the finance holding company, and not to any of the operating companies. Furthermore, the administrator is only appointed when the transaction is implemented, at which point the message to general, unsecured creditors, employees, customers, and other crucial stakeholders in the operating companies is that the reorganization of the complex, leveraged capital structure has been completed. In other words, insofar as all of these other parties in the operating business are concerned, the message will be that it is business as usual. And the expectation will be that, as the reorganization will be implemented immediately on appointment, it will not linger for long in the broadcast and print media.

[49] Molho (n 39) 64.

[50] As earlier chapters have noted, the Corporate Insolvency and Governance Bill, which has been introduced just as this book is going to press, inserts a new Part 26A into the Companies Act 2006, closely modelled on the scheme of arrangement but with a cross-class cram-down power: Corporate Insolvency and Governance Bill [HC] 2019–21, Sch 9, inserting new Part 26A into Companies Act 2006. The new Part 26A does not require appointment of an insolvency practitioner, and it will be noted that it is also a Companies Act procedure.

6.3.5 Summary of the argument in section 6.3

Overall, England's shift towards a more debtor-in-possession orientation has followed from a shift in the proximate finance field from resort to legal process where faith has been lost in management, to the use of legal process to solve failures in the bargaining process. Participants in the English process have arrived at this point untrammelled by particular concepts of debtor control. Instead, in a highly pragmatic fashion, they have remodelled existing tools to cope with the particular demands of the day. Perhaps precisely because filing for a corporate bankruptcy procedure has been so strongly associated with a loss of faith in management or the business, and with unsecured trade creditor loss, participants in the English process have focused on signalling in a reorganization of loan, bond, and equity finance. This provides more substance for the claim that the scheme of arrangement is particularly well adapted to achieve a reorganization limited to these financial liabilities. Not only does management remain in control, but the procedure is located in the Companies Act, avoiding negative signalling associated with a corporate bankruptcy filing. Moreover, it can be completed relatively rapidly and with little execution risk once it is launched.

6.4 Conclusion

This chapter has identified that the concept of debtor control in Chapter 11 was originally conceived of, in part, as a way of incentivizing proactive corporate bankruptcy filing. However, it has emphasized that Chapter 11 was enacted at the end of an era of steady, lifetime employment for senior managers. In this wider organizational and institutional setting, debtor control could be expected to appeal to senior managers preoccupied with retaining their jobs with the firm for the long term.

During the great era of US deregulation in the 1980s, debtor control continued to incentivize proactive mobilization of the Chapter 11 tool by directors in affected industries. Yet this was for the specific purpose of downsizing large, unionized workforces which benefitted from legislatively protected collective bargaining arrangements. In this chapter, the argument has been made that the rise of the private equity firm, and increasing alignment of director and shareholder interests in public companies through compensation arrangements, has fundamentally changed the incentives of directors so that debtor control no longer holds out much promise as a way of incentivizing proactive filing. However, it has been argued that the concept of debtor control continues to fulfil an important function in the reorganization of a complex, leveraged capital structure. Debtor control operates to avoid signalling to general, unsecured creditors, employees, customers, and other stakeholders which they may probabilistically associate with unsecured creditor loss. In this way, it is hoped to avoid the costs of action by general, unsecured creditors, employees, customers, or other stakeholders. Once again, both scholars adopting an economic approach and scholars sympathetic to a more progressive orientation ought to be able to agree on the debtor-in-possession concept in the context of the reorganization of a complex, leveraged capital structure.

Turning to England, the account in this chapter did not reveal a historical commitment to the concept of debtor control in legal process. Large corporate reorganization has historically been an out-of-court affair in England, with resort to legal process reserved for situations in which financial creditors have lost faith in management or the business, so that unsurprisingly legal procedure has tended to be management-displacing. The chapter explored how the issues of deregulation were handled in a different way in England in the 1980s. Yet, it also returned to the reasons why the calculus has changed as a result of significant shifts in the wider organizational and institutional environment, so that legal process may well be required to achieve a reorganization of a complex, leveraged capital structure in England, as in the US. Against this background, the chapter explored how participants in the English market have mobilized and adapted existing tools to achieve a functionally management-in-possession process. Once again, this performs a crucial function in a reorganization of financial liabilities, avoiding the signalling associated with a corporate bankruptcy filing, and thereby limiting the indirect costs and risks of general, unsecured creditor and customer action. And it has been suggested that participants in reorganization cases in England are particularly sensitive to this signalling issue, precisely because resort to legal process has traditionally signalled a loss of faith in management or the business and the sale or break-up of the firm, and the likelihood of losses to general, unsecured creditors. Once again, to the extent that a concern arises, it will be for the capacity of this conceptual framework to be adapted where efforts to achieve a reorganization of the loan, bond, and equity financing arrangements fail, and distress spreads to the operating liabilities of the group—the issue which is explored in Chapter 9.

7
The Fall of the Gentleman Banker

7.1 Introduction

A specific approach to corporate reorganization is now being built in the book. First, close attention has been paid to the ways in which shifts in logics, practices, and identities in the fields of finance and non-financial corporates have produced a new type of capital reorganization case. Secondly, close attention has been paid to the extent to which the new patterns of fact which emerge demand that existing concepts used to analyse corporate reorganization law are replaced, supplemented, or unravelled and reformulated. As this exercise is systematically undertaken, common ground is emerging, whether a scholar adopts an economic analysis or a progressive approach, in cases limited to sophisticated financial institutions. The financial creditors, the equity holders, and the debtor each foresee that the leveraged capital structure may be maladapted to future economic change. They are able to think about the mechanism by which the capital structure would be renegotiated *ex ante*, but implementation will depend on the circumstances prevailing *ex post*, and on potentially subjective and contentious inputs. It is these aspects of mechanism design which motivate the use of either a market-based system with credible threat, such as the exchange offer with exit consent, or a hybrid system of court supervision of largely privately ordered bargains. This brings the account in the book to the next complex concept, which will be re-evaluated in the context of a

Corporate Reorganization Law and Forces of Change. Sarah Paterson, Oxford University Press (2020). © Sarah Paterson.
DOI: 10.1093/oso/9780198860365.001.0001.

reorganization contained within the financial liabilities: the concept of bargaining and litigation at the heart of Chapter 11.[1]

The argument, thus far, has demanded that attention is paid to the relevance of the concept of the unsecured creditor as a party implicitly lacking bargaining power, voice, and loss-absorbing capacity, when the unsecured creditor is a sophisticated financial institution or shareholder in a complex, leveraged capital structure. The first step was to replace the concept of 'unsecured creditor' with 'sophisticated financial creditors and investors'. The case was then made for a simpler approach to valuation, offering fewer possible approaches and (where possible) drawing on market valuation techniques, in reorganizations of the debtor's loan, bond, and equity finance. This argument has been advanced on the basis that it will reduce the transaction costs associated with this type of reorganization, while only creditors who have already benefitted from the complex, leveraged capital structure suffer the compromise. And the argument has been made that both scholars adopting an economic approach and scholars sympathetic to a progressive vision ought to be able to agree on simpler methods of valuation in these types of cases. In this chapter, a further reason is advanced for promoting a simpler approach to valuation in cases which reorganize debt and equity finance. This relates to the changing nature of reputation for financial creditors in modern markets at both the firm and individual level, and the impact which that changing nature of reputation has on the bargaining and litigation concept in Chapter 11. Certain specific arguments will be made relating to the absolute priority rule, and some further comments will be made on the role of the finance documents which are negotiated when the leveraged financing is originally raised.

As is explored in this chapter, reputation is not a fixed quality. Indeed, the type of reputation which finance and non-financial market participants seek to cultivate may depend on the overall organizational and institutional environment in which they are embedded. The argument is made that shifts in the socially constructed identities of the financial creditors who participate in the reorganization of a complex, leveraged capital structure undermine some of the assumptions made in Chapter 11 about concern for reputation, and the way in which it will interact with corporate reorganization law to motivate bargaining. Overall, the argument is that, far from making litigation less likely and incentivizing bargaining, sophisticated financial creditors and equity are more likely to seize litigation opportunities which are offered by Chapter 11's relatively complex valuation approach. By unravelling the bargaining and litigation concept, and reformulating it by reference to the conditions likely to arise in a modern reorganization case among financial institutions, a further reason emerges to prefer a simpler approach to the valuation question.

[1] For the concept of bargaining and litigation, see Lucian Arye Bebchuk and Jesse M Fried, 'A New Approach to Valuing Secured Claims in Bankruptcy' (2001) 114 Harvard L Rev 2386, 2393.

Once again, the account in this chapter reveals why the comparatively recent development of corporate reorganization law to achieve a reorganization of a complex, leveraged capital structure in England means that the same assumptions are not made about the identities of the participants in the process, the role of reputation, and the bargaining environment in general. As a result, the English courts have developed a conceptual framework in which to approach a reorganization among financial institutions which is well adapted to disincentivize court challenge. Nonetheless, various aspects of the wider organizational and institutional environment in England incentivize bargaining. Once again, to the extent that there is a concern about English corporate reorganization law, it is whether key concepts which have developed in the decade since the financial crisis will prove sufficiently flexible if ongoing shifts and extensions in logic, practice, and identity in the fields of finance and non-financial corporates demand that they are adapted. This wider issue is explored in detail in Chapter 9, but this chapter considers the immediate need to consider how current reforms may impact the delicate bargaining environment in a reorganization in England.

7.2 United States

7.2.1 The concept of bargaining and litigation

Chapter 11 was originally conceived of as creating the right incentives to motivate bargaining among the parties. It sought to achieve this by setting up the possibility of a relatively complex valuation dispute and, ultimately, of an unpredictable cramdown of the reorganization plan. This is sometimes referred to in the literature in the United States (US) as the bargaining and litigation concept.[2] In other words, a key objective of the structure of Chapter 11 is to motivate structured bargaining, through the threat of an expensive and unpredictable, lengthy, and costly valuation fight in court. Complex valuation is thus a key element of a governance system designed to encourage parties to agree to a bargain, because the legislative regime's very uncertainty is designed to provide, as Daniel Bussel and Kenneth Klee put it, 'an environment where parties are encouraged to compromise rather than to stand on their legal rights'.[3]

In a generally cooperative finance market, where participants compete on reputation and not on price with a stable group of loyal clients, small sacrifices to strict legal rights are possible in order to get the deal through. Reputation can act as a strong constraint because bad behaviour by a market participant can be punished

[2] ibid.

[3] Daniel J Bussel and Kenneth N Klee, 'Recalibrating Consent in Bankruptcy' (2009) 83 Am Bankr LJ 663, 694.

by others. To borrow a term from Oliver Williamson, these markets purported to be '"High Minded" organizational forms' in which trustworthiness was assumed and bargaining was on 'nonopportunistic principles'.[4] Moreover, in a cooperative market, where the players met each other repeatedly, the threat of exclusion from the community encouraged the market to discipline itself. To borrow from Oliver Williamson again, 'Viable cooperatives will attempt to screen against, socially recondition, and otherwise penalize opportunistic invaders.'[5] A key concern of any governance mechanism for renegotiation is to deal with threat risk in order to secure commitment to the new bargain. Thus, the interaction between the ways of thinking about the bargaining process and the legal rules which influence the bargaining process is a critical part of the enquiry into the system for renegotiating capital structures in financial distress. In the past, relatively homogeneous markets enforced communal standards of bargaining behaviour: standing by bargains already struck; not taking more than one's due in the bargain; being prepared to give away a little to others in order to get the deal through; and behaving with dignity and courtesy in the bargaining room. In this environment, the central concept of Chapter 11 of encouraging voluntary bargaining against the threat of litigation could provide an effective method of getting the deal done. As this chapter explores, there have been dramatic changes in the sociology of financial markets, and in the type of reputation which participants in the market seek to cultivate. In order to understand the implications of this for the corporate reorganization case, it is first necessary to chart some of the shifts in the institutional environment.

7.2.2 The fall of the gentleman banker

As previous chapters have already explored, at the end of the nineteenth and the beginning of the twentieth centuries, J P Morgan and his successors played a major role representing debt security holders in distressed railroads and large industrials. While J P Morgan pioneered the use of the equity receivership procedure to create the moratorium within which a deal could be put together, the details of the corporate reorganization bargain itself were worked out privately under the auspices of the reorganization committee. The values, beliefs, and norms of behaviour which J P Morgan adhered to thus provided an important element of the corporate reorganization process. J P Morgan would have regarded it as vital that he maintain his reputation with his bondholders, in order to secure continued access to the British capital markets. In this way, the reputation which he and other investment

[4] Oliver E Williamson, *The Economic Institutions of Capitalism: Firms, Markets, Relational Contracting* (The Free Press 1985) 65.

[5] ibid 65.

bankers sought to cultivate would have been recognizable to the investors which they sought to represent.

As beautifully captured in both the title of Susie Pak's work *Gentlemen Bankers* (borrowed for the title of this chapter),[6] and in Ron Chernow's term the 'Gentleman Banker's Code',[7] J P Morgan, and other investment bankers of his day, strongly identified with gentlemanly ethics, and with discrete deal-making conducted behind closed doors. Moreover, the concentration of power in the hands of a small group of investment bankers provided a mechanism for excluding those who were not seen to play by the gentlemanly rules from the investment banking community. Criticisms were made of the deals which J P Morgan brokered. Yet there seems little doubt that he regarded himself as the honest broker for his clients, bound by gentlemanly obligations to protect their interests and to act in the interests of stability. What emerges in the literature is a portrait of investment bankers with formidable, concentrated power in the bargaining process, but who regarded themselves as bound by codes of behaviour perhaps best captured by the familiar exhortation, 'My word is my bond'.

As Chapter 2 explored, and as Chapter 8 will develop, investment bankers lost their role as honest brokers in the corporate reorganization bargaining process. This occurred, first, as a result of organizational change in the field of finance and, secondly, as a result of the New Deal legislative reforms. Yet the social dimension of the finance market did not change immediately. When the Glass-Steagall reforms prohibited commercial banks from engaging in security underwriting, and the J P Morgan firm made the (fateful) decision to remain as a commercial bank, Morgan Stanley effectively took over its securities business. The bond market then continued to operate on recognizably genteel principles. Morgan Stanley dominated the bond market, putting together groups, or syndicates, of investment banks to underwrite bond issues. If a participant in a Morgan Stanley syndicate did not meet the standards of behaviour which Morgan Stanley expected, then Morgan Stanley had the power effectively to expel that participant from the bond market for some time. Thus, Morgan Stanley did not have to, or expect to have to, compete on price with its rivals. At the same time, clients benefitted from Morgan Stanley's position, both as a result of Morgan Stanley's ability to select syndicate participants based on their knowledge of behaviour in previous deals, and as a result of their ability to enforce good behaviour through the exercise of exclusion from future syndicates.[8] The overall result was that the long-term bond market of the 1950s and 1960s could enforce its own gentlemanly codes of conduct. It seems likely, given the inevitable time lag between the studies which investigated the structure of reform

[6] Susie J Pak, *Gentlemen Bankers: The World of J.P. Morgan* (Harvard University Press 2014).

[7] Ron Chernow, *The House of Morgan: An American Banking Dynasty and the Rise of Modern Finance* (Grove Press 1990) 24.

[8] ibid 517.

of corporate reorganization law and the implementation of revised Chapter 11 in 1978, that this is the bargaining environment which would have been present in the reformers' minds.

However, fundamental change was afoot. The world of J P Morgan and Morgan Stanley had been made possible by an environment of low inflation, stable currencies, and weak corporate managers who were dependent on their investment bankers for access to capital. It has become apparent, by this stage in the book, that from the late 1960s onwards almost every aspect of this environment was to shift. Crucially, US industrialists had access to a wider range of capital, including Eurodollar loans, commercial paper, private placements, and domestic floating rate loans, at a time when the long-term bond market was unattractive. The abolition of fixed commissions by the New York Stock Exchange on 1 May 1975 (Mayday) was the first nail in the coffin of a market based on reputation with a loyal customer base.[9] Morgan Stanley attempted to control the market by excluding those who undercut on price from securities syndicates. It demanded the exclusive right to lead the syndicates which it organized, and to be represented in the highest position on the so-called 'tombstone advertisements' which listed the syndicate members.[10] Yet US management was no longer willing to condone this type of cartel-like behaviour, and Mayday and the other changes in the finance field meant that the market lacked the infrastructure to enforce it. The high-water mark came in 1979 when IBM refused to afford Morgan Stanley the top spot on a bond underwriting and handed the mandate to Salomon Brothers instead.[11]

At the same time, rapid technological advances mitigated the difficulties of making and retaining client relationships, so that some of the barriers which had effectively prevented banks from competing on each other's turf began to break down.[12] Technology generally, and computerization specifically, led to the commoditization of large areas of finance which formerly rested on judgement and instinct. A 'good' reputation became a reputation for mathematical ability and a sound knowledge of price movements in the secondary markets to inform clients about strategy and next steps. As Morrison and Wilhelm point out, computerization also made it increasingly possible to separate out advisory, trading, and other functions of investment banks. This further contributed to competition for advisory mandates.[13]

Rapid and fundamental change in the organizational and institutional structure of the finance market followed. First, as commercial and investment banks competed on price, and could no longer be assured of a client's business,

[9] ibid 602.
[10] ibid 623–24.
[11] ibid 626.
[12] Much of this section draws on Alan D Morrison and William J Wilhelm Jr, *Investment Banking: Institutions, Politics, and Law* (OUP 2012).
[13] ibid 257.

investment banks moved from so-called relationship banking, in which they focused on maintaining the client relationships which they had, towards transactional banking, in which banks focused on maintaining a diverse range of business lines for old and new clients. As a result, the market became more segmented and focused on profit, rather than loyalty. Consequently, the need to maintain a particular reputation for fair dealing on behalf of the client over the long term assumed less significance than the need to demonstrate expert knowledge of the market and a formidable ability to strike the best deal.

This shift in logic and identity promotes a completely different sort of reputation: one in which aggressive bargaining tactics and pursuing every last cent is more important than codes of honour and gentlemanly behaviour. At the same time, it also promotes a short-term approach, because the focus is on the transaction at hand rather than long-term relationships. Two consequences follow. First, the type of reputation which is admired in the market undergoes a fundamental shift. Secondly, even if the new type of reputation is not admired in all quarters, the short-term nature of market dealings, and the focus on immediate price and profit by everyone in the market, reduces the power of the market to sanction behaviour through market exclusion. In other words, the clients of financial firms come to accept the legitimacy of the new banking business model, so that aggressive action carries limited adverse reputational consequences. This has significant explanatory power for the idea that foreseeable problems with high leverage need not undermine the implementation of the deal. Leveraging up as much as the balance sheet will bear makes good sense on the assumption that, if that capital structure proves unsustainable in times of stress, it will be adapted by changing debt terms or swapping into equity or equity-like instruments. None of this precludes the borrower from returning to the debt markets if credit conditions loosen again after the reorganization has been completed. Indeed, a continuous cycle of leveraging, deleveraging, and re-leveraging the balance sheet may emerge.

Thus, as the world of loyal bankers and loyal clients disappeared, bankers became risk seekers, agitating for business and using both aggression and imagination. Procedural rules, such as rules on the ordering of the names of the underwriters on tombstones, gave way to competition based on price. William Cohan gives several examples of allegations of investment bank–client conflicts of interest in the corporate reorganization field.[14] Yet Cohan makes the argument that, even if conflicts do exist, clients are prepared to tolerate them. Whereas the investment bankers of the past had offered clients a steady advocacy for their interests at the cost of fixed prices in a stable economic environment, clients, like their bankers, now want

[14] William D Cohan, *Money and Power: How Goldman Sachs Came to Rule the World* (Penguin Books 2011) 168–74 (allegations of conflicts of interest in the Penn Central collapse); 323 (allegations relating to the Maxwell collapse); 298 (establishing and closing the Water Street Fund); 400–01 (allegations surrounding the LTCM collapse); 11–15 (allegations relating to the ABACUS trade); 599 (allegations surrounding the Hudson Mezzanine Funding).

keenly priced deals which are successfully marketed. In other words, an investment bank which has access both to capital to put to work and to a good distribution channel can have the reputation which clients want, even if the presence in the secondary markets which gives the investment bank these capabilities also gives rise to the potential for conflicts of interest.

Thus, for so long as the investment bank can offer deal flow and access to investment opportunities, Cohan suggests that its clients will live with bargaining behaviour which would not have been regarded as tolerable by clients in a past era.[15] At the same time, the leading investment banks (other than a limited number of advisory-only firms) argue that a presence in secondary markets is essential to help them to meet modern client needs. It provides investors with comfort that positions are liquid and can be traded in the secondary market. Specifically, secondary market presence provides the investment bank with the market knowledge it needs to service its clients' more sophisticated demands. In other words, far from undermining the investment bank's reputation through the conflicts of interest which arise, presence in the secondary market enhances the investment bank's reputation for the skills which are more pressing for the modern client. In short, what Morrison and Wilhelm call 'liquidity networks' are more important than avoiding all conflicts of interest.[16] In his work, Mitchel Abolafia frames this point explicitly in terms of different types of reputation:

> While reputation is important, reputation for providing profit opportunities may take precedence over reputation for opportunism, especially if the uncertain cost of opportunism is less than the presumed or real profit opportunities offered by a relationship with a top firm.[17]

Other forces have also undermined what might be called collegiality at the level of the individual in the finance field. First, the long working hours in modern finance have undermined the ability to participate in the political and cultural activities which bound together financiers of earlier times.[18] Secondly, the genteel world of bankers and clients meeting at social clubs and sporting events has broken down, as banking ceases to rely on social contacts. Thirdly, modern finance markets are populated by a much wider range of investors. Before the 1950s, US capital was raised from retail investors, supported by working capital lines from banks. Yet, the story of the late twentieth century and the early twenty-first century is the rise

[15] ibid 444.

[16] Morrison and Wilhelm (n 12) 83.

[17] Mitchel Y Abolafia, *Making Markets: Opportunism and Restraint on Wall Street* (Harvard University Press 1996) 37.

[18] As Chernow puts it, 'People now wore beepers, worked ninety-hour weeks, and remained on call over weekends, restricting their outside cultural and political activities—hallmarks of partners in the old House of Morgan': Chernow (n 7) 628.

of a diverse range of institutional investors, specializing in particular segments of the market, inevitably reducing homogeneity. Finally, individuals no longer expect to spend their entire career with a particular employer, and may even expect to work for a shorter number of years, so that firm–employee loyalty has significantly diminished. This shift has occurred, in part, because of the gruelling demands of working for maximum profit, deal by deal: constant contact with the office, long working weeks, remaining on call over the weekend, and the risk of job loss if a transaction is unsuccessful. There has been a declining focus on sociability and on the job training, and an increasing focus on skills of financial analytics, gained in the classroom, and portable from firm to firm.[19] At the same time, the increasing use of technology to facilitate the financial analysis which steers modern markets has resulted in further standardization between firms. This has had the result that it is quicker for an individual to grasp how things work on moving from one firm to another.

One significant consequence of this breakdown in firm–employee loyalty has been that, in order to attract, retain, and motivate the talent, the entire finance industry has come to focus on performance-related pay rather than salary alone. Spectacular bonus payments are available for the right results. At the same time, modern financiers are seeking to succeed in what Karen Ho calls 'a culture of "survival of the smartest" '.[20] As Ho identifies, this idea of smartness in the finance world involves both risk-taking and what she calls 'entrepreneurial resourcefulness'.[21] An individual demonstrates that they have been smart, taking risks in negotiation and exhibiting their superior knowledge of the market and of the relevant legal regime, by achieving a high pay award. Thus, it is important to understand that individuals do not just desire bonus payments in order to buy material goods. Bonus payments are also important for what Jean-Pierre Hassoun calls 'professional self-valuing'.[22] As Mitchel Abolafia puts it, money becomes, '... more than just the medium of exchange; it is a measure of one's "winnings." It provides an identity that prevails over charisma, physical attractiveness, or sociability as the arbiter of success and power.'[23]

Thus, the concept of a meritocracy based on smartness rewarded by high pay has taken the place of previous norms of behaviour rooted in class, religion, sporting ability, and sociability. The financiers who emerged, through the 1970s and into the 1980s, saw much to be critical of in what they regarded as the complacent markets which had existed before them. Investment bankers who had relied on a social address book and gentlemanly ideas loosely based on motifs from religion, sport, and

[19] Morrison and Wilhelm (n 12) 27.
[20] Karen Ho, *Liquidated: An Ethnography of Wall Street* (Duke University Press 2009) 59.
[21] ibid 104.
[22] Jean-Pierre Hassoun, 'Emotions on the Trading Floor: Social and Symbolic Expressions' in Karin Knorr Cetina and Alex Preda (eds) *The Sociology of Financial Markets* (OUP 2005) 102, 107.
[23] Abolafia (n 17) 30.

the gentleman's club, were to be disdained. Similarly, finance in old-world America based on contacts and the old school tie was seen as corrupt, rooted in ideas of race, class, and gender.[24] In this worldview, modern financial markets have replaced class-based, complacent finance with finance based on skill and merit, objectively measured by the economic outcome of the case and rewarded in financial terms.[25] Thus, while it is true that modern finance markets are more diverse and more global than before, and unarguably less collegiate, it is not the case that they do not exhibit any common values. Indeed, it is an organizing principle of this book that modern finance markets share a commitment to the concept of leverage, and the importance of adapting the capital structure if it gives rise to financial distress.

7.2.3 The fall of the gentleman banker and the corporate reorganization case

This profound shift in the informal norms, values, and beliefs of the finance market has had a critical impact on the renegotiation of the complex, leveraged capital structure as the new norms, values, and beliefs interact with a legal regime which was designed to facilitate bargaining by the threat of litigation. As this chapter has explored, modern finance markets no longer adopt a cooperative model, but are characterized by high levels of competition. In this competitive world, modern financiers are more likely to be opportunistic when the debtor faces financial distress. Modern financiers are considerably less likely to give away an allocation of debt or equity, and considerably more likely to enforce their strict legal rights, or to exploit uncertainties in the application of a complex code to a particular unforeseen situation. Enforcement of strict legal rights, right down to the last cent, is to be admired in markets which are focused on profit over stability, and on performance over connections. And as this chapter has explored, the market may be weakly positioned to enforce sanctions, even against what is objectively very bad behaviour. It may be the case that the reputations of those in the bargaining process facilitated bargaining outside the court room in times gone by. Yet, the argument here is that the detailed provisions of the US Bankruptcy Code, with the possibility of significant litigation success and the absence of other alternative methods of dealing with holdouts, may actually promote litigation in modern markets. This is compounded by specialization and segmentation in the market, because a number of participants will have traded into the situation at a significant discount to the par value of the debt, so that they will be able to bear significant risk and transaction costs in the litigation process.

[24] Ho (n 20) 108.
[25] ibid.

Developments in technology have also contributed significantly to attitudes to litigation in a debt and equity reorganization case. Developments in computing, coupled with cheap computing power, mean that it is relatively straightforward to project corporate cashflows and discount them back for current valuation purposes. Thus, the analyst can manipulate inputs towards the desired outcome with relative ease. In former times, such an exercise would have been done at worst with pencil and paper, and at best with a complex Hewlett Packard calculator. And the development of formulas such as the Black-Scholes model has, as Daniel Beunza and David Stark put it, 'given traders precision tools previously reserved for engineers'.[26] This means that a participant in the process can work out the maximum amount which they consider they are due in the case, and defend it with complex, mathematical modelling. These participants then take the job of understanding their legal rights seriously, in order to work out how to achieve their maximum return in the case.[27] In this environment, litigation becomes another tool to achieve the strategic objective, rather than something to be avoided.

7.2.4 Implications for the bargaining and litigation concept

The suggestion here is that the bargaining and litigation framework of Chapter 11 may have lost its force. In what Sebastian Mallaby calls the 'fighter pilot culture',[28] individuals are comfortable to take big risks in the hope of big rewards, and are likely to pursue their strict legal rights. Thus, once again, there may need to be less focus on protecting a sophisticated minority playing a high-risk, high-reward financial game. Instead, the focus should perhaps be on facilitating the deleveraging of the capital structure with minimum risk to the rest of the contract, trade, labour, and other creditors, customers, and employees. In this way, the borrower-level and, possibly, economy-level social costs can be avoided which may otherwise be incurred. Once multiple, complex points of reference increase the chances of disagreement, and reduce the prospect of a bargain, there is greater public interest in simplifying the process. In this way, the chances of flexing the complex, leveraged capital structure at an affordable price are maximized, in circumstances where the parties would otherwise embrace, rather than avoid, a complex and expensive litigation fight. This provides support for the argument already made in favour of simplifying the approach to valuation in Chapter 11, at least in a reorganization limited to debt and equity finance provided by financial institutions.

[26] Daniel Beunza and David Stark, 'How to Recognize Opportunities: Heterarchical Search in a Trading Room' in Cetina and Preda (eds) (n 22) 84.

[27] Sebastian Mallaby, *More Money than God: Hedge Funds and the Making of the New Elite* (Bloomsbury 2011) 274: 'These guys studied legal labyrinths . . . They could judge how a particular slice of subordinated debt was likely to be treated by a particular bankruptcy judge in a particular court.'

[28] ibid 251.

And, once again, both economically and progressively minded scholars ought to be able to agree to the approach. It also has implications for another vexed issue in Chapter 11 practice: the extent to which violations in the so-called absolute priority rule should be tolerated.

The absolute priority rule (APR) has developed through judicial decisions. Very broadly, it provides that no junior class should recover in a corporate reorganization until a more senior class has recovered in full and, as a corollary, that no senior class should recover more than it is owed. There is considerable empirical work in US corporate reorganization scholarship identifying deviations from the APR, and extensive comment on the desirability or otherwise of these deviations. For the purposes of this book, the work of Douglas Baird and Thomas Jackson is particularly interesting.[29] Baird and Jackson identify different motivations for deviations from the APR. First, there are deviations motivated simply out of a desire to speed up the bargaining process. Secondly, there are deviations which essentially represent a payment, for example, to management to continue with the firm after reorganization, or to equity to provide a necessary service. Baird and Jackson broadly do not support deviations from APR for the first purpose, but broadly support deviations in the second category. One benefit of simplifying the Chapter 11 bargaining process is that it maximizes the chances that deviations will be for the second purpose (essentially paying for a service), rather than simply to speed up or reduce the costs of doing the deal. While arguments can be made to defend the first type of payment, there is a risk of cronyism which is difficult to interrogate from the outside. On the other hand, when the bargaining environment is simplified, and the legal rights are clearer, it is less likely that entirely strategic payments will be made. In other words, it is more likely that payments will be made for the purpose of securing a necessary service or contribution. Thus, simplifying the bargaining environment is likely to reduce debate around APR deviations.

Furthermore, the changing nature of the bargaining environment in Chapter 11 suggests a need to revisit the incentives for financial parties to bargain *ex ante* over control rights in distress. This requires some unpacking. Chapter 11 is based on a strong, normative preference for a consensual bargain. Nonetheless, even in the heyday of consensual bargaining, concerns were raised with this approach. Scholars adopting an economic approach worried that Chapter 11 bargaining was costly and inefficient, and some of these scholars suggested alternatives to bargaining rooted in *ex ante* contracts.[30] Progressive scholars were critical of these

[29] Douglas G Baird and Thomas H Jackson, 'Bargaining after the Fall and the Contours of the Absolute Priority Rule' (1988) 55(3) U Chi L Rev 738.

[30] Robert K Rasmussen, 'Debtor's Choice: A Menu Approach to Corporate Bankruptcy' (1992) 71(1) Tex L Rev 51; Alan Schwartz, 'Bankruptcy Workouts and Debt Contracts' (1993) 36 J L & Econ 595; Barry E Adler, 'Finance's Theoretical Divide and the Proper Role of Insolvency Rules' (1994) 67 S Cal L Rev 1107; Alan Schwartz, 'A Contract Theory Approach to Business Bankruptcy' (1998) 107(6) Yale LJ 1807; Barry E Adler and Marcel Kahan, 'The Technology of Creditor Protection' (2013) 161 U Pa L Rev 1773.

plans to replace the corporate bankruptcy system with a privately ordered contractual system, out of fear that it would result in shifts of value from non-adjusting or weakly adjusting creditors to strongly adjusting creditors.[31] Less prosaically, a contractual system was simply not very practical as a method of addressing full financial and operational reorganizations of large corporates because of obvious problems of foreseeability and complexity in attempting to legislate for the uncertain future. However, there is no reason why sophisticated financial creditors and equity cannot bargain *ex ante* for control rights in a reorganization of loan, bond, and equity finance. As argued throughout this book, both economic and progressive scholars ought to be able to agree to mechanisms which implement a rapid and low-cost reorganization of an unsustainable, complex, leveraged capital structure. Concerns for minority protection have less salience in this type of transaction, whatever political or ideological position is adopted. At the same time, both the nature of the problem (that a capital structure which is complex and leveraged may prove unsustainable if the group's earnings deteriorate even temporarily), and the inputs which are required to solve it, can be worked out and negotiated in advance.

One option would be to have a contingently complete contract governing reorganization of the capital structure in financial distress. One scholar, Barry Adler, has advanced the idea of what he calls 'chameleon equity': in essence a convertible bond-type structure in which debt automatically converts into equity if the capital structure becomes unsustainable, not wholly unlike the contingent convertible bonds (CoCos) which have been proposed for financial institutions after the 2008 financial crisis.[32] The difficulty with this idea is that the principal input into any formula to determine which debt converts, and at what rate, is likely to be firm value. As this book has noted in a number of places, whatever approach is adopted to firm value, it is always likely to be a contentious and, to some extent, subjective input. It is for this reason that the financial parties are unlikely to commit to a contingently complete contract pursuant to which debt automatically converts into equity. Yet, as this book has already noted and as developed in the second part of this chapter, financial creditors in England nonetheless agree detailed allocation of control rights in financial distress in the intercreditor agreements which they enter into when the finance arrangements are put in place. Among other things, the intercreditor agreement mandates an independent third party (the security trustee) and, if necessary, the bankruptcy judge to implement the contractually worked-out mechanism. If Chapter 11 were to recognize and enforce similar intercreditor arrangements, it would encourage efficient *ex ante* bargaining over control rights in distress and reduce the inefficiencies which are created by the

[31] For a discussion of this point and other aspects of the contractual solution, see Susan Block-Lieb, 'The Logic and Limits of Contract Bankruptcy' (2001) U Ill L Rev 503.

[32] Barry E Adler, 'Financial and Political Theories of American Corporate Bankruptcy' (1993) 45 Stanford L Rev 311.

current bargaining environment. Oliver Williamson describes the effect in the following way, 'Transactions that are subject to *ex post* opportunism will benefit if appropriate safeguards can be devised *ex ante*.'[33]

The first, important point is the limited scope of the intercreditor agreement in US leveraged finance deals. As Chapter 5 noted, and as the second part of this chapter develops, it is usual for an English law intercreditor agreement to regulate all of the financial creditors in the capital structure. In contrast, in the US an intercreditor agreement is only likely to be put in place if there is more than one group of lenders secured over a common collateral pool.[34] This is most likely to occur, in a US deal, when there is a so-called 'second lien' layer in the capital structure. This is a layer of senior debt which usually shares all or some of the senior collateral pool, but which is subordinated to the rest of the senior debt. In this case, the intercreditor agreement will provide for the relative priority of the lender groups, but is increasingly likely to cover a range of other issues. These can include: agreements not to challenge the validity, perfection, or priority of the senior lenders' collateral; provisions addressing the release of liens outside corporate bankruptcy; rights to buy out the senior lenders; and extensive voting restrictions and blanket agreements designed to give the senior lenders control of any corporate reorganization process.[35] On the other hand, in the many US capital structures in which there is only a senior secured loan tranche and subordinated, unsecured bond debt, there is very likely to be no intercreditor agreement at all.[36]

The US Bankruptcy Court has grappled with the extent to which it should enforce intercreditor agreements along two dimensions. The first appears to be a concern for the protection of creditors' statutory rights.[37] Junior creditors, exhibiting high levels of opportunistic behaviour, have sought to challenge the binding nature of the state-contingent provisions of the contract in distress. This is to be expected because, as Williamson identifies, in contract renegotiation involving highly opportunistic parties, the spirit in which the parties approach the contract renegotiation is as important as the terms of the contract itself.[38] The courts have shown concern for the fact that the US Bankruptcy Code sets up detailed and complex creditor protection rules, and that there may be public policy reasons to make these mandatory. Junior financial creditors, identifying the courts' intellectual reticence, have been only too happy opportunistically to challenge the negotiated

[33] Williamson (n 4) 48.

[34] Danelle le Cren and Jeff Norton, 'Problems at the Border' (2015) 34(4) Int'l Fin L Rev 52, 54.

[35] George H Singer, 'The Lender's Guide to Second-Lien Financing' (2008) 125 Banking LJ 199.

[36] Tom Young, Lukas Becker, and Danielle Myles, 'Brother, Can you Spare Me a Loan?' (2012) 31(2) Int'l Fin L Rev 20; Le Cren and Norton (n 34) 54.

[37] See eg *Beatrice Foods Co v Hart Ski Manufacturing Company* 5 BR 734 (Bankr D Mins 1980); *Bank of America v North LaSalle Street Ltd Partnership* 246 BR 325 (Bankr ND Ill 2000); *In Contrarian Funds LLC v Westpoint Stevens, Inc* 333 BR 30 (SDNY 2005).

[38] Williamson (n 4) 76, citing Stewart Macaulay, 'Non-Contractual Relations in Business: A Preliminary Study' (1963) 28 Am Soc Rev 55.

terms of the bargain. It will come as no surprise, by this stage in the book, that a challenge is raised here to the approach of the courts. Where financial creditors are sophisticated and well advised, there would seem to be little reason not to uphold the bargain they have struck, even if it amounts to a waiver of statutory protection. This amounts to what Williamson calls a 'market-assisted governance structure'.[39] There would seem to be no paternalistic basis for denying the effect of the contract, as these financial creditors can be taken to have fully consented to, and understood, the contract which binds them.

A more nuanced argument relates to the impact of the waivers on the rest of the debtor's estate and on its other creditors. As Edward Morrison identifies in his work, the concern appears to be that concentrated, senior secured creditor power risks senior creditors taking action which is not in the best interests of creditors as a whole.[40] In other words, this is a variation of the concerns for secured creditor power covered in Chapter 5. However, in this book, the argument has been made that social welfare is most likely to be damaged if a reorganization of complex, leveraged loan, bond, and equity finance arrangements cannot be achieved sufficiently quickly or at an affordable cost so that distress spreads to the group's operations. In this context, an intercreditor agreement which simplifies the bargaining environment and reduces hold-out power is to be applauded. Where the transaction amounts to a reorganization of loan, bond, and equity finance arrangements, not only should courts uphold intercreditor arrangements, but they should also go further. They should actively encourage innovation and development of intercreditor technology to encompass a wider group of financial creditors and a wider range of issues. In this way, private bargaining can go some way towards assisting with simplification of the bargaining environment, given the different role that reputational concern plays in twenty-first-century deals. Nonetheless, this assumes a sophisticated group of financial creditors who can organize and defend themselves as the case demands. As Edward Morrison's thesis suggests, and consistent with the rest of this work, different concerns may arise if the corporate reorganization plan implicates general, unsecured creditors and employees.

7.2.5 Summary of the argument in section 7.2

The core argument here is that encouraging the finance market to discipline itself is an entirely legitimate objective when the focus is on the reorganization of complex, leveraged loan, bond, and equity finance arrangements. A good example of this has already begun to emerge in the US in another area: the so-called empty voting problem. Empty voting occurs when the party with the legal right to vote in the

[39] Williamson (n 4) 80.
[40] Edward R Morrison, 'Rules of Thumb for Intercreditor Agreements' (2015) U Ill L Rev 721.

corporate reorganization has no economic interest in the corporate reorganization case. It is most commonly identified with the situation in which a debt holder has purchased credit default swap protection. If the borrower defaults on the debt, the credit default swap holder may be in a better position if the debtor is liquidated rather than reorganized, because it will be able to recover the face amount of its debt from the credit default swap provider. In the most egregious cases, this may actually cause the debt holder to pursue a strategy to defeat an otherwise value-maximizing corporate reorganization transaction. There is a rich literature identifying the empty creditor voting problem.[41] Yet, interestingly, there are also signs that the loan market at least is beginning to take steps to address the problem for itself by disenfranchising so-called 'empty voters' in certain, identified circumstances in the finance documents.[42] This is exactly as it should be. While the reputational changes considered in this chapter increase the prospect of contestation, and reduce the effectiveness of market exclusion, the market does still possess the power to police behaviour which it determines is outside the bounds of acceptability. And it should be encouraged to do so. Thus, more inclusive intercreditor arrangements, which affect only the financial creditors' rights and not the debtor's rights, should be encouraged, at least where flexing of the complex, leveraged capital structure is the transaction in prospect.

7.3 England

7.3.1 Why England did not adopt the bargaining and litigation concept

As discussed in Chapter 2, after the bank mergers of 1918 the 'Big Five' clearing banks of Midland, Westminster, Lloyds, National Provincial, and Barclays operated as a virtual oligopoly in British banking.[43] The Big Five clearing banks (now the Big Four) were formed through the amalgamations of the private banking partnerships of nineteenth-century Britain, dominated by certain powerful families. At first, it was important to continue to attract senior members of powerful families into the banks for the inherited capital which they brought with them. Even when

41 Frank Partnoy and David A Skeel Jr, 'The Promise and Perils of Credit Derivatives' (2007) 75 U Cin L Rev 1019, 1035; Daniel Hemel, 'Empty Creditors and Debt Exchanges' (2010) 27 Yale L J Reg 159, 161; Henry T C Hu and Bernard Black, 'Equity and Debt Decoupling and Empty Voting II: Importance and Extensions' (2008) 156 U Pa L Rev 625, 731; Douglas G Baird and Robert K Rasmussen, 'Anitbankruptcy' (2010) 119(4) Yale L J 648, 681; David A Skeel Jr and Thomas H Jackson, 'Transaction Consistency and the New Finance in Bankruptcy' (2012) 112 Colum L Rev 152.

42 Milbank Client Alert, 'Net Short Lender Disenfranchisement: Is the New Anti-CDS Vaccine Safe and Effective?' (11 June 2019)—discussed in more detail in Chapter 9.

43 For one account of the merger movement, see Michael Collins and Mae Baker, *Commercial Banks and Industrial Finance in England and Wales 1860–1913* (OUP 2003, repr 2011) 107–11.

this ceased to be the case, family members continued to occupy the most powerful positions within the banks. In order to get any position within a clearing bank, a connection or introduction was needed: positions were rarely advertised.[44] City attitudes were dominated by the idea of the gentlemen and the players (those who actually did the work), and by the idea of the talented amateur, rather than the expert. Indeed, there was something of an anti-intellectual prejudice in the City, where qualities of 'clubability' and decent antecedents could be more important than intellectual ability. As Ackrill and Hannah identify:

> Ministry of Labour guidance in 1936 was unabashed by its matter-of-fact class snobbery. While acknowledging the need for arithmetical skill and English qualifications, it put stress on the social and athletic attainments of a 'good mixer' and 'the necessity for unimpeachable antecedents'. In effect, working-class boys need not apply.[45]

The business model was remarkably straightforward: personal and corporate deposits were the main source of funds, and business overdrafts accounted for the bulk of loans.[46] This simple business was made possible by the virtual cartel-like agreement between the banks on the appropriate range for rates of interest on deposit accounts and advances.[47] At the same time, until the 1970s, British banks benefitted from exemptions from disclosure obligations in successive Companies Acts, so that there was very little focus on actual levels of profitability.[48] Banks were assumed to have hidden reserves, and great comfort was taken in the sheer size of the biggest players.[49] This, then, was a scarcely competitive industry and what little competition there was, was based on service levels rather than price. British banks enjoyed a highly cartelized oligopoly.

The Bank of England and the Government tolerated this arrangement for a number of reasons. First, it was thought that the benefits which it provided in terms of a strong and stable banking system outweighed the problems for customers.[50] Secondly, it enabled the Government to borrow cheaply because banks could invest in Treasury Bills and gilt-edged stock at a low interest rate, and could pass the low rate on to customers in terms of a low interest rate on deposits.[51] Thirdly, it enabled the Bank of England to interfere relatively actively in the lives of the banks, with the threat of greater regulation against their interests if they did not comply

[44] See Margaret Ackrill and Leslie Hannah, *Barclays: The Business of Banking 1690–1996* (CUP 2001) 76.
[45] ibid 76.
[46] ibid 90.
[47] ibid 96.
[48] ibid 68.
[49] ibid 65.
[50] ibid 106.
[51] ibid 99.

with 'requests'. When the Bank of England was concerned about inflationary risks in the economy they could 'request' the Big Five to show restraint in lending policies, and they could require the Big Five to place special deposits with them as a way of controlling money in the economy.[52] A close and respectful relationship developed between the Bank of England and the Big Five, so that it was said that the Governor only needed to raise his eyebrows to indicate his displeasure in order to bring the banks into line.[53] The Bank of England was nationalized in 1946, and gained statutory powers which it could enforce against the banks. Yet, the informal and deferential relationship between the banks, which wished to maintain their cartel, and the Bank of England, which wished to exercise direct credit control, appears to have been just as important.

As explored in earlier chapters, the first significant modern crisis for British banking arose in the early 1970s. So-called secondary banks had grown up advancing large loans to the commercial property sector. Eventually, rising interest rates caused a crisis for the sector when the secondary banks no longer recovered enough interest on their commercial property loans to cover their interest payments on their external debt. And it turned out that the Big Five banks were heavily exposed to the secondary banks. Barclays was the lead banker and issuing house to a Morrison family investment, Cedar Holdings. The Bank of England held a lengthy meeting from 19–20 December 1973, at which it prevailed upon the Morrisons to relinquish control, upon Barclays to provide rescue finance, and upon the firm's institutional investors to top it up. The next day it launched a 'lifeboat fund' to provide greater help to the sector.[54] Crucially, the Bank saw the risks to systemic stability if the commercial property exposures of the secondary banks were all liquidated at fire sale prices with consequent losses for the Big Five. Instead, the Bank of England and other market players cooperated to promote the gradual realization of assets and the rescue and reconstruction of the commercial property trusts.

Earlier chapters explored how this experience persuaded the Bank of England of the need to seed some principles which banks should observe in order to facilitate the successful restructuring of financially distressed companies. These principles were promulgated by the Bank of England and became known as 'The London Approach'.[55] By this time, the cartel arrangement was ending. The Competition and Credit Control mechanisms, implemented in 1971, terminated the interest rate cartel. Moreover, they brought to an end a whole range of other agreements

[52] ibid 116–18.
[53] ibid 118.
[54] The account of the Cedar Holdings meeting is drawn from Ackrill and Hannah (n 44) 207.
[55] Pen Kent, 'The London Approach' (1993) Q1 Bank of England Q Bull 110; John Flood, Robert Abbey, Eleni Skordaki, and Paul Aber, 'The Professional Restructuring of Corporate Rescue: Company Voluntary Arrangements and the London Approach' (1995) ACCA Research Report 45; Alice Belcher, *Corporate Rescue: A Conceptual Approach to Insolvency Law* (Sweet & Maxwell 1997) 116–22; John Armour and Simon Deakin, 'Norms in Private Insolvency: The "London Approach" to the Resolution of Financial Distress' (2001) 1 J Corp Law Stud 21.

between the major banks.[56] The direct system of credit control (which required the cartel-like structure of the market to function) was giving way to control of money in the economy through the short-term interest rate,[57] while foreign banks and other types of institution actively began to compete for the Big Five's traditional business.[58]

Nonetheless, the Big Five continued to pay high regard to the Bank of England's wishes. For some time, therefore, the London Approach was enforced through the risk of incurring the Bank of England's displeasure if a bank did not observe it.[59] In other words, reputation for observing the rules of the game remained crucial for the clearing banks. However, monetarism established itself more firmly; competition increased from incoming foreign banks and new entrants to the finance field; Bretton Woods came to an end; and money began to flow more freely across borders. At this point, the Bank of England stepped away from its role as informal enforcer of good banking practice in a corporate reorganization case.

For a time, however, reputation for observing the rules of the club continued to be important. As discussed in Chapter 4, the syndicated loan had developed. Banks feared that if they gained a reputation for bad behaviour in corporate reorganizations they would no longer be invited to join syndicates when new loans were arranged.[60] Given that British and European banks had organized themselves into informal 'clubs' to cooperate in cross-border business for clients, market discipline operated even as against overseas banks.[61] Although the era of relationship banking was coming to an end, reputation for observing the informal rules remained crucial for continued participation in the primary markets. As a result, the London Approach continued to operate to incentivize bargaining and agreement in corporate reorganization transactions. In a sense, the London Approach operated as a version of what Oliver Williamson terms a 'general clause', whereby parties to a contract promise to 'disclose all relevant information candidly and to behave in a cooperative fashion', in contract renegotiation.[62] Thus social norms continued to be significantly more important than the threat of litigation in England.

[56] Committee of London Clearing Bankers, *The London Clearing Banks: Evidence by the Committee of London Clearing Bankers to the Committee to Review the Functioning of Financial Institutions* (Longman, Inc 1978) 175–76, referring to termination of the agreement relating to group terms for employees' bank accounts; agreement on charges for encashment of cheques by customers of non-clearing banks; agreement on charges for status enquiries by hire purchase companies; agreement on commissions on the issue of travellers' cheques; agreement on scales of minimum commission for customers abroad; and agreements not to certify cheques, guarantee trade debts, or carry on business outside banking premises.

[57] Ackrill and Hannah (n 44) 209.

[58] ibid 218.

[59] Armour and Deakin (n 55) 40.

[60] ibid 46.

[61] Committee of London Clearing Bankers (n 56) 143.

[62] Williamson (n 4) 66.

7.3.2 The fall of the gentleman banker in England

However, times were changing. As explored in Chapter 4, the development of actively traded secondary markets in loan debt gave birth to traders specializing in trading the debt of financially distressed borrowers. These lenders did not need access to the primary loan syndication markets and, in any event, benefitted from a more hard-bitten reputation for pursuing their legal rights. At the same time, the new era of competition, coupled with genuine disclosure of banks' profits, had caused the banking industry to focus on becoming profit-maximizing entities. During the era of the highly cartelized oligopoly, as Carnevali and Hannah put it, British 'Bankers were satisficers or, in expanding their branches, growth-maximizers; they were not, in general, profit-maximizers'.[63] Indeed, it was essential that the cartel operated in this way if the Bank of England were to be able to extract benefits in imposing soft controls which would often reduce the price of credit below the profit-maximizing price. The end of the cartel and increasing competition put pressure on bank margins, but also promoted the need for profit, so that banks were highly focused on how to maximize it. In these new, profit-maximizing times it was no longer acceptable to leave money on the table in order to get a deal done. Profit was more important than reputation for gentlemanly behaviour approved of by the authorities. Thus, the process of bargaining became more challenging in England, just as it had already become in the US, and gentlemanly bargaining came to be regarded as inherently complacent. The distressed debt traders brought the same forceful approach to the deal, shaking the English market when they voted down a consensual restructuring of Barings bank. Yet these changes occurred, in England, in a different context.

7.3.3 The fall of the gentleman banker and English corporate reorganization law

As explored in Chapter 3, until comparatively recently leveraged capital structures in England have comprised senior bank debt and mezzanine loans. Usually, both loans are secured over the same assets, with priority regulated by an intercreditor agreement. As a result, the intercreditor agreement ordinarily covers the whole of the leveraged capital structure, and provides what Williamson calls 'complex conditional responses' to the contingent event of financial distress.[64] Thus, the English intercreditor agreement goes further than

[63] Francesca Carnevali and Leslie Hannah, 'The Effects of Banking Cartels and Credit Rationing on U.K. Industrial Structure and Economic Performance Since World War Two' in Michael D Bordo and Richard Sylla (eds) *Anglo-American Financial Systems: Institutions and Markets in the Twentieth Century* (Irwin Professional Pub 1995) 74.

[64] Williamson (n 4) 346.

intercreditor agreements in US corporate reorganization in cutting down on (socially wasteful) renegotiation cost, and provides a credible threat given the English courts' willingness to enforce it. The intercreditor agreement ordinarily provides a stop on payments to, and action by, the junior creditors. Furthermore, as discussed in Chapter 5, it provides a detailed mechanism by which majority, senior lenders can issue an instruction to the security trustee to release the guarantees and security granted in favour of junior creditors by the operating companies, if the market price or current market value of the firm does not provide sufficient value to repay some or all of their claim. As this book has already argued, this provides a more predictable benchmark for senior lenders to justify the offer to junior lenders, bondholders, and equity, particularly if market price can be established via a short auction process.

7.3.4 The concept of the predictable court emerges in England

English courts have coupled their predictable willingness to enforce the intercreditor agreement with a general scepticism about junior creditor and shareholder attempts to hold up the reorganization transaction. Thus, as explored in earlier chapters, the English courts have placed considerable store by the counterfactual (what will happen if the reorganization cannot be achieved) in considering whether junior lenders, bondholders, and shareholders have been treated fairly. As the counterfactual is likely to be a going concern sale of the operating group, or even a break-up sale of the assets, junior lenders, bondholders, and shareholders have less capacity to contest a corporate reorganization case than in a Chapter 11 case. Overall, the approach which will be adopted by the court in any legal challenge is more predictable than the approach of the US bankruptcy court, while the English courts have shown themselves alive to the risk of hold-out litigation by junior financial creditors. In the *Bluebrook* case, the junior creditors argued that the directors of the scheme companies ought to have bargained harder on their behalf. They based this claim on the assumption that the senior lenders would have no interest, in reality, in taking enforcement action which would have destroyed value. Thus, they argued, the senior lenders lacked a credible threat which provided the mezzanine lenders with hold-out value. It was this hold-out value which, they argued, the directors ought to have exploited on their behalf. Mr Justice Mann dispensed with the argument on the basis that it seemed 'somewhat unreal'.[65] Among other things, the group would have continued to have difficulties in meeting its financial covenants, and a reorganization was plainly required. Mr Justice Mann also commented at some length on the sophisticated and engaged nature of the

65 *Re Bluebrook Ltd* [2009] EWHC 2114 (Ch); [2010] BCC 209 [60].

mezzanine financial creditors who 'seem at all material times to have been fighting their own corner'.[66] In short, the English courts have shown themselves aware of the incentives for junior financial creditors to hold up a reorganization, and equal to the task of containing that hold-out threat by creating a predictable litigation environment.

Other aspects of the English system also disincentivize litigation. First, England is a loser-pays jurisdiction, so that there can be real cost implications in relatively speculative efforts at litigation. At the same time, there are some comparatively strict rules on how claims are pleaded. These restrain some of the livelier claims which junior lenders, bondholders, and investors might otherwise seek to bring. In particular, if claims brought against other participants are seen to be challenging their good faith, then the court is likely to look closely at how much notice the defendants had of the allegations, and the opportunity which they had to respond to them properly.[67] Moreover, the claim may engage particular professional conduct rules for counsel advancing it. On the other hand, if the claim is raised late or weakly articulated, then it is unlikely to find much favour with the court, which will be alive to backdoor attempts to implicate directors and others, without giving them proper opportunity to respond to the allegations. Overall, the litigation environment is not very hospitable to junior financial creditors and investors seeking to hold up a reorganization transaction.

At the same time, it is important to note that, in most cases, the senior creditors will hope to avoid pursuing the pre-packaged administration sale implementation route. First, as discussed in Chapter 6, this route is more unsettling for general, unsecured creditors, employees, and customers of the operating group companies. Secondly, it raises liability concerns for the security trustee (in implementing the guarantee and security release) and the administrator (in implementing the pre-packaged sale transaction), raising cost. Thirdly, it has the result that the directors will have been directors of a company which has been placed into a corporate bankruptcy process: something which many will wish to avoid, if possible. Fourthly, an administration of the intermediate finance company may be more likely to default contracts in the operating group than a scheme of arrangement. And finally, the transaction raises difficult accounting and tax considerations. The ability credibly to threaten implementation of the transaction is vital, in the new world of reputation which has been identified in this chapter. This is because it is the convincing threat of a legal solution which incentivizes creditors to agree to the scheme of arrangement transaction, rather than the old-world reputational concerns which existed prior to the 1990s. At

66 ibid [56].
67 ibid [54]–[55].

the same time, it is highly unlikely to be the senior secured creditors' preferred course of action.

7.3.5 Summary of the argument in section 7.3

Overall, a delicate bargaining environment is created in England. Junior lenders, bondholders, and shareholders are disincentivized from litigating speculatively because of the relatively pro-senior orientation of the intercreditor agreement and the courts' willingness to uphold it; the risk of a costs order; and the general scepticism of opportunistic litigation. At the same time, the senior secured creditors are incentivized to bargain because of the undesirable consequences of resorting to an insolvency process in order to implement the reorganization.

Earlier chapters touched briefly on the new Part 26A to the Companies Act 2006, which is included in the new Corporate Insolvency and Governance Bill (the Bill) introduced just as this book is going to press, and which the UK Government has indicated it intends to fast-track through Parliament.[68] Part 26A is heavily based on, although separate from, the scheme of arrangement, and is intended to facilitate cross-class cram-down of a corporate reorganization plan, without resort to the pre-packaged administration transaction. It, therefore, avoids some of the risks of that transaction identified above. At the same time, it potentially provides a powerful threat to hold-out junior creditors, particularly given that cram-down would be dependent on demonstrating that dissenting creditors were no worse off under the Part 26A plan when compared with the 'relevant alternative'.[69] As already explored, in most cases, this is likely to be an administration sale of the shares in the parent of the operating group. In other words, in most cases it is likely to be on all fours with the existing intercreditor agreement release mechanics. Thus far, therefore, it has been suggested that it is unlikely to alter radically the landscape of the reorganization. The focus, instead, has been on whether English scholars, practitioners, judges, and the legislature will be able to replace, supplement, or reformulate concepts laid down in an era of reorganization of financial liabilities if expanding and shifting logics, practices, and identities in finance and non-financial corporate fields impact the ways in which corporate reorganization law is mobilized and adapted in the future.

However, a more immediate concern arises relating to the impact which the new Part 26A procedure may have on the delicate bargaining environment in an

[68] Corporate Insolvency and Governance Bill [HC] 2019–21, Sch 9, inserting new Part 26A into Companies Act 2006.

[69] New Part 26A Companies Act 2006, s 901G, which provides that 'the "relevant alternative" is whatever the court considers would be most likely to occur in relation to the company if the compromise or arrangement were not sanctioned'.

English reorganization case. At first sight, Part 26A would appear to place even more constraints on junior lender, bondholder, or shareholder power in a reorganization case. Thus, the question arises as to whether it disincentivizes senior creditor bargaining. A sanction hearing is always held in a scheme of arrangement case, even when no party appears to contest the scheme. Moreover, debtor's counsel retains an obligation of full and frank disclosure in taking the judge with carriage of the case through the scheme documents. Yet, it remains the case that an uncontested scheme of arrangement absorbs considerably less court time than a contested case. Furthermore, as already explored, in a scheme of arrangement case the court is alive to the question of whether there is reason to doubt that the majority exercised its vote in the interests of the class of which it forms part. More difficult questions about valuation associated with the wider concerns for objective fairness are infrequently implicated. On the other hand, it is possible that, if Part 26A is mobilized and adapted by senior creditors, it will offer fewer risks for them than the pre-packaged administration route in certain types of case. The question then arises as to whether the senior creditors have an incentive to avoid the bargaining stage entirely, and move straight to the court-implemented cram-down plan. If this were to come to pass, it may have implications for court time and resource. In this context, it is worth noting that the English courts which hear these cases are significantly less well resourced than US bankruptcy courts. It is too early to know how participants will mobilize and adapt the new Part 26A tool, and the extent to which participants will turn to Part 26A rather than the scheme twinned with pre-packaged administration as a method of imposing a plan on a dissenting class. Yet, assuming participants do turn to the tool, it is suggested that judges should be alive to the impact which it may have on the overall bargaining environment, in interrogating a Part 26A plan at sanction.

7.4 Conclusion

In this chapter, the argument has been made that the end of gentlemanly reputation in the US and England has significant implications for the bargaining environment in financial distress in both jurisdictions. It has been argued that this requires the unravelling and reformulation of the bargaining and litigation concept in Chapter 11. It has been suggested that the litigation and bargaining environment created by complex Chapter 11 rules is well adapted to a collegiate, gentlemanly market in which parties have significant reputational reasons, as Klee and Bussel put it, not 'to stand on their legal rights'.[70] However, the argument has also been advanced that it is less well adapted to an environment in which investment bankers

[70] Bussel and Klee (n 3) 694.

and their clients put more weight on transactions than on long-run relationships, and on mathematical ability and capacity in secondary markets than on a social address book and gentlemanly norms of behaviour. As a result, it has been suggested, first, that a simpler bargaining environment is to be preferred and, secondly, that there is good reason to support the market's attempt to discipline itself through contract rather than providing complex, but contestable, mandatory rules of law. Overall, the argument is that US bankruptcy courts should be more willing to uphold intercreditor agreements, so that parties are encouraged both to negotiate them seriously and to focus on developing a market consensus as to their terms. Moreover, it has been suggested that US courts should encourage intercreditor agreements which cover the whole of the capital structure, enabling them to play a more serious role in developing standards of acceptable engagement.

A very different story has unfolded when the account turned to consider England. The same shift is visible, from collegiate, gentlemanly markets, in which parties had incentives not to stand on their strict legal rights, to heterogeneous, competitive markets in which parties have every incentive to insist on them. Yet, the account in this chapter has revealed the vital role which the intercreditor agreement has played in the new environment in facilitating complex, deleveraging transactions. While it is apparent, by this stage in the book, that both the scheme of arrangement and the pre-packaged administration sale lack all of the tools which are necessary for successful implementation of a capital reorganization, it is also clear that the intercreditor agreement has developed to fill the gaps. At the same time, the English court has shown a high degree of willingness to enforce the contractual intercreditor arrangements. As a result, the intercreditor agreement has fulfilled a more significant function than it has hitherto enjoyed in the US. Crucially, it has created a predictable litigation environment in an era of more aggressive negotiation and litigation. At the same time, the English courts have shown themselves alive to the risk of junior lender, bondholder, or shareholder hold-out action, and other aspects of English litigation also act to restrain speculative litigation efforts and to create a predictable litigation environment. Yet, the account in this chapter has also revealed that senior creditors are unlikely to prefer a pre-packaged administration sale as a method of implementation in most cases, so that a delicate environment in which bargaining can take place is created.

One specific concern which has arisen is whether the new Part 26A to the Companies Act 2006 will have significant implications for the analysis in this book.[71] Thus far, earlier chapters have concluded that this is unlikely to be the case, at least in the short term. The concern has been raised in this chapter, however, that the reform proposal might impact on the bargaining environment more generally, with implications for court time and resource. In particular, the concern has been

[71] The Bill (n 68).

raised that senior creditors may have fewer concerns about immediate resort to the new Part 26A procedure in certain types of case, when compared with immediate resort to a pre-packaged administration to impose a cram-down plan on a junior class. Thus, it is suggested that this is an issue meriting immediate attention by judges when they are considering how they will approach sanction of a Part 26A plan. Part 26A is considered further when the reform agenda is examined in more detail in Chapter 10.

8
The Fall of the Honest Broker

8.1 Introduction

Earlier chapters have already discussed the crucial intermediation role which J P Morgan and other investment bankers played at the end of the nineteenth and the beginning of the twentieth centuries, between the railroads and the other corporates in the United States (US) who needed capital, and the British investors who were able to provide it. Morgan saw it as vital to his ability to continue to access British capital markets to be able to look after British investors for the entire life cycle of their investment. Thus, Morgan and other bankers of his ilk not only negotiated but also fundamentally shaped the reorganization transaction. The New Deal reforms decisively shifted power in corporate reorganization away from the investment banks, and Chapter 11 reforms decisively shifted that power towards debtors. However, as this chapter explores, debtors do not play a central honest broker role in determining the shape of a reorganization implicating sophisticated financial creditors and shareholders in modern cases. Most of the participants in these cases prize their superior ability to value assets, and will have their own strongly held views on firm value, unmediated by other parties. In order to deleverage the complex, leveraged loan, bond, and equity capital structure, it is vital that significant financial creditors with particular, expert views on the shape of the transaction are able to participate in the renegotiation.

Corporate Reorganization Law and Forces of Change. Sarah Paterson, Oxford University Press (2020). © Sarah Paterson.
DOI: 10.1093/oso/9780198860365.001.0001.

Thus far, the book has focused on concepts which have played a crucial role in formulating the debate between economically minded and progressively minded scholars about the policy and content of corporate reorganization law. In contrast, this chapter is concerned with a concept which has not divided corporate reorganization law scholars to date, but which interacts with another corporate law field in new ways. The relevant concept is the concept of transparency and disclosure, and the proximate field in question is the field of insider trading. This chapter explores why shifts in identities in the finance field raise entirely new questions about the implications of transparency and disclosure for insider trading and market abuse liability. It advances the argument that this gives rise to a new need to focus on insider trading laws in distress, and to create new safe harbours which enable reorganizations among financial institutions to be implemented as rapidly and at as low cost as possible, without requiring increased levels of disclosure and transparency by debtors. This chapter is different, too, because very similar concerns emerge in the US and English analyses.

8.2 United States

8.2.1 The concept of transparency and full disclosure

Both economically orientated and progressively orientated scholars agree on the need for transparency and disclosure in the corporate reorganization process. For scholars adopting an economic approach, transparency and disclosure enables bargaining to work efficiently to arrive at the most value-maximizing option. For progressive scholars, transparency and disclosure promotes equal access to information among all stakeholders, and thus promotes fairness. Similarly, most economically orientated and progressively orientated scholars have some commitment to equal access to information in the capital markets. Economically minded scholars typically focus on the need to promote confidence in the capital markets. Progressively minded scholars typically focus on fairness concerns for equal access to information. Yet the level of transparency and disclosure at the heart of Chapter 11 raises new issues in modern markets. In order to understand this, it is necessary to trace the history of the role of the intermediary in the corporate reorganization bargaining process.

8.2.2 The fall of the honest broker

Ron Chernow tells us something of J P Morgan's negotiating strategy when a firm in which he had marketed securities faced distress, and a reorganization needed to be agreed. First, Morgan would adopt what Chernow calls a 'no exit situation'. In many cases, the situation was literally no exit as Morgan frequently hosted negotiations at sea on his yacht, the Corsair. Secondly, Morgan adopted a policy of saying little in order to reinforce his role as honest broker. And finally, as Chernow identifies, Morgan '... performed the kind of task of industrial arbitration that would later be left to courts and public commissions'.[1] Modern scholarship has endorsed the effectiveness of Morgan as the broker between the parties in corporate reorganization cases.[2] Yet he exerted considerable power, and his role excited considerable controversy.

As this book has explored in a number of places, Morgan-sponsored reorganizations often concerned US railroads. A particular feature of Morgan's reorganizations was that he calculated the minimum earning capacity of the railroad after reorganization, and issued new, fixed-rate bonds and preferred shares against that earning capacity. This had the result that common stockholders (who Morgan often did not represent, and who were often local (US) investors, rather than British investors) had little or no prospect of receiving a dividend. After a reorganization had been implemented, Morgan typically established a voting trust pursuant to which Morgan nominees effectively controlled voting power. This left the common stockholders with no practical ability to protest against the lack of dividends. In other words, coupled with control concentrated in the hands of Morgan, domestic investors who held common stock ranked behind so many other securities that there was no practical likelihood of seeing a financial return, while foreign bond investors, whose interests were advanced by Morgan, prospered in the restructured road.[3] Moreover, this situation was only likely to deteriorate over time. This was because, with so little prospect of dividend payments on common stock, restructured railroads were forced to issue more bonds each time they wanted to raise new finance—bonds which ranked ahead of the stock and thus depressed its value still further. When more generalized concerns about the legitimacy of investment banking power were raised in the New Deal reforms, power was decisively shifted away from investment bank intermediaries in corporate reorganization.

As discussed in earlier chapters, the Trust Indenture Act of 1939 was designed to protect the holders of publicly issued bonds, debentures, and other debt securities, and arose directly out of a concern that investment bank 'brokers' would prioritize the interests of their clients in the reorganization plan over the interests of other investors. Among other things, by requiring that every bondholder agreed to changes to the interest rate, principal amount, or maturity of the outstanding bonds, it drove corporate reorganization into the US bankruptcy courts, effectively

[1] These descriptions of J P Morgan's negotiating style are all drawn from Ron Chernow, *The House of Morgan: An American Banking Dynasty and the Rise of Modern Finance* (Grove Press 1990) 55.

[2] J Bradford De Long, 'Did J.P. Morgan's Men Add Value? A Historical Perspective on Financial Capitalism' NBER Working Paper Series August 1990.

[3] Edward Gross Campbell, *The Reorganization of the American Railroad System 1893–1900: A Study of the Effects of the Panic of 1893, the Ensuing Depression etc* (sn) 160.

neutering much of the investment banker's power. As part of the sweeping package of New Deal reforms to corporate law, Congress passed the Chandler Act of 1938, which required the appointment of a trustee at commencement of a Chapter X case. This was undoubtedly a decisive shock to the organizational and institutional structure of corporate reorganization. Transparency and disclosure were also put at the very heart of the process, so that all creditors had access to equal information.

It is interesting to speculate on what might have happened to investment banker power without the legislative intervention of the 1930s. As it was, the US emerged from the First World War firmly as a creditor nation, so that J P Morgan's successors would not, in any event, have continued to mediate between US corporates seeking capital and foreign investors providing it. J P Morgan and his ilk had been in a powerful position because capital was in short supply and they were able to provide access to it for US corporates. Yet, as US capital became plentiful and easy to access, this kind of influence was naturally in decline. Nonetheless, the New Deal reforms are significant in providing a sudden, exogenous shock to an organizational and institutional environment. In England, the field of finance was consolidated in the hands of a few large commercial banks, just as power had been consolidated in the hands of J P Morgan and the other investment bankers in the US. The continuing consolidation of power in the hands of these so-called clearing banks, together with some other aspects of the institutional structure which are explored in the second part of this chapter, enabled the informal approach to continue to dominate in England for some time. Yet, there was no consolidated power base to broker such an informal approach in the US and, in any event, the New Deal reforms had driven the process into court.

It is also worth touching briefly on why accountants do not seem to have secured a significant role as an intermediary in US corporate reorganization when, as revealed in the second part of this chapter, they were the main intermediary during this period in England. The answer may be no more prosaic than the very slow development of accountancy in the US compared with England. In his review of the rise of the accounting profession in the US, John Carey tells us that there were no certified public accountants in 1896.[4] Indeed, it is the arrival of chartered accountants from England, at the end of the nineteenth century, which sows the seeds of a US accountancy profession. These accountants arrived because US industries were raising capital from British investors and these British investors despatched their trusted advisers to investigate the details of their investments. Thus, accountants did produce expert reports on US distressed situations for their British investors, but acted as a third-party expert for those controlling the reorganization process, rather than taking an active role in the process itself. While native, US firms began

[4] John L Carey, *The Rise of the Accounting Profession: From Technician to Professional 1896–1936* (American Institute of Certified Public Accountants 1969) 2.

to emerge at this time, English and Scottish accountants still tended to handle the most prominent investigations.[5] These visiting accountants would have been remote from the rest of the corporate field, and were arriving at a time when England, as the former colonial power, was generally unpopular. Thus, they acted as third-party experts for those promoting the corporate reorganization, and played little part in the development of the equity receivership in the US, which became the provenance of US investment bankers and lawyers.

In the meantime, accountancy continued to develop as a profession very slowly in the US. For a long time, accountants were not held in high public esteem, being 'indistinguishable from bookkeepers',[6] while the familiar battle between state rights and federal interests meant that the profession faced serious issues of organization for the first fifty years of its existence. The slow development of the profession meant that employment in it was somewhat precarious, so that it struggled to attract candidates of sufficient calibre.[7] By the time many of the principles and procedures of the equity receivership came to be codified in modern US corporate reorganization law, it is scarcely surprising that there was no central role for the accountant in the US way of doing things. When investment bankers were initially cast aside as the powerful intermediary in a corporate reorganization case, US accountants were not standing ready to fill the void.

By the time of the bankruptcy reforms of the 1970s, it had become obvious that debtors lacked incentives proactively to file for Chapter X protection, given that this would result in the appointment of a trustee, and they would lose control. Indeed, medium-sized corporate debtors had turned to Chapter XI for corporate reorganization, notwithstanding that it was intended as a small company tool, because it did not necessitate the appointment of a trustee. As a result, in the bankruptcy reforms of 1978, Chapter 11 became a single corporate reorganization gateway, and debtors remained in control. Part of the argument for the concept of debtor control was that the debtor was, of the available options, the most neutral party, and therefore best able to promote a corporate reorganization in the interests of creditors, shareholders, and other stakeholders. As Chapter 6 explored, US management did play a significant role in developing, proposing, and pushing through plans of reorganization during the 1980s and 1990s. Yet earlier chapters have already explored how the shift from a hold-to-maturity, working capital debt market to a traded, leveraged market eventually led to secured transactions reform which has, in turn, dramatically enhanced secured creditor power, while the changing identities of debtors and their senior managers has dramatically changed debtor and managerial incentives.

[5] ibid 38.
[6] ibid 46.
[7] ibid 151–52.

8.2.3 The fall of the honest broker and the corporate reorganization case

In short, this chapter arrives at a world in which financial creditors exercise control over, and shape, a reorganization of the debtor's loan, bond, and equity finance. In this new world, there is no real capacity for a so-called honest broker to hold the ring between the different classes of financial creditor in shaping and implementing the reorganization of the loan, bond, and equity capital structure.[8] The financial creditors are sophisticated institutional investors who will hire their own investment bank and legal advisers to help them to evaluate the options, and to craft an acceptable plan and implementation strategy. The debtor, and its advisers, perform a vital function in pulling the threads together, but there is no ring master as in the days of J P Morgan and the reorganization committee, or even as in the days of the debtor-driven corporate reorganization plans in the 1980s and 1990s. In a complex, multi-tiered, leveraged loan, bond, and equity capital structure it is likely that each tier of financial creditor will organize itself, appointing a committee to represent the interests of the class in negotiating a reorganization of the financial liabilities with the debtor. It is vital that these committees are established to facilitate negotiation, but as Douglas Baird and Robert Rasmussen put it, 'The current environment is one in which there are no natural leaders (or followers) among the creditors to perform the shuttle diplomacy required to build a consensus.'[9] This new organization of the reorganization process creates very different issues from the concerns for concentrated creditor power or, indeed, debtor control.

8.2.4 Implications for the concept of transparency and full disclosure

The first significant issue is the risk that participating in a formal or informal committee will prevent a financial creditor from being able to trade during the course of the case, as a direct result of the disclosures which will be made to the committee, during the course of the bargaining process. Financial information obviously lies at the heart of any attempt to agree a restructuring of a complex, leveraged loan, bond, and equity capital structure. Financial creditors will spend considerable time modelling and stress-testing the group's cashflow projections in determining crucial issues such as where the value breaks in the current capital structure and how much debt is sustainable going forwards. Yet, the debtor company will not wish to release this information to the public market until a reorganization of the financial

[8] For the inability of management to drive the process as a result of the presence of hedge funds, see Wei Jiang, Kai Li, and Wei Wang, 'Hedge Funds and Chapter 11' (2012) 67(2) J Finance 513.

[9] Douglas G Baird and Robert K Rasmussen, 'Antibankruptcy' (2010) 119(4) Yale LJ 648, 652.

liabilities has taken shape, so that the information may be material information for the purposes of trading in the debtor's listed securities in the meantime. As a result, a member of an official Chapter 11 committee, or a member of an informal or ad hoc committee in possession of information which is material and non-public, faces securities laws risk of insider trading liability if it continues to trade in listed securities. At the same time, while there is what Daniel Sullivan calls an 'unstable judicial and academic consensus' that securities laws do not apply to trading in other types of bankruptcy claim, there is some doubt about the position.[10] Thus, the concern arises that potential insider liability may arise when the committee member trades other types of unlisted bankruptcy claims.

This causes significant difficulties for most financial creditors in leveraged loan, bond, and equity capital structures. The creditor may wish to be free to trade in order to meet orders from clients, or for general portfolio balancing. It may also wish to be free to trade if it determines that it no longer wishes to support the reorganization effort or, conversely, that it wishes to consolidate its position in the debtor company's debt, in anticipation of a debt-for-equity swap as part of a strategy to take control of the debtor. The situation is very different from the days when security holders turned their securities over to a reorganization committee until closing of the case, or when debtor-driven plans of reorganization were concerned with trade debt and employee claims. Thus, the concern arises that the most able financial creditors may not be willing to sit on creditors' committees for fear that this will impede their ability to trade. In this case, the vital force needed for a plan of reorganization to emerge is not present at the bankruptcy negotiating table.

The US analysis is difficult and murky because of the complex development of common law US insider trading liability. For the purposes of this chapter, the important point is that liability may arise if the debtor has passed material non-public information to the creditor in confidence, and the creditor has traded on the basis of that information. Yet, a method of addressing the issues has been arrived at, at least where the US bankruptcy courts are already engaged. In this case, financial creditors have asked the US bankruptcy courts for orders permitting them to continue to trade, provided that they put in place a so-called Chinese, or ethical, wall between the trading arm of the creditor and those who are sitting on the relevant creditors' committee. Furthermore, sometimes it is a requirement that the counterparty to any trade is sufficiently sophisticated to understand the arrangement, and signs a so-called 'big boy letter' acknowledging that the creditor may be in possession of material, non-public information. These two solutions are designed to address the concern that either the company or the market counterparty may raise an insider trading claim relating to the trade. However, while this approach

[10] Daniel Sullivan, 'Big Boys and Chinese Walls' (2008) 75 U Chi L Rev 533. For a comprehensive analysis of the debate, see Robert D Drain and Elizabeth J Schwartz, 'Are Bankruptcy Claims Subject to the Federal Securities Laws?' (2002) 10 Am Bankr Inst L Rev 569.

has been adopted with some success in a number of cases, there have been cases in which problems have persisted.

In his seminal work in the 1960s, Manne suggested that there may be inefficiencies in the ban on insider trading which may prevent the market from moving towards a proper or intrinsic price for the asset.[11] A spirited debate on the economics of insider trading liability has followed, but the detail of this wider argument goes beyond the scope of this book (and there must be very little prospect of a general overturning of the ban on insider trading in light of recent controversies and scandals). Nonetheless, specific considerations do arise in the context of reorganizations of loan, bond, and equity finance. First, Chapter 4 has already established that one of the functions which the distressed debt market fulfils, and which increases the prospect of a rapid flexing of the capital structure, is that it enables creditors who do not want to support the reorganization plan to trade out, and enables those who do want to support it to trade in. As a result, preventing a member of a creditors' committee who does not wish to support the emerging reorganization plan from trading, because it is in possession of material non-public information, may limit the plan's chances of success.[12] Secondly, the chances of a successful reorganization of the debt and equity finance may be maximized where a creditor who wishes to take over the debtor is able to consolidate its position in the debtor company's debt. Once again, this may not be possible if the creditor is prevented from trading. In other words, distressed debt trading may be vital to the effective reorganization of the capital structure. At the same time, while insider trading rules generally are intended to protect the wider investing public, once the fact of financial distress is known, only a limited range of constituents is likely to be in the market as buyers. Existing investors may suffer if there is no liquidity for their securities in the distressed debt market,[13] while the wider public interest concern is that reorganization of the loan, bond, and equity capital structure can be achieved, so that financial distress does not spread to the operating group.

One answer, of course, would be for the debtor company to undertake regular cleansing of the information by publishing it to the market. In this way, the market is in possession of the relevant information. Thus, no distortion ought to arise if the financial creditor, who has been party to the reorganization negotiation, trades. Yet, this gives rise to a more general concern with the amount of information which is already disclosed in the Chapter 11 process.[14] A key objective of a rapid

[11] Henry G Manne, *Insider Trading and the Stock Market* (Free Press 1966).

[12] Stuart Gilson points out that there are a number of potential liabilities for investors in distressed debt in US bankruptcy, so that investors 'who are more familiar with the borrower's operations and management' have a comparative advantage—see Stuart C Gilson, *Creating Value through Corporate Restructuring: Case Studies in Bankruptcies, Buyouts, and Breakups* (John Wiley & Sons, Inc 2001) 207.

[13] Chaim J Fortgang and Thomas Moers Mayer, 'Trading Claims and Taking Control of Corporations in Chapter 11' (1990) 12 Cardozo L Rev 1, 4.

[14] Mark D Bloom, David M Olenczuk, and Richard L Wynne, 'Reorganizing in a Fish Bowl: Public Access vs Protecting Confidential Information' (1999) 73 Am Bankr LJ 775.

reorganization of the debt and equity financing arrangements is to prevent distress spreading to the operations of the group. In other words, by swiftly reorganizing the loan, bond, and equity finance the group ought to be able to continue to meet its operating liabilities. If significant amounts of private information are disclosed, in a way which is easily accessible given the rise of online filing, competitors may be able to obtain valuable intelligence on how to damage the debtor company and attract business away from it. Enhanced disclosure also risks shining a light on certain aspects of the group's business which attract the attention of general, unsecured creditors and customers who would otherwise have assumed that the transaction was limited to financial creditors and equity. These general, unsecured creditors and customers may react to business information which is disclosed, putting pressure on the operations and challenging the debtor's ability to limit the discussions, and the reorganization, to its debt and equity finance. Thus, for as long as the case is limited to a reorganization among financial institutions, the debtor is likely to be legitimately reluctant to disclose information generally.

As a result, it is suggested that a conflict arises between two competing policies. This is similar to the conflict between the policy of protecting collective bargaining, and the policy of promoting corporate reorganization, which was explored in Chapter 6. In the present case, the conflict is between 'ensuring a "level playing field" for investors, bolstering "confidence in the fairness of markets," and preventing the exploitation of "unerodable informational advantages"',[15] and the policy of promoting reorganizations of debt and equity finance. It is suggested that this competition between policy objectives should be determined in favour of promoting the reorganization of the debt and equity finance. Moreover, it is suggested that further work is needed on clarifying and scoping specific safe harbours for parties which may possess material non-public information and which trade financial liabilities during the course of a reorganization case. A bidder who knows it is about to make a tender offer can acquire target shares in the market. There are parallels between this and a distressed debt trader seeking to take control of a financially distressed debt company through a debt-for-equity swap. The debt trader attempts to acquire debt in the market with a view to consolidating its position, and ultimately taking over the firm (albeit that it is likely to seek to do so at a discount rather than the premium offered to shareholders in a public bid). Crucially, these safe harbours should be articulated in such a way that committee members can rely on them, before the US bankruptcy courts are engaged, but while renegotiations are in course.

The first problem with the Chinese, or ethical, wall as a complete solution, is the expense and structural challenges in establishing the relevant partitioning

[15] Selective Disclosure and Insider Trading: Final Rule, 2000 WL 1200556 (24 August 2000) as cited in John P Anderson, *Insider Trading: Law, Ethics, and Reform* (CUP 2018) 55.

of trading and non-trading parts of the organization.[16] This may make it practically impossible for smaller funds to erect such a barrier. As a result, if a Chinese, or ethical, wall provides the only solution to insider trading risk, they may choose to stay outside the negotiations, even where their participation is crucial to success. Furthermore, the Chinese, or ethical, wall does not address the fact that a committee member may discover, during the course of the negotiations, that it does not wish to support the emerging reorganization plan. In this case, it may be desirable for the committee member to be able to trade on that information with another, sophisticated distressed debt investor willing to buy in the market. Daniel Sullivan has suggested that specific safe harbours should be developed for participants trading in possession of inside information, in a corporate reorganization case. It is suggested here that Sullivan is right, and that these safe harbours should go beyond either agreeing not to trade or the successful establishment of a Chinese, or ethical, wall.[17]

The new safe harbour could require the parties to the trade to execute so-called big boy letters which inform the purchaser that the seller may be in possession of inside information. Furthermore, the purchaser could be placed under an obligation to inform any subsequent purchaser that it was party to such a big boy letter in the original trade. This would ensure that the fact that trades had occurred while parties were in possession of material, non-public information is disseminated down the trading chain.[18] It could also be a condition that the market is aware that the debtor company is in financial distress. In this way, participants would be put on notice that the safe harbour provisions are engaged. It is already the case that the price at which debt trades in distress is subject to a considerable number of variables. These include the liquidity and regulatory needs of sellers, which may mean they are in effect forced sellers; the number of purchasers in the market; and whether one or more funds is pursuing a consolidation strategy, with the ambition of gaining control of the debtor in the reorganization transaction. Thus, it is already possible that the distressed debt price will move a long way from what might be called the intrinsic, or fundamental, value of the security. Indeed, this is why caution is advisable in using the debt trading price as a reference point for firm value in assessing a reorganization plan. In short, caution is needed in deciding what weight should be given to preserving market confidence when trading occurs in the securities of a distressed firm. And caution is certainly needed in according it significant weight when it is balanced against the need for active, engaged creditors'

[16] For a useful description of what is involved in erecting a Chinese wall, see Glenn E Siegel and Davin J Hall, 'Confidentiality and Disclosure in Distressed Investing' (2008) 24(1) Rev Banking & Finan Ser 1, 5–6.

[17] Sullivan (n 10) 533.

[18] For problems which can arise if this is not done, see Siegel and Hall (n 16) 2.

committees in order to facilitate the rapid negotiation of a flexing of the loan, bond, and equity capital structure.

One difficult question is the extent to which the debtor company should be required to agree that a member of the committee, who is in receipt of material, non-public information, is free to trade. Where the company gives its agreement, it is difficult to see that a big boy letter alone should not suffice to protect the creditor, because there is no breach of obligation to the company not to trade while in possession of the information. On the other hand, if company consent is required, the company may opportunistically use insider trading risk to lock creditors in, effectively deadlocking the reorganization negotiations. As the second part of this chapter explores, this has been a real concern in the English market. Dispensing with company consent will also have the further benefit, as Sullivan puts it, of treating 'like investments alike'.[19] As discussed at the beginning of section 8.2.4, it is generally thought that the insider trading rules do not apply to unlisted bankruptcy claims. This would include trading in loan participations in the secondary market. Given the depth of this market, there seems very little distinction between trading in the loan participations and trading in a listed bond, in a large reorganization case. And, as Sullivan identifies, the Loan Syndications and Trading Association already includes big boy language in its suite of documents for trading in distressed loans.[20] On balance, therefore, it is suggested that in most cases company consent should not be required, provided that only the fact that the creditor may be in possession of material, non-public information, and not the information itself, is disclosed to the market.

Once again, this is not to say that no normative concerns arise in the new environment. Even though the relevant market participants are sophisticated, financial institutions and not retail investors, there is still a need for confidence in the capital markets for the parties to be willing to trade. And perhaps more importantly, there is the risk that an unscrupulous distressed debt fund trader exploits the safe harbour in order to manipulate the course of the loan, bond, and equity capital structure reorganization case in a way which the market would not regard as legitimate.[21] However, it is suggested here that, for the most part, this can be handled by the market marking out the acceptable boundaries of the safe harbours, and the court policing these boundaries, when it comes to confirmation of the reorganization plan. Even if the reorganization is implemented

[19] Sullivan (n 10) 566.

[20] Loan Syndications and Trading Association, *User's Guide for LSTA Distressed Debt Trading Documentation* referred to in Sullivan (n 10) 560 n 134 and accompanying text.

[21] This was the claim in *Washington Mutual* 461 BR 200 (Bankr D Del 2011) vacated in part 08-12229 (MFW), 2012 WL 1563880 (Bankr D Del Feb 24, 2012) discussed in Matt Porcelli, 'Bankrupting the Inside Job: Alternatives to the Washington Mutual Approach to Policing Creditor Committee Insider Trading' (2012) 9 NYU J L & Bus 295.

via an exchange offer, rather than a Chapter 11 plan, creditors have the ability to complain to the court. It has also been suggested in earlier chapters that the analysis in this book supports Bratton and Levitin's thesis that courts should concern themselves with whether there is reason to doubt the motives of the parties who voted on the exchange offer.[22] Specifically, Bratton and Levitin suggest that courts should consider whether the majority had reasons to vote for the offer which are unrelated to their investment in the class of debt securities in question. The members of a formal committee in the Chapter 11 process owe fiduciary duties to the creditors they are representing.[23] The members of an informal or ad hoc committee may owe fiduciary duties to other creditors, depending on the circumstances. It is suggested here that committee members should not be able to exclude liability to other financial creditors entirely, where they improperly access safe harbour provisions.

Similarly, in a Chapter 11 case, the US bankruptcy courts have a range of equitable powers available to address the situation where it doubts the motivation of the party voting in favour of a reorganization plan, including subordinating or disallowing the offending creditor's claim.[24] The US bankruptcy courts have also shown themselves willing to make highly unpopular disclosure orders, such as disclosure of the price at which a claim was purchased, in order to exercise their policing powers.[25] While these powers are not used frequently, they can be mobilized to address the situation in which particular concerns arise as a result of trading while in possession of material non-public information. Thus, if new safe harbours were developed to address trading in financial claims while in possession of such information, in a reorganization among financial institutions, the court could act as guardian of what would emerge as accepted market practice through its equitable powers. There is some debate in the literature about the extent of the US bankruptcy court's equitable powers, and specifically whether the scope of the powers is limited by the US Bankruptcy Code.[26] It is suggested here that if new safe harbours were established, the US Bankruptcy Code should clearly set out the powers of the US bankruptcy courts to police them. A creditor who remained concerned about the potential impact of these powers on its trading strategy would still be free to trade provided a Chinese, or ethical, wall was also in place. And there is unlikely to be concern for unsophisticated creditors if the safe harbour is limited to financial claims which will (or should) be owned by sophisticated financial creditors in modern markets.

[22] William W Bratton and Adam J Levitin, 'The New Bond Workouts' (2018) 166 U Pa L Rev 1597.
[23] 11 USC § 1102(a)(1).
[24] Sullivan (n 10) 533, 546–58.
[25] For a more general discussion of the disclosure issue, see Douglas G Baird, 'The Bankruptcy Exchange' (2009) 4 Brook J Corp Fin & Com L 23.
[26] Sullivan (n 10) 547 n 60 and accompanying text.

8.2.5 Summary of the argument in section 8.2

Overall, the culture of transparency and full disclosure in Chapter 11 may prevent the parties who need to be involved in bargaining, in order for a reorganization to be achieved, from participating in the process. This is because receipt of non-public information may prevent them from trading in the debt capital markets. It has been suggested that the solution to this problem lies in the field of insider trading proximate to the corporate reorganization field, and that there is a compelling need to focus on whether safe harbours can be developed to facilitate active financial creditor participation. Unusually, for the argument in this book, very similar issues arise in the English context.

8.3 England

8.3.1 Transparency and disclosure in England

As foreshadowed in the first part of this chapter, an entirely different form of intermediation in distress originally arose in England. By the middle of the nineteenth century, a new class of 'accountant' had found valuable work in commercial distress. Where a commercial concern had not adopted the corporate form, it was subject to the bankruptcy regime. From 1831, the court appointed 'official assignees' with responsibility to collect and distribute bankrupt's assets, and leading accountants of the era were amongst the very first official assignees. Thus, in his history of Ernst Whinney (a predecessor to the modern accountancy firm of Ernst & Young), Edgar Jones records that the father of William Turquand (founder of Turquand, Youngs which was later to merge with Whinney, Smith & Whinney), was one of the first official assignees appointed under the Bankruptcy Act of 1831.[27]

Important legislation in the 1840s first made the process of incorporation easier, and later legislation introduced the concept of limited liability, so that companies began to emerge in more significant numbers. At the same time, industrialized Britain embarked on the development of railway construction to provide much needed infrastructure, and significant numbers of railway companies were incorporated. The Joint Stock Companies Winding-Up Act of 1848 allowed any contributory to petition the Lord Chancellor or Master of the Rolls for winding up. The Master's office would then appoint an official manager, in consultation with the contributors, to gather in and dispose of the assets and distribute the proceeds. Public accountants took this role as official manager, and

[27] Edgar Jones, *Accountancy and the British Economy 1948–1980: The Evolution of Ernst & Whinney* (Batsford 1981) 34.

the early English accountants recorded significant work in company winding up. Bankruptcy work became even more lucrative for the early accountants in 1869, when Parliament abolished the position of official assignee, and created the position of the trustee in its place who could be appointed directly by the courts. This effectively cut out the middle man of the official assignee, and enabled a greater number of accountants to benefit from bankruptcy appointments.[28] Parliament reversed course again in 1883, introducing the concept of the Official Receiver so that employment in bankruptcy work was once again at the discretion of a middleman, and the direct link between the courts and accountants was broken. However, a number of leading accountants were appointed as Official Receivers, and an increasing amount of work was, in any event, moving into winding up as incorporation gained in popularity following the adoption of limited liability.[29]

All of this meant that by the end of the nineteenth century accountants had firmly established themselves in the business of investigating companies in distress and taking appointments if the need arose. Early, lucrative bankruptcy work for accountants also meant that increasingly their sons, who often followed them into the profession, had been educated at some of the best public schools and universities, so that the profession was held in higher social regard in England than in the US.[30] As the process of bank amalgamation produced the Big Five banks, it was entirely natural that the banks would establish close contacts with particular accountancy firms, to advise when customers ran into trouble, and to take appointments where necessary. This gave rise to a practice in which accountants would be appointed by the bank to investigate the affairs of the company, and to provide advice on whether the bank should continue to provide support. If the bank concluded that it had lost faith in the management or that the company was not viable, the accountant would be appointed as receiver of the company. At that point, the receiver would either replace the management, or sell the business and assets or assets of the debtor and distribute the proceeds to the bank. A symbiotic relationship developed between the banks and the accountants in financial distress, which placed the accountant at the very heart of the English system.

Until the 1970s, much of this work was undertaken by small, specialist firms because large corporate distress was a comparatively rare event. Yet, as Britain's manufacturing and industrial companies struggled in the face of technological development and international competition, and Britain experienced the volatile and damaging inflation of the 1970s, large corporate distress became a

[28] ibid 48.
[29] ibid 49–50.
[30] ibid 137.

more frequent concern. This had two impacts. First, the fees involved made the work interesting for larger accountancy practices on a more regular basis. Secondly, where an appointment was necessary, the number of individuals needed to supervise the trading of the business increased. As a result, the larger accountancy practices became more regular players in late twentieth-century restructuring, often buying smaller provincial or specialist firms to acquire the necessary connections to establish themselves more firmly in the field.[31]

Accountants continued to act as trusted advisors to their relationship banks during the era of the London Approach (explored in earlier chapters in the book). They typically produced what became known as independent business reviews (IBRs) for the bank syndicate. The IBR reported on the debtor's cashflow forecasts; its assets and liabilities; its operations; its market position; the capabilities of its management team; and similar issues. The overall purpose of the IBR was to provide advice on whether the syndicate should continue to support the debtor, or whether the debtor should be placed in a corporate bankruptcy procedure. However, the IBR would only be made available to the bank lenders. Confidentiality was seen as a key benefit of the London Approach procedure, and the ambition was to restrict disclosure of the company's difficulties to the financial creditors, to the greatest extent possible. Writing in 1995, John Flood and his co-authors put it this way:

> The whole process takes place outside the glare of publicity. One banker said the last thing he wanted to see was the unsecured creditors jumping out at the news. The cloak of secrecy also helps the banks to work together rather than in competition with each other.[32]

As discussed in Chapter 2, England experienced two periods of modern insolvency reform. The first, in 1986, primarily aimed to address the situation where there was no bank with a floating charge willing or able to appoint a receiver. However, the second, in 2002, aimed primarily to address what were seen as serious deficiencies in the receivership system. In the event, the accountants were able to maintain their hegemony through both of these reform efforts. The 1986 reform followed the work of a committee of investigation led by Kenneth Cork, probably the leading insolvency accountant of his day. Thus, it is scarcely surprising that apparent gaps in the system were plugged by a new role for the licensed insolvency practitioner, who was most likely to be a practising accountant. Things might have turned out quite

[31] Edgar Jones, *True and Fair: A History of Price Waterhouse* (Hamish Hamilton 1995) 270.

[32] John Flood, Robert Abbey, Eleni Skordaki, and Paul Aber, 'The Professional Restructuring of Corporate Rescue: Company Voluntary Arrangements and the London Approach' (1995) ACCA Research Report 45, 29.

differently in 2002, given that this reform effort was more hostile to the existing system, and the role of the insolvency practitioner within it. However, the accountants, perhaps failing to sense the rapid organizational and institutional change in the proximate field of finance that was just occurring, singularly failed to grasp the opportunity to refashion both the system and their role in it, which the reforms potentially offered. As a result, the accountants and the clearing banks cooperated together to adapt the way in which the new law on the books functioned. As a result, there was little discernible difference between the way in which the system was perceived and used by market participants after the reforms and the way in which it had been perceived and used before they took effect.

Yet, rapid organizational and institutional change was afoot in the proximate field of finance. The clearing banks were to move, increasingly, from the dominant system of relationship banking to regarding loan business as transactional business which formed part of a traded portfolio. Through the course of the 2000s, this was to open loan business up to other types of institutional lenders, other than banks. At the same time, as explored in Chapter 4, specialist distressed debt players entered the market. And bond debt gradually became a more significant part of leveraged capital structures. Thus, the relationship between the bank and the accountant ceased to be as significant.

Nonetheless, the idea of adapting a highly leveraged capital structure to changing economic conditions emerged as a dominant idea in the UK, just as it had in the US. If the accountants had approached the 2002 reforms differently, they could have inserted themselves into these reorganizations. As the book has touched on many times, the scheme of arrangement began to emerge as the main legal procedure to implement a reorganization of the debtor's loan, bond, and equity financing arrangements. In defending the allocation of consideration in the scheme, borrowers frequently provide evidence on what will happen if the scheme is not sanctioned. Most commonly they argue that the only alternative option will be an administration sale, which will produce lower returns than those offered in the scheme. This might have opened a door for accountants to insert themselves into scheme practice. In other words, accountants could have appeared in court to confirm that, if the scheme did not go ahead, and they were asked to take an administration appointment, they would not have any option but to move to a sale transaction which they anticipated would produce lower values. If this step had been included as a regular feature in early cases, it could rapidly have become accepted practice. Indeed, the English courts might have welcomed this development, because the court has significantly fewer resources to preside over complex loan, bond, and equity capital structure reorganizations than US bankruptcy courts. Furthermore, there is a long tradition of the English courts relying on accountants for commercial judgments in corporate bankruptcy. In the event, accountants made little effort to carve out a regular role of this nature in the new transactions to flex the loan, bond, and equity capital structure of the leveraged borrower. Indeed, most schemes have proceeded without much input from the accountancy profession at all.

Instead, the work has passed almost entirely into the hands of investment banks in England. In part, this is because the investment banks are regarded as having the pre-eminent corporate finance teams, and the problems of valuation implicated in proposing a new capital structure are essentially problems of corporate finance. The detailed operational investigations, at which English accountants excel, are often seen as largely irrelevant to this process. Indeed, many of the new non-clearing bank lenders express bewilderment at the types of traditional reports into the business which the accountancy profession produces. Accountants are sometimes called upon to produce expert evidence as part of a scheme application. Usually, however, this is as the hand maiden of the investment banks (who have provided the detailed financial analysis for the new capital structure) and the lawyers (who have navigated the legal procedures needed to implement the transaction).[33]

8.3.2 The fall of the honest broker in England

However, the investment banking community has not emerged as the honest broker to hold the ring in place of the trusted accountancy adviser in the sorts of multi-tiered leveraged loan, bond, and equity capital structures with which this part of the book is largely concerned. In England, just as in the US, there is unlikely to be a single individual undertaking, to borrow from Baird and Rasmussen again, the sort of 'shuttle diplomacy' and deal-doing role which accountants fulfilled for their clearing bank masters until the late 1990s.[34] Instead, it is likely that the creditor classes in the multi-tiered leveraged loan, bond, and equity capital structure will organize themselves into separate committees, or will appoint financial creditors from within their own number to act as coordinators. As before, the debtor company will have its own investment bank adviser and lawyers, and will meet regularly with the committee members or coordinators in an attempt to hash out a reorganization deal. Yet when it comes to detailed analysis, English creditors are doing it for themselves.

[33] Earlier chapters have touched on the new Part 26A to the Companies Act 2006, which is included in the Corporate Insolvency and Governance Bill introduced just as this book is going to press, and which the UK Government has indicated it intends to fast-track through Parliament. As discussed in earlier chapters, new Part 26A is closely modelled on the existing scheme of arrangement procedure, but includes a cross-class cram-down power which would be available where the court is satisfied that the members of a dissenting class would not be worse off under the compromise or arrangement than they would be under the 'relevant alternative'. The 'relevant alternative' is whatever the court considers would be most likely to occur in relation to the company if the compromise or arrangement were not sanctioned. It will be interesting to see whether the accountancy profession carves out a role for itself in the new Part 26A procedure, providing evidence on the most likely alternative if the compromise or arrangement fails: new Part 26A Companies Act 2006, s 901G, inserted by the Corporate Insolvency and Governance Bill [HC] 2019–21, Sch 9.

[34] Baird and Rasmussen (n 9) 652.

8.3.3 The fall of the honest broker and the English corporate reorganization case

It is possible to establish formal creditors' committees in administration in England, but the role of these committees is quite different from the role of the unsecured creditors' committee in a Chapter 11 case. The committees' views are advisory only, and, crucially, the committee members do not owe fiduciary duties to other creditors. Moreover, it is unlikely that the relevant committee for the purposes of renegotiating a complex, leveraged loan, bond, and equity capital structure in England will be a formal administration committee. As already established, this sort of transaction is likely to mobilize the scheme of arrangement. If the scheme is to be 'twinned' with an administration, for the purposes of achieving a functional cram-down of an entire class of creditor, it will be a pre-packaged administration in which the administrator has only a walk-on part, and the transaction is used for the purposes of implementing the negotiated reorganization plan. As a result, committees in England will almost always be established in accordance with market practice rather than corporate reorganization law.

As earlier chapters have explored, the Loan Market Association (LMA) was established in 1996 for the purposes of encouraging the trading of loan participations in the secondary market. In their excellent book on UK corporate restructuring, Chris Howard and Bob Hedger describe two sets of documents which the LMA has issued for use in establishing creditors' committees. First, they describe an informal 'non-authoritative' coordinator letter. Secondly, they describe a coordinator 'with authority' letter.[35] Generally, creditors on a committee in an English corporate reorganization negotiation will seek to describe their role in mechanical terms. This includes functions such as circulating information, coordinating feedback, and generally acting as the liaison between the company and the rest of the creditor class. They are likely to have their own legal and financial advisers and may insist on indemnity protection, both from the debtor company, and from the other creditors. They are also likely to insist on extensive disclaimer provisions, and acknowledgments of non-reliance from other financial creditors who will confirm that they are reaching their own decision based on their own skill and expertise. It is also possible that a committee of major financial creditors will be established more rapidly, perhaps with indemnity cover only from the company. This is likely to be described as an ad hoc committee, and may be replaced by a more formal committee in due course (albeit still without fiduciary liability).[36]

[35] These descriptions of the LMA and other arrangements in the UK, are drawn from Chris Howard and Bob Hedger, *Restructuring Law and Practice* (2nd edn, LexisNexis 2014) Chapters 3 and 4.

[36] ibid 214–15 paras 4.94–4.99.

It is interesting that, when the issue is left to the market, the market is generally content to proceed on the basis of no fiduciary obligations to other creditors. Even so, the significant transaction costs absorbed in establishing and running the relevant committees should not be underestimated. While the LMA letters may act as a starting point, they are also likely to be subject to negotiation for the specific concerns of particular committee members. The debtor company is likely to be meeting all of the costs of each of the constituent committees. It will be focused on who the committee members are; their ability to represent the interests of the class; and their skill, sophistication, and overall contribution to the process. The debtor company may also wish to establish caps on adviser fees, reporting schedules etc. Moreover, the indemnity provisions are likely to be hotly contested. First, there will be a concern that creditors who have not signed up to committee membership may be able to freeride on its negotiating efforts without meeting indemnity obligations. Secondly, some fund committee members may argue about their ability to provide indemnity cover, citing constitutional issues. As Howard and Hedger note, this is particularly likely to be the case where a fund is closed or in run off.[37] At the very least, the fund may attempt to limit its obligations with non-recourse or non-petition language.

Nonetheless, an effective committee structure is usually essential to the successful negotiation of a flexing of a complex loan, bond, and equity capital structure. As INSOL puts it:[38]

> The interests of relevant creditors are best served by coordinating their response to a debtor in financial difficulty. Such coordination will be facilitated by the selection of one or more representative coordination committees and by the appointment of professional advisers to advise and assist such committees and, where appropriate, the relevant creditors participating in the process as a whole.[39]

The concern is, therefore, to ensure that the financial creditors most able to facilitate the reorganization transaction are incentivized to act on the relevant committee. Once again, this leads to tensions between the policies of England's insider trading and market abuse regimes, on the one hand, and the desire to facilitate a rapid reorganization of the loan, bond, and equity finance before financial distress spreads to the operating group, on the other.

[37] ibid 198–99 para 4.35.

[38] INSOL International is a worldwide federation of national associations for accountants and lawyers who specialize in turnaround and insolvency, <https://www.insol.org/about/> accessed 1 May 2020.

[39] INSOL International, *Statement of Principles for a Global Approach to Multi-Creditor Workouts II* (INSOL 2017) 2.

8.3.4 Implications for the concept of transparency and disclosure in England

England's insider trading regime divides into two, broad buckets. First, there is the domestic regime for insider trading, in the Criminal Justice Act 1993, which carries criminal sanctions. Secondly, at least for the moment, pending the outcome of Britain's Brexit negotiations, English listed companies are subject to the EU Regulation on Market Abuse (MAR).[40] Listed companies must also observe the continuing disclosure obligations in the Disclosure Regulations issued by the Financial Conduct Authority, pursuant to the Financial Services Act 2012. As conceived in MAR, listed companies may delay announcements in order to protect their legitimate interests, and a specific example is provided where announcing 'ongoing negotiations' would affect their 'outcome or "normal pattern"'.[41] This is developed with the case of a company whose solvency is threatened where public disclosure would 'seriously jeopardise' the interests of existing and potential shareholders by undermining negotiations designed to ensure long-term financial recovery.

However, while the wording of MAR would appear to enable the company to delay both announcing the fact of financial distress, and the reorganization negotiations which have commenced with the financial creditors, the UK Financial Conduct Authority's position is that the company may delay announcing the negotiations, but must announce the underlying problem.[42] This arguably super-equivalent interpretation is controversial in the UK, and has arguably led to rapid deterioration in the fortunes of listed companies, which would have fared better if they had been able to keep the fact of distress and early negotiations confidential for longer. However, it does at least mean that the market will be aware of the fact of financial distress, and that participants will be on notice when they deal in the listed securities of the company. It will be suggested here that this should make it easier to establish specific safe harbours for those who trade while in possession of inside information, during a reorganization of the debt and equity financing arrangements. Once again, the argument is that active participation by significant financial creditors in committees is vital in order to secure a flexing of a complex, leveraged loan, bond, and equity capital structure. Moreover, it is argued that this militates against a rigid approach to insider trading rules. This is because of the vital importance of trading in the debt of distressed companies for securing the renegotiation, and preventing distress from spreading to the operating group companies.

40 Regulation (EU) No 596/2014 on market abuse [2014] OJ L173/1.

41 MAR, recital 50.

42 Financial Conduct Authority Disclosure and Transparency Rule 2.5.4(G).

As before, one approach in England is to establish a Chinese, or ethical, wall between the trading parts of the organization and the parts of the organization participating in the reorganization negotiations. However, it is important to remember that this is not straightforward, and may be impossible for smaller organizations. At the same time, given the potentially draconian liability for insider trading in England, many organizations simply prefer to sit outside the committee in order to be sure of their ability to trade. Complex, alternative arrangements have also been put in place. For example, in some transactions all information has been provided to the lawyers for the particular creditor class, who filter it for anything which could be regarded as 'price sensitive', and thus inside information. Only the sanitized information is then provided to the relevant committee member. In other cases, the debtor company has been required to ensure that it indicates ahead of any meetings or circulation of documents whether price sensitive information is included. The relevant committee member can then recuse itself from the discussions or receipt of documents.[43] It will be readily apparent, however, that this is unlikely to facilitate efficient negotiation of the reorganization plan.

Similarly, whatever approach is adopted, it is likely that the debtor company will need to agree a detailed regime for so-called 'cleansing'. This means that any price sensitive information is disclosed to the wider market. An enormous amount of time and cost can be wasted in agreeing these cleansing regimes. The creditors are likely to want a reasonably short timeline by which the cleansing must occur. In this way, they can be confident that, even if they are unable to trade, the restriction will only last for a short period of time. On the other hand, the company will not want to be bound by a cleansing obligation before the reorganization plan is negotiated, or at least well advanced. In this way, it can be assured that it only discloses sensitive information when it can also reassure the market. Delayed disclosure is also in the interests of the wider constituency of the general, unsecured creditors, employees, customers, and other stakeholders, if it maximizes the chances that the reorganization plan can be implemented without affecting the operating group companies which can continue to trade. Secondly, there is likely to be widespread (and ill tempered) debate about precisely what needs to be cleansed. The company is likely to want to keep close control over this. It would be something of a pyrrhic victory if, having successfully completed reorganization negotiations, the company's cleansing statement rattles operating company customers, suppliers, or employees, or provides information which competitors are able to exploit.

All of this, it is suggested here, gives rise to the need to think more seriously about the implications of the transparency and disclosure concept for specific safe harbours for reorganization cases. MAR also contains specific safe harbours to facilitate bids, where a party trades on the basis of inside information in the context

[43] For an excellent account of these, and other, methods of addressing the disclosure challenges, see Howard and Hedger (n 35) 107–08 paras 3.40–3.43.

of a public takeover bid or merger, for the purpose of gaining control of that company. Once again, it is suggested here that this can be used as a starting point for thinking about how to craft specific safe harbours for reorganization cases among financial institutions. In the English market there have been attempts to establish insider trading regimes for private companies which are not listed on a regulated exchange, and which only have loan debt. Loan debt is not a debt security for the purposes of either the Criminal Justice Act 1993 or MAR. To the extent that these guidelines can be seen as the guidelines which the market participants themselves regard as legitimate, they may prove a useful starting point in crafting safe harbours, which can be adopted for companies with equity or debt listed on a relevant exchange, which are experiencing financial distress.

As the LMA was established with the express purpose of encouraging secondary trading in loan participations, in general it describes its mission as reflecting, rather than leading, the market. In other words, the LMA aspires to represent generally accepted market practice. Its comprehensive suite of model documentation for leveraged loan transactions is almost universally adopted as a starting point in negotiations in the English market, albeit that it is then often subject to intense negotiation, particularly at borrower-friendly moments in the credit market cycle. The LMA has published guidelines on 'Transparency and the Use of Information' which, although they only have the status of guidance, are taken seriously in the English loan market, given the LMA's stated role as arbiter of accepted market behaviour.

Howard and Hedger identify that the LMA guidelines start with the general proposition that market participants should not trade on material information which has not been made available to the whole of the loan syndicate.[44] For these purposes, material information will generally be information which, if it were known by the entire syndicate, would significantly impact the price of the loan. They report that the LMA guidelines then establish certain, specific safe harbours. The first is the now familiar idea of a Chinese, or ethical, wall in which those within the institution making the decision to trade the loan are separated from those possessing the material information. Yet, as the account in this chapter has established, this may not work for many smaller institutions. The LMA guidelines, therefore, also introduce the idea of big boy letters. Howard and Hedger identify that they set out certain requirements which must be met before the party possessing the material information can trade in reliance on such a letter:

(i) the fact that it was in possession of such information when it executes the trade is also disclosed further in any downstream trades;

[44] The description of the LMA guidelines in this part is drawn from Howard and Hedger (n 35) 100–03 paras 3.22–3.29.

(ii) it can reasonably make a judgement that its trade would be consistent with appropriate standards of professional integrity and fair dealing; and
(iii) it can reasonably make a judgement (consistently with appropriate standards of professional integrity and fair dealings) that the transaction will not adversely affect other members of the syndicate/market.[45]

The LMA guidelines have, however, been subject to criticism by market participants, who argue that they were not adequately consulted before the guidelines were issued, and that the guidelines seek to lead the market, rather than reflect it. Howard and Hedger advance two main criticisms. The first is that the guidelines do not place enough emphasis on the obligation of the debtor company to disclose what it can. In other words, the concern arises that the company may use the threat of insider trading liability effectively to lock up the debt by restricting or delaying disclosure. Secondly, it will be seen that some elements of the big boy letter provisions are, to say the least, vague and subjective. Accordingly, there has not been overwhelming support for these guidelines in the market, and they may not be the best place to start for inspiration in developing specific safe harbours for trading in possession of inside information on regulated markets.

A rival set of guidelines has been issued by the Alternative Investment Management Association (AIMA), with the stated objective of more accurately reflecting market practice, and responding to concerns raised with the LMA guidelines.[46] These guidelines are described as the 'AIMA Note on Sound Practice in Secondary Loan Markets', and Howard and Hedger report that the guidelines suggest that participants will be acting in accordance with accepted market practice where they:

(a) rely on the 'big boy' representations as a means to address asymmetry of information between seller and buyer;
(b) continue to trade with fellow coordinating committee members where both seller and buyer have the same level of Borrower Confidential Information; and
(c) execute a trade as a purchasing lender having elected not to receive any Borrower Confidential (or other information) from a selling lender in line with the treatment of Syndicate Confidential Information set out in the LMA Guidelines.[47]

45 Howard and Hedger (n 35) 103 para 3.28.
46 The description of the AIMA guidelines in this part is drawn from Howard and Hedger (n 35) 103–04 paras 3.30–3.32.
47 ibid 104 para 3.30.

Indeed, as Howard and Hedger note in their comprehensive treatment of these issues:

> ... the LMA Guidelines acknowledge and permit loans to be traded by parties holding Syndicate Confidential Information, and accept that this is the case even where the party has chosen not to receive or does not, in practice, hold such information. There is no logical reason why the same principle could not be extended to Borrower Confidential Information, provided that the parties to the trade enter into the trade with their eyes open and subject to enhanced 'big boy' language.[48]

It is suggested here that the AIMA guidelines would provide a useful starting point in developing specific safe harbours for trading while in possession of price sensitive information on a regulated market, as well as in private, secondary loan markets. This would depend on the debtor company having made the fact of financial distress public. Once again, it is acknowledged that this risks behaviour which would not be regarded as legitimate by either the market or normal standards of common decency, within the cover of the technical boundaries of the safe harbour. Yet, it is suggested that the English courts have shown themselves equal to this challenge. While the normal position is that a creditor is free to act in its own interests, the English courts have shown that creditors may owe a duty to the minority in certain circumstances.[49] And part of the purpose of the sanction stage of a scheme of arrangement is to ensure that the English court always has the power to decline to sanction a scheme, on the basis that the scheme is not just and equitable. These powers should act as a brake on efforts to exploit the safe harbours in unacceptable ways, while facilitating participation in the committees which are essential to the negotiation of a modern restructuring of a complex, leveraged loan, bond, and equity capital structure, and reducing the transaction costs currently absorbed in negotiating complex cleansing provisions.

8.3.5 Summary of the argument in section 8.3

Overall, the argument is made that transparency and disclosure to the participants in the corporate reorganization process in England was uncontroversial during the era of the London Approach for two reasons. First, the bank participants in the process did not typically seek to trade their participations. And, secondly, wherever possible it was an ambition of a London Approach process to confine disclosure to these bank participants and to avoid, to the greatest extent possible,

[48] ibid 104 para 3.30.

[49] *Assenagon Asset Management SA v Irish Bank Resolution Corp Ltd (formerly Anglo Irish Bank Corp Ltd)* [2012] EWHC 2090 (Ch); [2013] 1 All ER 495.

wider disclosure. During this era, accountants played a vital coordination role, investigating the business and affairs of the company and providing advice to the bank syndicate on the feasibility of a reorganization process. Yet, almost every aspect of this wider organizational and institutional environment has changed. It is now likely that banks will wish to trade; that they will be joined as lenders by hedge funds and direct lenders, who critically rely on trading flexibility in managing their portfolios; and it is much more likely that participants will come to their own view on value and strategy. It has been suggested that this leads to a need to focus on the interaction between the corporate reorganization field and the proximate field of insider trading and market abuse in England. Specifically, it has been suggested that, as in the US, there is a need to focus on developing specific safe harbours from insider trading and market abuse liability.

8.4 Conclusion

This chapter has explored how changes in the proximate fields of finance and non-financial corporates have led to the rise of creditors' committees as the fulcrum of reorganization negotiations. It has explained why this gives rise to new concerns for the implications of the concept of transparency and disclosure and the constitution of the committee, its duties, and the costs of establishing it. The chapter has also explored why this leads to a tension between the concept of transparency and disclosure to facilitate a flexing of a complex, leveraged loan, bond, and equity capital structure before financial distress spreads to the operating group, and the policy goal of securities laws to ensure equal access to information on regulated markets. The chapter has advanced the argument that the balance should be tipped in favour of corporate reorganization law's concerns. This should be achieved through the development of specific safe harbours to facilitate trading while in possession of inside information. This would enable creditors to trade out when they no longer wish to support the reorganization transaction, or to consolidate a position in the company's debt for the purposes of acquiring control of the operating group through an eventual debt-for-equity swap transaction. It has been suggested that England's AIMA note on sound practices in the secondary loan market would prove a useful place for scoping a suitable safe harbour, and that the US bankruptcy court and the English courts should be equipped with the necessary tools to monitor egregious exploitation of the safe harbour provisions.

9
Looking to the Future

9.1 Introduction

Chapters 3–8 examined how shifts in logics, practices, and identities in the fields of finance and non-financial corporates have affected the ways in which corporate reorganization law is mobilized and adapted by the participants in the process. Specifically, the chapters focused on reorganizations of over-leveraged firms' loan, bond, and equity finance arrangements among sophisticated financial institutions. Significantly, it was suggested that scholars viewing United States (US) corporate reorganization law through an economic lens and scholars viewing it through a progressive lens ought to be able to agree on the content of corporate reorganization law when it is mobilized and adapted to deleverage a complex financial capital structure.

However, it is not the purpose of this book to suggest that these financial reorganizations have replaced all other types of corporate reorganization in the US. Indeed, it is an organizing principle of this book that modern corporate reorganization law responds to different patterns of fact in diverse and complex ways. As a result, economically minded and progressively minded scholars are likely to continue to disagree about the appropriate content of US

Corporate Reorganization Law and Forces of Change. Sarah Paterson, Oxford University Press (2020). © Sarah Paterson.
DOI: 10.1093/oso/9780198860365.001.0001.

corporate reorganization law when it is mobilized and adapted to respond to different types of situation. It is the first purpose of this chapter to explore some of these other types of situation, starting with full financial and operational reorganization cases.

The analysis of these types of cases begins with what will be described as the 'end of corporate reorganization law' debate. This is the argument advanced by some economically minded scholars that, as US firms move from a model of horizontal and vertical integration to a bundle-of-contracts business model, there is no need for full financial and operational reorganization. As this chapter explores, readers' perspectives on this argument are likely to depend, to a very great extent, on the particular lens through which they view the case. Indeed, there is likely to be a significant degree of disagreement about the implications of the bundle-of-contracts business model for corporate reorganization law between scholars viewing the issue through an economic lens and those viewing it through a progressive lens.

The chapter then considers reasons to suspect that there may be an increase, rather than a decline, in full financial and operational US corporate reorganization cases over the next decade. At the time at which the book was being written, there was a particular focus on the implications of the progressive loosening of credit terms since the financial crisis. As is explored in the chapter, there has been an explosion of loans written on so-called covenant-lite terms. Covenant-lite loans are loans which do not have financial covenants which are tested on an ongoing basis or periodically, but which either have no financial covenants at all or have covenants which are only tested if the borrower incurs further debt outside permitted indebtedness baskets. Furthermore, new definitions of earnings before interest, tax, and depreciation (EBITDA) have radically increased the potential for further leveraging of the capital structure. Moreover, the rest of the covenant package in both loan and bond debt has provided the borrower with considerable flexibility, for example, in moving assets outside the security net. At first sight, covenant-lite and covenant-loose loans would appear to impact only the financial creditors. Yet, it is suggested in this chapter that they increase the likelihood that a corporate reorganization will implicate a wider group of financial and operating creditors than a reorganization limited to the debtor's loan, bond, and equity financing arrangements. Moreover, as the book goes to press, companies in both the US and England have experienced enforced government shutdowns and social distancing measures in response to the COVID-19 crisis, so that they have continued to accrue operating liabilities while generating no, or substantially less, cashflow. In other words, there may be an increase in the number of cases which are full financial and operational reorganization cases implicating financial creditors, general, unsecured creditors, employees, and customers, as opposed to reorganizations of financial liabilities limited to sophisticated financial institutions. Once again, readers' views of the way in which corporate reorganization law can and should be mobilized and adapted in these types of cases are also likely to depend on the theoretical perspectives which they bring to bear on the analysis.

After sketching out the different contours of the debate in full financial and operational reorganization cases, something of a hybrid case, falling between a financial reorganization and a full financial and operational reorganization, is examined. Kevin Delaney's label for these types of cases is adapted, so that they are referred to in this chapter as 'strategic corporate reorganization' cases.[1] Once again, as the broad outlines of these types of cases are sketched out, difficult questions arise for economically minded and progressively minded scholars. And, once again, there is likely to be some disagreement among them when it comes to determining the policy and content of strategic corporate reorganization cases. The position is different in the final type of corporate reorganization case which this chapter explores: the reorganization of what Kenneth Ayotte has labelled 'fragmented capital structures'.[2] In this type of case, very similar issues arise, whether the case is viewed through an economic or a progressive lens. Some tentative suggestions for addressing these issues are offered.

Overall, the first part of the chapter describes types of US corporate reorganization case other than reorganizations of loan, bond, and equity finance arrangements among sophisticated financial institutions. It begins to connect economic and progressive theoretical perspectives to the diverse patterns of fact which emerge. The second part of the chapter examines the same types of situations as they emerge in England, and considers the implications for English corporate reorganization scholars. As the book has already explored, until the 2000s corporate reorganization was largely an out-of-court affair in England, so that English scholars did not develop conceptual frameworks which matched those of their US peers with which to assess English corporate reorganization law and practice. Since the 2000s, as the book has identified, large corporate reorganization has moved into court, and a new conceptual framework for evaluating corporate reorganization has emerged. Thus far it has been argued that, because this conceptual framework has been developed without a priori commitments to other concepts developed at a different time in response to a different, wider, organizational and institutional environment, it is particularly well adapted to the dominant corporate reorganizations of the past decade: reorganizations of complex, leveraged capital structures among sophisticated financial institutions.

The second part of this chapter considers the extent to which this new conceptual framework for analysing corporate reorganization cases may need to be adapted to meet new patterns of fact, as English corporate reorganization law is mobilized and

[1] Kevin J Delaney, *Strategic Bankruptcy: How Corporations and Creditors Use Chapter 11 to Their Advantage* (University of California Press 1998).

[2] Kenneth Ayotte, 'Disagreement and Capital Structure Complexity' (*SSRN*, 1 February 2019) 1 <https//ssrn.com/abstract=3276779> accessed 30 July 2019.

adapted in diverse ways to meet diverse types of situations. In short, the concern is that English corporate reorganization scholars, practitioners, judges, and the legislature may all struggle to adapt a conceptual framework which has developed in response to the deleveraging of complex capital structures among sophisticated financial institutions, for cases which implicate general, unsecured creditors, employees, customers, and the community. For the reasons already developed in this book, to date English corporate reorganization scholarship has not divided along economic and progressive lines in debating the content of corporate reorganization law. However, it may be that a version of the US economic versus progressive debate will come to England, as corporate reorganization law is mobilized and adapted in new ways.

9.2 United States

9.2.1 Full financial and operational reorganizations in the US

In the early 2000s, Douglas Baird and Robert Rasmussen argued that corporate reorganization would disappear.[3] They based their analysis on the rising popularity of section 363 sales arguing, as Mark Roe puts it, that 'Today we sell firms in bankruptcy to the highest bidder.'[4] However, this book has already noted that many more public companies have reorganized than have been liquidated or sold since 2012,[5] and that there is emerging evidence, in the academic literature, that the rise of section 363 sales is counter-cyclical.[6] While much of this book has concentrated on the mobilization and adaptation of corporate reorganization law to achieve a reorganization of loan, bond, and equity finance arrangements among financial institutions, full financial and operational corporate reorganization cases do still occur in the US.

This gives rise to the more fundamental question of whether the changing nature of US corporates should lead to the end of full financial and operational corporate reorganization transactions. The argument in favour is essentially that, as firm structure has moved from a vertically integrated model to a contract-based model, there is less need to keep firms together through a corporate reorganization transaction.[7] As Mark Roe identifies, it is considerably more likely today that a

[3] Douglas G Baird and Robert K Rasmussen, 'The End of Bankruptcy' (2002) 55 Stanford L Rev 751; Douglas G Baird and Robert K Rasmussen, 'Chapter 11 at Twilight' (2003) 56 Stanford L Rev 673.

[4] Mark J Roe, 'Three Ages of Bankruptcy' (2017) 7 Harvard L Rev 187, 205.

[5] Jones Day, 'The Year in Bankruptcy: 2018' (February 2019) <https://www.jonesday.com/en/insights/2019/02/the-year-in-bankruptcy-2018>.

[6] Stuart C Gilson, Edith S Hotchkiss, and Matthew G Osborn, 'Cashing Out: The Rise of M&A in Bankruptcy' (*SSRN*, 6 March 2016) <https://ssrn.com/abstract=2547168> accessed 18 May 2020; Jared A Wilkerson, 'Defending the Current State of Section 363 Sales' (2012) 86 Am Bankr LJ 591, 600 n 45 and accompanying text.

[7] Roe (n 4) 214–15.

firm's value is represented by intangible assets, rather than by physical assets. Many businesses are located in the service sector, and so are naturally organized around contracts with their employees and their clients. Yet, even in the manufacturing sector, it is more likely that a company will sub-contract fundamental aspects of its operations, rather than carrying them out itself within a vertically integrated firm. The argument is that, as a result, there is no real social need to keep the operations within the firm. If the firm is broken up, other companies can just as easily pick up the operations. The argument continues that there is likely to be a good reason why the firm which originally housed the contracts fell behind. Thus, in the final analysis, resources will move to higher and better use if the firm is allowed to fail. However, the view one takes on this issue is firmly dependent on the lens through which it is viewed. Here, the distance between economically minded and progressively minded scholars is likely to be very wide indeed.

As Jonathan Haskel and Stian Westlake identify in their excellent analysis of the rise of the intangible economy,[8] there are several uniquely important features of intangible assets. One crucial feature which Haskel and Westlake focus on, and which is highly relevant for the future of corporate reorganization law, is the concept they call 'sunkenness'.[9] This is the idea that it is harder to recover the value of intangibles by selling them. There may not be markets for many intangibles and it is hard to form a realistic estimate of their value. Haskel and Westlake give the examples of the failure of British Coachways (set up as a challenger firm to the incumbent National Express when Britain deregulated coach travel), and the failure of Maxjet, a discount business-class airline. Both companies had significant physical assets (coaches and planes, respectively). In the case of British Coachways, the assets retained value, and, in the case of Maxjet, the planes reverted to a leasing company and were put back into operation. Haskel and Westlake contrast these cases with Toyota's lean production systems, which add considerable value to Toyota but could not be separated from its factories and sold off. They provide Starbucks as a further example, focusing on Starbucks's voluminous handbook which its branches and franchises follow, and which provides the homogeneity and customer experience which seems to produce the overall value in Starbucks when compared with other operators, but which could hardly be realized as a separate asset.[10] Thus, consistent with the examination of the rise of reorganization limited to financial liabilities among financial institutions in Chapters 3–8, there are strong incentives for lenders and bondholders, in firms with significant intangible assets, to reorganize.

[8] This section draws heavily on the arguments made in Jonathan Haskel and Stian Westlake, *Capitalism without Capital: The Rise of the Intangible Economy* (Princeton University Press 2018).

[9] ibid 68–72.

[10] ibid 162–63.

Baird and Rasmussen acknowledge that intangible investments can be valuable assets of the firm, but imply that a firm with valuable intangibles of this type will naturally be a success.[11] This ignores, of course, the other developments explored in this book which may give rise to distress, such as the high fixed costs associated with a complex, leveraged capital structure or the potential challenge of refinancing leveraged finance arrangements at maturity if conditions in credit markets have changed. And it ignores other, wholly unexpected, extraneous shocks to a firm's cashflow which may emerge at any time, such as the loss of cashflow as a result of the US and UK response to the COVID-19 crisis. At the same time, a problematic feature of firms with significant value in intangible assets is that they can be particularly vulnerable to financial distress spreading to the operating parts of the business. This is because these types of business are heavily reliant on the confidence of their suppliers and customers. It is often relatively straightforward for the parties who contract with them to contract elsewhere, while the traditional actions which a firm can take to address a liquidity crisis are not open to them: there are few fixed assets which can be sold to raise cash; it may be extremely difficult to extend supplier days or to reduce debtor days, as suppliers and customers are already seeking to take contracts elsewhere; and there is no inventory level to reduce.[12] Thus, firms operating in sectors which are not traditionally associated with customer confidence may be more prone to the risk of sudden loss of confidence if they have adopted a bundle-of-contracts business model. At the same time, although the financial creditors may have every incentive to agree a reorganization, it may be difficult to contain the reorganization in the finance arrangements if the distress is spreading rapidly to the operations. If the liquidity crisis becomes acute, and no new financing can be found then, consistent with Haskel and Westlake's thesis, it is more likely that a piecemeal liquidation of parts of the business, or the assets, will follow.

Economically minded scholars, who consider that the role of corporate bankruptcy law is to facilitate the allocation of assets to highest and best use in the economy may not regard liquidation in these circumstances as problematic. For these scholars, there is no particular reason why the contracts need to be deployed in the distressed firm any more than in any other firm, and employees can simply move to work for the firm which takes over the relevant contracts from the liquidated firm in the market. If the existing financial creditors are not willing to provide new money to stabilize the situation, then it may be that the firm has moved beyond the point at which it can realistically be saved. A progressive scholar, on the other hand, will point out that it can be very challenging for contracts to shift

[11] Baird and Rasmussen, 'The End of Bankruptcy' (n 3) 763.

[12] These actions, which an industrial or manufacturing company can take to address cashflow difficulties, are drawn from Stuart Slatter, *Corporate Recovery: Successful Turnaround Strategies and their Implementation* (Penguin Books 1984) 122–23.

seamlessly to new providers, and the collapse of a large, leveraged contract firm is likely to result in significant dislocations for employees and communities. Indeed, as the second part of this chapter discusses, a number of high-profile corporate bankruptcies of large, leveraged contract businesses in the UK have implicated significant state resource in attempting to alleviate these dislocations. For the progressive scholar, this may mean that new tools should be mobilized when financial distress spreads to the operations of a large, leveraged contract business, in order to avoid the costly dislocation and to preserve state resource. A scholar approaching the issue from an economic perspective is likely to be less concerned if the state chooses to use resource to reduce frictions in the transfer of contracts to new parties, and to help the displaced employees to find new jobs. Economically minded scholars are likely to see the decision to assist as a political choice to respond to a political problem (the risk that the dislocations will damage public support at the next election), rather than a financial response to an economic problem (that the assets are not being put to their highest and best use). In other words, a debate among economic and progressive scholars opens up again. This is particularly significant because there are reasons to suspect that both the current rise of covenant-lite lending, and the shocks of the COVID-19 crisis, may result in an increase in full operational and financial reorganization cases over the course of the next decade.

9.2.2 The rise of covenant-lite lending and corporate reorganization law

A covenant-lite loan has no, or only very few, financial covenants. If it does have financial covenants, these covenants are not tested on an ongoing basis, or maintained, but are only triggered if the borrower positively raises further debt. Provided the borrower does not raise further debt, no financial ratios are tested. This type of covenant is known as an incurrence covenant, rather than a maintenance covenant, because it does not need to be maintained. In other words, it is only triggered if further debt is incurred. Covenant-lite loans first began to appear in the years before the 2008 financial crisis,[13] but have exploded in popularity in the years since that crisis in leveraged loans to the private equity industry. This appears to pose something of a puzzle. As identified throughout this book, a leveraged borrower may struggle to cope with financial distress when compared with a less leveraged borrower. This means that even a relatively small drop in earnings may starve the borrower of vital cash to invest in its business. In the recent collapse of

[13] Billett, Elkamhi, Popov, and Pungaliya date the introduction of covenant-lite loans as 2005, noting that they 'rose in popularity with issuance of $140 billion in 2007': Matthew T Billett, Redouane Elkamhi, Latchezar Popov, and Raunaq S Pungaliya, 'Bank Skin in the Game and Loan Contract Design: Evidence from Covenant-Lite Loans' (2016) 51(3) J Finan Quant An 839, 840, 862.

the leading US nationwide toy retailer, Toys R Us, a number of newspaper reports identified that one consequence of the retailer's highly leveraged capital structure was that it had put very little cash into the business, so that the store experience had declined and customers had little reason to choose to shop in one of the stores.[14] The benefit of a maintenance financial covenant is that it tests ratios which indicate the borrower's financial condition on an ongoing or regular basis. Thus, appropriately crafted maintenance financial covenants can act as a relatively early warning of potential liquidity issues, so that the borrower and lenders can come to the table before cash has been diverted from operations over a significant length of time, damaging the business. It might be expected, therefore, that there would be a significant number of carefully drafted maintenance financial covenants in a highly leveraged loan.

Against this background, a number of explanations have been offered to explain why the covenant-lite leveraged loan has become a regular feature of the landscape. These include: sufficient confidence in private equity governance to facilitate permissive credit terms;[15] features of private equity firms which mean they will come to the table to negotiate, even without maintenance financial covenant triggers which force the parties together;[16] the need to reduce transaction costs in negotiating complex covenant packages;[17] that the firm may be bound by covenants in other parts of its capital structure;[18] and competition for deals in loose credit conditions and a low interest rate environment, as a result of quantitative easing and monetary policy more generally.[19] The author, in other work,[20] has also focused on the explanation of Kenneth Ayotte and Patrick Bolton that the benefit of covenant-lite loans is that they reduce 'contract reading costs of potential buyers'.[21] Furthermore, as Uday Rajan, Amit Seru, and Vikrant Vig put it, the rise of debt as a traded instrument has increased the 'distance between the originator of the loan and the party that bears the default risk'.[22] In other words, the party originating the loan and negotiating the contractual terms no longer assumes that it will hold the loan at maturity and bear the risk of default. Overall, the institutional changes as a

[14] Bryce Covert, 'The Demise of Toys 'R' Us Is a Warning' (*The Atlantic*, July/August 2018) <https://www.theatlantic.com/magazine/archive/2018/07/toys-r-us-bankruptcy-private-equity/561758/> accessed 18 May 2020.

[15] Cem Demiroglu and Christopher M James, 'The Role of Private Equity Group Reputation in LBO Financing' (2010) 96(2) J Finan Econ 306, 307–08.

[16] Billett and others (n 13) 843.

[17] ibid 843.

[18] Latham and Watkins, 'Key Issues in Leveraged Lending' (2015) 96(2) Private Debt Investor 29.

[19] Demiroglu and James (n 15) 307.

[20] Sarah Paterson, 'The Rise of Covenant-Lite Lending and Implications for the UK's Corporate Insolvency Law Toolbox' (2019) 39(3) Oxf J Legal Stud 654, 663.

[21] Kenneth Ayotte and Patrick Bolton, 'Covenant Lite Lending, Liquidity and Standardization of Financial Contracts' in Kenneth Ayotte and Henry E Smith (eds) *Research Handbook in the Economics of Property Law* (Cheltenham, UK and Northampton, MA USA, 2011) 174.

[22] Uday Rajan, Amit Seru, and Vikrant Vig, 'Statistical Default Models and Incentives' (2010) 100 Am Econ Rev 506.

result of traded debt, explored in Chapter 4, offer considerable explanatory power both for the rise of the covenant-lite loans and for a general loosening in credit standards, with more permissive consents to raise further debt, and more flexibility of action for the borrower. One particularly high-profile example was the J Crew case, in which it was reported that the private equity borrower was able to navigate the covenant package in the leveraged debt, in order to move valuable intellectual property rights out of the senior creditors' security net, for the purpose of raising new debt to refinance junior debt which was trading at distressed prices.[23]

The first concern with this covenant-lite environment is that borrowers will be able to avoid coming to the table to renegotiate until they face liquidity issues, so that they cannot service their debt. While, in theory, the discipline of high leverage should force them to the table, in reality, the borrower may be able to starve the business of investment for a considerable period of time, in order to meet debt service costs and in the hope that trading conditions will improve. This increases the risk that, by the time the borrower and financial creditors come to the table, the borrower is experiencing severe stress in its operations, so that it is not possible to agree a reorganization which is limited to the debtor's debt and equity financing arrangements, and the corporate reorganization case engages both financial and trade creditors.

As Chapter 6 of the book explored, notwithstanding debtor control rights in Chapter 11, the private equity borrower has little incentive to come to the table any earlier than is strictly necessary. This is because it knows, in modern markets, that once a corporate reorganization is triggered, it is highly likely to lose its equity investment in the corporate reorganization plan. Directors are closely aligned with this view of the case through their own equity holdings. A similar analysis was also identified, in Chapter 6 of this book, for leveraged, publicly traded firms. However, if efforts to divert cash towards debt service drain the business of investment; operating conditions do not improve; general, unsecured creditors become nervous about the health of the company so that they start to refuse supply, or reduce debtor days, or demand cash on delivery; and customers start to take their business elsewhere, eventually the business will face a liquidity crisis which will drive it to the bargaining table. As Chapters 3–8 of the book have explored, in a reorganization limited to the debtor's debt and equity finance the purpose of the Chapter 11 filing is to impose the new capital structure on any hold-out financial creditors. In the situation under consideration here, the purpose of the Chapter 11 filing is very different. The Chapter 11 filing is likely to be made for the purposes of stabilizing the situation so that the debtor can attempt either a corporate reorganization or a going concern sale. Furthermore, it must reduce liquidity pressure so that the operations can continue and the negotiations can take place. Thus, a much wider

[23] Sujeet Indap, 'Investors in Debt-Laden Companies Face Messy Workouts' *Financial Times* (New York, 22 January 2019).

range of tools is likely to be used than in a debt and equity finance reorganization among sophisticated financial institutions. And Chapter 11 provides a particularly wide range of tools which can be adapted by the participants for this very different type of case.

First, Chapter 11 has a strong automatic stay, which prevents a counterparty from terminating its contract with the debtor because of the Chapter 11 filing and seeking recovery of its pre-filing debts. This enables Chapter 11 to be mobilized both to stabilize the situation (preventing the loss of contracts) and to act as what Kenneth Ayotte and David Skeel call 'a liquidity provider'.[24] Before the Chapter 11 filing, the debtor may be experiencing severe liquidity problems in its business as a result of general, unsecured creditor action (refusing supply; reducing debtor days; or demanding cash on delivery). The automatic stay is designed so that it can be mobilized to ease these liquidity pressures, both by enabling the debtor to avoid paying for pre-filing supply without the risk of losing contracts and by preventing the counterparty from taking informal steps to change delivery terms, which put pressure on cashflow. Moreover, this architecture means that a Chapter 11 filing can be used to stem a cycle of termination as suppliers lose confidence and terminate their contracts; other suppliers react to news of these terminations by terminating in their turn; and customers lose confidence in the firm's ability to supply and move their business to new providers. This is a form of collective action problem: if too many suppliers and customers take this type of action, it may become impossible to save the firm. And it is likely to be more significant in the modern era in many sectors of the economy than the 'grab' race, because the firm may have very few hard assets susceptible to enforcement action.

At the same time, the right to prevent contract termination on bankruptcy (the so-called ban on ipso facto clauses) may need to be used circumspectly. If counterparties are not paid for pre-filing supply they may, in turn, face their own financial difficulties; or they may find commercial excuses to avoid supply (the van has broken down, stock has not arrived etc); or they may prefer to take the risk that the debtor will proceed against them for damages, over the risk of continued supply. Furthermore, counterparties may refuse to deal with the debtor once their existing contract expires, so a long-term reorganization becomes impossible. Or the firm's reputation may be damaged to such an extent by its treatment of commercial counterparties that it simply cannot recover, once it emerges from reorganization. Moreover, the automatic stay only bites if the supplier has a contract with the debtor, rather than trading on running account terms.[25] Chapter 11 practice has developed to address all of these problems by opening up the possibility of

[24] Kenneth Ayotte and David A Skeel Jr, 'Bankruptcy Law as a Liquidity Provider' (2013) 80 U Chi L Rev 1557.

[25] Donald Wayne, 'Postbankruptcy Refusals to Deal with the Debtor and the Automatic Stay: A Fresh Approach' (1994) 72 Wash U L Q 507.

obtaining so-called critical vendor orders from the US bankruptcy courts as part of the Chapter 11 filing, entitling the debtor to pay certain creditors' pre-filing claims in full.[26] This enables the debtor to keep crucial, general, unsecured creditors on-side, while freeing up cash by adopting a more hard-line approach to others, or to use the Chapter 11 filing to prevent loss of contracts, without necessarily seeking to create liquidity through general, unsecured creditors. Moreover, as Chapter 5 of the book explored, recent developments in debtor-in-possession (DIP) financing, such as roll-ups and cross-collateralization, have developed to incentivize existing lenders to provide new money which is highly likely to be needed rapidly in these types of corporate reorganization cases. Finally, section 365 of the Bankruptcy Code provides the debtor with the ability to assign, assume, or reject executory contracts, providing it with powerful tools to reorganize operating liabilities, as well as financial liabilities.

It will be immediately apparent that these full financial and operational reorganization cases implicate directly many of the traditional debates between scholars adopting an economic approach and scholars adopting a progressive approach. The economic perspective sees a limited role for corporate reorganization law, and is sceptical of Chapter 11's efforts to shift bargaining power in order to influence the nature of the bargain. Scholars adopting a progressive approach, on the other hand, are concerned for widespread job losses if this type of thoroughgoing financial and operational reorganization cannot be agreed, and advocate for a wide range of flexible tools to shift bargaining power. New battlegrounds also open up as practice develops. Critical vendor orders remain controversial, as they straightforwardly prefer some general, unsecured creditors over others. And controversies with roll-up and cross-collateralization in DIP finance take on a different character, when the lack of genuinely new money advanced in the DIP financing, and the priority jumps which result for the DIP financiers, implicate general, unsecured creditors and employees.

Once again, time and space do not permit a full analysis in this book. The short point is that the distance between economic scholars and progressive scholars is not fixed or universal but contingent on the particular pattern of facts in the corporate reorganization case, and the ways in which corporate reorganization law is mobilized and adapted to address them. Thus, the distance between scholars is likely to be wider and rockier in these types of full financial and operational corporate reorganizations than in the deleveraging of a complex, financial capital structure. In other words, while the argument has been advanced in this book that scholars adopting an economic approach and scholars adopting a progressive approach ought to be able to find common ground in reorganizations which are limited to the firm's loan, bond, and equity finance arrangements, other types of full financial

[26] Mark J Roe and Frederick Tung, 'Breaking Bankruptcy Priority: How Rent-Seeking Upends the Creditors' Bargain' (2013) 99 Vand L Rev 1235, 1254–57.

and operational reorganizations continue to stand on contested ground. And shifts in logics, practices, and identities in the fields of finance and non-financial corporates, proximate to the corporate reorganization field, have different implications in these full financial and operational reorganizations going forward. Thus, specificity is needed in describing the particular type of corporate reorganization case, and in determining the contours of the debate between economic and progressive scholars, and many rich new areas of inquiry open up for theorists. This will be equally true when cases which fall somewhere between a financial reorganization and a full financial and operational reorganization are considered.

9.2.3 Modern strategic corporate reorganization cases in the US

Chapter 6 of the book explored how debtors mobilized and adapted Chapter 11 in the 1980s in order to reduce the size of the labour force, or to address mass tort liabilities. As Chapter 6 of the book also identified, a Chapter 11 filing is still used to address renegotiation of the labour contract and mass tort liability. Two further modern examples of strategic corporate reorganizations are the use of Chapter 11 to address the size of the rental estate in the retail sector and the use of Chapter 11 to tackle defined benefit pension costs. While these modern cases may also involve a reorganization of loan, bond, and equity finance between financial creditors and investors, the important point is that other (unsecured) creditors are implicated in the case. Notably, however, only specific, unsecured creditors are likely to be implicated, with most classes of ordinary, unsecured claim unaffected by the plan.

In the retail example, the problem is not confined to a complex, leveraged capital structure (although that is often a factor), but also relates to changing shopping habits. These changing habits include the shift to online shopping, with the result that the retailer has too many physical shops, and has rental costs which it can no longer afford. As a result, it is not only necessary to reduce the fixed costs associated with debt finance, but also to reduce the size of the rental estate and the rental bill. Thus, the corporate reorganization is likely to implicate landlords, as well as financial creditors, and is likely to take a different shape from the transactions discussed in the book thus far. In the second case, the problem is a defined benefit pension scheme established in a different era, when markets were less volatile and participants in the scheme had shorter life expectancies. As a result, the ratio of so-called active members (members of the defined benefit pension scheme who are still working), to retired members could support the payment of the pension benefit. Both changing market conditions and longer life expectancy have fundamentally affected the viability of many of these pension schemes. Of course, where the purpose of a corporate reorganization is to reorganize the defined benefit pension scheme, current and future employees will be implicated in the transaction.

In the second edition of his case study book, Stuart Gilson explores the Chapter 11 case of the major US retailer, Kmart Corporation.[27] First, he highlights how Kmart's problems had spread to its operations. As rumours circulated that Kmart was facing liquidity problems, its suppliers started to delay shipping goods, or even stopped shipping. Furthermore, a number of factoring firms began to withdraw credit from suppliers to Kmart. Secondly, he shows how operational issues relating to terminating unprofitable leases were part of the corporate reorganization plan in Chapter 11. This lease reorganization was coupled with a reorganization of the financial liabilities, through a debt-for-equity swap. Finally, he shows how Chapter 11's DIP financing regime enabled Kmart to raise financing for the reorganization case. More recent cases, such as Mattress Firm, have attempted to develop strategic corporate reorganization cases which are something of a hybrid between a debt and equity finance reorganization and a full financial and operational reorganization in order to address these issues. On the one hand, Mattress Firm needed to address lease liabilities as well as its debt and equity finance structure. On the other hand, to the greatest extent possible, its plan of reorganization sought not to interrupt general suppliers and customers. The objective was to keep the business trading as well as it could, and to preserve a 'business as usual' message.[28] As is explored in the second part of this chapter, this has also been typical in English strategic corporate reorganization cases which have sought to include landlords within corporate reorganizations, without disrupting general supplier and customer behaviour.

A wider range of Chapter 11's tools is mobilized in a real property lease reorganization: the ban on ipso facto clauses; the tools in section 365 of the US Bankruptcy Code for addressing so-called executory contracts; and the ability, in Chapter 11, to sell 'designation rights' to a third party who determines which leases to assume and which to reject (made possible, in the Kmart case, by the ability for the firm to assign leases in Chapter 11 even if the lease contract prohibited it). These tools tip the bargaining power towards the debtor, with the objective of facilitating the reorganization of the real property leases. Where leases are terminated as part of a corporate reorganization plan, the landlord retains a claim for damages. However, the damages claim is unsecured, paid out at the rate of distribution under the plan of reorganization, and capped at the greater of one year's rent or the rent for 15 per cent, not to exceed three years, of the remaining term of the lease.[29] In other words,

[27] Stuart C Gilson, *Creating Value through Corporate Restructuring: Case Studies in Bankruptcies, Buyouts, and Breakups* (2nd edn, John Wiley & Sons, Inc 2010) 85–128.

[28] Mattress Firm, 'Mattress Firm to Strengthen Balance Sheet and Optimize Store Footprint through Court-Supervised Prepackaged Financial Restructuring' (Mattress Firm, 2018) <http://newsroom.mattressfirm.com/press/mattress-firm-to-strengthen-balance-sheet-and-optimize-store-footprint-through-court-supervised-prepackaged-financial-restructuring/> accessed 4 May 2020.

[29] 11 USC § 502(b)(6).

the debtor has powerful tools to limit the recovery of landlords and promote the corporate reorganization case. The question, of course, is whether allocating the losses suffered by a struggling retail business in a changing retail environment to the landlord can be regarded as objectively fair. Chapter 11 also contains specific rules governing the debtor's ability to reject or modify retirees' benefits in section 1114 of the US Bankruptcy Code (modelled on the negotiation rules for collective bargaining agreements introduced after the *Bildisco* decision, which was discussed in Chapter 6). Here, too, the question is whether the Code pushes too far in favour of corporate reorganization, and against the interest of the workforce, particularly where rank-and-file employees suffer losses, and management is incentivized by the financial creditors to deliver the corporate reorganization plan.[30]

In a reorganization of debt and equity finance, only sophisticated financial creditors are implicated, which have the capacity and ability to bargain. In a strategic corporate reorganization, a particular class of general, unsecured creditor (landlords; the labour force; the pension fund) is selected to absorb the loss, raising wider questions of equitable pain sharing.[31] Time and space do not permit a full analysis in this book. The crucial point is that this is a different type of modern corporate reorganization case, in which Chapter 11 is mobilized and adapted in a particular way, and it raises new issues for both economically minded and progressively minded scholars. A great deal of specificity is needed here: progressive scholars may react differently to commercial landlord-only cases, where commercial landlords have the benefit of off-market rents, than they would to cases designed to address retiree benefits. Thus, in strategic corporate reorganization cases it is wise to be specific about the class of creditor implicated in the plan. And the view which one takes of these strategic corporate reorganization law cases may very well depend on the lens through which they are viewed. This leads to the final innovation discussed in this section. This is the reorganization of what Kenneth Ayotte has termed 'fragmented capital structures'.[32]

9.2.4 Fragmented capital structure reorganizations

In a fragmented capital structure, the borrower bundles up particular subsets of its assets to act as security for particular loans. Ayotte provides a number of examples, but the most straightforward is a group, such as a retail group, which has a

[30] 'Chapter 11 at the Crossroads—Does Reorganization Need Reform? A Symposium on the Past, Present and Future of US Corporate Restructuring' (2010) 18 Am Bankr Inst LJ 365, 379–88.

[31] For strident criticism of a variant on strategic reorganization in the coal industry, in which a wide range of claims is compromised but regulatory, environmental, and retiree liabilities receive dramatically lower payouts, see Joshua Macey and Jackson Salovaara, 'Bankruptcy as Bailout: Coal Company Insolvency and the Erosion of Federal Law' (2019) 71 Stanford L Rev 879.

[32] Ayotte (n 2) 1.

large real estate portfolio of stores. In this case, the retail group can offer real estate loans or securities, secured over the real estate portfolio, while offering different loans or securities against its other assets, such as its receivables. Some investors will already have exposure to real estate in their portfolios, or will not pursue real estate investment strategies at all, and they will prefer to invest in other loans and securities, which may carry higher pricing. On the other hand, other investors will be attracted to a real estate loan or security, and will potentially offer lower pricing if they are confident in the value of the physical assets on default. If the real estate assets are bundled with the rest of the group's assets in a vertical capital structure, the investment is not a pure property investment, and the pricing of the loans or debt securities will reflect that fact. However, if the real estate is split out, then investors who are expert in valuing and enforcing against real estate security may be prepared to reduce pricing for what, from a credit perspective, is purely a real estate exposure.[33]

Earlier chapters have discussed why senior lenders and junior lenders have an incentive to disagree about value in distress. Senior lenders have an incentive to argue for a low value for the firm, in order to avoid other creditors diluting their stake in the new capital structure. On the other hand, junior lenders have the incentive to argue for a high value, in order to participate in the new capital structure. The analysis thus far has also revealed that these lenders have the incentive to argue their respective cases on value in distress even if they might privately agree on the value of the firm. An important part of the narrative was that practices and identities in modern markets might increase the prospect of valuation fights. Thus, it was suggested in earlier chapters that simpler valuation approaches are needed.

However, in a fragmented capital structure, value flows differently to different groups of investors in different types of transaction. For example, in a liquidation, the lenders secured against the real estate assets may be confident of making a recovery on their loan because, as already noted, physical assets typically hold their value better in a liquidation than intangible assets. On the other hand, other investors secured against the group's other assets may face a very poor recovery on a break-up of the business. Of course, this will depend on market prices at the time. Nonetheless, the important point is that the very reason for the fragmented capital structure is that some investors consider they will make a better recovery on default because they are secured by particular assets. Thus, incentives to disagree not only about firm value, but also about the appropriate transaction in distress, are embedded in the capital structure from the start. This opens up a category of case in which the form of the transaction is actively contested, raising complicated issues for the analysis in this book.

[33] See also Edward M Iacobucci and George G Triantis, 'Economic and Legal Boundaries of Firms' (2007) 93 Virg L Rev 515.

In the Toys R Us Chapter 11 case, no corporate reorganization could be agreed, notwithstanding the number and sophistication of the tools available in Chapter 11 for dealing with operational issues. Ayotte suggests that, in part, this was because Toys R Us had a fragmented capital structure, with senior and junior debt, parent and operating company debt, and secured property debt.[34] This made it extremely complex to agree not only firm value, but also how value would flow among the different classes of investor in different types of transaction. Lenders with security over commercial property may have assessed their ability to make a recovery on a liquidation more highly than other lenders. While the stores backing the $512 million real property bond in 2016 were reported to have fallen in value by one-third, if they were vacated and released,[35] enforcement over the real estate assets may still have made economic sense for at least some of the real property bondholders. Thus, fragmented capital structures reintroduce the risk that some secured lenders may prefer an enforcement and sale over a corporate reorganization transaction, while others prefer a reorganization. In other words, in a fragmented capital structure, the form of transaction may be open to contest in a way which is less likely in a reorganization of debt and equity in a vertical capital structure in traded markets. Once again, there is a need to remain alert to shifts in logics, practices, and identities in the finance and non-financial corporate field; to the implications which those shifts may have on the nature of the corporate reorganization case; and to the concepts which are chosen to describe and analyse the issues which arise.

Having identified the discriminating fact of a fragmented capital structure, the question is what to do about the risk that financial creditors, invested in different loans and bonds backed by different guarantee and security arrangements, will prefer different forms of transaction. Unlike the other examples considered in this chapter, this would appear to be a problem for both economically minded scholars and progressively minded scholars. For economically minded scholars, the concern will be that the fragmented capital structure prevents bargaining for the transaction which promotes the highest and best use of the assets. For progressively minded scholars, the concern will be that the real losers are not the sophisticated, strongly adjusting financial creditors who traded into the debt, but the non-adjusting or weakly adjusting creditors who find themselves exposed in a corporate reorganization effort of byzantine complexity, cost, and delay. Indeed, the ultimate liquidation of Toys R Us had dramatic consequences for thousands of employees who lost their jobs without, as a strict legal matter, any entitlement to severance payments. Thus, the problems of a complex, leveraged capital structure, with the attendant problems of fragmentation, highly permissive terms, and

[34] Ayotte (n 2) n 2 and accompanying text.

[35] Bloomberg, 'Some Toys R Us Stores May be Worthless, Deutsche Bank Says' (*Fortune*, 22 March 2018) <https://fortune.com/2018/03/22/toys-r-us-stores-value-retail-properties> accessed 18 May 2020.

exceptionally loose monitoring, were ultimately visited on thousands of non-adjusting or weakly adjusting employees. Once again, although they approach the problem differently, it seems likely that both economically minded and progressively minded scholars would strive to find a solution to the particular problems posed by fragmented capital structures.

Kenneth Ayotte has suggested that one solution may be to simplify valuation procedures in Chapter 11, in order to reduce disagreement.[36] However, it has already been suggested that, in the case of a fragmented capital structure, the problem is not just agreeing the value of the firm. A problem arises from the fact that value flows differently to different classes of investor in different transactions, so that some creditor classes have a rational preference for a liquidation. As Chapter 6 explored, the response to the general policy concern of secured creditor liquidation bias has traditionally been to engage the concept of debtor control in US bankruptcy. By providing the debtor with the exclusive right to propose the corporate reorganization plan, Chapter 11 seeks to tip the balance in favour of a corporate reorganization, and away from a liquidation. However, in this book it has been suggested that debtors have little incentive to come to the table early for a Chapter 11 filing where they have ample liquidity. Indeed, in the Toys R Us case, the filing was prompted by a liquidity crisis as a result of supplier action. Once the borrower is facing a severe liquidity crisis in its operating business, it may be unable to sustain itself in Chapter 11 long enough to frame and rally support for a plan. Jared Ellias and Robert Stark have suggested that the answer is to impose greater risk of personal liability on the directors if they continue to trade in distress.[37] Focusing on the absence of 'norms that formerly restrained managerial opportunism',[38] they use a case study approach to illustrate aggressive tactics by private equity sponsors to try to retain their investment, including the J Crew example, described in section 9.2.2 'The rise of covenant-lite lending and corporate reorganization law' above. However, it is extremely difficult to promote just the right incentives through this type of personal liability regime.

It is suggested, instead, that the answer must be for creditors to pay more attention to these leviathan structures, and to ensure that they have the correct monitoring tools to force the directors to the table at an early stage of distress. In other words, the covenant-lite and covenant-loose phenomenon makes little sense here. If the property assets are spun off into a separate subsidiary, then lenders and bondholders at other levels in the group need to ensure that they can get to the table before the property-backed debt defaults, and that they have the right tools to reorganize the rest of the capital structure. Rating agencies also play a part here.

[36] Ayotte (n 2) 27–28.

[37] Jared A Ellias and Robert J Stark, 'Bankruptcy Hardball' UC Hastings Research Paper No 308 (*SSRN*, 19 January 2019) <https://ssrn.com/abstract=3286081> accessed 8 March 2020.

[38] ibid 1.

In rating the bonds, the rating agency should require a convincing explanation of how the structure would be reorganized if it were to become unsustainable. In a working paper in 2013, Thomas Jackson and David Skeel borrow the concept of a so-called 'living will' from recent innovations in dealing with distressed financial institutions.[39] The analysis in this chapter supports this suggestion: the application of the new concept of the living will to large corporates, other than financial institutions, as a way of mitigating the issues which arise with fragmented and other highly complex, leveraged capital structures.

9.2.5 Summary of the argument in section 9.2

Overall, it is apparent that there are still corporate reorganization cases in which the traditional concerns of progressive scholars, for operational restructuring and distributional fairness, remain at least as salient as transaction cost concerns. Indeed, this chapter has explored the ways in which the loosening of credit terms and the rise of fragmented capital structures raise many of the policy concerns with which the original drafters of Chapter 11 grappled. Moreover, just as the book goes to press, US Government action in the face of the COVID-19 crisis increases the prospect of a rise in the number of traditional Chapter 11 corporate reorganization cases. However, the concept of debtor control holds little promise as a solution. This is not because it could not be entrenched again, but because debtors lack other incentives to come to the table early. More care needs to be taken, instead, at the structuring stage, to include monitoring rights and to design a structure which, while complex, is capable of reorganization. This is the idea behind the new concept of living wills. The history of leveraged finance suggests that eventually these steps will need to be taken, in order for a deal to trade in secondary markets.

9.3 England

9.3.1 Modern strategic corporate reorganization cases in England

The US Bankruptcy Code has specific chapters for particular types of cases (Chapter 9 relating to municipal bankruptcies; Chapter 12 for farmers and fishermen; and Chapter 13 for individuals), and has a separate Chapter 7 procedure for liquidation. However, outside these specific cases, Chapter 11 acts as a single gateway for corporate reorganization cases. In contrast, England has a range of

[39] Thomas H Jackson and David A Skeel Jr, 'Bankruptcy and Economic Recovery' University of Pennsylvania Law School Institute for Law and Economics Research Paper No 13-27 (July 2013) 14–15.

tools which can be adapted to assist with a reorganization case: the scheme of arrangement; a company voluntary arrangement; administration; fixed charge receivership; and, where a relevant exemption applies in the Enterprise Act 2002, administrative receivership.

England also has a specific regime to protect defined benefit pension liabilities in an insolvency situation.[40] If a pension scheme employer enters an insolvency process, then the defined benefit pension scheme is transferred to the Pension Protection Fund (PPF), which protects many of the defined benefit pension rights of the members (funded by a levy on all defined benefit pension scheme providers in the UK). Of course, there is a concern that this regime may result in so-called 'moral hazard' behaviour: that the pension scheme employer will seek to engineer a transfer of the defined benefit pension scheme to the PPF. As a result, the Pensions Regulator, who oversees the regime, has a number of powers to pursue associated parties for contributions, known as moral hazard powers. Thus, a relatively complex and specific regime is engaged, which participants in a corporate reorganization must navigate where the underlying problem implicates an underfunded defined benefit pension scheme.

There have been examples of debtor companies using a scheme of arrangement to deal with defined benefit pension fund liabilities.[41] The participants in the process might also consider what is known as a regulated apportionment agreement (RAA), which is available with the Pension Regulator's consent, where the employer will otherwise become insolvent in the next twelve months. However, typically, the Pension Regulator will demand a significant equity allocation as part of an RAA. This may dilute financial creditors beyond acceptable levels, if a debt-for-equity swap is also required. Alternatively, the parties may consider a pre-packaged administration sale transaction, along the lines explored in Chapters 3 and 4, in which the business and assets of the operating group are transferred to a new company as a going concern, and the defined benefit pension scheme liabilities are left stranded in the empty company. The attraction of this is that it avoids the dilution of the equity allocation to the financial creditors, which is likely to be necessary in a regulated apportionment agreement. The challenge is establishing that the Pensions Regulator will not be able to use its moral hazard powers after the transaction to seek financial contributions from the parties.

Overall, different concerns for distributional fairness emerge than in a case limited to sophisticated, strongly adjusting financial creditors, who had the full range of investment opportunities available to them, and the opportunity to allocate detailed control rights in distress in their finance documents. There is persistent concern that the right balance has not been struck in England between the interests of the

[40] Pensions Act 2004.

[41] *Re Uniq Plc* [2011] EWHC 749 (Ch); [2011] 3 WLUK 846.

unsecured pension fund and the interests of the financial creditors. Indeed, as this book was being written, proposals were being developed to significantly strengthen the Pension Regulator's powers,[42] and, as the book goes to press, a new Pensions Schemes Bill has been introduced in the House of Lords.[43] Thus, while participants in the corporate reorganization process have found ways to adapt English law's corporate reorganization tools to achieve a strategic reorganization of both the capital structure and pension liabilities in large cases, the ways in which concepts, which have developed for capital structure reorganization cases, are applied to this very different type of strategic corporate reorganization remain open for debate.

Financially distressed retailers also pose a challenge, because it is usually necessary, at a minimum, to deal with rental liabilities as well as financial liabilities. As section 9.2 'United States' explored, in the US, debtors have used the powers in section 365 of the US Bankruptcy Code to terminate leases which are no longer needed and cannot be sold; to transfer valuable leases to third parties; and to assume leases where the debtor wishes to continue in occupation. Moreover, the threat of termination in section 365 can be used as bargaining leverage to win concessions from lessors in return for assuming leases, and landlords who have been terminated are left with a capped damages claim which is paid at the rate of distribution in the plan of reorganization. English law does not have a specific regime for dealing with executory contracts of this type, and the scheme of arrangement is poorly adapted for reorganizing a real property estate. This is because the scheme requires that creditors are divided into classes according to their rights going into, and coming out of, the scheme, and does not provide a power to cram the plan down on a dissenting class. This means that landlords who are to be terminated in the corporate reorganization case would be likely to form a separate class. They would be expected to vote against the proposal, given that they have nothing to gain from it. Thus, they would be able to hold up the rest of the transaction. As a result, participants have mobilized and adapted the company voluntary arrangement (CVA) in retail restructuring.

CVAs were designed as a small business tool, although nothing in the statute limits their use to small companies. They suffer from the limitation that they cannot affect secured creditor rights without secured creditor consent,[44] so that they cannot be mobilized to reorganize a complex, secured leveraged capital structure. Rental liabilities are, however, unsecured liabilities. Moreover, and crucially, the CVA does not require creditors to be divided into classes for voting purposes. It simply requires a 75 per cent vote of all creditors present and voting (subject to certain restrictions on connected party creditors).[45] And the CVA is not investigated

[42] Department of Work & Pensions, *Government Response to the Consultation on Protecting Defined Benefit Pension Schemes—A Stronger Pensions Regulator* (*Gov.UK*, February 2019) <https://assets.publishing.service.gov.uk/government/uploads/system/uploads/attachment_data/file/777758/response-protecting-defined-benefit-pension-schemes.pdf> accessed 18 May 2020.

[43] Pensions Schemes Bill [HL] 2019–21.

[44] Insolvency Act 1986, s 4(3).

[45] The Insolvency (England and Wales) Rules 2016/1024, rule 15.34.

by a court, unless a creditor challenges the transaction after voting has been concluded and the CVA has been passed. As a result, participants have mobilized the CVA to impose a reorganization of the retail estate on landlords with leases which are to be terminated or amended as part of the corporate reorganization plan, sometimes in combination with a scheme of arrangement or a pre-packaged administration sale where a loan, bond, and equity reorganization is also required.

These cases are further examples of what this book has called, following Kevin Delaney, strategic corporate reorganizations.[46] They not only address loan, bond, and equity finance arrangements, but also reduce liabilities to a specific group of creditors of the firm. It is immediately apparent that, unlike the situation in which senior creditors have been able to argue for a low value for the firm and no value has flowed down the capital structure to junior creditors or shareholders, the compromise of landlords raises different issues. The landlords did not foresee explicitly that their rental agreements with the tenant might be unsustainable. They did not enter into contractual arrangements allocating control rights in distress to the creditors who have now imposed the compromise on them. In a strategic corporate reorganization, they may be the only class of non-financial unsecured creditor affected by the plan. While the CVA does not require separate classes for voting as a procedural matter, the debtor cannot ignore class issues completely. Indeed, a creditor may challenge a CVA on the grounds of unfair prejudice.[47] However, in the most significant case on the use of the CVA to compromise rental liabilities to date, Mr Justice Norris upheld the use of a landlord-only CVA on the basis that it was objectively fair.[48] He contrasted the position of the landlords, who had historic rental agreements on terms which no longer reflected terms available in the market,[49] with other, general unsecured trade suppliers which, he said, had generally contracted on market terms.[50] As the effect of the CVA was only to impose current market terms on the landlords, he held the arrangement to be fair.

Nonetheless, questions persist. In the Debenhams case, while the court considered the fairness of the CVA as between the landlords and trade creditors, it did not consider explicitly whether it implicated a transfer of value to financial creditors who had swapped debt claims for equity in the business. And there are clearly alternative arguments which could be made about allocating all of the loss in the case to the retail landlords. Doubts have also been raised over the ways in which landlord claims have been calculated for the purposes of voting on landlord-only CVAs. Furthermore, while the court will not ordinarily consider whether another,

46 Delaney (n 1).
47 Insolvency Act 1986, s 6(1)(a).
48 *Discovery (Northampton) Ltd v Debenhams Retail Ltd* [2019] EWHC 2441 (Ch); [2020] BCC 9.
49 The leases had thirty-five-year terms with automatically escalating rents for the first ten years of the term, thereafter the rent being reviewed on an 'upwards only' basis at five-yearly intervals—see ibid [4].
50 ibid [66].

fairer scheme could have been implemented in assessing the scheme before it, it is more inclined to do so where there are good arguments that the alternative scheme in question was clearly capable of implementation.[51] This is particularly relevant in certain retail CVAs, where equity retain their stake. This is because, while a shareholder vote is required in a CVA, it cannot override the decision of the creditors, and only leaves the shareholder with the right to apply to court for review.[52] Thus, there are good arguments that shareholders would not be able to hold up an arrangement which compromised retail liabilities but also diluted shareholders' equity. And, finally, there are many questions over the precise effect of a CVA on other aspects of the rental agreement. Overall, then, while participants have mobilized and adapted the CVA tool for a specific purpose, different issues arise from those examined in the context of capital structure reorganizations. Many of these issues are yet to be heard by the courts, and may eventually be determined in ways which undermine existing practice. Thus, while creative lawyers and advisers in England have found ways to adapt English law corporate reorganization tools to meet the challenges of a strategic corporate reorganization, there is a great deal here for corporate reorganization scholars to analyse and debate. Difficult questions about the adaptability of the English law concepts arise where a thorough financial and operational restructuring is required. As mentioned in earlier chapters, just as the book is going to press, the Government has introduced new legislation which includes a new restructuring plan procedure, closely modelled on a scheme of arrangement, but with a cross-class cram-down power. This new procedure may be mobilized and adapted to terminate and compromise unprofitable leases going forwards. Section 9.3.3 below 'The rise of covenant-lite lending and English corporate reorganization law' touches briefly on the new legislation, and it is considered further in Chapter 10.

9.3.2 Full financial and operational reorganizations in England

A series of recent cases in the UK have illustrated the practical difficulties of keeping a large, modern corporate together, in which the value in the business is embedded in intangible assets, once the liquidity crisis has spread from meeting financial liabilities and into operating liabilities. Chapter 6 identified that, to the extent scholars have debated the orientation of English corporate bankruptcy law, the debate has historically focused on whether the right incentives existed to rescue the business as a going concern, as opposed to a break-up sale of the assets. English scholars have spent less time debating whether English corporate bankruptcy law

[51] *Inland Revenue Commissioners v Wimbledon Football Club Ltd* [2004] EWCA Civ 655; [2004] 5 WLUK 746.
[52] Insolvency Act 1986, s 4(A)(3).

is sufficiently tilted towards incentivizing corporate reorganization. In part, this is because large corporate reorganization operated outside court right up until the early 2000s and, where corporate reorganization efforts failed, going concern sales frequently preserved the economic operations of the business. The UK is geographically smaller than the US, and has fewer 'mega' companies, so that it has historically been easier to achieve a going concern sale of the business in which employees transfer, and operations remain intact, in the UK than in the US. Thus, the dislocations for employees, small suppliers, and customers which promote debate among scholars viewing US corporate bankruptcy law through an economic lens, and those adopting a more progressive approach, have historically only arisen if a going concern sale could not be achieved.[53]

Since the 2000s, it has been possible to confine most large corporate reorganizations to the financial liabilities, and concepts have emerged to govern these capital structure reorganizations. In this book, it has been suggested that because the new concepts have emerged unbounded by historically inherited assumptions related to full financial and operational reorganizations, the new field of action has been more clearly visible in England. It has also been argued that once this field of action is revealed, it is clear that there should be a shorter distance between economically minded scholars and progressive scholars on how to deal with it. However, once the financial distress has spread to the operating liabilities of a large, modern, contract business new policy concerns emerge.

As already discussed, it can be extremely difficult to hold contract businesses together, during a reorganization effort. This is because they are vulnerable both to increasing supplier action (withholding supply; reducing debtor days; demanding cash on delivery etc) and increasing customer action (as there are often other providers in the market who can fulfil customer needs). While it is arguable that there is no policy case for keeping the assets (the contracts) within any particular company, the dislocation which employees, suppliers, and customers who have stayed with the business can experience if a reorganization cannot be achieved can be dramatic. The reorganization effort tends to collapse because the liquidity crisis has become acute. At this point, it can be extremely difficult to keep the business intact as a going concern, given the fact that the assets are intangible assets of the type which Haskel and Westlake identify as difficult to realize.[54] At the same time, the funding needs for any corporate bankruptcy process can be very large indeed. Thus, progressive scholars who consider that corporate bankruptcy law should concern itself with temporary dislocations for weakly adjusting creditors and employees, are likely to take a very different view of these cases from scholars adopting

[53] See eg what John Armour and Rizwaan Jameel Mokal describe as a parting of company on English banks' incentives to purse a going concern rescue in their joint article 'Reforming the Governance of Corporate Rescue' [2005] LMCLQ 28, 30.

[54] Haskel and Westlake (n 8) 68–72.

an economic approach. As already identified, England has experienced dramatic collapses of contract businesses which promote debate about the case for different tools in the toolbox.[55] And there is reason to believe that more of these cases are likely to occur over the next decade.

9.3.3 The rise of covenant-lite lending and English corporate reorganization law

The covenant-lite phenomenon was not a significant feature of the leveraged finance landscape in England before the financial crisis, but it has exploded in recent years. As this book was being written, most leveraged finance deals were concluded on covenant-lite terms. And England experienced the same loosening of credit terms more generally, already encountered in the first part of this chapter. It has already been suggested that it is more likely that debtors, lenders, and borrowers will come to the negotiating table later where debt has covenant-lite and covenant-loose terms. Moreover, as this book is going to press, companies are experiencing a sudden shock to their cashflows while operating liabilities continue to accrue during the COVID-19 shutdown, so that some of the corporate reorganization cases which follow may well implicate operating, as well as financial, liabilities.

The first part of this chapter explored why cases which are closer to a traditional financial and operational reorganization case may result in mobilization of a wider range of Chapter 11's tools. It has already been argued that the English law scheme of arrangement has proved best in class for a reorganization of loan, bond, and equity finance in a finance holding company. And the chapter has also already explored how participants have been able to adapt and combine other tools to deal with the specific issues of defined benefit pension scheme liabilities and retail rental liabilities. Yet, to date, few tools have been available in the English corporate reorganization law toolbox to stabilize a liquidity crisis in the operations of the business and to create further liquidity for a full financial and operational reorganization. While most large reorganizations in the UK since the financial crisis have been loan, bond, and equity reorganizations, as already identified, there have been high-profile examples of businesses with very tight liquidity and the need for greater operational reorganization which have failed. These businesses have had few physical assets, and have been largely 'a good idea, a handful of people ... and a bunch of contracts'.[56] These types of contract businesses may be difficult to save, outside a corporate reorganization transaction. Yet, England's corporate reorganization law

[55] Notably Carillion Plc and Thomas Cook Group Plc.

[56] John Micklethwait and Adrian Wooldridge, *The Company: A Short History of a Revolutionary Idea* (The Modern Library 2003) 183.

toolbox has, to date, been smaller than the rich and varied toolbox for a full financial and operational reorganization in the US.

The first, striking difference has been the relative weakness of available moratorium (or stay) protection in English corporate reorganization law when compared with the US. Earlier chapters have already explored why this has not proved particularly problematic in the financial capital structure reorganizations of the past decade. However, very different problems arise if the reorganization implicates financial and operating liabilities, and both the finance holding company and operating subsidiaries. This is because, as the Toys R Us example illustrated in the first part of the chapter, where trade creditors become concerned about the financial viability of their customer, they have a range of actions available to them. These actions include ceasing to supply, or changing supply terms, and can cause immediate liquidity issues for the debtor company. In other words, supplier action can significantly increase the scale of the company's financial distress. Furthermore, customers may also react by cancelling orders or stretching debtor days. To date, the scheme of arrangement has not offered a moratorium. The CVA has provided optional moratorium protection pursuant to Schedule A1 to the Insolvency Act 1986 but, as already identified, a CVA does not bind secured or preferential creditors without their consent.[57] Even more significantly (in part because the CVA was designed as a small company procedure and the Government wished to encourage the use of other tools by large corporates), the Schedule A1 moratorium has only applied when the company satisfies one of two conditions for a small company,[58] and does not fall within any of the relevant eligibility exceptions.[59] The English law administration procedure does offer a moratorium,[60] but, to date, it has also suffered from a number of significant disadvantages.

As emphasized throughout the account in the book, administration has historically signalled the end of the prospects for a reorganization, and a shift to an insolvent sale of the business and assets, or assets, of a distressed company in England. Ian Molho describes how counterparties form 'probabilistic beliefs' in response to particular signals,[61] which they can subsequently verify by reference to the outcome of the case. Over the long run, administration in England has been associated with a sale or break-up transaction, and the prospect that some unsecured creditors will not recover for their pre-administration supply. Thus, creditors are likely to respond to the administration signal by considering what action they can take to protect their position, increasing operational pressure on the business. As the first part of the chapter explored, creditors may respond in the same way if a debtor

[57] Insolvency Act 1986, s 4.
[58] Companies Act 2006, s 382(3).
[59] Insolvency Act 1986, Sch A1 paras 2, 3, and 4.
[60] ibid Sch B1 para 43.
[61] Ian Molho, *The Economics of Information: Lying and Cheating in Markets and Organizations* (Blackwell Publishers Ltd 1997) 64.

seeks Chapter 11 protection in the US while continuing to trade, in an attempt to hash out a financial and operational plan of reorganization (as opposed to proceeding by way of exchange offer, or pre-packaged Chapter 11 plan, or section 363 sale transaction). However, at this point, Chapter 11 offers the debtor tools to keep control of the case, so that the financial and operational reorganization remains a possibility. In other words, if a debtor is experiencing intense pressure from general, unsecured creditors, destroying value in the estate, and increasing liquidity pressure, it can turn to Chapter 11 to attempt to stabilize the situation. In contrast, English administration has traditionally had a strong, normative commitment to freedom of contract. Thus, to date, neither the administration moratorium nor the CVA small company moratorium has prevented a counterparty from terminating valuable contracts triggered by the decision to file for the procedure,[62] other than a utility or IT provider,[63] or from seeking to exert a ransom position to try to secure payment for pre-filing liabilities.[64] The concern has been that all of these actions will significantly increase liquidity pressure. In other words, whereas, in the US, Chapter 11 can be used to create valuable breathing space for the debtor from general, unsecured creditor action, such action may very well increase in an English administration case, and the administrator has had very few tools available to prevent it. Moreover, administration does not offer any tools to impose a corporate reorganization on dissenting, general, unsecured creditors, such as the ability to adopt, assign, or terminate executory contracts offered by Chapter 11 in the US. While administration may be combined with a scheme of arrangement or CVA, the difficulties with those procedures identified above would persist.

The second major difficulty has been the lack of an explicit cross-class cramdown provision in any of the procedures, other than the pre-packaged administration workaround, which has already been considered. As earlier chapters have identified, the pre-packaged administration workaround gives rise to a number of operating, tax, and accounting concerns, and it has not been mobilized in a significant number of large corporate reorganization cases since the financial crisis. To date, the threat of a pre-packaged administration sale has typically been used to provide bargaining leverage to the debtor and senior creditors to incentivize junior creditors and shareholders to consent to the capital structure reorganization plan. The pre-packaged administration strategy is also heavily reliant on well-drafted intercreditor agreements, and is vulnerable to even small drafting errors in the finance documents. Yet, if forces of change such as the covenant-lite and covenant-loose phenomenon or the COVID-19 crisis do cause borrowers and creditors to come to the table when distress is more advanced, and has moved beyond purely

[62] *Re Olympia & York Canary Wharf Ltd American Express Europe Ltd & Ors v Adamson & Ors* [1992] 7 WLUK 374, [1993] BCC 154.

[63] Insolvency Act 1986, s 233 and Insolvency (Protection of Essential Supplies) Order 2015, SI 2015/989.

[64] Insolvency Act 1986, Sch B1 para 66.

financial distress, more radical capital structure reorganizations may be needed. This may make it harder to reach a quasi-consensual deal in each class. Overall, then, the lack of an explicit cram-down power may become more of an issue in the future.

As noted in earlier chapters, in 2018 the UK Government published proposals to reform corporate bankruptcy law,[65] which impacted on some of these issues. As the book is going to press in the midst of the COVID-19 crisis, the UK Government has introduced a new Corporate Insolvency and Governance Bill (the Bill) which takes forward some of the reform proposals, and which it plans to fast-track through Parliament.[66] The Bill includes a new free-standing moratorium procedure (which also replaces the Schedule A1 moratorium),[67] a ban on the exercise of insolvency termination clauses in supply agreements, among other circumstances in both the new moratorium procedure and administration,[68] and a new cross-class cram-down procedure.[69] These reforms are considered in Chapter 10, when the approach which has been developed in this book is connected to current reform efforts in the US and England.

The 2018 reform proposals indicated that the UK Government had decided not to progress plans to introduce a rescue finance regime,[70] and no new regime is included in the Bill. Thus, none of the English corporate reorganization law tools currently offers an explicit financing tool. Once again, this has not proved particularly problematic in the years since the financial crisis. This is because, for the most part, the borrower and creditors have been driven to the negotiating table by a maintenance financial covenant breach when the group still has operating liquidity. Nonetheless, it may become a more significant problem if the parties come to the table later in the next decade. In the days of the London Approach, large banks would readily supply financing for the corporate reorganization case on a priority basis, observing the informal rules of the game which prevailed in that era.[71] The question arises as to how priority financing for the case will be arranged if it becomes necessary more frequently, in the next era. This issue is also revisited in Chapter 10.

[65] Department for Business, Energy & Industrial Strategy, *Insolvency and Corporate Governance: Government Response* (Department for Business, Energy & Industrial Strategy, 26 August 2018).

[66] Corporate Insolvency and Governance Bill [HC] 2019–21.

[67] ibid s 1, inserting new Part A1 into Insolvency Act 1986 (Moratorium) and ibid Sch1, inserting new Part ZA1 into Insolvency Act 1986 (Moratorium: Eligible Companies).

[68] ibid s 12, inserting new s 233B (Protection of Supplies of Goods and Services in Great Britain) into Insolvency Act 1986, and Sch 12, inserting new Schedule 4ZZA (Protection of Supplies under s 233B: Exclusions) into Insolvency Act 1986.

[69] ibid Sch 9, inserting new Part 26A into Companies Act 2006.

[70] Department for Business, Energy & Industrial Strategy (n 65) para 5.177.

[71] John Flood, Robert Abbey, Eleni Skordaki, and Paul Aber, 'The Professional Restructuring of Corporate Rescue: Company Voluntary Arrangements and the London Approach' (1995) ACCA Research Report 45, 28.

Overall, in England as in the US, full financial and operational reorganizations give rise to new and significant areas for debate between economically minded scholars (who may continue to assert England's strong commitment to freedom of contract and worry about the *ex ante* incentive effects of an ipso facto ban) and progressively minded scholars (who are likely to be shocked by the scale of the dislocations seen in recent cases, and to advocate for a more varied toolbox). The account in the book has revealed why the economic versus progressive debate did not develop in England in the same way in the 1980s and 1990s, and why this has enabled corporate reorganization law to emerge, in the 2000s, in a way which is well adapted to the reorganization of financial liabilities among sophisticated financial institutions. Yet, the new shape of full financial and operational corporate reorganizations of large, leveraged contract businesses raises new issues for English corporate reorganization law scholars. It will be essential that these scholars keep in mind both the historic reasons why going concern sales were a largely acceptable last resort in England until the 2000s, and why the distance between the economic analysis and the progressive analysis has not narrowed since the financial crisis. This will help scholars to construct context-sensitive conceptual frameworks to interrogate the new order of full financial and operational reorganizations. In short, a new version of the economic versus progressive debate may be coming to England.

9.3.4 Summary of the argument in section 9.3

Throughout the book, it has been argued that US bankruptcy scholars face challenges in reframing concepts in corporate reorganization law in a changing organizational and institutional environment. Indeed, it has been suggested that, in some cases, they have clung to concepts which apply in full financial and operational corporate reorganization cases but have less salience, or require significant reformulation, in the context of a capital structure reorganization. This has arisen because Chapter 11 was worked out, and applied, in a very different, wider organizational and institutional setting than that which prevails today. Insofar as England is concerned, the book has consistently hinted that the challenge may lie ahead.

English corporate reorganization law has largely developed in the decade since the financial crisis to implement quasi-consensual, financial capital structure reorganizations. The concepts which have emerged are thus well adapted to reorganizing financial liabilities owed to strongly adjusting financial creditors and shareholders, which had the full range of investment possibilities open to them. And participants in the process have also been able to mobilize and adapt corporate reorganization law to achieve a strategic corporate reorganization, limited to pension fund or rental liabilities. The challenge for England is whether concepts such as the market price and current market value concepts; the concept of majority rule; and deference to the finance documents will prove sufficiently adaptable for the challenges which lie ahead. It may be necessary to adjust the ways in which these concepts are used, if shifts in the proximate fields of finance and non-financial corporates lead to new adaptations and mobilizations of corporate reorganization law, including new adaptations and mobilizations of the newly announced tools which are discussed in Chapter 10. This is particularly the case if these adaptations impact directly weakly adjusting, general, unsecured creditors, employees, and customers, and give rise to new concerns for social cost . There may be spirited debate on the horizon.

9.4 The potential for more radical change

Thus far, the shifts in logics, practices, and identities which have been discussed are already visible in the US and England. However, as noted at the beginning of the book, time and again sophisticated predictions by truly expert corporate reorganization law scholars about the future of corporate reorganization law turn out to be partly or wholly incorrect. It was suggested that this is probably because not all of the relevant shifts in logics, practices, and identities come into view at the same time. Moreover, even if they do, it is extremely difficult to predict how they will interact with each other. The first chapter of the book noted that significant change is currently on the horizon, with environmental concerns looming large; significant debate about the shareholder value conception of the firm; unease about leverage, private equity firms, and hedge funds; and at least one candidate who was, at the time the book was being written, in the race for the democratic nomination to the White House with an explicit agenda to regulate modern finance more stringently. The suggestion was made that it is impossible to predict accurately the future of corporate reorganization law, in either the US or England, in the face of this tsunami of potential change. This observation has assumed even greater significance as the book goes to press against the background of the paradigmatic example of an unforeseen force of change— the enforced business shutdown and social distancing measures introduced in response to the COVID-19 crisis. Nonetheless, this chapter considers a couple of speculative possibilities for how these changes may influence the real world of corporate reorganization and, accordingly, corporate reorganization law in the long term.

9.4.1 The potential for further shifts in reputation

The first possibility is that concern for public reputation may become more significant as a motivating mechanism in corporate reorganization cases. The principal reason for suggesting this is that many of the fund investors, introduced during the course of this book, are becoming somewhat more establishment figures, rather than iconoclastic innovators. Toys R Us was owned by two giants of the private equity industry: the mighty Kohlberg Kravis Roberts (KKR) and Bain Capital. When KKR started out in 1976, it had two small offices in New York and San Francisco.[72] In 2006, it took the first step in raising permanent capital on the stock market, and today it has over 1,400 employees, consultants, and advisers working across sixteen industries in offices across the world.[73] US state pension funds have been investors in KKR since the early 1980s. After job losses were announced in the Toys R Us bankruptcy, state pension funds, such as the Minnesota state pension fund, started to put pressure on KKR to offer severance pay to the workers who had lost their jobs. While they did not identify what motivated their decision, in November 2018 Bain Capital and KKR agreed to fund $20 million in severance payments to the employees of bankrupt Toys R Us.[74] As a matter of the order of distributional priorities in a US bankruptcy, the workers would not otherwise have received this payment.

This is not an isolated example of renewed concern for public reputation. Larry Fink started out running his bond business for Blackstone, before it was spun off as Blackrock Financial Management in the 1990s. Stellar growth followed, and Blackrock listed as a publicly traded company in 2006.[75] Larry Fink used his 2019 annual letter, to the chief executive officers of the companies in which Blackrock is invested, to focus on the importance of 'sustainable long-term growth',[76] and of the importance of corporate purpose. He wrote, 'Profits are in no way inconsistent with purpose—in fact, profits and purpose are inextricably linked.' As public opinion increasingly focuses on the legitimacy of the shareholder value approach, investment firms are increasingly unable to ignore public opinion. In the same letter, Fink is clear that he is motivated by a wider debate which has been gathering considerable force, not only in scholarship but in wider public opinion, about the shareholder value conception of the firm:

> Unnerved by fundamental economic changes and the failure of government to provide lasting solutions, society is increasingly looking to companies, both public and private, to address pressing social and economic issues. These issues range from protecting the environment to retirement to gender and racial inequality, among others. Fueled in part by social media, public pressures on corporations build faster and reach further than ever before.

[72] George P Baker and George David Smith, *The New Financial Capitalists: Kohlberg Kravis Roberts and the Creation of Corporate Value* (CUP 1998) 3.

[73] <https://www.kkr.com/our-firm/team> accessed 18 May 2020.

[74] Sujeet Indap, 'Unexpected Victories for Unorthodox Shareholder Activists' *Financial Times* (London 17 December 2018).

[75] David Carey and John E Morris, *King of Capital: The Remarkable Rise, Fall, and Rise Again of Steve Schwarzman and Blackstone* (Crown Publishing Group 2010) 124.

[76] Larry Fink's 2019 letter to CEOs, 'Purpose and Profit' <https://www.blackrock.com/corporate/investor-relations/2019-larry-fink-ceo-letter> accessed 15 May 2019.

It is possible, of course, to be cynical about these public statements of concern for social and economic responsibility. Yet there is no doubt that there is considerable focus on the twin pillars of leverage and shareholder value, on which modern finance and non-financial corporate markets have been built, which is feeding directly into the attitudes of institutional investors in the investment fund industry. As this book has consistently shown, it is changes in the logics, practices, and identities in the fields of finance and non-financial corporates which ultimately change the ways in which corporate reorganization law is mobilized and adapted. If institutional investors become reluctant to invest in firms with complex, leveraged capital structures, or which adopt aggressive, risk-taking behaviour, then fundamental change might be expected to follow. As this book goes to press, it appears likely that experience of highly leveraged capital structures in the aftermath of the COVID-19 crisis may further inform the public debate. In this account, change occurs because, without it, the firms will no longer be able to attract investment in the market

In a fascinating piece on attitudes to insider trading, Dan Kahan and Eric Posner consider an alternative, sociopsychological explanation, to explain how fundamental changes in attitude come about.[77] The core of the argument is nicely summarized by John Anderson.[78] The first stage is for a significant event, such as a stock market crash, to occur, which is blamed by some constituencies on insider trading (possibly without much in the way of empirical support). As public attitudes harden against insider trading, participants avoid it, both for reputational reasons and to avoid liability in a changing regulatory environment. At this point, they see nothing wrong with it *per se*. Gradually only what Kahan and Posner call 'bad types' engage in insider trading, reinforcing the incentives for everyone else to refrain from it. Ultimately, as Anderson puts it, 'to avoid cognitive dissonance (ie engaging in action inconsistent with one's beliefs), those who originally believed there was nothing wrong with insider trading will actually revise their beliefs about the morality of such trading to cohere with the reputational and criminal consequences they impose on others for such behaviour'.[79] In the words of Kahan and Posner, they 'convince themselves through a psychological process that is not well understood, that not only do bad people engage in insider trading, but that insider trading is morally wrong'.[80]

It is possible that this type of fundamental shift may occur in the fields with which this book is concerned, particularly as a (delayed) result of the 2008 financial

[77] Dan M Kahan and Eric A Posner, 'Shaming White-Collar Criminals: A Proposal for Reform of the Federal Sentencing Guidelines' (1999) 42 J L Econ 365. The description of Kahan and Posner's thesis as offering a 'sociopsychological explanation' is from John P Anderson, *Insider Trading: Law, Ethics and Reform* (CUP 2018) 226.
[78] Anderson (n 77) 225–26.
[79] ibid.
[80] Kahan and Posner (n 77) 378.

crisis and renewed debate as a result of the COVID-19 shock. There was already a sense that some of the fundamental causes of the 2008 financial crisis had not been fully understood and that, where they had been understood, they had not necessarily been resolved. Certainly, as this book has explored, some of the core ideas in the finance field before the crisis (such as leverage, the central role of risk and diversification in the investment decision, the need for liquidity in traded securities, and the need to generate outsized returns) do not seem to have changed after it. Before COVID-19 struck, there was growing focus both on the concept of leverage and on the concept of shareholder value among regulators, media commentators, and the general public. Indeed, in both the US and the UK certain high-profile recent failures have been blamed, in part, on these two, core ideas. This interrogation of both the consequences of a highly leveraged capital structure and of the concept of shareholder value seems only likely to increase, as the US and the UK attempt to get to grips with the economic consequences of the COVID-19 crisis.

As this book was being written, Elizabeth Warren had proposed the 'Stop Wall Street Looting Act', which took aim specifically at the private equity leveraged acquisition model by making the private equity sponsor liable for the debts of bankrupt portfolio companies in certain circumstances, and reducing permitted dividends and fee charges.[81] The Business Roundtable (a group of 180 of the chief executive officers of some of the US's most influential companies) had issued a new statement on corporate purpose, committing to provide value for customers; invest in employees; deal fairly and ethically with suppliers; support the communities in which the companies work; and generate *long-term* (emphasis added) value for shareholders.[82] In the UK, Colin Mayer launched a British Academy project to investigate the purpose of the company.[83] And since 2015, the Big Innovation Centre's purposeful company taskforce consortium of FTSE 100 companies, investment houses, business schools, business consultancy firms, and policymakers has been, 'examining how the governance and capital markets environment in the UK can be enhanced to support the development of value-generating companies, acting with purpose to the long-term benefit of all stakeholders'.[84] While it is too early to hazard a view on how the economic consequences of the COVID-19 crisis will unfold, both the interests of shareholders versus other stakeholders,[85] and the

[81] Elizabeth Warren, 'End Wall Street's Stranglehold on Our Economy' (Medium,18 July 2019) <https://medium.com/@teamwarren/end-wall-streets-stranglehold-on-our-economy-70cf038bac76> accessed 5 May 2020.

[82] Business Roundtable, 'Statement on the Purpose of a Corporation' (*Business Roundtable*, 19 August 2019) <https://www.businessroundtable.org/business-roundtable-redefines-the-purpose-of-a-corporation-to-promote-an-economy-that-serves-all-americans> accessed 5 May 2020.

[83] The British Academy, *Future of the Corporation* research project <https://www.thebritishacademy.ac.uk/programmes/future-of-the-corporation> accessed 5 May 2020.

[84] The Purposeful Company Project, *The Big Innovation Centre* <http://www.biginnovationcentre-purposeful-company.com/> accessed 18 May 2020.

[85] Stephen Morris, David Crow, and Chris Giles, 'British Lenders Suspend Dividends after BoE Pressure' *Financial Times* (London, 1 April 2020).

increased risk to recovery posed by the types of highly leveraged capital structures which have been put in place in recent years,[86] are already attracting comment.

It is possible, therefore, that real and meaningful pressure for change will emerge. This may trigger a process, similar to the one which Kahan and Posner describe,[87] in which leverage multiples drop and new and more conservative approaches are taken to bargaining. Initially, this occurs to avoid legal challenges and reputational issues in the changing environment. Eventually, it occurs because attitudes fundamentally shift among all participants in the field. Of course, this is highly speculative. Yet, it is important to remain alive to the fact that fundamental shifts in logic and practice may occur. If they do, it is essential to focus on which of the concepts used to describe the corporate reorganization field may need to be replaced, supplemented, reformulated, or contested once again.

9.4.2 The potential for the market to discipline itself

Change may be coming, too, in the willingness of the market to find new ways to discipline itself. Chapter 7 briefly discussed attempts to address perverse incentives created in corporate reorganization by the credit default swaps market. It has been argued that the rise of an active distressed debt market increases the prospect that a borrower in financial, and not economic, distress will successfully implement a capital structure reorganization. Yet, the position may be different if a major financial creditor holds credit default swap protection against the borrower. In a recent example, a hedge fund was reported in the media as having pursued litigation against the issuer of bonds which it held, when it was rumoured to have the benefit of credit default swap protection which would pay out if the issuer defaulted.[88] Yet, there are signs that the market is taking steps to impose discipline, through the use of so-called 'net short lender disenfranchisement provisions', which seek to disenfranchise empty voting in a distressed scenario.[89] These provisions are difficult to draft, and doubts have been raised about their effectiveness, but they are coupled with other shifts in the wider institutional environment in which the credit default swap market is embedded.

Demand for action has also followed reports of an even more high-profile case. A credit fund is reported to have promised a borrower cheap financing, but only on the condition that the borrower defaulted on a bond, which would

[86] Joe Rennison, 'Rating Agencies Put 1,000 CLO Slices on Review for Downgrade' *Financial Times* (London, 23 April 2020).
[87] Kahan and Posner (n 77) 376–78.
[88] Sujeet Indap, 'Windstream Debt Battle Opens Up "Pandora's Box" for Hedge Funds' *Financial Times* (New York, 22 February 2019).
[89] Milbank Client Alert, 'Net Short Lender Disenfranchisement: Is the New Anti-CDS Vaccine Safe and Effective?' (11 June 2019).

trigger credit default swap protection which the credit fund had purchased.[90] Regulators have roundly condemned the behaviour, warning that it may constitute market manipulation, and taking the prospect of regulatory intervention seriously. The industry body which administers the market, the International Swaps and Derivatives Association, has made changes to its terms in an attempt to address the issues. And the threat of legal action by the credit default swap provider is reported to have been sufficient to end the planned default. What is clear is that so-called manufactured defaults are pushing the boundaries of what the market regards as acceptable, and that steps to impose discipline are being taken. This is consistent with Mitchel Abolafia's work examining the relationship between finance participants' pursuit of self-interest, and what he calls 'the nature of restraint in the marketplace',[91] in which he concludes, 'When extreme acts of opportunism exceed the level of tolerance of various powerful stakeholders inside and outside the market, pressures rise to restrain the extremes.'[92]

This also applies to more general attempts to impose discipline through the use of black lists and white lists in the loan market. A black list details financial institutions to whom a lender is not permitted to transfer its loan participation, while a white list details the only financial institutions to whom a lender is permitted to transfer its loan participation. As Chapter 4 explored, to date black lists and white lists have been notoriously difficult for a borrower to negotiate, because loan transferability has become a key lending criteria for all financial institutions, including banks. And even where they have been negotiated, they have traditionally fallen away on a default, so that they do not prevent loans trading into the hands of distressed debt funds. However, as a result of increasingly aggressive behaviour by certain funds, and the borrower-friendly lending environment which persisted before the COVID-19 crisis, not only have transfer restrictions reappeared, but they are drafted in such a way that they would continue to apply on default.[93] This is hugely significant for corporate reorganization, because it potentially prevents the entrance of certain distressed debt funds into the case. And yet, it also reintroduces a mechanism by which the market may impose some discipline in corporate reorganization, in ways which are reminiscent of the era of the London Approach. A fund, which does not play by what are seen as the acceptable rules of the game, may find itself on black lists or omitted from white lists in future deals.

[90] Joe Rennison and Sujeet Indap, 'Wall Street Tries to Clean Up $8 trn Market for Credit Derivatives' *Financial Times* (New York, 14 March 2019).

[91] Mitchel Y Abolafia, *Making Markets: Opportunism and Restraint on Wall Street* (Harvard University Press 2001) 3.

[92] ibid 11.

[93] Gibson, Dunn & Crutcher LLP, 'Transfer Restrictions—A Delicate Balance?' (11 September 2018).

9.5 Conclusion

It has been argued, for much of this book, that the concepts used to frame corporate reorganization law need to be re-evaluated where only sophisticated, strongly adjusting finance creditors and shareholders are implicated in the transaction. Yet, it has also been acknowledged that cases still exist which require both financial and operational reorganization. In general, Chapter 11 still offers a richer and more varied toolbox for these types of transaction. Yet, these types of transaction not only give rise to many traditional questions between economic and progressive scholars, but also give rise to new issues for debate. And there is reason to believe that the covenant-lite, permissive, and loosely monitored capital structures of the past few years may result in an increase in full financial and operational reorganizations over the next decade. At the same time, the development of what Ayotte calls 'fragmented capital structures' potentially raises new challenges, for both economically and progressively minded scholars.[94] The market is best placed to deal with these issues and, while lessons may be learnt slowly, experience suggests that they will be learnt eventually. There are also embryonic signs that market participants may wish to cultivate a different sort of reputation, and that the market is beginning to develop mechanisms to police the boundaries of acceptable behaviour, and it may be that experience of the COVID-19 crisis may have an impact on both of these developments. Ultimately, as argued throughout the book, it is the interaction of law with the underlying logics, practices, and identities of the participants which drives real change.

Insofar as England is concerned, concepts in corporate reorganization law are well adapted to achieve a capital structure reorganization or a strategic corporate reorganization. Yet, it remains to be seen whether they will prove sufficiently adaptable to permit analysis of full financial and operational reorganizations which implicate a wider range of participants, and to address new concerns for social cost. The Government's new Bill adds some new tools to the corporate reorganization law toolbox,[95] and Chapter 10 considers the implications of this for corporate reorganization law reform.

Of course, much more radical existential shocks are always possible. As this chapter has noted, there is growing focus in the broadcast and print media, scholarship, and wider public debate about the finance and non-financial corporate markets, with a particular focus on the risks of leverage and the purpose of the company. For the moment, however, crystal ball gazing has been limited to expanding and changing logics, practices, and identities which are already visible in the fields of finance and non-financial corporates. As the much-attributed aphorism goes, prediction is very difficult, especially about the future.

94 Ayotte (n 2) 1.
95 The Bill (n 66).

10
The Approach in the Book and Implications for Reform

10.1 Introduction

It is a central argument of this book that the distance between scholars adopting an economic approach to corporate reorganization law and scholars adopting a progressive approach should depend on the fact pattern of the corporate reorganization case. It has been suggested that shifts in logics, practices, and identities in finance and non-financial corporate fields have resulted in new fact patterns, and that participants in the process have mobilized and adapted corporate reorganization law in new ways to address them. However, it has also been suggested that scholars in the United States (US) have continued to mobilize old concepts in analysing these new adaptations. This book has argued that this has obscured the boundary between parts of the field where the distance between economically minded and progressively minded scholars ought to have narrowed, and the parts of the field where traditional or new debates among them remain salient, or have even opened up. Chapters 3–8 revealed a new field of action for corporate reorganization law. They suggested ways in which existing concepts could be replaced, supplemented, or unravelled and reformulated in analysing this new field of action. And they argued that, once this exercise was completed, there ought to be consensus between economic and progressive scholars on the content of corporate

Corporate Reorganization Law and Forces of Change. Sarah Paterson, Oxford University Press (2020). © Sarah Paterson.
DOI: 10.1093/oso/9780198860365.001.0001.

reorganization law in this context. In contrast, Chapter 9 examined other types of corporate reorganization case, and revealed that the goals and policy advanced for corporate reorganization law depended very much on the particular lens through which it was observed.

Overall, as a result of the rise of leverage, tradeable debt, and blanket security in large corporate loan and debt capital markets, corporate reorganization cases emerge which are limited to claims owed to sophisticated, strongly adjusting financial creditors. In these cases, the dominant policy goal should be to facilitate the rapid deleveraging of the complex capital structure. For economically minded scholars, this facilitates the allocation of assets to highest and best use. For progressively minded scholars, it prevents distress spreading to the operations of the business, implicating weakly adjusting general, unsecured creditors, employees, customers, and other stakeholders. Changing identities in the fields of finance and non-financial corporates have also changed the corporate reorganization bargaining environment, and new policy concerns emerge for corporate reorganization law as a result. Once again, however, there ought to be common ground here between economically minded scholars, focused on a procedural conception of corporate reorganization law, and progressively minded scholars, focused on promoting the public interest, or limiting social cost.

In contrast, Chapter 9 considered corporate reorganization cases, which continue to implicate both strongly and weakly adjusting creditors directly, and in which old policy debates continue to arise. It considered how expanding and changing logics, practices, and identities in the financial markets may call for different policy objectives, and new or adapted corporate reorganization law content to meet them, over the next decade. Overall, the call has been for a context-sensitive approach in the corporate reorganization law debate. Both the US and the UK have common law systems, which allow considerable room for bankruptcy judges to adapt their approach to suit the changing ways in which corporate reorganization law is mobilized and adapted by the participants in the process. In this book, it is suggested that judges will need to continue to embrace this challenge, as corporate reorganization law is mobilized and adapted in different ways to meet the demands of the day.

This chapter considers the implications of the approach in the book for the reform debate in the US and England. US bankruptcy scholars, practitioners, and commentators have identified the significantly different ways in which corporate reorganization law is mobilized and adapted in twenty-first-century financial markets. Nonetheless, this chapter suggests that the US reform debate has persisted in measuring and debating the extent to which these new adaptations of Chapter 11 have moved it from the way in which it was originally conceived. Thus, the debate has continued to revolve around identifying the original policy objectives, and the content of corporate reorganization law which is needed to achieve them, and, for the most part, has continued to divide along economic and progressive lines. In this chapter, the aim is to show how this approach can lead to policy missteps, and the implications of using the approach established in this book, instead, for the reform agenda.

Moreover, the book explores the ways in which the US has sought to export the original policy goals of Chapter 11 as what Michael Power calls 'world level norms'.[1] This has occurred via the World Bank Doing Business Report; US institutions seeking to make foreign investments; and US lawyers working in foreign markets. As a result, in this chapter it is suggested that the English reform debate has dedicated too much focus to responding uncritically to pressure to adopt traditional US policy goals and specific US corporate bankruptcy tools. It is argued that what is needed, instead, is a bottom-up analysis of how English corporate reorganization law interacts with the new logics, practices, and identities in the fields of finance and non-financial corporates, and of the types of corporate reorganization case which emerge as a result. It is argued that this approach reveals where English corporate reorganization law may lack particular tools, and the arguments for and against providing them in the toolbox. This is not to say that England has nothing to learn from US Chapter 11. The previous chapter of this book identified that, where a full financial and operating reorganization is required, Chapter 11 still offers one of the richest toolboxes in the world. Yet this chapter examines how a bottom-up analysis would more accurately reveal which tools to borrow from the US, how to adapt them to meet modern market conditions, and how to incorporate them coherently into the rest of the English corporate reorganization law toolbox. The chapter starts, however, with the US reform debate.

10.2 United States

10.2.1 The ABI Commission and the LSTA

In 2012, recognizing that changing financial markets have radically changed the ways in which Chapter 11 is mobilized and adapted, the American Bankruptcy Institute (ABI) launched a Commission to study reform of Chapter 11 (the Commission). The Commission identified thirteen broad topics to study, each relating to a particular component of Chapter 11, and enlisted the help of over 150 volunteers from insolvency practitioners, expert judges, lawyers, financial advisors, academics, and consultants to serve on advisory committees for each of these topic studies. The Commission also formed an international working group, and held sixteen public field hearings in eleven different US cities at which collectively almost ninety individuals testified. It published its final report in 2014,

[1] Michael Power, 'Enterprise Risk Management and the Organization of Uncertainty in Financial Institutions' in Karin Knorr Cetina and Alex Preda, *The Sociology of Financial Markets* (OUP 2005) 262.

running to over 390 pages, and making recommendations on almost every aspect of Chapter 11 practice.[2]

The introduction to the report contains a useful, potted summary of some of the changes in the financial markets explored in this book which have had an important impact on the way in which Chapter 11 is mobilized and adapted by the participants in the process. Indeed, the Commission's mission statement explicitly refers to changing conditions in financial markets:

> In light of the expansion of the use of secured credit, the growth of distressed-debt markets and other externalities that have affected the effectiveness of the current Bankruptcy Code, the Commission will study and propose reforms to Chapter 11 and related statutory provisions that will better balance the goals of effectuating the effective reorganization of business debtors—with the attendant preservation and expansion of jobs—and the maximization and realization of asset values for all creditors and stakeholders.[3]

Part III of the ABI report (Background on the Commission and on the Study Project) starts with a useful summary of the history of US business reorganization law. It highlights the emergence, in the late nineteenth century, of the idea that 'a business generally is more valuable to creditors and society as a whole if it rehabilitates rather than liquidates'.[4] It highlights Congress's view, at the time at which the 1978 Bankruptcy Code was enacted, that 'the purpose of a business reorganization case … is to restructure a business's finances so that it may continue to operate, provide its employees with jobs, pay its creditors, and produce a return for its stockholders', and thus, crucially, that 'reorganization, in its fundamental aspects, involves the thankless task of determining who should share the losses incurred by an unsuccessful business and how the values of the estate should be apportioned among creditors and stockholders'.[5] It then sets out the case for reform:

> … today's financial markets, credit and derivative products, and corporate structures are very different than those existing in 1978 when Congress enacted the Bankruptcy Code. Companies' capital structures are more complex and rely more heavily on leverage, which is secured under state enactments of the Uniform Commercial Code that encumber vastly more assets than in 1978; their asset values are driven less by hard assets … and external business models

[2] American Bankruptcy Institute Commission to Study the Reform of Chapter 11 2012–2014, *Final Report and Recommendations* (American Bankruptcy Institute 2014) (henceforth in this chapter referred to as 'the report' or 'the ABI report').

[3] ibid 3.

[4] ibid 9.

[5] ibid 10, citing Harvey R Miller and Shai Y Waisman, 'Is Chapter 11 Bankrupt?' 47 BCL Rev 129, 181 (quoting S Rep No 95-989, at 10 (1978)).

> are increasingly multinational. In addition, claims trading and derivative products have changed the composition of creditor classes. Although these developments are not unwelcome or unhealthy, the Bankruptcy Code was not originally designed to rehabilitate companies efficaciously in this complex environment.[6]

Of course, much of this description echoes the shifts in logics, practices, and identities in the fields of finance and non-financial corporates which have already been explored in this book. However, while the report does periodically refer to these changes, in many places it rehearses what it sees as the traditional Chapter 11 policy goals. It does not always undertake a sustained inquiry into how the changing environment in the fields of finance and non-financial corporates interacts with corporate reorganization law, and the implications which this may have for the concepts used to frame the corporate reorganization law debate. As the US Loan Syndications and Trading Association (LSTA) points out in its response to the ABI report, the Commission tends to approach changes in financial markets as undermining the effectiveness of Chapter 11.[7] The LSTA response focuses on what it calls the 'narrative' of the ABI report, and its 'central plot-line ... that the evolution of the financial markets, including the increased use of secured credit, has fundamentally changed the bankruptcy process, rendering the existing Code outdated'.[8] It raises three specific criticisms: the lack of empirical evidence to support the claim that secured creditor control has undermined the effectiveness of the Bankruptcy Code; what it calls the potentially 'harmful real-world consequences' of the Commission's proposals; and what it sees as a significant analytical flaw in the ways in which the proposals seek to rebalance rights between secured and unsecured creditors in the corporate reorganization process.

The LSTA response does spend more time articulating the detail of the changes in financial markets than the ABI report: the rise of the non-investment grade leveraged market; reform of Article 9 of the Uniform Commercial Code (UCC) (and the rise of the blanket lien); the growth in the high-yield bond market; the rise of the distressed debt market; and the ability for creditors to sell their claims. There is also a greater focus in the LSTA response on the different mindsets of the participants in the process, and it hints at other changes in the sociology of financial markets. Moreover, in the detail of its analysis, the LSTA considers the boundaries of the secured credit market for non-investment grade firms,[9] and the changing contours of the debtor-in-possession (DIP) finance market.[10] Yet the LSTA's central

6 ABI report (n 2) 12.

7 The Loan Syndications and Trading Association, 'The Trouble with Unneeded Bankruptcy Reform: The LSTA's Response to the ABI Chapter 11 Commission Report' (LSTA October 2015) 7 (henceforth referred to in this chapter as the LSTA response).

8 ibid 13.

9 ibid 29.

10 ibid 29.

mission appears to be to push back against the contention in the ABI report that things have changed in a way which requires reform of the Chapter 11 process. As a result, it dedicates its efforts to querying 'whether increased secured creditor control has in fact led to inefficient decisions that are systematically skewed in favor of the secured creditor',[11] focusing in particular on whether recent literature empirically supports the proposition that it has done so.[12] Furthermore, it focuses on potential increases in the cost of the bankruptcy process, and on the cost and availability of finance for non-investment grade firms if the Commission proposals are implemented.[13]

The LSTA also takes issue with the ways in which the ABI report frames traditional US bankruptcy concerns. It reasserts a focus on the role of Chapter 11 in staying creditor action and, for the most part, distributing assets according to non-bankruptcy rights and priorities except 'where necessary to serve some *bankruptcy* purpose'.[14] In other words, it frames its objections to the Commission report in terms of traditional Chapter 11 concepts. It criticizes the ABI report for suggesting that it is an explicit policy objective of traditional Chapter 11 to tip the balance of the case in favour of corporate reorganization, and for suggesting that Chapter 11 embraces a norm of distributional fairness.[15] As the aim of the response is to push back against the case for reform, it does not attempt its own, comprehensive reframing of the ways in which corporate reorganization law is mobilized and adapted by participants in the process as a result of the shifts in logics, practices, and identities in the field of finance which it touches on. The LSTA acknowledges that shifts have occurred, but the thesis of its response is that these shifts have not undermined the effectiveness of Chapter 11, and no reform is needed.

Thus, a polarized debate emerges, in which one side reasserts the traditional policy goals and content of Chapter 11 and argues that changes in financial markets have undermined them, while the other side acknowledges changes in financial markets but argues that they do not undermine the traditional policy goals of Chapter 11, so that no reform is needed. Moreover, the bifurcation of the debate reflects the traditional divisions between scholars adopting an economic analysis (who argue for a limited role for corporate reorganization law in providing the automatic stay, market-based approaches to valuation, and distribution in accordance

[11] ibid 20.

[12] See references on pages 20–23 of the LSTA response (n 7) to Kenneth M Ayotte and Edward R Morrison, 'Creditor Control and Conflict in Chapter 11' (2009) 2 J Legal Analysis 511; Jay Lawrence Westbrook, 'Secured Creditor Control and Bankruptcy Sales: An Empirical View' (2015) U Ill L Rev 831; Stuart C Gilson, Edith S Hotchkiss, and Matthew G Osborn, 'Cashing Out: The Rise of M&A in Bankruptcy (*SSRN*, 16 March 2016) 31 <http://ssrn.com/abstract=2547168>; Mark Jenkins and David Smith, 'Creditor Conflict and the Efficiency of Corporate Reorganization' (*SSRN*, 4 June 2014) <http://ssrn.com/abstract=2444700>; and Jared A Wilkerson, 'Defending the Current State of Section 363 Sales' (2012) 86 Am Bankr LJ 591.

[13] LSTA response (n 7) 27–31.

[14] ibid 31.

[15] ibid 35.

with non-bankruptcy rights and priorities, all reflected in the LSTA response) and progressive scholars (who argue for an explicit role in tipping the outcome of the case in favour of corporate reorganization and for a norm of distributional fairness, shifting bargaining rights, and engaging a norm of post-reorganization value, all evident in the ABI report). This book has argued, of course, that a sustained and micro-analytical review of the interaction between corporate reorganization law and the changes in the fields of finance and non-financial corporates suggests that different concerns may emerge in different types of large corporate reorganization cases, demanding context-sensitive concepts and trade-offs. A significant part of the field has emerged where there ought to be common ground between scholars adopting an economic analysis of corporate reorganization law, on the one hand, and progressive scholars on the other. It is scarcely surprising that this common ground does not emerge clearly in the debate between the ABI and the LSTA, given the terms in which it is undertaken.

10.2.1.1 The debtor-in-possession

The ABI report starts with the DIP model.[16] It runs through the traditional debate between those who argue that this model retains the knowledge and expertise of the company's existing management and those who point to the fact that managerial mistakes may have caused the Chapter 11 filing in the first place. It debates alternatives to the DIP model, and the case for reform of fiduciary duties of directors in distress. Ultimately, the Commission broadly supports the status quo, for both the DIP model and the appointment of a trustee in certain Chapter 11 cases.

This book has advanced a more nuanced argument, focusing particularly on the incentives of debtors in modern deleveraging cases. Specifically, it agrees with those who have noted that debtors have very little incentive for early action in many deleveraging cases, focusing in particular on the private equity industry and the close alignment of management with the interests of the private equity investors. Early in the case, the private equity firm has little incentive to come to the table unless it is compelled to do so, because in modern markets it is highly likely that a deleveraging corporate reorganization transaction will result in the reallocation of the private equity firm's existing equity stake. Directors, with equity-based compensation, have an identity of interest with the private equity firm in delaying the case, if possible. However, once a corporate reorganization becomes inevitable, management has an interest in supporting the deleveraging transaction, provided it receives an allocation of equity in the reorganization case, or at least compensation related to successful completion. At the same time, the DIP model may perform a crucial signalling function to general, unsecured creditors, employees, customers, and other stakeholders that a reorganization is in prospect and that

[16] ABI report (n 2) 22–25.

they should continue to deal with the firm. Thus, the wider institutional environment has undergone significant changes since Chapter 11 was introduced in the late 1970s. It is suggested here that the ABI report could usefully have dedicated a little more time to this complex picture in analysing the role of debtor control in twenty-first-century markets.

10.2.1.2 The estate neutral

More radically, the report does suggest replacing the current examiner (who can be appointed in appropriate cases with a specific mandate to investigate the debtor's affairs), with what it describes as the more flexible 'estate neutral'.[17] Notwithstanding some criticism of the examiner role, and the fact that academic research suggests that examiners are infrequently appointed (even when, arguably, they ought to be appointed in strict compliance with the US Bankruptcy Code),[18] the report identifies benefits in the role of the examiner in providing 'an independent assessment of the matter at hand', and identifying value, encouraging 'parties to recognize the strengths and weaknesses of their respective positions in the case, facilitat[ing] quicker resolutions of disputes'.[19] However, it concludes that appointments should not be mandatory, but made only where the court determines that the best interests of the estate would be served by officer appointment, and should take the more flexible form of the estate neutral. After considering the argument that mandatory, unsecured creditors' committees should no longer be required, 'given that the fulcrum claims are now secured claims in many debtors' capital structures',[20] the report continues to advocate for mandatory unsecured creditors' committees in large cases.[21]

Once again, however, the report dedicates surprisingly little time to examining the significant changes in the bargaining environment explored in this book. For example, it does not consider in any detail the changing identities of the financial creditors, and how that may impact both their approach to valuation and the usefulness of introducing a new role for the estate neutral. In common with the rest of the analysis, the report does not draw a distinction between cases which involve only sophisticated, strongly adjusting financial creditors and cases involving both financial and general, unsecured creditors, employees, or tort creditors. Furthermore, it does not draw a distinction between cases where the purpose of the Chapter 11 filing is to implement a capital structure or strategic reorganization and cases where the purpose of the Chapter 11 filing is to stabilize the debtor's operations and create liquidity. Thus, once again, it is suggested that more thought

17 ibid 32–38.
18 Jonathan C Lipson, 'Understanding Failure: Examiners and the Bankruptcy Reorganization of Large Public Companies' (2010) 84(1) Am Bankr LJ 1.
19 ABI report (n 2) 36.
20 ibid 41.
21 ibid 38–43.

needs to be given to the precise role which the estate neutral can play, and in which circumstances. Moreover, as argued in this book, it is suggested that the new bargaining environment requires us to consider the precise contours of the creditors' committee role, including issues of non-bankruptcy law relating to insider dealing legislation. Finally, the section of the ABI report discussing the estate neutral is also the first of many places in the report in which the Commission refers to the need to critically analyse 'the debtor's proposed reorganization plan to ensure that the enterprise value would not be artificially depressed'.[22] This is an issue which is returned to in section 10.2.1.5 'Valuation' below.

10.2.1.3 Post-petition finance

Insofar as post-petition finance is concerned, the Commission recommends that section 364 of the Bankruptcy Code is amended to prohibit the roll-up of pre-petition debt, and that pre-petition contractual prohibitions on subordinated pre-petition junior secured creditors offering or providing post-petition financing should, subject to certain exceptions, be unenforceable.[23] Once again, the report starts with the traditional ways in which Chapter 11 seeks to incentivize new money loans. It identifies the difficulties, touched on in Chapter 5, in 'priming' existing secured lenders, and suggests that these difficulties explain why debtors often seek to negotiate post-petition financing facilities with existing secured lenders.

However, the report does not explore other shifts in logic and practice analysed in this book on the cost and availability of DIP finance: the changing regulatory capital position and the fact that few large, leveraged estates now have unencumbered assets. There are footnoted references to the lack of available post-petition financing in 2008; references to differing evidence at field hearings on the case for incentivizing Chapter 11 post-petition lending; and a reference to the use of pre-petition finance documentation to gain control rights for lenders pursuing a loan-to-own strategy. It is suggested here that what is missing is a more sustained and detailed examination of the changes in the finance field, and the implications for the present and future of post-petition financing. These are key issues in determining whether opportunities for roll-up and cross-collateralization provide necessary incentives to the likely limited pool of lenders of post-petition financing to contribute new money in post-financial, or COVID-19, crisis cases. The LSTA response does focus on the incentives which roll-ups and cross-collateralization provide,[24] but largely from the perspective that current DIP financing practice has not affected the debtor's ability to reorganize, and on the risk that banning roll-ups and other tools may increase DIP finance pricing. What the LSTA does not do

[22] ibid 41.
[23] ibid 73–79.
[24] LSTA response (n 7) 55–56.

is consider why the changes in the finance field may make methods of incentivizing DIP lending, such as roll-ups, more important than they might have been in earlier eras.

Similarly, the ABI report does not consider the wider reasons for incentivizing more thorough negotiation of intercreditor arrangements between financial creditors in complex, leveraged capital structures. As a result, a somewhat blunt suggestion is made with reference to post-petition financing. Furthermore, the report recommends (later) that provisions in intercreditor agreements waiving junior creditor voting rights, or assigning them to senior creditors, should not be enforced.[25] The analytical structure in this book would support enforcement of pre-petition intercreditor arrangements, at least where the corporate reorganization implicates only sophisticated financial creditors. Indeed, it has been suggested that courts should go further and incentivize more fully worked out allocation of control rights in intercreditor agreements for reorganizations among financial institutions. Once again, many of the issues only emerge clearly when time is dedicated to unpacking the changing relationship between corporate reorganization law and the environment in which it is embedded.

10.2.1.4 Breathing space for the debtor

As part of a more general proposal to introduce a sixty-day breathing space for debtors, the report recommends that the court should not approve post-petition financing under section 364 of the Bankruptcy Code that is 'subject to milestones, benchmarks, or other provisions that require the trustee to perform certain tasks or satisfy certain conditions within 60 days after the petition date'.[26] The milestone idea is then discussed in more detail in the section relating to timing of section 363 sales, summarized as follows:

> The trustee should not be permitted to conduct an auction of, or to receive final approval of a sale transaction involving, all or substantially all of the debtor's assets within 60 days after the petition date or date of the order for relief, whichever is later. The court should not shorten this 60-day moratorium unless (i) the trustee or a party in interest demonstrates by clear and convincing evidence that there is a high likelihood that the value of the debtor's assets will decrease significantly during such 60-day period, and (ii) the court finds that the proposed sale satisfies the standards set forth in the principles for section 363x sales.[27]

In examining the case for the new 'breathing space', the report starts with the principal concerns with section 363 sales: that they facilitate debtor avoidance of

[25] ABI report (n 2) 261–63.
[26] ibid 79.
[27] ibid 83.

disclosure obligations and deny creditors the chance to vote on proposals. It also concentrates on concerns that section 363 sales may have the result that assets are not properly valued and marketed, and that 'other restructuring alternatives' may not be fully explored.[28] The Commission summarizes the central concern as follows, 'whether value is being removed from the estate by permitting a value realization event such as a sale too early and too quickly in a chapter 11 case'.[29]

Yet, once again, there is almost no discussion of the changes in logic and practice which may have contributed to both the rise of the section 363 sale and to quicker timetables. This book has drawn a distinction between the use of a section 363 sale to implement a reorganization of debt and equity finance affecting only sophisticated, strongly adjusting financial creditors and of a section 363 sale which implicates general, unsecured creditors and employees. In the first case, the dominant policy concern should be to facilitate the reorganization as quickly as possible. This will limit the potential for the distress to spread to the operating subsidiaries, ensuring that value is preserved in the business, and preventing losses spreading to weakly adjusting trade creditors and employees. For scholars viewing corporate reorganization law through an economic lens, this reduces transaction costs which may prevent bargaining. For progressive scholars, social cost is avoided by rapid implementation of the section 363 sale transaction as a means of reducing leverage. Insofar as value is concerned, this book has argued for a simpler approach to valuation in these capital structure reorganization cases, not only in section 363 but also in Chapter 11, paying more attention to current market price at the time of the crystallizing event. Provided the sophisticated financial creditors understand that this will be the approach, they can make their lending, pricing, hedging, and other portfolio decisions accordingly, while, from a theoretical perspective, a current market price approach to valuation at the moment of the crystallizing event is perfectly justifiable. Thus, it will become clear that, where there is a chance to implement a rapid reorganization of the financial liabilities, preventing it by the introduction of a sixty-day breathing space is more likely to increase transaction costs and, potentially, social cost.

Moreover, the report spends very little time on the problems of trading in bankruptcy: high advisory costs of the lawyers, investment bankers, and other financial advisors necessary to guide the company through the corporate reorganization process; management distraction; lost customers as a result of uncertainty around the company's future and on service levels during a bankruptcy process; lost opportunities for new business during the bankruptcy case; and the implications of having resorted to bankruptcy for the recovery of the company when it emerges. Chapter 9 explored the rising number of businesses in distress which are contract

[28] ibid 84.
[29] ibid 86.

businesses. Even in a full financial and operational restructuring, it has been identified that time will very often be of the essence.

10.2.1.5 Valuation

The Commission analyses questions of valuation in section 363 sales in detail later in the report, when focusing on provisions relating to exiting the bankruptcy case.[30] Once again, the report draws no distinction between: (i) a section 363 sale which is functionally implementing a reorganization of debt and equity finance and which implicates only sophisticated, strongly adjusting financial creditors and investors; and (ii) a section 363 sale which also implicates weakly adjusting creditors. Thus, it draws no differences in policy objectives between types of cases (with reduction of transaction costs more salient in the first example for all scholars, and minority protection more salient in the second example for scholars pursuing a progressive agenda). It states:

> In a case where the debtor's assets are sold for less than the value of the secured claims asserted against the estate, junior creditors—including those holding prepetition unsecured claims and, potentially, postpetition administrative claims relating to the administration of the case following the sale—may not receive any distributions.[31]

No distinction is made between weakly adjusting, general, unsecured creditors and employees, who may have had little practical ability to protect their position, and who otherwise lack voice in the proceedings, and large, US hedge funds. Yet these hedge funds had the full range of investment opportunities available to them and chose to invest in unsecured subordinated bonds in a highly leveraged capital structure, which they knew may well prove unsustainable if the debtor suffered a shock to its earnings.

The analysis then leads to one of the most complex of the recommendations in the report, that: 'The valuation date set by the effective date of a plan or the date of a section 363x sale order should not foreclose, in appropriate cases, a distribution in the Chapter 11 case on account of the possibility of future appreciation in the firm's value due to the firm's continuation as a going concern.'[32] The report identifies the valuation debate, which was explored earlier in the book: that although a market price for a business at any point in time will reflect value for future growth, if the sale happens to be occurring when similar businesses are distressed, or the economy is depressed generally, then sale prices may be particularly low.[33] It raises

[30] ibid 201–06.
[31] ibid 204.
[32] ibid 207.
[33] ibid 207, 213–14.

the familiar argument that this will result in 'a reallocation of the reorganized firm's future value in favour of senior stakeholders and away from junior stakeholders in a manner that is subjectively unfair'.[34]

Thus, once again, the traditional policy goal emerges of enabling junior creditors in Chapter 11 to share in any future upside potential, achieved by engaging the concept of post-reorganization valuation. This book has argued that this policy goal is intimately related to the policy goal of minority protection, and that it may continue to appeal to progressive scholars where unsecured and junior creditors are unsophisticated retail investors, or trade creditors, or employees. Yet, all scholars ought to be able to coalesce around a dominant policy goal of reduction of transaction costs in a corporate reorganization which implicates only sophisticated, strongly adjusting financial creditors, achieved by engaging the concept of current market price in valuation. This will certainly not solve all disputes between senior and junior creditors in a reorganization of financial liabilities, but it should make the process somewhat simpler, and therefore faster and cheaper. For scholars viewing corporate reorganization law through an economic lens, it attempts to replicate the results which the market would have produced if cooperative bargaining had been possible. For progressive scholars, it reduces the risk that financial distress will spread to operating subsidiaries, increasing social cost.

Yet the report spends very little time analysing either the character of the participants in the process or the nature of the corporate reorganization case. There is no sense that the nature of either is relevant to the analysis. Indeed, frequently the footnoted evidence which supports the text covers both more traditional cases, implicating the full range of creditors, and disputes which appear to be between secured loan providers and unsecured bondholders, in reorganizations limited to the financial structure of the firm. As a result, no context-sensitive policy goals emerge clearly for the reform agenda. Instead, the report proposes the highly complex idea of allocating consideration to junior creditors by means of calculating what it calls 'redemption option value'.[35]

Essentially, the redemption option value concept provides that, in a cram-down, the junior creditors would be entitled to consideration if a hypothetical option, with an option value equal to the amount of the senior claims and a redemption period of three years from the plan date or section 363 sale, would have value. The first step is to calculate the 'redemption price': the aggregate amount of all senior claims (together with interest at the non-default rate and allowable fees and expenses). As already discussed, the redemption period would be the period starting on the effective date of the plan or the date of the section 363 sale, and ending on the third anniversary of the petition date. The next step would then be to determine whether an option having these features would have any value in the market,

[34] ibid 207.
[35] ibid 208–11.

using models for pricing options such as the Black-Scholes option pricing model. If the hypothetical option would have value, according to this calculation, then the junior class would receive an allocation of consideration in the corporate reorganization case equal to that amount. It is not envisaged that this would take the form of an option: the report suggests that it could be paid in cash, debt, stock, warrants, or in some other form. The Commission appears to hope that this approach will reduce the cost of valuation disputes, because it engages options pricing methodology which the Commission implicitly regards as easier to apply than discounted cashflow methodology. Moreover, the Commission attempts to incentivize agreement, and reduce valuation disputes, by making allocation of redemption option value conditional on the fact that the junior class did not object to the valuation of the firm for the purposes of the sale or plan of reorganization. The report does, however, acknowledge that complexities could arise, and that the principle requires further working out.

Several scholars, starting with Lucian Bebchuk, have suggested some form of options approach as a solution to the valuation dispute challenge in Chapter 11.[36] However, it is difficult to see that the particular version which is set out in the ABI report will reduce complexity and, once again, this book has argued that in many applicable cases the dominant policy concern should be rapid implementation of the deleveraging transaction. While Black-Scholes and other option pricing models are well established, they would carry their own, significant difficulties in a distressed situation. For example, as the LSTA response notes,[37] Black-Scholes would require the parties to agree the volatility rate. This is likely to be highly contested in a distressed scenario. It is difficult to believe that such a complex idea will solve current challenges. Moreover, the ABI report suggests that in some cases it may be necessary to turn to other models, such as 'The Binomial Options Pricing Model, Monte Carlo options models, and other formulas'.[38] As the LSTA response notes, this might be expected to increase costs and introduce further, complex disputes about the appropriate approach.

Nonetheless, the LSTA response particularly focuses on the application of redemption option value in a sales transaction, where senior creditors will not receive any future upside even if it is realized. In common with its general approach to the ABI report, the LSTA response draws no distinction between a section 363 sale which implements a reorganization of debt and equity finance and a sale of the business and assets of the debtor to a third-party trade buyer. At the very

[36] Lucian Arye Bebchuk, 'A New Approach to Corporate Reorganizations' (1988) 101(4) Harvard L Rev 775; Philippe Aghion, Oliver Hart, and John Moore, 'The Economics of Bankruptcy Reform' (1992) 8(3) J Law Econ & Org 523; Oliver Hart, *Firms, Contracts and Financial Structure* (OUP 1995); Lucian Arye Bebchuk, 'Using Options to Divide Value in Corporate Bankruptcy' (2000) 44(4) Eur Econ Rev 829.

[37] LSTA response (n 7) 27.

[38] ABI report (n 2) 221 n 795.

end of its analysis of the redemption option value the LSTA response states, 'The Commission's concern with fairness to junior creditors is also somewhat odd in light of the realities of modern finance.'[39] It states, citing from a law firm client alert:

> In today's chapter 11 cases, "[t]he contest is most often among seasoned investors (banks, hedge funds, and other institutional investors) who hold debt at different levels of the debtor's capital structure." Particularly in light of the evolution of a sophisticated market in high-yield bonds, the junior creditors the Commission seeks to protect "are sophisticated financial institutions or investment funds that *choose* to invest in a particular part of the debtor's capital structure fully aware of the risk (lower recovery) and rewards (increased interest rate) associated with such choice." Thus, "[t]his proposal could reward those creditors that chose to receive higher interest payments and agreed to take on additional risk while hurting those creditors that chose to receive lower interest rates and invest in a safer portion of the capital structure." Establishing a complex new procedure simply to move value from secured lenders to unsecured bondholders—when both are large institutional investors that chose the risk profile of the debt in which they invested—makes little sense.[40]

However, this point is made almost in passing in the LSTA response, while it emerges as a central concern from the analysis in this book. This arises because of the failure to reframe the debate explicitly around how changes in logics, practices, and identities in modern finance change the ways in which corporate reorganization law is mobilized and adapted by the participants in the process. The first step, not the last step, should be to set corporate reorganization law explicitly in the context in which it is used by modern markets. If this is done, it becomes apparent that a context-sensitive approach is appropriate, and it is clear that different trade-offs may be necessary in different types of case. In particular, both progressive scholars and scholars adopting an economic analysis ought to be able to coalesce around more market-based valuation approaches where only sophisticated, strongly adjusting financial creditors and investors are implicated, whether in a corporate reorganization plan or a section 363x sale.

10.2.2 Summary of the argument in section 10.2

The ABI report is an extremely impressive document. It seeks to review almost every aspect of Chapter 11 and, for a wide range of issues, the Commission

[39] LSTA response (n 7) 63.

[40] ibid 63, citing Chapman & Cutler LLP, Client Alert, 'Redemption Option Value: Broad Implications for Secured Lenders' (*Chapman and Cutler LLP*, 5 January 2015) <https://www.chapman.com/insights-publications-373.html> accessed 15 May 2020.

manages to arrive at a consensus position. It is an invaluable survey of the terrain, and is undoubtedly a source of inspiration for the reform debate. However, it is suggested here that a more sustained inquiry into how corporate reorganization law interacts with the logics, practices, and identities of the participants in the fields of finance and non-financial corporates is needed, in order to identify convincingly the concerns of corporate reorganization law in the twenty-first century. The LSTA response does dedicate a little more time to the detail of changes in the finance field but, perhaps because its mission is to push back against the case for reform, it focuses on the lack of empirical evidence for the ABI Commission's claims; the cost implications of the proposal; and disputes over the correct analysis of Chapter 11's traditional policy objectives. This book has suggested a different approach, which reveals the need for context-sensitive concepts, paying close attention to the participants in the process, the nature of the corporate reorganization case, and the way in which the participants mobilize and adapt corporate reorganization law as a result. The implications of this approach for the reform debate in England are now considered.

10.3 England

10.3.1 The World Bank Doing Business rankings and the UK Government review

In May 2016 the UK Government launched a review of the corporate insolvency framework, consulting on various options for reform.[41] The consultation sought 'views on whether the UK's regime needs updating in light of international principles developed by the World Bank and the United Nations Commission on International Trade Law (UNCITRAL), recent large corporate failures and an increasing European focus on providing businesses with the tools to facilitate corporate rescue'.[42]

Crucially, before the incumbent Conservative party won the 2015 general election in the UK, they had made an explicit manifesto commitment to, 'aim to be number one in Europe and in the top five worldwide in the World Bank's Doing Business rankings by 2020'.[43] This refers to the influential World Bank 'Doing Business' rankings, which rank economies on their ease of doing business. Each economy achieves an overall ranking, calculated from a range of

[41] The Insolvency Service, *A Review of the Corporate Insolvency Framework: A Consultation on Options for Reform* (The Insolvency Service May 2016) (henceforth the UK review).
[42] ibid 4.
[43] The Conservative Party Manifesto 2015, 17.

indicators, from starting a business to getting electricity. In 2015, the UK's overall ranking was nine, but one important indicator is the 'resolving insolvency' indicator, for which the UK was only ranked fourteen. Thus, it was an explicit objective of the UK review to improve its own ranking for resolving insolvency, thus improving its overall Doing Business ranking with a view to meeting the manifesto commitment.

The World Bank methodology for resolving insolvency adopts a case study approach. It assumes a limited liability company, operating in the economy's largest business city, which is 100 per cent domestically owned, with the founder owning 51 per cent of the shares. The company's major asset is a hotel, which has 201 employees and fifty suppliers, and which is in financial difficulty. It has a ten-year bank loan, secured over the hotel and, where it is possible in accordance with local laws, a charge over the rest of the company's business and assets. The business is now experiencing liquidity difficulties, and the business has too many creditors to agree an informal reorganization. The World Bank methodology tests the availability of the following options: a judicial procedure aimed at the rehabilitation or reorganization of the company to permit its continued operation; a judicial procedure aimed at the liquidation or winding-up of the company; or a judicial debt enforcement procedure (foreclosure or receivership) against the company. It derives its information to test the availability of these procedures via a questionnaire, completed by local insolvency practitioners, which it then seeks to verify by studying local laws and regulations, as well as other public information on the relevant corporate bankruptcy system.[44]

It will be immediately apparent that this methodology has a number of difficulties for the account in this book. First, the case study is of a medium-sized business with physical assets, and the questionnaire very much assumes a full financial and operational reorganization. This means that the type of contextual analysis of large corporate reorganization which has been undertaken in this book is never engaged. Secondly, questionnaire responses are coded '0' or '1', so that other, alternative ways of achieving functionally the same result are unlikely to emerge. Most problematic of all, the questionnaire very much adopts the traditional policy and principles of Chapter 11 as, to adopt Michael Power's term, 'world level norms'.[45] Thus, the UK has historically fallen down in a number of areas: whether the debtor (or an insolvency representative on its behalf) can continue performing contracts essential to a debtor's survival; whether the insolvency framework requires the approval by the creditors for the sale of substantial assets of the debtor; and whether the insolvency framework provides that a creditor has the right to request information from the insolvency representative. Yet, in each case, more nuanced analysis

[44] The World Bank, 'Resolving Insolvency Methodology' <https://www.doingbusiness.org/en/methodology/resolving-insolvency> accessed 8 March 2020.
[45] Power (n 1) 262.

would produce more nuanced results. As Antonio Nicita and Simona Benedettini put it:

> ... given a certain theoretical framework defining what business regulation is, what its objectives should be, and what main interests it should satisfy, it follows that a definition of what should be measured (i.e. the unit of measurement), and of the coding to be used to transform a qualitative matter into a quantitative indicator is automatically derived.[46]

Nonetheless, the Doing Business rankings do have political significance, and they formed a substantial motivation for the 2016 UK review. As a result, the corporate reorganization review was very much framed in terms of adding the tools which were apparently missing in the UK corporate reorganization law toolbox from a Doing Business perspective. The hope must have been that this would enable local insolvency practitioners to respond positively to more of the questions. If this happened, the UK would rise in the rankings as a result. This was not a very auspicious way to begin the process of reform. This general approach was reinforced by US practitioners living and working in London, or representing US investors in the UK. As the UK has increasingly become what Sefa Franken terms a 'dependent state',[47] (that is a state which has become increasingly dependent on importing US capital) it has had an interest in adapting its corporate reorganization laws to reflect the laws which US investors understand, and are comfortable with. This has added to the pressure to approach the reform exercise by incorporating tools familiar to US practitioners and investors.

Thus, the 2016 consultation considered the case for introducing four new tools. The first was a new, free-standing moratorium which would act as a single gateway to any of the existing English law corporate reorganization tools (a contractual workout, a company voluntary arrangement (CVA), an administration, or a scheme of arrangement). The second was a new measure which would enable a company entering into a moratorium, administration, CVA, or a new restructuring plan (discussed below) to designate certain supplies as essential, with the result that the relevant suppliers would be prevented from relying on termination clauses. The third was a new restructuring plan procedure, closely modelled on a scheme of arrangement but permitting cross-class cram-down. The final suggestion was the possibility of further development of rescue finance. The Government then published the extensive responses which it received to the consultation, and took some time to consider and discuss them.

[46] Antonio Nicita and Simona Benedettini, 'Towards the Economics of Comparative Law: The *Doing Business* Debate' in Pier Giuseppe Monateri (ed) *Methods of Comparative Law* (Edward Elgar 2012) 294.

[47] Sefa M Franken, 'Cross-Border Insolvency Law: A Comparative Institutional Analysis' (2014) 34(1) Oxf J Legal Stud 97.

The Government response was finally published in 2018.[48] The response indicated that nothing further would be done with respect to rescue finance. It indicated that the moratorium proposal would be taken further, but would exclude companies that were already insolvent and would take the form of a general moratorium, modelled on the existing administration moratorium. The essential supplies idea was replaced by a plan to introduce a general ban on insolvency termination clauses in supply contracts. And the response indicated that proposals for the new restructuring plan procedure incorporating cross-class cram-down powers would be taken forward. When this book was being written, there was no sign that the proposals would be taken forward; the vote of the British people to leave the European Union had raised significant challenges for UK legislative time. However, as the book goes to press, the Government has introduced the Corporate Insolvency and Governance Bill (the Bill) which takes forward some of the reform proposals in the midst of the COVID-19 crisis.[49] The Bill provides for a new free-standing moratorium,[50] a ban on the exercise of insolvency termination clauses in supply agreements, among other circumstances in both the new moratorium procedure and administration,[51] and a new cross-class cram-down procedure.[52] What is of particular interest, for the purposes of the argument in this book, is the approach taken in the reform effort, specifically the lack of context provided in any of the consultation documents for the case for reform.

This book has argued that the English scheme of arrangement procedure has proved itself best in class for rapid reorganization of a complex, leveraged capital structure in a finance holding company, implicating only sophisticated, strongly adjusting financial creditors and investors who had the full range of investment opportunities open to them. It has argued that the policy objective for these cases should be to promote a rapid reorganization of the loan, bond, and equity finance: for scholars with an economic viewpoint, in order to reduce transaction costs preventing a reorganization bargain, and for scholars sympathetic to a progressive agenda, in order to reduce the risk that distress spreads to the operating subsidiaries, implicating non-adjusting or weakly adjusting creditors, and thereby increasing social cost. It has also been suggested, however, that expanding and changing logics, practices, and identities in the finance field mean that corporate reorganizations may not follow the same model

[48] Department for Business, Energy & Industrial Strategy, *Insolvency and Corporate Governance: Government Response* (Department for Business, Energy & Industrial Strategy 26 August 2018) (henceforth the Government response).

[49] Corporate Insolvency and Governance Bill [HC] 2019–21.

[50] ibid s 1, inserting new Part A1 into Insolvency Act 1986 (Moratorium), and ibid Sch1 inserting new Part ZA1 into Insolvency Act 1986 (Moratorium: Eligible Companies).

[51] ibid s 12, inserting new section 233B (Protection of Supplies of Goods and Services in Great Britain) into Insolvency Act 1986, and ibid Sch 12, inserting new Schedule 4ZZA (Protection of Supplies under section 233B: Exclusions) into Insolvency Act 1986.

[52] ibid Sch 9, inserting new Part 26A into Companies Act 2006.

in the next decade as that which they have typically adopted since 2008. Specifically, Chapter 9 focused on the risk that covenant-lite and covenant-loose lending increases the prospect of the parties coming to the table later to negotiate, perhaps when distress has already affected operations and when operating liquidity is a serious issue. And it highlighted that the enforced business shutdown and social distancing measures implemented in response to the COVID-19 crisis have significantly increased the likelihood that both operating liabilities and operating liquidity will be implicated in corporate reorganization cases. The scheme of arrangement is much less well adapted to deal with these types of corporate reorganization cases. Furthermore, Chapter 9 suggested that, consistent with the principle of a context-sensitive approach, unsecured and junior creditor protection may have more salience for progressive scholars in cases implicating operating liabilities than in a reorganization among financial institutions. Finally, it noted that new debates may emerge, related to the specific facts of these new types of cases.

However, because the consultation did not start with the English law case for reform, it did not focus on what function any new tools would be required to perform. It has already become apparent that, in a reorganization limited to financial liabilities, it may be possible to manage without moratorium protection: the intercreditor agreement contains a stay against junior lender, or bondholder, action; it is not entirely clear what action the junior lender, or bondholder, can take while preserving its value; and lenders and bondholders who do not want to support the reorganization effort are typically able to trade out in the distressed debt market. However, if trade creditors are unsettled by distress, they have a wider range of options available to them: terminating contracts; stopping supply; delaying supply; shortening payment days; or increasing pricing. All of these actions increase liquidity pressure on the distressed group, and potentially destroy the prospects for a reorganization. Moreover, where the group is facing both financial and operational distress, it is more likely that it will need to reshape its operating contracts, as well as its financial contracts, if it is to survive. As has become clear, because it was conceived of as a tool to restructure both financial and operating liabilities, US Chapter 11 offers a full range of tools to achieve these objectives: a strong automatic stay with an ipso facto ban, and powerful debtor rights to determine whether to assume, reject, or assign contracts. As Chapter 9 explored, England's toolbox is considerably slimmer in comparison.

Thus, if England's corporate reorganization law is examined in the context of expanding and changing logics and practices in the finance field, the focus is likely to be on cases in which the parties come to the table later than has habitually been the case since the financial crisis, when the group is facing liquidity issues in its operations, as well as in servicing its debt. Progressive scholars would thus want a full suite of powerful, coordinated, and well-supervised tools for use in this more precarious situation. However, because the consultation did not approach the case for reform in this way, but was rather influenced by traditional US narratives, it drew no distinction between large and small cases. It did not distinguish between cases which reorganize debt and equity finance among sophisticated financial institutions and cases implicating financial and operating liabilities. It drew no distinction between cases where corporate reorganization law is mobilized and adapted to implement a reorganization and cases where it is mobilized and adapted to stabilize a deteriorating operating environment and to create liquidity. Overall, the consultation appeared to be influenced by the traditional US policy concern of promoting early action. Yet, the argument has already been made that early action is unlikely in modern, large leveraged cases. This is because coming to the table risks the private equity sponsor or investors in a publicly traded company losing their equity investment. At the same time, the English toolbox is relatively well adapted for early mobilization. As a result, it is suggested here that a number of policy missteps occurred in the reform proposals, some of which have been replicated in the Bill.

10.3.1.1 The moratorium

First, the moratorium, as initially proposed, was a pre-insolvency moratorium.[53] Yet, for the reasons outlined here, stronger moratorium protection is more likely to be needed when the group is in a more advanced state of distress, implicating operating liabilities as well as financial liabilities. Secondly, as initially proposed, the moratorium lasted for a period of twenty-eight days, subject to extension for a further twenty-eight days.[54] This appeared to be too short for the types of large corporate reorganizations with which this book is concerned to be worked out. And, finally, the moratorium placed some pressure on an insolvency practitioner (to be known as the monitor) to supervise the moratorium, while giving the insolvency practitioner comparatively few powers, and offering creditors very little by way of convincing supervision.[55] The Bill appears to recognize the challenges with the moratorium as a solely pre-insolvency procedure, so that the broad solvency condition has been dropped.[56] However, for the most part, the challenges identified here persist. Although complicated mechanics for extension by creditors or the court are included in the Bill,[57] the basic period of the moratorium is twenty

[53] The Government response (n 48) 47 para 5.28.

[54] ibid 51–52 paras 5.46–5.56.

[55] ibid. The insolvency practitioner was required to: confirm they have assessed the eligibility tests and qualifying conditions and are satisfied that these are met (para 5.19); assess whether the company has sufficient funds to carry on its business during the moratorium (paras 5.33–5.34); confirm that the qualifying conditions are met on an extension (para 5.52); terminate the moratorium if the qualifying conditions cease to be met (para 5.65); and sanction asset disposals outside the normal course of business and the granting of any new security over company assets (para 5.65), while the Government response was explicit that, '... the moratorium is a debtor-in-possession process' and that the insolvency practitioner 'is not running the company' (para 5.40) and that, 'while the company's directors remain in control of the company's operations during the moratorium, the Government intends the role of the monitor to be limited in scope to functions necessary to support the integrity of the moratorium process and ensure creditor interests are protected' (para 5.65).

[56] New Sch ZA1 (Moratorium: eligible companies) Insolvency Act 1986.

[57] New Part A1 Insolvency Act 1986, s A11 and s A13.

business days,[58] subject to extension without creditor consent (provided certain conditions are met) for a further twenty business days.[59] The monitor continues to have relatively onerous obligations to supervise the moratorium,[60] and relatively few powers. There is an obligation to pay rent falling due during the moratorium,[61] and debt service obligations,[62] so that the ability to use the moratorium to create liquidity is limited. And many types of large company are excluded from access to the procedure altogether.[63] Overall, because the moratorium was conceived of as a procedure to encourage early filing, the new tool arguably cannot be mobilized and adapted for all the purposes for which participants might have hoped to use it.

10.3.1.2 Reorganizing corporate contracts

Furthermore, while the proposals envisaged a ban on insolvency termination clauses, they did not go on to offer tailored tools for reshaping corporate contracts. This is also the position in the Bill, which introduces a ban on insolvency termination clauses in contracts for the supply of goods and services, among other circumstances, in the new moratorium procedure and in administration,[64] but which does not offer an explicit regime for acceptance, rejection, or assignment of contracts. It is possible that existing tools, such as the administrator's powers in relation to pre-administration contracts, the scheme of arrangement, the company voluntary arrangement (CVA), or the new Part 26A procedure (discussed below), can be adapted for this purpose, but there are complexities here. It would have been preferable to articulate why the tools are needed, to debate the new trade-offs which arise, and then to design the tools explicitly for their identified purpose. Similarly, given the argument in this book that the tools are needed for a thoroughgoing large corporate reorganization implicating both financial and operating liabilities and when the group is facing liquidity issues in both its financial and its operating companies, more work is needed on the possibilities for rescue finance with priority status in England. The author has suggested in other work that it is possible

58 ibid s A9.

59 ibid s A10.

60 Among other things, the monitor is required to confirm that, in the monitor's view, it is likely that the moratorium would result in a rescue of the company as a going concern (ibid s A6(1)(e)); confirm that, in the monitor's view, it is likely that the moratorium will result in the rescue of the company as a going concern on an extension (ibid s A10(1)(d), s A11(1)(d), and s A13(2)(d)); during the moratorium monitor the company's affairs for the purpose of forming a view whether it is likely that the moratorium will result in the rescue of the company as a going concern (ibid s A35(1)); terminate the moratorium, among other things, if the monitor thinks that the moratorium is no longer likely to result in the rescue of the company as a going concern or the company is no longer able to pay any debts which are due for payment in the moratorium (ibid s A38((1)(a) and (d)); and sanction the granting of any new security over company assets, the payment of certain pre-moratorium debts, and asset disposals outside the normal course of business (ibid s A26, A28, and A29).

61 New Part A1 Insolvency Act 1986, s A18(3)(c).

62 ibid s A18(3)(f).

63 New Sch ZA1 (n 56).

64 New s 233B Insolvency Act 1986 (n 51).

that this can be achieved by adapting the administration procedure.[65] Once again, working out how the tools fit into the existing toolbox, and for what purpose they are to be used would help significantly with the design process.

10.3.1.3 Assessing the fairness of the plan

Finally, as noted in the introduction to section 10.3.1 'The World Bank Doing Business rankings and the UK Government review', the Bill introduces a new Part 26A into the Companies Act 2006 (Arrangements and Reconstructions for Companies in Financial Difficulty), which is defined in the Explanatory Notes to the Bill as a 'restructuring plan'.[66] The new restructuring plan procedure is closely modelled on the scheme of arrangement procedure, but introduces a new cross-class cram-down feature so that it can be mobilized and adapted in very different circumstances.[67] As discussed in Chapter 4, the scheme of arrangement is based on the principle of majority rule. If a majority of similarly situated creditors has agreed to a proposal, then the court is likely to need to find some reason to suspect the motivations of the majority, before interfering with its decision. Otherwise, a minority creditor is bound by the view of the majority of similarly situated creditors, and the English court will be reluctant to interfere with the view of the majority in most cases, and is likely to sanction the scheme. This approach is particularly well adapted to a reorganization of debt and equity finance, in which creditors have invested in a loan or debt security as a member of a class of creditor, and the majority has determined the appropriate compromise when the capital structure is no longer sustainable.

However, the power to cram a plan down on an entire, dissenting class introduces an entirely different question: whether it is objectively justifiable to impose the plan on that class. This explains why a US court, faced with a cram-down decision, concerns itself with the detail of the plan of reorganization, and whether it is objectively fair to the dissenting class. Where the cram-down implicates only sophisticated, strongly adjusting financial creditors and investors, then provided the treatment of the class was foreseeable, and the junior creditors and investors were able to make their investment decision and price their advance accordingly, the court may still be able to adopt a relatively light touch. Yet, if distress has spread to non-adjusting or weakly adjusting creditors' claims, and the plan is to be crammed down on a wider range of types of creditor, the court may wish to roll up its sleeves and look at the detail of the plan. Thus, it might be expected that the English court will need to develop different principles for sanction in a cross-class cram-down

[65] Sarah Paterson, 'Finding Our Way: Secured Transactions and Corporate Bankruptcy Law and Policy in America and England' (2018) 18(2) J Corp L Stud 129, 247, 253–4, Sarah Paterson, 'The Rise of Covenant-Lite Lending and Implications for the UK's Corporate Insolvency Law Toolbox' (2019) 39(3) Oxf J Legal Stud 654, 675.

[66] Explanatory Notes to the Corporate Insolvency and Governance Bill, para 10.

[67] The Bill (n 49) Sch 9, inserting new Part 26A into the Companies Act 2006.

restructuring plan, notwithstanding the close relationship between the new procedure and its nineteenth-century ancestor.

Once again, the argument is for a policy objective of rapid flexing of the capital structure, and a norm of reducing transaction costs, where a reorganization is limited to loan, bond, and equity finance. Thus, arguments have been advanced for simpler valuation methodology in these types of transactions. As currently proposed, in order to sanction a Part 26A plan, the court would need to be satisfied that creditors were not worse off than the 'relevant alternative'.[68] This will often be a sale of the business and assets as a going concern by an administrator, although in the immediate aftermath of the COVID-19 crisis it may be a break-up sale of the assets. To all intents and purposes, therefore, the new Part 26A broadly adopts a current prevailing market price or value approach, rather than a post-restructuring market value approach. While the argument in this book would support this approach for a reorganization limited to financial liabilities among sophisticated financial institutions, there may be a need to consider the fairness of the case where the reorganization not only implicates sophisticated, strongly adjusting financial creditors and investors, but also implicates non-adjusting or weakly adjusting general, unsecured trade creditors, landlords, employees, customers, tort creditors, or even the community. To this end, the Explanatory Notes to the Bill make clear that:

> As is the case with Part 26 schemes, the court will always have absolute discretion over whether to sanction a restructuring plan. For example, even if the conditions of cross-class cram down are met, the court may refuse to sanction a restructuring plan on the basis that it is not just and equitable.[69]

This is particularly important because, as English corporate bankruptcy law becomes increasingly statute-based, English judges have defined their role in increasingly narrow terms.[70] In this age of complexity, the ability of US and English judges to flex their approach to meet expanding and changing logics, practices, and identities in the fields of finance and non-financial corporates, which continuously reshape the ways in which corporate reorganization law is mobilized and adapted, is an important asset. It is crucial that any reforms provide judges with the confidence to adapt their approach in this way. This is also important in light of the argument

[68] New Part 26A Companies Act 2006, s 901G, which provides that 'the "relevant alternative" is whatever the court considers would be most likely to occur in relation to the company if the compromise or arrangement were not sanctioned'.

[69] Explanatory Notes (n 66) para 15.

[70] Lord Neuberger, Keynote Speech at the International Insolvency Institute Annual Conference 2017 (*Supreme Court UK*, 19 June 2017) <https://www.supremecourt.uk/docs/speech-170619.pdf> accessed 9 March 2020; Mr Justice Hildyard, 'Mind the Gap: Insolvency, Interstitial Innovation and Implications of Brexit' speech at the Insolvency Lawyers' Association Annual Dinner 2017 (26 September 2017) <https://www.ilauk.com/docs/insolvency_and_interstitial_innovation__final_draft_26_september.pdf> accessed 18 May 2020.

in Chapter 7 that the new restructuring plan provisions may affect the delicate bargaining environment which is currently achieved in England.

10.3.2 Summary of the argument in section 10.3

It is a central argument of this book that English corporate reorganization law is generally well adapted for the reorganization of complex, leveraged, financial capital structures. However, it is a controlling principle of this book that participants in the process adapt corporate reorganization law so that it addresses particular problems which occur as a result of shifts in the proximate fields of finance and non-financial corporates. For the reasons explored in Chapter 9, as the book was being written there were already reasons to suspect that an increase in corporate reorganization cases implicating both financial and operating liabilities might be on the horizon. As the book goes to press, it seems even more likely that a greater number of cases will implicate both financial and operating liabilities as a result of the business shutdowns and social distancing measures imposed as a result of the COVID-19 crisis. However, neither the UK review nor the Government response engaged in any detail with the case for reform. This may be, in part, because the original motivation for the review appears to have been a somewhat instrumental approach to rising in the World Bank Doing Business rankings. As a result, it has been suggested here that there is a risk that the tools provided by the new Bill will not be as well adapted to meet the challenges ahead as they might have been.

10.4 Conclusion

This brings to a conclusion both this chapter and the book as a whole. The goal of the book has been to suggest a new approach to US and English corporate reorganization law. The first step was to identify significant shifts in logic, practices, and identities in the fields of finance and non-financial corporates, and to focus on the ways in which these shifts have reshaped how corporate reorganization law is mobilized and adapted by the participants in the process. Specifically, a new type of corporate reorganization case has emerged from the account in the book, limited to a reorganization implicating only financial liabilities owed to sophisticated, strongly adjusting financial creditors who had the full range of investment opportunities open to them. This book has argued that the dominant policy goal in this type of case should be to promote a rapid reorganization of the complex, leveraged capital structure, before distress moves from the finance holding company into the operating subsidiaries. New concepts and new trade-offs have emerged from this account: prioritizing reduction of transaction costs over unsecured or junior creditor protection and prioritizing reduction of hold-out power over staying creditor action. It has been suggested that there is a need to reformulate the concern for secured creditor control. And it has been argued that changes in identities in the finance and non-financial corporate fields have changed the bargaining environment in which corporate reorganization law is embedded, and that this has implications for the concept of debtor control rights, the concept of an uncertain litigation environment to promote bargaining, and the concept of transparency and disclosure.

Nonetheless, it is emphatically not the case that new universal or fixed contours for corporate reorganization law analysis have emerged. First, the book only addresses large cases. Secondly, it draws sharp distinctions between different types of corporate reorganization case, and the different ways in which corporate reorganization law is mobilized and adapted as a result. And thirdly, expanding and changing logics, practices, and identities in the continuous process of change in modern finance and non-financial corporate fields are likely to change the dynamic yet again, so that new debates emerge. Indeed, Chapter 9 attempted some tentative forecasting of how currently expanding and changing logics, practices, and identities in the fields of finance and non-financial corporates may change the landscape and, as this book goes to press, COVID-19 has emerged as the paradigmatic example of an unexpected force of change. Overall, the demand is for a context-sensitive approach to the different ways in which corporate reorganization law is mobilized and adapted by the participants in the process.

Finally, in this chapter, the approach in the book has been applied to current reform efforts in both the US and the UK. In both the US and the UK, it has become apparent that significant changes in the finance and non-financial corporate fields have changed the ways in which corporate reorganization law is mobilized and adapted. This chapter has suggested that, in the US, debate about the implication of these changes for reform has all too easily become a debate about how to promote the traditional policy goals of Chapter 11, framed using concepts which have been used by scholars since the 1980s. Thus, the ABI report has put forward proposals which are largely designed to reassert traditional concerns for unsecured creditor protection, without regard for the different types of corporate reorganization cases which emerge in modern markets. The LSTA has put more emphasis on the changing nature of corporate reorganization cases, but because its mission seems to be, largely, to advocate for no reform, it tends to assert a different universal or fixed analytical framework for Chapter 11, and to argue that Chapter 11 is still effective in meeting these concerns. Thus, the debate remains divided along roughly economic and progressive lines. As a result, this book has argued that a good deal of common ground is missed by both sides.

Insofar as England is concerned, the reform agenda was driven, initially, by a concern to rise up the World Bank Doing Business rankings. The analysis in this chapter has identified that the World Bank methodology is heavily based on the policy objectives and concepts of a traditional Chapter 11 case, and certainly does not draw the type of context-sensitive distinctions which emerge from the approach adopted in this book. It has been suggested that the UK reform effort required a more detailed analysis of the case for reform, in order to promote better identification of the gaps in the toolbox, and the arguments for and against filling them. The approach of borrowing tools from the US, while dedicating less time to thinking about how they fit with the rest of the English system, has also been encouraged by US practitioners working in London, or advising US clients looking to make an inward investment into the UK. These practitioners have tended to advocate traditional US Chapter 11 policy goals and content for English corporate reorganization law. This, it is suggested, increases the risk of policy missteps.

Finally, one of the great merits of both the US and the UK systems is the presence of highly able corporate bankruptcy judges, capable of adapting their approach as expanding and changing logics, practices, and identities in the finance and non-financial corporate fields reshape the ways in which corporate reorganization law is mobilized and adapted by the participants in the process. In the US, there has been lively debate about the extent of the bankruptcy courts' equitable powers, given the detailed statutory framework of the US Bankruptcy Code. In England, leading judges have described their capacity for innovation in increasingly narrow terms, as corporate bankruptcy also becomes steadily more statute-based in the UK. Yet, corporate reorganization law is increasingly mobilized and adapted in continuous cycles of change by participants embedded in dynamic and innovative proximate fields. The US and England should protect judicial innovation to ensure that the conceptual framework within which corporate reorganization law is assessed keeps pace with the effects of changing logics, practices, and identities in the fields of finance and non-financial corporates on the ways in which the participants in the process use the corporate reorganization law toolbox. The book ends with a rallying cry for scholars, practitioners, judges, and the legislature to abandon the search for a fixed or universal conceptual framework for analysing corporate reorganization law. The claim is that they should turn, instead, to adapting their conceptual frameworks to the different ways in which corporate reorganization law is mobilized and adapted by the participants in the process, as those participants respond, in their turn, to changes in the wider, shifting landscape in which corporate reorganization is embedded.

Index

For the benefit of digital users, indexed terms that span two pages (e.g., 52–53) may, on occasion, appear on only one of those pages.